THE
BLACK
COMMUNITY
Diversity
and
Unity

ROBERT BIERSTEDT
Professor of Sociology, University of Virginia
Advisory Editor to Dodd, Mead & Company

THE
BLACK
COMMUNITY
Diversity
and
Unity

JAMES E. BLACKWELL
University of Massachusetts at Boston

DODD, MEAD & COMPANY
New York   1975

TO MYRT

Contents

List of Tables

Preface

This book grew out of my long-standing professional interest in the field of racial and ethnic relations and observations made during my years as a civil rights activist. It reflects my viewpoint that neither the immense diversity nor implications of intragroup differentiation within American minority groups have been adequately treated by social scientists. This is especially true in the case of the black community, which, invariably, is treated as an undifferentiated categorical mass of sameness. Although some readers will claim that I have a point of view and a value position relative to the presence of diversity and factors that create hetereogeneity as well as unity— and they are right—I have attempted to remain faithful to my training as an objective sociologist permitting the empirical evidence to speak for itself in this analysis of the black community.

In a book like this some aspects of institutional life are not treated as extensively as some would like. I acknowledge this shortcoming with the observation that the constraints of space precluded the inclusion of a number of relevant topics. However, my purpose is not necessarily to pour old wine in new bottles but to augment our knowledge by focusing more generally on contemporary issues and institutional concerns. Hopefully, the reader will emerge with both a better understanding of the American black social structure and new insights into the dynamic character of the American black community.

In the preparation of this study I am indebted to a large number of people who assisted me in so many ways. My sincere appreciation is expressed to my colleagues T. Scott Miyakawa and Douglas Davidson, who read the entire manuscript during its formative stages and offered constructive criticisms that added strength to subsequent drafts, and to Stan R. Nikkel, who also offered advice on the chapter on housing. Appreciation is also expressed to Ronald Lembo, who served as my research assistant during the early stages of this project. I also owe a great deal to other scholars whose meticulous readings of the manuscript and cogent analyses of some of the issues I raised were of inestimable value to me. Included in this group of scholars are my sociology editor, Robert Bierstedt, Charles E. King, Wilson Record, and Doris Y. Wilkinson.

Special appreciation is noted for the highly commendable job performed by Maureen Hayes, who was particularly diligent in typing the manuscript and its revisions, and my sincere thanks to Anne Knight and Kathleen Kelleher, who also typed various portions of the manuscript. Above all, I owe a profound debt of gratitude to Myrt, my wife, whose sensible insights, humaneness, and understanding sustained me throughout this project.

JAMES E. BLACKWELL

Foreword

The Black Community: Diversity and Unity addresses itself to nine essential questions: (1) What is the black community? (2) How is the community formed, structured, and held together? (3) What functions do white racism and oppression of black people perform in creating and sustaining a black community in America? (4) In what theoretical terms should this community be perceived—as a parallel structure or as an internal colony or as a social system? (5) To what extent has sociological research dealt with the heterogeneity and intragroup distinctions within the black community? (6) What are the sources of the diversity prevalent in the black community today? (7) What factors account for the unity that binds black people together into a social bond called the black community? (8) What are the urgent problems confronting black communities, and to what extent are the solutions advanced contravened by conflicting issues and competing demands? and (9) Is the black community moving toward integration or separation or revolution or liberation—what is its future in American society? Implicit in these questions are a number of issues that provide both the study focus and illustrations of the book's primary theme.

The major theme of this study is that the black community is a highly diversified, interrelated aggregate of people who unite into relatively cohesive structures in response to white oppression, racism, and patterned repression. The diversity within the black community manifests itself in economic life, occupational pursuits, earned income, and business ventures and in their successes and failures. It is evident in family structures, educational attainment, residential distribution, and political behavior—including active participation in community politics and voting behavior in general. Diversity is apparent in different life styles, disparate political ideologies, and orientations toward the government and its responsibilities to the masses of people. It appears in distributive justice, perceptions of justice, health-care systems, and individual roles in medical and health-care institutions. Indeed, diversity does not end with this litany of factors affecting the lives of black people. It reaches beyond these factors to a diversity of interpretations of the power of white oppression in shaping and molding what is now identified as black community.

The black community is also a response to white racism and to the accompanying historical aspects of that oppression; and it is the overwhelming force of that oppression that has moved black people in America to a semblance of unity and cohesive social structure. At the same time, I have indicated that diversity can be found in the black community and is to some degree accepted by the black community, as slogans such as "unity without uniformity" show. Here the factors of class, color, and race intersect and unite black people on the one hand and stratify them on the other. The factors of race and color coalesce to produce group solidarity in the face of confrontation or opposition from members of another race or from people who are of a different "color." Even this behavior, however, is a response pattern to the behavior of members of outgroups, who in this case are nonblack. Thus the history of black people in America is a history of accommodation and adjustment to white oppression and white racism. It is this history that is now becoming the fundamental basis for developing a sense of unity and community among black people in America.

Both the unity now sought and that of the past have found profound expression in organizations elaborated by black people to serve black interests, in institutions developed and strengthened in response to the needs of black people, and in the articulation of shared goals for communal life. The unity that has resulted from these experiences is further clarified in the strategies devised or skills required for dealing with white oppression and for achieving self-liberation. The search for black unity and social cohesion is neither unexpected nor without precedent. A basic sociological axiom is that groups tend to achieve greater degrees of ingroup solidarity when confronted with threats from members of an outgroup or from the totality of the outgroup itself. The threatened groups organize to form strategies for self-maintenance, group survival, and protection of their rights and privileges, no matter how limited and imperfectly formed or how extensive or entrenched the threatened groups may be.

Because of its disinclination to share its values, attainments, and wealth with others who are singled out as being different, the dominant group finds it convenient to categorize minorities—that is, to lump them together and regard them as homogeneous entities. It is a most compelling fact that the literature in sociology is replete with such homogeneous interpretations of minority groups. When the literature does recognize diversity, it usually does so in simplistic Marxian terms, such as when dealing with the relationship between economic condition and class position. In this framework explanations of diversity are frequently deterministic and dogmatic. This approach allows for exceptions to the rule, since use of the concept of social class can facilitate an understanding of the degree to which minorities have been socialized into adhering to the dominant group's values or whether they have accepted the normative structures of the dominant group as their own. Social class can clarify how minorities have allocated their roles, distributed their resources, or effected role-management systems. This approach may lead to the conclusion that minority groups, including the black community, are fragmented, but one should be cautioned against interpreting fragmentation as disorganization.

Given these observations, we can now repeat our major theme: *The black community is a highly diversified set of interrelated structures and aggregates of people who are held together by the forces of white oppression and racism.* Unity within the black community is a function of the strategies developed to combat white racism and to strengthen black social, economic, and political institutions for group survival and advancement. The development of this theme requires an explication of various aspects of group life within the black community. The indispensability of theoretical perspectives, both for understanding black-white relations and as frameworks for analyzing the very nature of the community, is the central issue of the general introduction in Chapter 1. Here the concept of community is assessed in terms of its applicability to the black population today, and each succeeding chapter concentrates on contravening variables that serve either to unite or to separate black community members.

Chapters 2 through 8 analyze the diversity and unity found within the social structure of the black community. This analysis leads in Chapter 2 to a discussion of the black family, patterns of family life, the impact of slavery and urbanization on the black family, and such controversial issues as illegitimacy, divorce, and the myths, realities, conceptualizations regarding blacks on welfare. In Chapter 3, the stratification system within the black community is described, and mobility patterns are examined in terms of traditional and nontraditional criteria for upward movement and status achievement in the social system. The primary focus is on the unique characteristics of that system as a parallel form to the larger dominant group stratification system but one that typifies features that distinguish it from that larger system. This chapter examines social class both as a factor contributing to increasing diversity or heterogeneity within the black community and as an instrument for effecting greater cohesion among black people. Special attention is devoted to the relative salience of blackness for conferring status on black community members.

Chapter 4 assesses the impact of education on social change within the black community. Beginning with an analysis of institutional and systemic segregation, it continues with an examination of selected strategies called upon to break down barriers of de facto segregation and discrimination. Both positive and dysfunctional consequences of integration and desegregation of school systems are treated from the perspective of special interest groups within the black community. Contemporary issues, such as busing to achieve school integration, community control of schools, and neighborhood school concepts, come under close scrutiny. The final section of this chapter draws attention to other current issues, including the role of traditionally black colleges in higher education, problems of black students in white colleges, and implications of increasing competition between predominantly white colleges and universities and traditionally black colleges for black professionals. The major theoretical controversy here concerns the orthodox view of education as an instrument for eventual assimilation of blacks into the American society versus the view of education as a tool for elaborating and defining a black culture.

The internal colonialism model is the basic theoretical framework used in Chapter 5 for analyzing the issues of housing and the ghettoization of blacks. Simultaneously, the existing black ghettos are examined in terms of the power of territoriality as a factor of special importance in sustaining a community. In this sense the chapter treats housing as a boundary-maintenance system that both the colonizers and the colonized employ but for vastly different reasons; the techniques of boundary maintenance are analyzed as well. Attention is also given to those responses made by blacks who seek changes in the system, who are determined to develop open housing as a reality, and whose mission is to eradicate barriers related to this process.

Despite the disproportionate amount of poverty existing in the black community, it does a $51-billion consumer business each year. However, the black people do not control this market, but people who live outside the black community administer and manipulate it. The capital gains earned in the black community rarely benefit it and rebound instead to the advantage of a sometimes invisible power structure made up of absentee owners of resources and managers of finance. Black power advocates have called upon black people to alter this traditional pattern of money outflowing. Thus Chapter 6 examines black businesses and compares them to businesses found outside the black community. It also gives some attention to black economic unions and to self-help organizations at the local and national levels that claim to strengthen black economic development. Organizations such as black cooperatives, Operation Breadbasket, Opportunities Industrialization Center, People United to Save Humanity (PUSH), and the Black Muslims are highlighted. The second section of this chapter shifts to the issues of manpower needs and resources, especially in law, business, higher education, medicine, dentistry, and allied health services, and calls for development of middle-range manpower skills that, once acquired, may help to elevate a substantial number of blacks above the poverty level.

Chapter 7 deals with black political power and racism in the American political structure. It examines voting rights legislation as it affects the political participation of blacks. The theme of diversity and unity emerges again in the discussion of the civil rights and black liberation movements. Confrontation politics and perspectives on coalitions with other Third World groups and with American whites are also described in this chapter.

The following chapter shifts attention to another area of increasing concern to the black community in America—blacks in the military. Historical roles of blacks in the military, changing patterns of segregation and discrimination, and the impact of generalized racism on blacks in the armed services form the central elements of this discussion. An effort is made to demonstrate the relationship between economic deprivation and the enlistment of blacks in the military as well as to demonstrate the relationship between racism and experiences of blacks in the Vietnam War. Adjustment patterns of the ex-military man to the American society are discussed. Chapter 8 also considers how the tensions and dilemmas of armed conflict affect the interpersonal relations among forced comrades in arms. This discussion leads to the hypothesis that the racism experienced by blacks in the military on foreign terrain is a manifestation of racism learned and internalized through the socialization process at home.

Chapter 9 is devoted to deviance and is divided into two parts for analytical purposes. The first section discusses criminality—not in the traditional perspective of the pathology of the black community but as an adaptive response to white domination and black subordination. A social-psychological theoretical framework permits the treatment of both acquisitive and aggressive criminal behavior, as reflected in discussions of the hustler syndrome and of victims of black criminal behavior. Following a discussion of racism in the administration of criminal justice is an analysis of ghetto crime-control programs initiated by black people. The second section examines problems of mental health and health-care systems. The interrelatedness of economic factors and external control of drugs used to debilitate ghetto blacks is also treated here.

Chapter 10, "The Black Community in a White Society," recalls the theoretical frameworks that are the basis of the book and focuses attention on the current ideological issues that both divide and unite the black community: integration, assimilation, separation, and liberation. It outlines the positions assumed by advocates of cultural nationalism and those who espouse revolutionary nationalism in dealing with the radicalization of black protest movements.

Although this book illustrates a major thematic structure, it is not committed to a single theoretical perspective in race relations. Single-factor theories are emphatically rejected, since the forces that produce multiplicative interaction patterns both among and within racial and ethnic groups are far too complex for satisfactory analysis by singular theories. In using this open approach, an effort has been made to demonstrate both the extensiveness of intragroup differentiation within the black community and the force of categorical treatment, based upon race, color, and class, in creating unity out of diversity.

JAMES E. BLACKWELL

1 | INTRODUCTION: TO BE BLACK IN AMERICA

To understand fully the meaning of being a black American we must assess the impact of representative institutional structures on members of the black community. This assessment describes the formidable role of prejudice in patterning systems of denials to black people as manifested in institutionalized racism—both de jure and de facto. Historical evidence shows that there has been a significant qualitative change in the categorical treatment of blacks when compared to treatment patterns a few years ago. This does not mean, however, that blacks are no longer subjected to categorical treatment as a low-status group, which would be a gross misrepresentation. It would be equally misleading to deny the progress, albeit limited, that blacks have made toward achieving equality and full participation as citizens. The apparent disjunction between these two perspectives lies in the ever-widening gap between white gains and the inaccessibility of societally shared values to the black population.

Four brief examples, elaborated in subsequent chapters, will help illuminate this point. First, public school segregation, mandated in its de jure form by the 1896 *Plessy* v. *Ferguson* decision, was overturned in the case of *Brown* v. *Board of Education of Topeka, Kansas*, in 1954. In its de facto form housing patterns seemed to have been the major culprit in perpetuating a dual educational system outside the South. But the promise of equal education envisioned in 1954 is unfulfilled. *While many school districts are desegregated, numerous schools within these districts are more segregated*

1

now than they were in 1954. Second, in the economic sphere a number of executive orders and equal-opportunity mechanisms were issued in the United States during and after World War II; they were designed to eradicate income disparities between the two major racial groups. Although some income-equalizing devices have led to significant income gains for blacks, they have not successfully closed the gaps in income distribution between black and white Americans. In fact, blacks are losing ground in the attainment of equal income, which, if earned, could be transformed into other economic, health, and educational benefits.[1] Blacks, moreover, are invariably the most seriously affected by economic recessions. Third, the rise of blacks as a major political force poses other dilemmas. This emergence occurred through the enactment of enabling legislation, such as the voting rights bills of the 1960s, and a reduction of violence against those blacks who sought participation in the political process. Perhaps it is unfortunate that blacks have forged onto the urban political scene, particularly at a time when resources are wanting, a federal administration is largely unsympathetic, and the fear of the consequences of active political involvement continues to prevail among many blacks. Thus the failure to bring about a more equitable redistribution of political power raises serious questions about the extent of black power in the United States in relation to white dominance. Housing provides a fourth illustration of the hiatus between white gains and the inaccessibility of shared values for black Americans. Since 1917 various Supreme Court decisions have attempted to curb housing discrimination. In some instances these decisions, along with limited enforcement by state, local, and federal governments, have caused neighborhoods to desegregate. But in all parts of the nation neighborhoods are becoming increasingly segregated. White flight from the city has occurred so rapidly that the inner city is almost all black. Only 4.7 percent of the nation's black population lives in the suburbs, while those residing in the 12 largest cities of the United States having 2 million or more people constitute 28 percent of their total populations.[2] The phenomenon of territorial segregation has enormous implications for institutional segregation and discrimination (for instance, all-black schools in the cities and all-white schools in the suburbs).

The patterns of denial found in institutional segregation and discrimination also imply patterns of denial in day-to-day living. Consequently, to be black in America now is an extension of what it meant to be black in the 1870s—it means a struggle for equality of opportunity, appropriate rewards, and access to the shared values of the nation—whether in housing, jobs, income, voting rights, political offices, good medical care and health services, schools, and protection from crime—and it means a struggle against the painful reality that rising expectations are relatively unfulfilled. But to be black now is qualitatively distinguishable from being black in the 1870s. Theoretically, laws are ideally color blind; but, actually, their implementation is not. The black person today confronts different historical experiences and sociopolitical forces than his forebears of a century ago. Unlike them, he has the benefits of voluminous scientific research about personality, the nature of self, and the roles that individuals play in social systems. He knows that other black people have won freedom from white domination and established independent political nation-states that suggest other alternatives to the traditional goals of assimilation within the American society. To be black today is to exist in a sociopsychological state of becoming, to be engaged in a quest for identity, a search for a universal meaning of being with other black beings. Being black today means creating new value systems that are peculiarly and distinctively indigenous to the black community; it means accepting and appreciating the self.

To be black is to acknowledge the principle that unity without uniformity is acceptable within the community of black people. It is confronting the often bitter reality that the majority of American whites feel that blacks are getting "too much too soon" and that a significant number of whites accept the stereotype of able-bodied, lazy blacks clogging the welfare rolls even when evidence to the contrary abounds.

To be black means claiming credit plus reparations for helping build this nation into the world's richest and most advanced technological society. It is neither cowed subservience nor acceptance of the status quo but acting to create meaningful social change. To be black is a realization by blacks as well as whites that the black community is a complex, heterogeneous entity whose strength and vitality emanate from its diversity. To be black means all of these things—it also means being a Justice of the United States Supreme Court, a judge in a lower court, a member of the presidential cabinet, a president of a black-owned bank or insurance company with millions of dollars in assets, a vice-president of a major "all-white" bank, or a professional employed by IBM, Dow Chemical, Polaroid, or McDonald's hamburger chain. Hence to be black also means for many an incontestable commitment to the Protestant ethic not indistinguishable from that of America's ruling class. How did these conditions come about? What factors account for the emergence of a black community as distinguished from any other American community? What theoretical models are useful for sociological interpretations of this community? What are the characteristics of the people who comprise this segment of the American population? The answers to these and other questions appear in subsequent sections in this chapter. We turn now to the theoretical issues.

A SEARCH FOR A
RELEVANT THEORY

The absence of theoretical models developed solely by black scholars for analysis of what is labeled as the authentic black experience in America is a vexing problem for ideologists of "blackness." The latter question the validity of most existing theoretical constructs because the white middle-class social scientists who designed them unavoidably based them on the white middle-class norm. According to this view, the norms of white America should not be equated with the norms of black America. There are wide divergencies and startling contrasts in the normative structures of white middle-class America and those of the black community; in fact, the majority of black people cannot be labeled middle class. This position, however, may be more political than scientific.

On a political level this claim achieves its greatest relevance, since as outsiders blacks are able to provide a perspective on the same phenomena different from interpretations made by white outsiders.[3]* It is this possibility of rectifying incorrect interpretations of the past that gives this view its greatest acceptability. On a more scientific level, though, such views encounter serious problems.[4] The utility of a theory, for example, does not lie totally and exclusively in such considerations as those posited by ideologists of blackness. Even if theories were dichotomized into black theories and white theories, similarities of functions would be inevitable. The search for a relevant theory would continue. The functions of sociological theory would not be dissimilar, black or white. Sociological theory explicates, defines, and provides generalizations about observable social phenomena as they exist—it does not prescribe what social behavior ought to be. The most advanced theories are based upon objective knowledge rather than upon social philosophy. They are, in effect, verified generalizations gained from repeated observations of social phenomena. Without verification generalizations might merely be speculative thought.

Sociological questions are raised both in terms of their theoretical relevance and as guidelines for ascertaining solutions to specific problems. In the latter instance the concern is an expression of a social value while in the former it focuses on the explanation of the regularities or patterns of social behavior as well as on the discontinuities or deviations from prescribed

---

* In the insider-outsider controversy, advocates of the insider doctrine maintain that members of a given racial or ethnic group, who are usually "outsiders" to the dominant group, are more uniquely qualified to provide meaning to their experiences than are individuals who are not members of that group. On the other hand, outsiders claim that, by not being members of such groups, they are able to bring intellectual objectivity to the analysis of the experiences of less favored and often oppressed groups.

social norms. Some problems defy analysis by a given single-theory formulation because it may be too narrow in scope to account for the complexities of the problem being studied. The problem of the black community is such an instance. No single theoretical model can adequately or appropriately explain the structural and organizational entities of this complex and diverse phenomenon. No single theory can explain fully the authentic black experience in America. Again the point should be stressed that there is no single authentic black experience in America except that which developed as a consequence of ubiquitous white racism and the prevalent color consciousness. Because of variations in manifestations of racism and color consciousness, multiple black experiences occurred, each one as authentic as the other. The common denominator for all of them, however, is the coalescence of racism and color. Because of the limitations of single-theory formulations and the absence of a fully developed black sociological perspective, three paradigms for developing a sociology of the black community follow. Used together they permit a juxtaposition of black and white interpretations of the same behavioral patterns when appropriate. The three theoretical paradigms are: (1) parallel structures and pluralism, (2) the more recently developed internal colonialism model, and (3) systems theory.

PARALLEL STRUCTURES AND PLURALISM

Minorities in America, it is typically assumed, will eventually assimilate into mainstream American society. According to this view, assimilation is tantamount to incorporation into the American system; in essence the incorporated group loses its identity and becomes similar to the group that engulfed it. This theoretical framework, endorsed by most liberal American sociologists, has persistently guided studies of race relations. It is founded upon the liberal belief that there are almost unlimited opportunities for all who are willing to do so to enter into the mainstream of the American society regardless of their cultural origins. The major flaw in this theory of incorporation, however, is that it was addressed largely to northern and western European immigrants rather than to *all* minorities. Even in their case, it did not anticipate the unfulfilled aspirations of European ethnics as evidenced in the contemporary resurgence of a new ethnicity among them. Its application to non-European immigrants is a recent phenomenon. Metzger calls attention to Reuter's influential pioneer study of racial problems in America, which makes clear that many early American sociologists did not view blacks as assimilable.[5] This is especially the case when we observe that assimilation is synonymous with equality or equal access to the shared values within the opportunity structure. There is, however, a significant caveat: Opportunity means also a mandate to discard one's ethnicity.[6] We should note that it is somewhat easier to discard one's ethnicity than to discard one's race, although much evidence exists showing that the latter occurs in the United States through the phenomenon of passing—that is, voluntarily relinquishing one's assigned racial identity to become a member of another race by virtue of possessing biological features common to the new race. Members of subordinate groups usually use passing to achieve access to shared values and better opportunity structures. Other questions such as the desirability of absorption of minority groups into the dominant culture or the possibility of assimilation as a manifestation of the democratic ethos as opposed to a form of containment of black minorities will be elaborated in succeeding chapters.

One of the more salient consequences of patterned discrimination and enforced segregation of black people in the United States has been the creation of dual but parallel structures presently giving way to pluralism within the black community. Pluralism in this case means the development of institutions (e.g., separate educational institutions and businesses, churches, banks catering specifically to blacks) that are similar to those found in the larger society but that were fostered by forces in the larger society in such a manner as to give rise to a black community. The institutions and, consequently, the community emerged from racial separation as well as from the exclusionary policies of the dominant group. Slavery, for example, was accompanied by racism. Racism in turn helped to legitimate discrimination and enforced segregation, which were instrumental in establishing boundary-maintenance systems. These systems then prevented the incorporation of blacks into the larger social system. In time blacks were forced to evolve institutional arrangements necessary to meet functional needs common to any other human group. Thus black people, being denied entry as equals into the mainstream social system, created their own institutional forms in religion, marriage and the family, education, government, economics, recreation, and so forth.

Slavery. As Jessie Bernard contends, slavery provided a model of integration predicated upon separation.[7] Blacks were in America physically but were only tacitly a part of the country. The policies of separation extended to all institutional forms, and because of them blacks were relegated to a position of inferiority within the social structure. The result of this situation was the institutionalization of white dominance and black subordination. The institutionalization was achieved through legislation and aided substantially by the inhumane treatment of black people.

The first step in the process was to provide a rationale for treating black people differently, and it came with the statutory recognition of slavery by Virginia in 1661. Virginia's bold step established a precedent for subsequent legislation enacted in most other colonies. Legalizing slavery was followed by interpretations of slaves not as human beings but as prized property. This definition justified behavior among slaveowners and their surrogates that ranged from maltreatment (such as extreme brutality, physical assaults, sexual exploitation, imposed roles as studs, and slave transfers that severed family units), on the one hand, to manifestations of concern for the welfare and protection of slaves, humane treatment of subordinated individuals, and generalized love, on the other. The efficacy of these options varied immensely from colony to colony and from plantation to plantation. Just as alternatives relative to the disposition and treatment of slaves varied, so did conceptualizations of slaves throughout the nation.

Despite divergent views of slaves and slavery, a common denominator remained—the perception of slaves as property. Chattels were used quite effectively to bolster the economic structure of the period. Similarly, they were also the foundation for the development of a society based upon white domination over a relatively defenseless black populace. Having rationalized the interrelationship between the economic necessity of slavery and the promotion of white superiority, the white power structure had to devise a method of maintaining that relationship. Black codes were invented for that purpose—the maintenance of white superordination and the protection of private property.

Black Codes. Thus containment, conformity, and subjugation reached their zenith perhaps in the articulation of the inhumane *code noir*, or the black codes, which spread with alarming speed throughout the colonies, especially those of the South. These codes underscore the magnitude of control that white colonists had over even the most mundane aspects of the lives of enslaved black people. Codes limited their movement on and off plantations and required written authorization from a master for off-plantation travel. The penalty for rape and murder was death by hanging and masters were then given financial compensation by the colony (as in Virginia, Maryland, and New Jersey) for this economic loss. Mutilation was the penalty for crimes of robbery and burglary as well as for generally petty offenses. Often the severing of an ear or the nailing of a slave's ear to a pillory post was accompanied by branding, floggings, and lacerations. Throughout the colonies, North and South, the major capital offenses were murder, rape (of white women), arson, escape from a plantation, robbery, and burglary.[8] Other laws forbade marriage without the master's permission[9] and denied blacks the privilege of engaging in any form of trade at all or to be in possession of any type of weapon without a permit.[10]

Some codes, as in Georgia, forbade teaching slaves reading and writing. Obviously, this law was often violated. Others forbade slaves the right to own and acquire property. In general, too, a child took the status of his mother so as to guarantee enslavement of children fathered by white men with black slave women. Planters rationalized these laws on the grounds that black people were barbaric, uncivilized, and in need of humanizing influences that only contact with Christian colonists could provide. Thus it was to the slave's benefit to be enslaved, brutalized, and dehumanized in the process. Kenneth Stampp argues that the slave codes were designed to socialize the slave into accepting a rigid discipline invoked by the white slave master, to render the slave completely dependent upon the owner, to force him into unequivocal submission, and to induce him to adopt the master's standard of acceptable behavior.[11]

Codes were initially significant first steps. However, the undeniable consequence of the codes was the establishment of a pattern of superordination and enforced subordination buttressed by a prevailing morality that permitted its occurrence. By reassuring white superordination through legal sanctions, the codes were instrumental in creating a sociopsychological state among most white Americans that is indelible and that has had far-reaching implications—that is, the belief in the inherent inferiority of the black race and the natural superiority of white people. In time, many blacks internalized this view. It remains among a significant number of whites today both as a deeply entrenched sense of group position and as an acceptance of notions of biological superiority—it is one explanation for the failure of many desegregation programs and other programs originated to eradicate segregation along with discrimination. This is maximum racism in its most expressive form.[12]

House Slaves and Field Slaves: Social Stratification. It is the contention of many historians that slavery rescued a dying economy in many parts of the American colonies.[13] Assuming that there is merit in this claim, we can further observe that the economic structure of the plantation, which is treated extensively by Ulrich Phillips and Kenneth Stampp,[14] evolved a complex division of labor among blacks that has profound implications for their lives today.

During slavery (1661–1865) the most important status distinctions stemmed from the occupational stratification of blacks as either house slaves (for instance, serving as maids, butlers, cooks, nursemaids, coachmen, laundry workers, and companions) or as field slaves (performing nonhousehold roles on the plantation such as that of a field hand). The distinction between house slaves and field slaves was paramount. The former were accorded a higher status than the latter. Not unexpectedly, they attempted to safeguard their high-status positions as much as possible. Thus some informed about other slaves; some attempted to delimit their contacts with field hands unless such contacts maximized their advantages with the masters. Urban blacks, including slaves, worked as skilled artisans, as bricklayers, carpenters, machine operators, mechanics, cotton-press operators, and cabinetmakers. The allocation of slave roles depended upon variables such as the size of the plantation, sex, the type of crops produced, and the work season.

House slaves had a much greater exposure to the dominant culture, greater opportunities to learn its customs, values, and life styles and to share, even though in a subordinate position, in its culture. Field hands, however, were more likely to retain their African heritage. We should keep in mind that the plantation structure crystallized the division between master and slave and bifurcated the slave social system. In each system institutions arose to meet certain socially defined needs. The differences among the institutions within these basic stratification subsystems were a function of the intensity of cultural homogenization or isolation between slaves and masters. The differences were greater among field slaves. As ethnolinguistic units among slaves were destroyed through the trade and transfers, the alternative available to slaves was to learn the culture of the master. This became both functional and necessary for survival. Where ethnolinguistic units remained relatively intact, institutional differences between the superordinates and subordinates were maximum. In both cases there occurred unique adaptations to the American experience that formed the framework for the development of parallel institutions and a form of pluralism. If it is a fundamental and incontestable truth that field hands, the true pariahs of the system, were more likely to retain their original culture, one must look to them for survivals of the African past. Similarly, is it also likely that some of these same cultural survivals in contemporary times are more probably located among the field hands of the rural South and the socially isolated of the urban ghetto?

It is this distinction between house slaves and field slaves that is so critical in the development of parallel institutions, in the assimilation of some slaves into the culture of the whites (acculturation), and in the argument for African cultural survivals among North American slaves.

African Survivals. The debates between E. Franklin Frazier and Melville Herskovits of over a quarter of a century ago framed the issues of African survivals. The debates involved much more than a discussion of the prevalence of African survivals, and indeed concerned the emergence from them of a distinctive black culture in America. Their ideas seem to have an uninterrupted continuance in the arguments advanced today by scholars like Andrew Billingsley[15] and Robert Blauner,[16] on the one hand, and Nathan Glazer and Daniel P. Moynihan[17] and Irving Kristol,[18] on the other. Like Herskovits, Billingsley and Blauner take the position that in spite of the harshness of slavery and its deliberate efforts to dispossess blacks of their cultural past, a black culture has survived in America.

Much of what has survived originated in an African past. Survivals include family patterns and attitudes, songs, dance, religious practices, superstitions, ways of walking, verbal expressions, orientations toward recreation and pleasure, epicurean traditions, sex-related role expectations, music, given names for children, and traditional foods. Thus Blauner and others[19] advance the notion that an authentic black culture survived slavery and is to be found today largely in the urban ghettos of black America. That culture has its roots in the parallel institutions that evolved and crystallized social relationships among the members of the black community.

Frazier claims that Herskovits and his followers overstate the case for African survivals and a black culture.[20] He maintains that the black American's African past was gradually "sloughed off" as a consequence of his experiences in America.

Glazer and Moynihan and, to some degree, Kristol extend this theoretical position in their claim that blacks are peculiarly and distinctly American, knowing no culture other than the American culture. The disagreement between Frazier and Herskovits is not so much over kind as degree. The issue is not whether there are any African survivals at all in the United States, but rather the degree to which these survivals persist and whether they persist in sufficient strength to influence current or contemporary patterns of black behavior. We shall return to this argument at various points in subsequent chapters.

It should now be easier to understand how the convergence of prejudice and mandates for segregation within the social structure fostered the development of parallel structures and cultural cohesion. As blacks were excluded and prevented from participation in institutions of the larger society, they developed their own institutional forms. This process was gradually abetted by the promulgation of numerous laws, beginning with black codes and continuing through the implementation of Jim Crow legislation at the turn of the twentieth century. These legal constraints, coupled with intimidation and violence, either threatened or actually visited upon black people by white Americans, created a boundary system that separated the races and gave rise to parallel structures. The more extreme the barriers were between the races, the greater was the tendency for blacks to establish their own institutional forms.

THE DEVELOPMENT OF PLURALISM

In time, parallel institutions became the foundation for pluralism. Immediately, it should be apparent, as Richard A. Schermerhorn argues, that there are different types of pluralism. He identifies four prevalent usages of the term pluralism: (1) as an ideological designation called normative pluralism, which refers to doctrinal beliefs ascribed to a minority group whose members wish to preserve their way of life despite its sharp differences from the dominant group patterns; (2) as a political designation called political pluralism, which refers to "the multiplicity of interest groups and associations" that exert pressure on the decision-making process as well as on the implementation of decisions through organizations such as political parties or lobbies and through a skillful use of mass media; (3) as a cultural designation, also called cultural pluralism, in which the cultural differences of a group set it apart from other groups, dominant or minority— these differences may be perceived in terms of language, religion, nationality, kinship forms, tribal affiliation, and other normative patterns that may heighten their distinctions—race may also become a potent variable in defining stratification patterns and express itself in the norm of cultural pluralism; and (4) as a structural designation, also called social pluralism, which refers to the presence of parallel institutional forms within a particular group that differ structurally from those of other groups existing in the same society. The differences in (4) are magnified when the factors of race and language are significant in the society. Schermerhorn also speaks of this type as institutional pluralism and admits its similarity to Milton Gordon's structural pluralism.[21]

Irving Rinder speaks of accommodative pluralism, which is characteristic of moderately deprived minorities that are able to retain much of their true or original cultures while conforming to the economic structure of the host country (as in the case of Jews).[22] Both accommodated pluralism and Schermerhorn's normative pluralism are new ways of expressing what Louis Wirth identified as a pluralistic minority based upon "the goal toward which the minority and the dominant group are striving."[23] It is in normative, cultural, and structural pluralism that the arguments for pluralism find expression today. In the black community the stress is upon cultural pluralism, although its advocates seem to use the term to include those attributes identified by Schermerhorn as pertaining to all three designations: normative, structural, and cultural. Structural pluralism is more apparent in terms of the diverse institutional forms that emerged throughout the black experience in America. Cultural nationalists would also claim that an identifiable black culture evolved through the medium of distinct black institutional structures. Thus there is, in their view, a black way of life that is to be distinguished from white culture. Like all other cultures, it is learned through a socialization process, undergirded by a system of norms and values that guides conduct and is transmitted both formally and informally. This is precisely the claim of advocates of a black sociology or a black psychology. But claims of pluralism are not new in American sociology. The term was popularized as it applied to American Jews in the works of its chief proponent, Horace M. Kallen, and of others including Isaac B. Berkson, Louis Adamic, and, more recently, Stewart and Mildred Cole and S. N. Eisenstadt and others. However, there is a fact of profound importance here. Although the black community (broadly defined) originated as a defense against white racism, it soon took on a special dynamism or character of its own, so that today even though its institutions may parallel those of the larger society, they possess their own uniqueness and intrinsic values.

On a theoretical level, then, the concept of pluralism can be employed for understanding the black community as a separate structure and distinctive cultural unit within the total American society.

INTERNAL COLONIALISM

A second theoretical perspective that can serve as a framework for understanding the black community and the experiences of black people in America is the internal colonialism model. The chief advocate of this perspective among sociologists is Blauner, whose provocative essay "Internal Colonialism and Ghetto Revolt" created considerable theoretical controversy among American sociologists.[24] The following discussion is based upon Blauner's theoretical formulation.

The central theme of internal colonialism is that black-white relations in the United States are essentially those of colonizer and colonized. The primary emphasis in this model is on domestic colonialization as a process or as an experience instead of the classical or traditional perspective of colonialization as a system. In theoretical terms it is an attempt to bring conceptual clarity to race relations theory by converging missing links from such frameworks as "caste and racism, ethnicity, culture, and economic exploitation" theory into an all-encompassing theme.[25]

Exploitation and control are essential elements in both traditional or classical colonialism and in internal or domestic colonialism. The colonizers seize and maintain control over all resources and over the land on which colonizers and colonized alike settle. Legitimated authority and power over the political processes are maintained through the establishment of formal mechanisms, which the colonizers also control. In the traditional sense, however, the colonizers are generally outsiders and numerical minorities who use superior technological power, skill, and know-how as instruments for subordinating the indigenous majority people, who by definition are technologically, if not culturally, inferior. Thus colonialism is quite similar to what Stanley Lieberson has termed migrant superordination.[26] In either case, racism is one of the more observable consequences.

Blauner asserts that colonialization involves an interplay of four variables or components: (1) the point of entry of the racial group (how it entered the dominant society); (2) acculturation, with culture loss by the colonized group; (3) administrative control of the affairs of the colonized group by the colonizing power; and (4) manifestations of racism. Therefore, internal colonialism is typified by situations in which a colonized group involuntarily enters the dominant society as, for example, through slavery; the destruction of its original culture through a systematic mechanism of denial; the control and manipulation of the internal affairs of the colonized group by forces external to its community (for example, control and manipulation of all institutions except perhaps the church); and the articulation of a racist structure in which notions of the superordinate group's alleged biological superiority rationalize oppression and subordination of the colonized. This process is often achieved through the institutionalization of legal structures evidenced in de jure segregation and discrimination.[27]

As applied to the black community, the internal colonialism model takes on a special meaning. Most American blacks have as ancestors former slaves who had little choice about being uprooted from their original homes for entry into a society as a subject people. Options available to European immigrants, as, for example, payment for their labor, were not available to them. One could argue that unfair labor practices and the relatively low position of blacks in the labor market today still attest to the limited options available to black laborers. Similarly, just as slave masters isolated slaves and denied them their culture with the resultant development of parallel institutions within the black community, new black cultural structures are maintained in part as a consequence of continued structural isolation and separation. Further, just as an external white power structure manipulated and managed the lives of preemancipation blacks, so today an external white structure manipulates and manages many facets of daily life among black people. The powerlessness of blacks in urban ghettos and rural farm areas all over the United States reduces them to a state of dependency. This condition is reflected in occupations and income, general economic state, politics, education, health care, and police protection—all controlled largely by people outside the black community. Decision-making power on issues of primary importance to them is beyond their pale. The limited opportunities for escape from the wall of the ghetto coupled with powerlessness in the several dimensions just cited typify a protracted state of domestic colonialization. Kenneth Clark in *Youth in the Ghetto*, Richard Schermerhorn in *Comparative Ethnic Relations*, and others also share this view.

James E. Blackwell and Marie Haug,[28] for example, using the evidence of cities like Gary and Cleveland, disproved the widely held belief that gaining control of the mayoralty results in significant social and political rewards for the black masses. The election of a black mayor does not necessarily lead to meaningful changes in the day-to-day living conditions. Political victories do not by themselves result in economic, educational, medical, or housing payoffs. Indeed, the cultural imperatives, to use Harold Cruse's term, of the white majority may still be mandated in the school system and the informal mechanisms or symbolic rituals that influence daily life.

The internal colonialization model is of value in providing insight into power conflict theory, especially when the focus shifts to present-day manifestations such as ghetto revolts, issues of ghetto control, and the stress on cultural nationalism. In this sense the primary concern is the struggle for a rearrangement of power structures in order to accelerate access of the black minority to legitimated privilege and to elevate the colonized blacks to a new status. This model is limited, however, in not being applicable to the situation of some white ethnics and in its inadequate treatment of the important variable of mobility among some blacks.

SYSTEMS THEORY AND
THE BLACK COMMUNITY

A third theoretical framework within which to study the sociology of the black community is that of systems analysis. Systems theoreticians, like Talcott Parsons, who advocate the notion of societies in a state of equilibrium, usually follow an organic model traceable to the pioneer works of Herbert Spencer. Those who oppose the organic model of equilibrium, such as George Homans, owe much of their theoretical formulations to the works of Valfredo Pareto. However, Parsons' views seem to have enjoyed wide popularity and greater influence on sociological thought in the United States.

In general, systems theory begins with the notion that societies can be viewed as a system in which the whole has predominance over all of its parts. Societies are viewed as "going concerns," dynamic as it were, but their survival or maintenance is dependent upon meeting important needs or functional imperatives. These functional imperatives are a necessary precondition of survival. A basic requirement for meeting these needs is the articulation of certain structures or uniformities of action that recur as particular situations demand. These structures are specified in the form of social organization as social institutions, such as the family, religion, education, economy, and government, called for by the society. However, societal needs dictate the organization of these structures into a system of interrelated activities that are, in turn, mutually supportive. It is this property of interdependence that creates order and cohesion within the system.

As long as they are of functional utility for maintaining the whole system, the components of the concept of order may include legitimized institutional patterns, deviance, conflict, and even subcultural forms. Boundary-maintenance devices are established to assure the maintenance of order and societal equilibrium. Such devices, that is, formal and informal socialization, structures for social control, and "mechanisms of defense," possess some degree of constancy or continuity about them. Thus societal units are interlocked in a network of mutually shared expectations, normative structures, sentiments, and value constructs.[29] The social system is, therefore, a configuration or a network of interrelated parts organized into a whole. These parts include values, norms, sentiments, roles, statuses, patterned behaviors, and institutions. In general, these components are expected to exist in a homeostatic relationship, but this is not always the case, since perfect equilibrium is never attained. Systems are always subject to stresses and strains. Deviance and conflict occur, but the ability of the system to survive as a whole rests on its success in handling those internal and external factors that create consensus and unity.

The black community can be perceived as a social system. Within the community value consensus and congruence exist; a significant segment of its constituents share norms, sentiments, and expectations. Structures are developed to meet defined needs and are hierarchically arranged according to their ability to respond to certain needs. Thus roles and statuses emerge in relation to societal expectations and differential rewards that are assigned. Even though diversity exists within the community, its members are held together by adherence to commonly shared values and goals.

In sum, each of the foregoing three theoretical schemes has much to offer in providing frameworks for the analysis of the black community, the nature of its present condition in relation to the larger social structure, and the dynamics of its organization. We see these frameworks not as totally independent constructs but as mutually reinforcing ones, providing understanding and linkage where a hiatus exists in the study of race relations today. They help provide better insights into the nature of the collective responses that black Americans have made in the past and continue to make to the conditions of subjugation, discrimination, prejudice, and institutionalized racism. These collective responses are typified by individual reactions to external conditions imposed upon the black community as a whole as well as to the internal state of affairs within the community itself. Responses crisscross a number of different boundaries. For example, such responses may be related to educational, economic, and familial variables found in the black social system or they may be a function of the administrative power exercised on that system from without. The interplay of these forces is of incontestable importance in terms of impact on the behavioral patterns within and among the members of the black community.

THE BLACK COMMUNITY
TODAY

In this work the black community is viewed as a social system engaged in a number of interrelated activities. These activities are organized around structures called social institutions, which function to meet specific needs and which parallel those institutions existing in the larger society. In many respects the community exists only in a colonized state, since much of what occurs in it is controlled and manipulated by a power structure that is external to the community itself. The manipulation from the outside is only partial, however, since a structure prevails within the black community itself. Nevertheless, the power exercised by the leadership there is at best relative, for it is neither fully autonomous nor fully a creation of the rank-and-file community member. Whatever the case, black people in America, in spite of the admitted diversity, find themselves in what Thomas C. Shelling aptly describes as "the same boat together."[30]

Components of Community. There are, of course, varied perceptions of the concept "community." The term embraces such factors as territoriality or spatial distribution, and human aggregates distributed within certain ecological boundaries who share common experiences, value systems, and social institutions. Community also connotes power distribution; it means how the members are organized at both formal and informal levels or in a social class structure; it also refers to associational character and friendship cliques.[31] Conceptually, then, community is not characterized by unidimensionality. It is multifaceted. It can be used in both an ecological sense (territoriality and propinquity) or in sociopsychological terms. In the latter sense we are speaking of the role of shared values in creating a sense of identity with a particular group that may or may not live within the same geographic boundary. People are brought together in community because they happen to share common interests and values. They have accepted sets of definitions of situations, life experiences, or other conditions that give them a uniqueness apart from others whose views, values, and experiences are dissimilar. Shared values, in the formation of a community, may supersede geographic boundaries; they may cross over social class and color lines. A community, therefore, may be considered as a "combination of social units and systems which perform the major social functions having locality reference."[32]

FUNCTIONS OF A
COMMUNITY

Roland Warren identifies five major functions of a community that have locality relevance. These are: (1) *production-distribution-consumption*, which concerns the availability of goods and services essential to daily living in the immediate locality (and includes all social institutions found in the community); (2) *socialization*, which refers to the transmission of basic values and behavioral patterns to the individual members of the system; (3) *social control*, which is the structural arrangement for influencing members toward behavioral conformity; (4) *social participation*, which refers to those structures that facilitate incorporation into the community by virtue of opportunities for participation in its life; and (5) *mutual support*, which describes the process of care and exchanges for help among the members of a group, especially in times of stress. Mutual support may be performed by socializing agents, family members, religious bodies, informal associations, friendship cliques, and so forth.[33]

This definition subsumes a number of important elements of community and permits the elaboration of other issues. For example, a constellation of such variables as resource availability and utilization, leadership structure, power distribution, community control, and access to shared values may be examined. We shall call upon these variables in appraising various structures within the black community throughout this book. The reader is reminded, however, that members of a community develop positive sentiments or feelings toward one another. These emerge from the interests they share as well as from the commonality of their experiences with an external, hostile environment. Just as sentiments may serve as the source of normative integration, they also show the diversity among a community's members. This diversity is particularly noticeable when sentiments are transformed into values, as, for example, the value of integration versus the value of separation, which threatened to polarize the black community during the late 1960s (see Chapter 10).

DEMOGRAPHIC CHARACTERISTICS

This section introduces a variety of characteristics and distinguishing features of the American black population today. When appropriate, historical comparisons will be drawn for illustrative purposes. Special attention is given to such characteristics as size of population, migration patterns, distribution of the population, fertility and mortality, and the age-sex structure. Subsequent chapters of the book will treat most of these characteristics in somewhat greater detail. The discussion that follows is drawn largely from an analysis of U.S. census data, which has the most reliable national statistics on population characteristics available.

Size. The slightly more than 23 million blacks in the United States in

1971 constituted approximately 11.2 percent of the total American population. The proportions of blacks in the total population have never remained
stable. Table 1-1 illustrates the number of fluctuations in population size
over a substantial time period. These fluctuations also illustrate how the black
population is increasing but at a decreasing rate. Changes in population size
may be explained by a number of factors that need not be elaborated here;
but they may be listed as: (1) termination of the slave trade; (2) the end
of slavery; (3) a decline in infant mortality and adult mortality rates; and
(4) changes in the birth rates among women of childbearing ages. Disparities in the proportion of blacks among the total population may only be partially explained by the preceding four factors, since the United States also
experienced a steady and unparalleled influx of people from Europe for
almost a century. This flow of immigrants led to a rapid increase in the population, which, in turn, reduced the proportion of blacks in the population
as a whole. The proportion has declined even though the black population
has more than tripled since 1820.

TABLE 1-1.

Population Growth of Black Americans
in Selected Years, 1790–1971

Year	Total U.S. Population	Total Black Population[1]	Percent Black
1790	3,929,214	757,000	19.3
1800	5,308,483	1,002,000	18.9
1820	9,638,453	1,772,000	18.4
1840	17,069,453	2,874,000	16.8
1860	31,443,321	4,521,000	14.1
1880	50,155,783	6,753,000	13.1
1900	75,944,575	9,185,000	11.6
1920	105,710,620	10,890,000	9.9
1940	131,669,275	13,454,000	9.8
1960	179,323,175	18,872,000	10.5
1966	195,000,000[1]	21,220,000	11.0
1967	197,000,000[1]	21,600,000	11.0
1968	198,900,000[1]	21,900,000	11.0
1969	200,900,000[1]	21,200,000	11.0
1970	203,200,000[1]	22,600,000	11.0
1971	205,700,000[1]	23,000,000	11.2

[1] Figures are rounded off.
SOURCES: U.S. Department of Commerce, Social and Economic Statistics Administration, Bureau of the Census—Current Population Reports; *Historical Statistics of
the United States*, Bureau of the Census, Department of Commerce, 1960; *Statistical
Abstracts, 1973*, Bureau of the Census, Department of Commerce, 1973.

Distribution and Nativity. For several centuries the black population was concentrated in the rural South, where agriculture was its principal occupational pursuit. As recently as 1900 almost 90 percent of the black population still remained in the Southern states. However, commencing with the 1915 exodus, when more than 250,000 blacks outmigrated, the rest of the nation has witnessed an almost unabated, though uneven, influx of blacks from region to region. As a result, slightly more than one-half (53 percent) of the black population remained in the South as of 1971. Thirty-nine percent of the black Americans are presently found in the North, including states subsumed under the regional categories as Northeastern and North Central areas, and, as Table 1-2 shows, the remaining 8 percent are located in the Western states.

The exodus of the black population from the South, which began in 1915, marked a turning point in the geographical distribution of black Americans. The movement signaled something greater than merely the shift of the population from one region to another—though that shift proved to be of profound consequences for structural changes in the black community —it brought about fundamental changes in the rural-urban distribution of

TABLE 1-2.

Percent Distribution of the Population by Region: 1950, 1960, and 1970

Subject	1950[1]	1960	1970
Black			
United States (millions)	15.0	18.9	22.6
Percent, total	100	100	100
South	68	60	53
North	28	34	39
Northeast	13	16	19
North Central	15	18	20
West	4	6	8
White			
United States (millions)	134.9	158.8	177.7
Percent, total	100	100	100
South	27	27	28
North	59	56	54
Northeast	28	26	25
North Central	31	30	29
West	14	16	18

[1] Data exclude Alaska and Hawaii.
SOURCE: U.S. Department of Commerce, Social and Economic Statistics Administration, Bureau of the Census.

the black population. Thus, according to the 1970 census, approximately three-fourths of American blacks now live in metropolitan areas of the United States. In becoming a metropolitan population blacks have tended to concentrate in the inner cities in every region of the country, except the South. As a general rule, the larger the metropolitan area, the greater the proportion of black people residing in the central cities. Simultaneously, the white population has become more suburbanized by moving away from all parts of the city. As a result, an ecological pattern of succession has already started as blacks replace whites in the cities and the cities of America are increasingly inhabited by blacks and poor whites.

T A B L E   1 - 3 .

Population Distribution and Change, Inside and Outside Metropolitan Areas: 1950, 1960, and 1970

(Numbers in millions)

Area	Population					
	Black			White		
	1950	1960	1970	1950	1960	1970
United States	15.0	18.9	22.6	135.1	158.8	177.7
Metropolitan areas[1]	8.8	12.8	16.8	85.1	106.4	121.3
Central cities	6.6	9.9	13.2	46.8	49.5	49.5
Outside central cities	2.2	2.9	3.7	38.3	56.9	71.8
Outside metropolitan areas	6.2	6.1	5.8	50.00	52.4	56.4

Area	Change, 1960 to 1970			
	Black		White	
	Number	Percent	Number	Percent
United States	3.7	20	18.9	12
Metropolitan areas[1]	4.0	32	14.9	14
Central cities	3.3	33	–	–
Outside central cities	0.8	27	14.9	26
Outside Metropolitan areas	–0.3	–5	4.0	8

–Rounds to zero.

[1] Includes Somerset and Middlesex counties in New Jersey, which are not part of any standard metropolitan statistical area (SMSA), but are in the New York, N.Y.-Northeastern New Jersey Standard Consolidated Area.

SOURCE: U.S. Department of Commerce, Social and Economic Statistics Administration, Bureau of the Census.

Four American cities now have black majorities—Washington, D.C., Atlanta, Georgia, Newark, New Jersey, and Gary, Indiana. At least six cities with a population over 100,000—Detroit, Baltimore, New Orleans, St. Louis, Birmingham, and Richmond—are between 40 and 50 percent black. One can assume that if the present migration trends continue, these six cities and, quite possibly, others in the 30-to-40 percent cohort will in all probability reach a black majority by 1980. This means a redistribution of a people that is almost 100 percent native-born Americans, for 99 percent of all black people in the United States are native-born. Only the American Indian population can make a similar claim. (See also the discussion of housing patterns in Chapter 5.)

Why did blacks emigrate from the South, and what have been some of the consequences for them? Mass movements of people from place to place are frequently explained by a combination of push-and-pull forces. In the case of the black population the major pull factors prior to the post–1954 civil rights era were the lure of improved living and working conditions and the possibility of better incomes and a life relatively free from the increasing difficulties and problems embodied in the Jim Crow social system of the South. The major push factor was, concomitantly, the oppressive, pernicious, and demoralizing life as second-class citizens in a quasi-caste social system that persisted like a "cake of custom" in the South. Unfortunately, the freedom sought was seldom gained and was at best only a relative phenomenon.

A push factor of major significance in the redistribution of blacks was of course the mechanization of agriculture. Not only did mechanization contribute to the great exodus of Southern blacks, it is of special importance in explaining the impoverished conditions of many rural Southern blacks today. In 1930, approximately two-thirds of American blacks were still engaged in agricultural pursuits. Then, there was still a need for black farm labor to support an essentially retrogressive and traditional method of farming. Mechanization brought with it tractors, harvesters, and other large-scale farm equipment as a basis for commercial farming. Black farm hands or laborers were one of its notable casualties. Thus, by 1973, according to the U.S. Department of Commerce, less than four per cent of black male workers were classified as farm workers. Nevertheless, some 4.5 million blacks still reside in the rural South, many of them jobless. In many ways, they are the true pariahs, the lumpen-proletariats of the American social and economic system. They lag behind others in educational attainment and other marketable skills so much so that when they do migrate to the city they become dependent upon public welfare for survival. Black rural residents comprise a large share of the sub-employed, unemployed, and the total number of persons living below the poverty line, often earning no more than $1.30 per hour whenever they are fortunate enough to find work—hence, their abject poverty, their abysmally inadequate housing, and their unimaginably poor nutrition. Their subservient economic condition is, in part, maintained by the inability of black small-scale farmers to obtain sufficient financial leverage through loans or assistance from the United States Department of Agriculture (USDA) to enable them to cope with increasing agricultural mechanization. In order to make ends meet thousands of rural Southern blacks have become the peripatetic migrant workers, following opportunities for seasonal employment in the harvesting of fruit, vegetables, and sugar cane. Rootless and often exploited, it becomes increasingly difficult for these black victims of mechanized agriculture to survive.

Most Southern black transplants to the North and West did not initially and do not now find living as easy as they previously envisioned; they have found somewhat more subtle prejudice and discrimination, nonetheless demeaning, when compared to that experienced in the South. Specifically, rural Southern blacks were lured—by promises of a better life by friends, relatives, and labor agents—from the share cropping system and tenant farms of the South only to become the modern new industrialized laborers and semiskilled operators in the factories of Detroit or Chicago or the menial workers in the manufacturing industries of Philadelphia and Newark or in the garment industry of New York or in the steel mills of Pittsburgh and Cleveland. And black women discarded the role of mammy to white Southerners only to become exploited household servants of the established rich and the ever-widening white middle classes of the urban North and West.

Fertility and Mortality. Tables 1-4 and 1-5 depict fluctuations in fertility and mortality rates among the black population. When speaking of fertility rates, we are referring to the total fertility rate, which is defined by the Bureau of Census "as the number of births that 1,000 women would have in their lifetime if, at each year of age, they experienced the birth rates occurring in the specified calendar year."[34] Inasmuch as 95 percent of all people categorized by the census as nonwhite are black, the statistics in these tables are of value in illuminating the fertility differentials between black and white Americans. They also support our claim that the black population is increasing but at a decreasing rate.

From birth onward *blacks have a higher death rate than do white Americans.* Table 1-5 shows that the number of deaths of babies under the age of 28 days per 1,000 live births for blacks and other nonwhites was 21.6 in 1970 in comparison to 13.5 for whites during the same year. The pattern repeats rates observed over the past several years. These data lead

TABLE 1-4.

Total Fertility Rates: 1955 to 1968

Year	Black and Other Races	Black	White
1955	4.55	(NA)	3.45
1956	4.73	(NA)	3.55
1957	4.80	(NA)	3.63
1958	4.73	(NA)	3.56
1959	4.77	(NA)	3.57
1960	4.52	(NA)	3.53
1961	4.53	(NA)	3.50
1962[1]	4.40	(NA)	3.35
1963[1]	4.27	(NA)	3.20
1964	4.15	(NA)	3.07
1965	3.89	(NA)	2.79
1966	3.61	3.58	2.61
1967	3.39	3.35	2.45
1968	3.20	3.13	2.37

Births 1955–1959 adjusted for underregistration of births.
NA Not available.
[1] Excludes data for New Jersey.

SOURCE: U.S. Department of Health, Education and Welfare and U.S. Department of Commerce, Social and Economic Statistics Administration, Bureau of the Census.

to the inevitable conclusion that black babies are twice as likely to die during infancy as are white children. This fact suggests a number of problems related to mother-child care, prenatal health care, the ability to afford proper diets during pregnancy and after parturition, and differentials in the quality of facilities and postnatal treatment available to white and black women in the United States. The general mortality rate is also higher among blacks than among whites; the life expectancy of whites is 71.0 years, whereas that of blacks is 64.1 years. There are significant differences in the causes of death among these two populations, which will be examined in greater detail in Chapter 9.

Age-Sex Structure. The black population is essentially young. As Table 1-6 shows, whites tend to be, on the average, about seven years older than blacks. The median age of black males and females in 1971 was 21.1 and 23.6, respectively. Forty-five percent of the males and 43 percent of the females were under the age of 20. Yet 6 percent of the men and 8 percent

TABLE 1-5.

Maternal and Infant Mortality Rates: 1940, 1950, 1960, and 1965 to 1970

(*Per 1,000 live births*)

| | *Maternal* | | *Infant* | | | |
| | | | Under 28 Days | | 28 Days to 11 Months | |
Year	Black and Other Races	White	Black and Other Races	White	Black and Other Races	White
1940	7.6	3.2	39.7	27.2	34.1	16.0
1950	2.2	0.6	27.5	19.4	16.9	7.4
1960	1.0	0.3	26.9	17.2	16.4	5.7
1965	0.8	0.2	25.4	16.1	14.9	5.4
1966	0.7	0.2	24.8	15.6	14.0	5.0
1967	0.7	0.2	23.8	15.0	12.1	4.7
1968	0.6	0.2	23.0	14.7	11.6	4.5
1969	(NA)	(NA)	21.6	14.1	10.0	4.4
1970	(NA)	(NA)	21.6	13.5	9.8	3.9

Note: 1969 and 1970 data are provisional.
NA Not available.
SOURCE: U.S. Department of Health, Education and Welfare.

of the women were over the age of 65. The youth of the black population can be observed by examining those 14 years of age and under. Of this group 35 percent are black as compared to only 27 percent that are white. The combination of the extreme age groups in the black population places almost half of its population outside the labor force. Hence this group is dependent because of age.[35]

The age distribution of American blacks differs from region to region. In the South and West the black population is considerably younger than it is in the Northeastern and North Central States. In 1970, for example, 43 percent of blacks were under the age of 18, but in the Northeastern and North Central states the percentages in this category were 40 and 42, respectively. This same pattern is reflected in comparative median ages according to regions of the country. The median age of blacks is 21.7 in the South; 22.5 in the North Central region; 22.7 in the West; and 24.0 in the Northeast.[36] These data show that the South has a larger proportion of age-dependent blacks, which of itself has a number of implications for

TABLE 1-6.

Black Population by Region and Age: 1960 and 1970

Subject	United States	North-east	North Central	South	West
1960					
Total population					
(thousands)	18,849	3,021	3,442	11,304	1,082
Median age (years)	23.5	27.2	25.3	21.6	24.7
Percent of Total					
Under 18 years	43	37	41	45	41
Under 5 years	14	13	15	15	15
18 years and over	57	63	59	55	59
21 years and over	53	59	55	51	56
65 years and over	6	5	6	7	4
1970					
Total population					
(thousands)	22,580	4,344	4,572	11,970	1,695
Median age (years)	22.4	24.0	22.5	21.7	22.7
Percent of Total					
Under 18 years	42	40	42	43	41
Under 5 years	11	11	11	11	11
18 years and over	58	60	58	57	59
21 years and over	52	55	52	51	53
65 years and over	7	6	6	8	5

SOURCE: U.S. Department of Commerce, Social and Economic Statistics Administration, Bureau of the Census.

family life, poverty structure, welfare, and institutional participation. These too, shall be examined in greater detail in subsequent chapters.

As shown in Table 1-7, there are more black females than black males.* In 1971 the black population consisted of 10,932,000 males and 12,029,000 females; therefore, for every dozen females there were only ten black males. In other words, there were 2 million more black females than males in the general population. This shortage of black males and the dis-

---

* Of course, the same is true of the sex distribution throughout the population as a whole. However, these proportions may be more significant in the black community because of adverse experiences of black males in comparison to white males.

proportionate distribution of females is more acute in some age groups than others. In the 20-to-24 age group, for example, there were 919,000 males and 1,036,000 females; and in the crucial ages of 25 to 34, as of 1971, black males numbered 1,247,000 while black females numbered 1,478,000. The larger number of women has certain implications for family life and the labor force, while will become apparent in subsequent discussions (See Table 1-7).

TABLE 1-7.

Population by Age and Sex: 1971

(*Numbers in thousands*)

Age and Sex	Black	White[1]	Percent Distribution Black	Percent Distribution White[1]
Male, All Ages	10,932	89,111	100	100
Under 5 years	1,251	7,585	11	9
5 to 9 years	1,363	8,572	12	10
10 to 14 years	1,409	9,219	13	10
15 to 19 years	1,248	8,608	11	10
20 to 24 years	919	7,559	8	8
25 to 34 years	1,247	11,242	11	13
35 to 44 years	1,080	10,070	10	11
45 to 54 years	990	10,273	9	12
55 to 64 years	735	8,143	7	9
65 years and over	689	7,843	6	9
Median age	21.1	27.7	(X)	(X)
Female, All Ages	12,029	93,402	100	100
Under 5 years	1,242	7,245	10	8
5 to 9 years	1,356	8,209	11	9
10 to 14 years	1,406	8,828	12	9
15 to 19 years	1,261	8,355	10	9
20 to 24 years	1,036	7,822	9	8
25 to 34 years	1,478	11,456	12	12
35 to 44 years	1,312	10,451	11	11
45 to 54 years	1,156	10,967	10	12
55 to 64 years	871	9,057	7	10
65 years and over	912	11,010	8	12
Median age	23.6	30.4	(X)	(X)

Note: Estimates of resident population
X Not applicable.
[1] Includes the category "other races."

SOURCE: U.S. Department of Commerce, Social and Economic Statistics Administration, Bureau of the Census.

CONTRAVENING
VARIABLES

The progress of the black community toward incorporation and assimilation or toward the construction of a separate but viable system is affected by such factors as income and occupational distribution, unemployment, and persistent poverty. Throughout the history of black people in America, these factors have contravened progress, exacerbated problems, and combined to create disillusionment, despair, and alienation among significant segments of the black communities. Income inequities, menial occupational distribution, and poverty provide extremely potent weapons for heightening group diversity and intensifying or solidifying class boundaries. While no attempt will be made at this time to discuss in detail the myriad factors that contravene progress and divide black people, attention will be called, in a more or less general way, to their relative importance in black community life.

Occupational Distribution. Historically, blacks have constituted a major proportion of the work force at the lower echelons of the occupational scale. Their experiences in the labor market illustrate what Sethard Fisher calls a process of halt, progress, and retardation.[37] Prior to emancipation a class of black artisans, including masons, carpenters, plumbers, painters, repairmen, and machinists, could be found largely in the urban areas. Following emancipation and with increasing educational opportunities, even though a disproportionate number of blacks were working in agriculture and domestic work, a select few blacks turned to the professions of teaching and preaching. This situation persisted for several decades after the end of the Civil War. Three factors, in a large measure, explain this situation: (1) the destruction of the artisan class of blacks, which came about as a consequence of the influx of 9 million members of white ethnic groups from Europe, who were given jobs, especially in the North, that would normally have gone to blacks; (2) the displacement of blacks by white artisans during the post–Reconstruction period, aided considerably by the failure to enforce post–Reconstruction civil rights legislation and by the enactment of Jim Crow legislation; and (3) the rise of the sharecropping and tenancy system, which was buttressed by a system of legalized peonage in the South.

The sharecropping system permitted white planters to exploit black farmers. The latter agreed to live and work on land owned by white planters with the understanding that the profits gained would be equally divided after expenses were deducted. The general practice was for white planters, who always kept the books, to subtract so much from the sale of the crops that black tenant farmers ended up owing them for the privilege of working from sunup to sundown on their land. Blacks could never get ahead and found themselves struggling under a new form of slavery. Moreover, the constraints and structure of Southern laws prevented blacks from moving from a given farm until all their debts had been paid to white landowners. Thus black farmers were cheated, exploited, and reduced to peonage. The conditions found in agriculture were equally applicable to other occupations in many parts of the South. Consequently, the black worker was denied access to money, technology, and jobs that would assure advancement and secure incomes.[38]

Since World War I the trend for black Americans has been away from agricultural pursuits toward broader representation in the occupational structure. This can be attributed to factors such as: (1) a greater need for black laborers following the curtailment of the immigration of certain white ethnic nationalities*; (2) pressure from professional and highly skilled predominantly black civil rights groups such as the National Association for the Advancement of Colored People (NAACP), the National Urban League, and the Congress of Racial Equality (CORE); (3) direct action in the form of pickets, boycotts, "don't buy where you can't work" campaigns, lobbying; (4) pressure tactics such as sit-ins and stand-ins; (5) the issuing of executive orders; and (6) the enactment of fair employment practices laws and civil rights legislation outlawing discrimination in hiring practices as well as in the more recent policies pronounced in the Philadelphia, New York, Chicago, and Boston plans. (Affirmative Action programs call for the hiring of a number of minorities equal to their percentage in the population of the particular locale. Though they were applied first to the construction industry, they now have a much broader application and cover any agency, including colleges and universities, holding a federal government contract of $50,000 or more.)

Nevertheless, in 1971 striking differences existed between nonwhites and whites in occupational distribution. A few examples illustrate this point. Twice as many employed whites (27 percent) held professional, managerial, and technical positions in comparison to the number of nonwhites (13 percent) who held positions in these categories. More than twice the number (41 percent) of all employed nonwhites were found in the service, private household, farm, and laboring jobs as were found among white workers (20 percent)) in 1971. The same type of disparity existed in the categories of craftsmen and kindred workers operatives in which only 8 percent of the nonwhites but 13 percent of the white population were employed. Compared to whites, twice as many blacks were service workers, seven times

* Immigration was curtailed through the enactment of highly restrictive legislation in 1917, 1921, and 1924, which was designed to limit the number of immigrants mainly from southern and southeastern Europe.

as many blacks were engaged in private household work, and twice as many blacks were farm workers. But whites outnumbered blacks by 300 percent as managers and administrators; there were almost twice as many of them in professional work and four times as many in sales work in 1971.

Income. Blacks still earn far less than white Americans. In 1971, Census data showed that the median income for black families is approximately $6,400, while that for white families is $10,670. Thus black families' incomes are 60 percent of those of white families.* Furthermore, the dollar gap between black and white families has steadily widened so that it would take extremely sharp rises in the total incomes received by black families accompanied by little or no increases in white family incomes for black families ever to approximate parity. Racist hiring practices, automation, and mechanization of agriculture conspire to keep the gap from closing. Although demonstrations and organized protests in the 1960s attacked unfair labor practices in the construction industry and in other aspects of labor, they helped to change the situation only slightly. The average black worker is still paid $1,200 less than the average white worker performing the same type of work.

As indicated in Tables 1-8 and 1-9, all across the country, from region to region, the income structure favors the white population and relegates the black population to a disadvantaged position. This bleak portrait of income disadvantages coupled with low occupational status and high rates of unemployment are the sources of numerous disabilities that characterize many segments of the black community. A faint glimmer of relief from this dismal situation may be observed in the close approximations of median incomes of younger blacks in their early twenties, when both husbands and wives are employed, with whites of the same age. However, it should be stressed that such families constituted only about one-tenth of the total 4.9 million black families in the United States in 1971. It is not to be assumed, as some have mistakenly done, that most blacks are now in the middle classes. (See the bibliographic reference to Ben J. Wattenberg and Richard Scammon.)

Unemployment. The unemployment rate among blacks remains about twice as high as that for whites. The unemployment picture is an extremely complex phenomenon consisting not only of those persons who are traditionally unemployed (those who are reportedly looking for jobs and cannot find them) but also those who constitute the subemployed (those persons who are so disenchanted that they stop looking for work or who are able to locate only part-time work that is inadequate to support either self or family, or who turn to whatever they can find that seems more promising).

---

* In 1974 the U.S. Department of Commerce reported that, in cases where only husbands were employed, the ratio of black to white income had climbed to 65 percent at the end of 1972.

TABLE 1-8.

Distribution of Families by Income in 1947, 1960, and 1970

(*Adjusted for price changes, in 1970 dollars*)

Income	Black and Other Races			White		
	1947	1960	1970	1947	1960	1970
Number of families (thousands)	3,117	4,333	5,413	34,120	41,123	46,535
Percent	100	100	100	100	100	100
Under $3,000	54	36	20	20	13	8
$3,000 to $4,999	25	22	17	24	13	10
$5,000 to $6,999	11	16	16	24	17	11
$7,000 to $9,999	7	15	18	18	26	20
$10,000 to $14,999	4	8	17		21	28
$15,000 and over		3	11	15	10	24
Median income	$2,807	$4,236	$6,516	$ 5,478	$ 7,664	$10,236
Net Change, 1947–1970:						
Amount	(X)	(X)	$3,709	(X)	(X)	$ 4,758
Percent	(X)	(X)	132.1	(X)	(X)	86.9

X Not applicable.
SOURCE: U.S. Department of Commerce, Social and Economic Statistics Administration, Bureau of the Census.

These are the discouraged workers who are unable to make ends meet, who work but do not earn a living wage. Their numbers have reached crisis proportions in the United States.

Although this topic will be expanded during the discussion of the welfare problem in Chapter 2, a few observations are germane for the present analysis: First, the jobless rate for blacks was almost 10 percent in 1971, whereas the unemployment rate for whites was about 5.4 percent. In February, 1975, the Bureau of Labor Statistics reported a national unemployment rate of 8.2 percent, the highest since the Great Depression. The unemployment rate for whites was 7.5 percent, while that for blacks and other races was 13.4 percent. The figure for blacks may be considerably more since in some states, such as Connecticut, rates for blacks had already jumped to 20.4 percent in December, 1974. In general blacks are twice as likely to be unemployed as whites. Second, the unemployment rate for black teenagers is considerably more critical than it is for adults. Almost

TABLE 1-9.

Families by Median Income in 1971, and Black Family Income as a Percent of White, by Region: 1959, 1966, 1970, and 1971

Area	Number of Families, 1972 (Millions)		Median Family Income, 1971		Black Income as a Percent of White			
	Black	White	Black	White	1959	1966	1970	1971
United States	5,157	47,641	$6,440	$10,672	51	58	61	60
North and West	2,581	33,544	7,596	11,057	71	71	74	69
Northeast	1,068	11,447	7,601	11,291	69	67	71	67
North Central	1,057	13,582	7,603	11,019	74	74	73	69
West	456	8,515	7,623	10,803	67	72	77	71
South	2,576	14,097	5,414	9,706	46	51	57	56

SOURCE: U.S. Department of Commerce, Social and Economic Statistics Administration, Bureau of the Census.

one-third (31.7 percent) of all black teenagers were unemployed in 1971 in comparison to 15.1 percent unemployment among white teenagers. Third, black women are more likely to be unemployed than white women; their unemployment rates are 8.7 and 5.3, respectively. This discrepancy exists even though 59 percent of the black women between the ages of 15 and 49 and 46 percent of all black women with children under the ages of five are in the labor force. Comparable figures for white women are 46 and 27 percents, respectively, as of 1971. Fourth, a most disturbing picture emerges when one examines data concerning Vietnam veterans. The black veteran has an unemployment rate of 17.5 percent while his white counterpart's rate is 11.6 percent. Both rates are considerably above the national unemployment rates. This indicates that a sizable number of Vietnam veterans fall into the category of the discouraged, alienated, subemployed worker. True measures of the unemployed, subemployed, and underemployed would reveal the depths of the employment crisis among black people in this country. Their plight is partially attributable to a lack of skills that are in demand and to limited education.

But the unemployment crisis is even more complex than the foregoing observations might suggest. It stems partly from recent federal anti-inflation policies under which the rate of economic growth has been slow with the resultant disproportionate effect on black workers. It is also a consequence of exclusionary practices that effectively keep black workers out of the labor market and unions that control high-paying blue-collar jobs. Discrimination in hiring, promotion, and retention conspires to reduce the number of blacks hired, especially at the better-paying jobs, to hinder their chances of promotion to higher status on the job, and to make them expendable during work curtailments. Thus low educational attainment alone cannot fully explain the plight of the black worker, as many would argue.

Poverty. As a result of relegation to the lower rungs of the occupational ladder, which are characterized by the lowest incomes and the highest unemployment, a disproportionate number of black Americans are living below the poverty level. One-third of all blacks live below the low-income level, and about one-half of the black population of the United States lives in poverty, although most of the poor people of America are not black. The low-income wage is fixed by the U.S. Department of Commerce on the basis of the estimated income needed to maintain a nonfarm family of four. In 1971 this figure was set at $4,137. But, at any given time the proportion of blacks below the low-income level is three or more times greater than that of whites.

In sum, the conditions of low income, inaccessibility to high-paying occupations, widespread unemployment, and pervasive poverty are pervasive in the black community today. If allowed to continue unchecked, they will have major consequences for the quality of life not only in the black community itself but for America as a whole. These conditions have a profound impact on the stability of the family and on those who are forced to seek public assistance and must suffer severe psychological trauma in the process. They create invidious stratification systems, inhibit the mobility of people from one social stratum to another, and determine to a large degree who shall and who shall not be educated. They combine with racism to keep blacks contained in the concrete ghettos of the inner cities or isolated in rural areas or spatially separated in the South and to restrict them to areas surrounded by white suburbanites who continually seek to block their exits. Low income, unemployment, and poverty effectively unite with racist practices to reduce the availability of black capital necessary for the construction and survival of black business. This situation, in turn, all but destroys the potential political power that could be generated in several black communities. For power is not only the possession of resources; among other things it is also a function of the mobilization of those available resources. Mobilization requires money. Finally, the problems of low income, poverty, unemployment, and racism may be directly interconnected to expressions of deviant behavior, whether in the forms of psychological disorders, mental health problems, or alcohol and drug abuse.

NOTES

1. See *The Social and Economic Status of the Black Population in the United States, 1971,* U.S. Department of Commerce, Bureau of the Census (July 1972), pp. 29–30.

2. *Ibid.,* p. 23.

3. For a discussion of the insider-outsider controversy see Robert K. Merton, "Insiders and Outsiders: A Chapter in the Sociology of Knowledge," *American Journal of Sociology,* 78 (July 1972), pp. 9–47.

4. I am indebted to Professor Walter Wallace for ideas concerning the dichotomization of perspectives on the insider-outsider controversy.

5. Paul L. Metzger, "American Sociology and Black Assimilation: Conflicting Perspectives," *American Journal of Sociology,* 76 (January 1971), p. 632.

6. *Ibid.,* p. 628.

7. Jessie Bernard, *American Community Behavior* (New York: Holt, Rinehart and Winston, 1949), p. 226.

8. John Hope Franklin, *From Slavery to Freedom* (New York: Alfred A. Knopf, 1952), pp. 77–78.

9. *Ibid.*

10. *Ibid.,* pp. 340–345.

11. Kenneth Stampp, *The Peculiar Institution* (New York: Alfred A. Knopf, 1956).

12. Richard A. Schermerhorn, *Comparative Ethnic Relations: A Framework for Theory and Research* (New York: Random House, 1970), p. 148.

13. This viewpoint is explored in considerable detail in Stanley Elkins, *Slavery* (Chicago: University of Chicago Press, 1959).

14. Cf. Ulrich B. Phillips, *Life and Labor in the Old South* (Boston: Little, Brown, 1929), pp. 194–217, and Stampp, *op. cit.*

15. Andrew Billingsley, *Black Families in White America* (Englewood Cliffs, N.J.: Prentice-Hall, 1968), Chap. 1.

16. Robert Blauner, "Black Culture: Myth or Reality," in Norman Whitten and John Swed (eds.), *Afro-American Anthropology* (New York: Doubleday, 1970), Chap. 19.

17. Nathan Glazer and Daniel P. Moynihan, *Beyond the Melting Pot* (Cambridge, Mass.: The M.I.T. Press, 1963), p. 51.

18. Irving Kristol, "The Negro Today is the Immigrant of Yesterday," *New York Times Magazine,* September 11, 1966, p. 50.

19. Blauner, *op. cit.*

20. Cf. arguments advanced by E. Franklin Frazier in both *The Negro in the United States* (New York: The Macmillan Company, 1949) and *The Negro Family in the United States* (Chicago: University of Chicago Press, 1939).

21. Schermerhorn, *op. cit.*, p. 122.

22. Irwin Rinder, "Minority Orientations: An Approach to Intergroup Relations Theory Through Social Psychology," *Phylon,* 26 (Spring 1965), pp. 5–17.

23. Louis Wirth, "The Problem of Minority Groups," in Ralph Linton (ed.), *The Science of Man in the World Crisis* (New York: Columbia University Press, 1945), pp. 347–372.

24. Robert Blauner, "Internal Colonialism and Ghetto Revolt," *Social Problems,* 16 (Spring 1969), pp. 393–408.

25. *Ibid.*, p. 394.

26. Stanley Lieberson, "A Societal Theory of Race and Ethnic Relations," *American Sociological Review,* 26 (December 1961), pp. 902–910.

27. Blauner. See note 24.

28. James E. Blackwell and Marie Haug, "Relations Between Black Bosses and Black Workers," *The Black Scholar,* 4 (January 1973), pp. 36–43.

29. Cf. Talcott Parsons, *The Social System* (New York: The Free Press, 1951), and Walter Buckley, *Sociology and Modern Systems Theory* (Englewood Cliffs, N.J.: Prentice-Hall, 1967).

30. Thomas C. Shelling, *The Strategy of Conflict* (Cambridge, Mass.: Harvard University Press, 1960), pp. 11–12.

31. Bernard, *op. cit.*, pp. 3–10.

32. Roland Warren, *The Community in America* (Chicago: University of Chicago Press, 1972), p. 9.

33. *Ibid.*, pp. 10–11.

34. *The Social and Economic Status of the Black Population in the United States,* 1971, p. 106.

35. *Ibid.*, p. 24.

36. *Social and Economic Status of the Black Population in the United States,* 1970, U.S. Department of Commerce, Bureau of the Census (July 1971).

37. Sethard Fisher, *Power and the Black Community* (New York: Random House, 1970), p. 217 and Chapter 29.

38. Lerone Bennett, "The Making of Black America: The Black Worker, Part X," *Ebony,* 27 (December 1972), pp. 73–79, and (November 1972), pp. 118–122.

2 | THE BLACK FAMILY IN AMERICAN SOCIETY

This chapter examines the family as the basic social unit in the structure of the black community. The major argument here is that, both structurally and functionally, the black family system further exemplifies the high degree of differentiation within the black community referred to earlier. Attention will be devoted to such topics as: (1) the impact of slavery on family life, (2) patterns of family life, (3) controversial issues such as illegitimacy, divorce, and welfare, especially in relationship to the Moynihan Report, and (4) urbanization and the changing family. The reader is cautioned here regarding the author's use of the definite article "the" in reference to black families. It is used here purely for the sake of convenience and not as a description universally characteristic of black persons.

THE IMPACT OF SLAVERY ON THE BLACK FAMILY

Some sociologists argue that the black family in contemporary America is heading toward increasing disintegration and that this process has its roots in slavery. The most common element in their theories is to regard slavery as the cause of all the pathologies that they say are "characteristic" of the black family today.[1] Undoubtedly, slavery did leave its mark upon black family patterns but not with the magnitude claimed by Frazier and

Moynihan. It has never been satisfactorily demonstrated that slavery is directly and exclusively accountable for *all* of the present-day attributes of the black family life. Slavery was responsible, however, for establishing a caste system that relegated blacks to an inferior status. The detrimental effects of this status, from which they have never fully recovered, profoundly affect black family life.

Slavery undermined the family as the fulcrum of the social order that blacks had known in West Africa, from which most slaves came, even though it never *completely* destroyed marriage and the family as important social institutions. The process of family erosion was slow and insidious but quite effective, nonetheless. To begin, some slaves did marry, of course. However, it is inescapable that whether or not marriages were voluntary affected black peoples' chances of remaining together until death. Their opportunities for relatively stable sexual unions outside the institution of marriage not only varied from region to region but also depended upon the willingness of slaveowners to adhere to the law regarding these unions. Whites in New England, for example, applied far more stringent regulatory norms to black people and to whites themselves than did whites in most of the Southern regions. Consonant with the Puritan ethic, they expected all who engaged in heterosexual activities to do so only after they had taken marital vows. The publishing of marital bans prior to marriage, which was conducted by a magistrate, was a further effort to regulate sexual norms. There is considerable evidence to support Franklin's argument that this explicit respect for the institution of marriage and the implicit regard for the family prevailed throughout New England.[2] Not unexpectedly, black people were eager to conform to these societal and legalistic expectations, since they had come from areas having carefully delineated proscriptions for the institution of marriage and the family. It was in the South, however, more so than in any other region, where Frazier's comment about the inimicality of economics for black family life takes on more explicit meaning. During the early stages of the slave trade, more men were recruited than women, largely because of the need for strong men to till the soil and work the land. This created a highly distorted sex ratio, but in time more black women were forced into American slavery, which not only balanced the sex ratio better but proved to be economically more profitable for slaveowners.

In the South and Middle Atlantic states, particularly, experiments with different forms of slave unions, both in and out of wedlock, occurred but largely as a means of strengthening economic life among large slaveowners. Thus legal marriages, casual unions, and stud farms—whose main purpose was the production and subsequent marketing of children like cattle were sanctioned by the prevailing social system. During this process, there developed a myth of black licentiousness and animalistic sexual behavior overlaid with a disdain for formalized marital unions. This myth was created by slaveowners who structured social situations that facilitated a self-fulfilling prophecy of sexual behavior between black men and women. It was convenient to rationalize, for instance, that blacks had no regard for marriage while whites were simultaneously forcing them into sexual unions on stud farms, often without benefit of marriage. Not infrequently, young girls of 13 became mothers. Once their fecundity had been established, they were used to bear more children with amazing regularity so that by the time they reached 25 at least a dozen children had been born.[3] Many of the children were traded or sold and separated from their families. Many fathers were never permitted an opportunity to play the role of husband-father. Casual, if not brittle, familial relationships were common. In many instances the extirpation of family life as we know it among slaves was a *sine qua non* for the maintenance of the economic system of slavery. Therefore, innumerable family units were destroyed by the persistent practice of selling fathers or mothers separately and children as well or by trading children for other property or cash.

The contempt for black family structures displayed by white slaveowners and overseers was engendered by a system that simultaneously made black women easily accessible to white men. In the American population the diversity of color found among persons legally identified as black is evidence of the extent to which cohabitation between the races occurred in the past. White men exploited their superior group status in taking advantage of black women. They began the practice of bedding black women, impregnating them, and then deserting them, leaving them to fend for themselves and their offspring. (White women, too, occasionally initiated secret liaisons with black mandangoes, sometimes at great personal risks to themselves and to the black males.)

When black men did leave their families, historical and sociological evidence shows that they usually did so under duress. The only alternative to forced separation was instant death. Indeed, numerous slave escapes were undertaken because of the unfailing determination of black men to reunite with their family members. Even their success at this endeavor *fails* to confirm the viewpoint that slaves welcomed separation because it permitted greater freedom to establish new sexual liaisons. Although white disregard for the black slave family seems to have been the norm, there were exceptions. In the South and Middle Atlantic states, for example, usually depending upon the size of the plantation, some slaveowners did make valiant attempts to protect and preserve the sanctity of the institution of the family among slaves. Smaller plantation owners were often more diligent in this regard than larger owners, among whom a callous disregard for black family life was particularly characteristic.[4]

PATTERNS OF FAMILY
LIFE

It is from the conditions mentioned previously that the diversity in black family life emerges. As we shall see, black family life varies by types of marriage, authority structure, household patterns, family functions, and the degree of stability. Chapter 3 will extend this diversity to include social class attributes and mobility patterns. Despite their persistent variation, these factors collectively become crucial elements in a family system.

Marriage. Monogamy is, of course, the norm among black families in America; that is, almost all black people conform to the law permitting one spouse at a time. *Serial monogamy* is a series of marriages of relatively short duration between a man and a woman; it also occurs among black Americans but is found predominantly in the lower socioeconomic groups. (However, it is quite widespread throughout the total American population as measured by the increasing proportions of second and third marriages.) *Common-law marriages* are informal marriages between a man and a woman who decide to live together as husband and wife without the benefit of more formalized marital sanctions such as a marriage license. Except in a few states common-law marriages are not recognized as legal, and the children resulting from such unions may not be considered legitimate unless paternity is legally acknowledged. Common-law marriage is similar to the practice of "taking up" with someone, in which case, an unmarried couple may live in a marital arrangement for an indefinite period of time. The various forms of boyfriend-girlfriend arrangements, discussed in a later section of this chapter, may be a derivative of the taking-up phenomenon. Nevertheless, even with this diversity, almost all black people who marry are united through some kind of formal and legitimate channel such as by taking out a marriage license and having a wedding ceremony performed before a minister, priest, or justice of peace.

Authority Structure. Black families vary considerably in the structure of family authority. The authority figure may be either the male or female, or both may share authority equally. If authority and decision-making responsibilities are either vested in or assumed by the husband or father, the family is patriarchal. If the wife or mother is the head, then the family is matriarchal. If both husband and wife share equally in these responsibilities, the family is equalitarian. Black families in America are characteristically stereotyped as matriarchal, but the equalitarian family pattern is actually the most common authority pattern found. Even at the low-income levels equalitarianism precedes in importance both matriarchy and patriarchy as dominant family types.[5] The trend toward equalitarian family structures has developed over a long period of time. Basically, the movement has been away from the traditional patriarchal structure, once characteristic of most American families, white and black, in which an overpowering male potentate ruled without much challenge from other family members. As patriarchies disappear, matriarchies are not replacing them. Again, sociologists like Andrew Billingsley,[6] Robert Staples,[7] and Robert Hill[8] argue quite forcefully that the universality of the black matriarchy is largely a myth and that female dominance is by and large class linked. And if David A. Schulz is correct, there is reason to question the notion of female dominance even in lower-class black families, especially when the quasi-father and the boyfriend exist as male norms.[9]

Household Patterns. Family patterns among black Americans vary in terms of household composition. Billingsley identifies three primary family types: (1) basic, characterized by the presence of husband and wife only; (2) nuclear, consisting of husband, wife, and children; and (3) attenuated nuclear families, characterized by the absence of one of the marital partners. He subdivides these primary types into extended families, subfamilies, and augmented families. Extended families are comprised of one or more relatives as members of the nuclear or basic families. Subfamilies consist of relatives who join another family as a basic family unit (for example, parents and children joining another nuclear family in the latter's residence). Augmented families form when persons having no consanguineal ties to the family join the family unit. These persons may be boarders, roomers, or extended guests. In addition, combinations and derivations of the primary family and their subtypes may arise. The most important feature of this typology is that it depicts the tremendous diversity in types and composition of black family structures. The apparent heterogeneity among black family structures is an adaptation developed to survive what has been an alien and hostile experience for a sizable proportion of the black population in America.[10]

Of all the types mentioned by Billingsley, the simple nuclear family—father, mother, and their children under one roof—is generally regarded as the most prevalent family structure found in the American society. It is the universally accepted model to which Americans are expected to aspire. Yet Billingsley has cited evidence that the proportion of simple nuclear families varies from 36 percent to 49 percent of the total number of black families studied or identified in the larger population.[11] Thus although the simple nuclear family may be regarded as an ideal type, it has not been achieved by a majority of the black families in the United States. One explanation for this situation is simply that a significant number of black family units are either extended or contain other subfamilies or fall into one or more of the other 12 family types identified by Billingsley. Other data, however, suggest that the nuclear family is the norm.

The 1970 census, for instance, reported a total of 4,863,401 black family units in the United States. Of that number approximately 70 percent were residing in simple nucleated households. It is interesting to note that some 326,163 subfamilies existed, including 218,093, or 67 percent, headed by females. But almost 90,000 of the subfamilies were basic family types, consisting only of a husband and wife. The remaining family units were either attenuated nuclear, extended, or augmented structures. Clearly, then, the two-parent, simple nucleated family is the dominant form found among black families in the United States, according to these data.[12]

TWO-PARENT FAMILIES

When people refer to the simple nuclear family as the norm, they really mean that a high premium is placed on families in which both parents are present. Thus two-parent families are regarded as the singularly most powerful indicator of family stability. It is assumed that such families can best serve the various functions of family units and meet the needs of individual members. Such family structures are less likely to be encumbered with social problems, and, even when problems occur, presumably, two-parent families have the wherewithal necessary for problem solving with minimal trauma. A logical corollary of this argument is that the attenuated nuclear family, in which only a single parent is present, is the opposite of the two-parent structure in terms of stability and finding meaningful solutions to the problems of daily life. A further extension of this argument is that single-parent families are a strong indicator of family disorganization or disintegration. This is a controversial viewpoint and one that is consciously being rejected by white participants, in the counterculture that supports single-parent structures. Though the issue is provocative, we will concentrate now on two-parent structures in the black community.

Although approximately 70 percent of all black family units have two parents living in the home, data reveal a declining trend of this type of family structure. The decline is gradual rather than rapid or alarming. Between 1950 and 1972, for example, the proportion of two-parent black families dropped by approximately 10 percent (that is, from 77.7 percent to 67.4 percent), while the percentage of two-parent white families remained relatively stable at about 89 percent. The decline among black families of this type does not necessarily signal an increase in family instability. It may mean the rise of other adaptive familial forms or an increase in family dismemberment due to factors proportionately more prevalent among blacks, such as early deaths, higher rates of imprisonment and military service, and "separating" as distinct from divorce.

MALE-HEADED FAMILIES

Men, not women, head the majority of black families. But the proportion of male-headed families varies markedly from city to city and from region to region. The number of such families is as low as 56 percent in Boston but increases to 62 percent in New York City, Philadelphia, and Pittsburgh. The ratio of male-headed black families rises slightly to 63 percent in Los Angeles, Baltimore, New Orleans, and St. Louis, and to highs of 70 percent in Indianapolis and 73 percent in Houston.[13]

TABLE 2-1.
Families by Sex of Head and by Income: 1969

Family Income	Negro			White		
	All Families (Thousands)	Percent of All Families		All Families (Thousands)	Percent of All Families	
		Male Head	Female Head		Male Head	Female Head
Total	4,774	72	28	46,024	91	9
Under $3,000	1,015	42	58	3,713	71	29
$3,000 to $4,999	947	61	39	4,453	81	19
$5,000 to $6,999	831	74	26	5,428	86	14
$7,000 to $9,999	934	88	12	10,098	93	7
$10,000 to $14,999	706	93	7	12,871	96	4
$15,000 and over	341	94	6	9,462	97	3

SOURCE: U.S. Department of Commerce, Bureau of the Census.

FEMALE-HEADED FAMILIES

The proportions of male-headed families and female-headed families differs strikingly according to income levels. From year to year, most persistently, an inverse relationship exists between the amount of income received and the proportion of female-headed black families. Similarly, there is a more direct relationship between the proportion of male-headed families or two-parent family structures and the amount of income received. Thus as income increases, the proportion of female-headed families decreases and, conversely, male-headed family structures increase. As a rule, and as Table 2-1 indicates, female-headed households are concentrated at the lowest income levels or at those in which the total amount of family income is less than $3,000 per annum. However, male-headed families are in a distinct majority when the annual income received reaches $3,000, while female-headed families decrease. At an annual income of $15,000 or more the proportion of such families is not distinct from the proportion of female- or male-headed families found in the white population at that income level.

The number of female-headed black families is increasing, nevertheless, and has almost doubled in slightly more than two decades. In 1950, for example, the proportion of such families had risen appreciably to 17.6 percent. As Table 2-2 shows, comparable figures on female-headed white families for 1950 and 1972 were 8.5 percent and 9.4, respectively. If these families are in trouble, the underlying causes are likely to be rooted in the systematic discrimination against women in regard to salaries, access to jobs, and occupational mobility. However, a single-parent family, male or female, is not necessarily any less organized than a two-parent family, and, indeed, the latter may have more trauma than the former. Whether or not instability characterizes this type of family is a function of any number of interrelated variables such as income, occupation, stability of employment, intrafamily harmony, and orientation toward children.[14]

TABLE 2-2.

Percent Distribution of Families by Type: 1950, 1955, 1960, and 1966 to 1971

Year	Husband-Wife		Other Male Head		Female Head[1]	
	Negro and Other Races	White	Negro and Other Races	White	Negro and Other Races	White
1950	77.7	88.0	4.7	3.5	17.6	8.5
1955	75.3	87.9	4.0	3.0	20.7	9.0
1960	73.6	88.7	4.0	2.6	22.4	8.7
1966	72.7	88.8	3.7	2.3	23.7	8.9
1967	72.6	88.7	3.9	2.1	23.6	9.1
1968	69.1	88.9	4.5	2.2	26.4	8.9
1969	68.7	88.8	3.9	2.3	27.3	8.9
1970	69.7	88.7	3.5	2.3	26.8	9.1
1971	67.4	88.3	3.7	2.3	28.9	9.4

[1] Female heads of families include widowed and single women, women whose husbands are in the armed services or otherwise away from home involuntarily, as well as those separated from their husbands through divorce or marital discord.

SOURCE: U.S. Department of Commerce, Bureau of the Census.

Boston has the highest proportion of female-headed households. Women head 73 percent of all black families in below the low-income levels. As Table 2-3 indicates, several cities, such as Chicago, Philadelphia, Cleveland, Newark, and Oakland, hover about the 66 percent level of the proportion of low-income black families headed by women.

T A B L E 2 - 3 .

Black Persons, Families, and Unrelated Individuals Below the Low-Income Level in 1969 for Cities with 100,000 or More Blacks

(*Numbers in thousands*)

Selected Cities	Persons		Families			Unrelated Individuals	
	Num-ber	Per-cent of All Black Per-sons	Num-ber	Per-cent of All Black Fam-ilies	Per-cent of Fam-ilies with Female Head	Num-ber	Per-cent of All Black Un-related Indivi-duals
New York, N.Y.	399	24	81	21	63	58	31
Chicago, Ill.	274	25	51	21	66	38	37
Detroit, Mich.	143	22	28	19	63	24	39
Philadelphia, Pa.	165	26	32	21	66	28	40
Washington, D.C.	103	19	19	16	60	20	30
Los Angeles, Calif.	127	26	25	21	65	20	30
Baltimore, Md.	112	27	21	23	65	17	43
Houston, Tex.	93	30	18	25	49	12	46
Cleveland, Ohio	77	27	16	23	66	12	42
New Orleans, La.	116	44	23	39	54	11	57
Atlanta, Ga.	72	29	14	25	55	11	48
St. Louis, Mo.	79	31	14	26	60	11	46
Memphis, Tenn.	99	41	18	36	49	10	59
Dallas, Tex.	62	30	12	25	53	7	43
Newark, N.J.	56	27	11	24	68	6	34
Indianapolis, Ind.	29	22	5	18	57	4	39
Birmingham, Ala.	50	40	10	34	48	7	61
Cincinnati, Ohio	39	32	7	27	60	7	50
Oakland, Calif.	31	25	6	22	66	5	35
Jacksonville, Fla.	47	40	9	35	53	6	58
Kansas City, Mo.	28	25	5	20	55	5	42
Milwaukee, Wis.	28	27	6	25	64	3	38
Pittsburgh, Pa.	33	32	7	27	65	6	48
Richmond, Va.	30	30	6	25	63	5	47
Boston, Mass.	29	28	6	25	73	4	30
Columbus, Ohio	25	26	5	21	62	5	44

SOURCE: U.S. Department of Commerce, Social and Economic Statistics Administration, Bureau of the Census.

Female-headed black families suffer tremendous economic disadvantages, which are often reflected in differences in their median incomes as compared to the median incomes of male-headed households. In families headed by men the median family income of $7,800 is twice the median family income of $3,900 received in families headed by women. Nationally, in urban communities, the percent of black families headed by women that are below the low-income level is slightly more than three times higher than that for families headed by black males. The percentages are 15 and 48 for men and women, respectively.[15] The low-income problem, continually compounded by widespread unemployment and underemployment, is especially serious. In the 1970 census 50 percent of the 26 cities having 100,000 persons and over reported one quarter or more of the black families in the low-income levels. Females head most of these families. In several of these cities, such as New Orleans, for example, the median family income of black families is appalling. At $4,745 New Orleans has the lowest black family median income of any city in the United States with a population over 100,000.[16] Moreover, 40 percent of its black families are living at low-income levels.

RESIDENCE OF CHILDREN

In every age group the majority of black children reside with their own parents. However, the proportion of black children living with their own parents in recent years is declining. As Table 2-4 shows, in 1960 three-fourths of all children classified by the U.S. census as Negro and other races, most of whom were black, resided with their natural parents; but in 1970 the proportion dropped to 67 percent. Comparable figures for the white population were 92 and 91 percents, respectively.

There is direct correlation between the amount of income annually received by black families and the proportion of children residing with their own families. As expected, the higher the family income level, the larger the number of children residing with their own families. Conversely, the lower the income, the fewer the number of children residing with their own families. At annual incomes of $3,000 or less slightly less than one quarter of black children reside with their own families, but the proportion reaches almost nine-tenths (89 percent) when the income level reaches $15,000 or more. The critical income watershed seems to be at the level of $5,000, for at that point and above the proportion of children residing with both parents does not fall below 71 percent. As Table 2-5 shows, below that point, the proportion of black children residing with both parents does not reach 50 percent.[17]

The differences in residential patterns of black children demonstrate

TABLE 2-4.

Own Children Living with Both Parents as a Percent of All Own Children: 1960 to 1971

Year	Negro and Other Races	White
1960	75	92
1961	76	92
1962	73	92
1963	70	92
1964	71	92
1965	71	91
1966	71	91
1967	73	92
1968	69	92
1969	69	92
1970	67	91
1971	64	90

Note: Unmarried children under 18 years old living in families.

SOURCE: U.S. Department of Commerce, Social and Economic Statistics Administration, Bureau of the Census.

the need of black families for financial assistance and social service in caring for their children and meeting their functions as family heads. Unable to meet these needs, some parents allow their children to live with other family members for a time until their economic situation improves. Thus such arrangements are often temporary ones and perhaps help to explain the increase in the proportion of children living with their own parents at the upper-income levels. The absence of children from the households of their parents may be further explained by family dismemberment because of death, desertion, divorce, or involuntary separation. It may also be due to a temporary arrangement whereby grandparents and other relatives take care of children while natural parents are working, or hospitalized, or in prison, or taking up with a girlfriend or boyfriend.

AUGMENTED FAMILIES AND BOYFRIENDS

Some husbandless women, in time, feel compelled to make more dependable arrangements for meeting their emotional or affectional needs as well as for augmenting their capacity to care for their children when the

TABLE 2-5.

All Own Children and Percent of Own Children Living with Both Parents, by Family Income: 1971

Family Income in 1970	Negro		White	
	All Own Children (Thousands)	Percent Living with Both Parents	All Own Children (Thousands)	Percent Living with Both Parents
Under $3,000	1,682	22	2,846	47
$3,000 to $4,999	1,684	41	3,842	64
$5,000 to $6,999	1,576	68	5,925	83
$7,000 to $9,999	1,733	80	12,726	92
$10,000 to $14,999	1,515	88	18,533	97
$15,000 and over	687	85	14,345	97

Note: Unmarried children under 18 years old living in families.

SOURCE: U.S. Department of Commerce, Social and Economic Statistics Administration, Bureau of the Census.

husband-father is absent. Similarly, some men who wish to avoid formalizing a liaison with women through marital bonds make tentative arrangements as boyfriends. One of the more important research studies in this area demonstrates that the diversity of the black family structure extends to the roles of boyfriends.

David Schulz addresses himself to liaisons between black men and women in the lower class.[18] Contrary to popular belief, he argues, such liaisons are much more stable than is commonly assumed. Black men and women are able to establish a kind of quasi-familial relationship in which men do express great concern for women and the care of their children. In this view the establishment of a boyfriend relationship is an adaptive response to oppression and deprivation experienced in the larger society. But boyfriends are obviously not all the same; they are dissimilar in the degree of financial and emotional support they bring into the relationship. They also vary in the types of relationships that they establish. Thus Schulz identifies four different types of boyfriends: (1) the quasi-father, (2) the supportive biological father, (3) the supportive companion, and (4) the pimp.[19]

A brief description of each type will help demonstrate the variations in degrees of concern for women and their children and will illuminate other distinguishing features as well. The *quasi-father* seems in many ways to epitomize certain aspects of exchange theory in sociology. He gives and expects something in return. There is kind of quid pro quo in his relationship with women that suggests that he is bargaining for more than a woman in a family context. In general, his distinguishing features are as follows: (1) regular and sustained support for his girlfriend and her children; (2) the establishment of an affective relationship with his girlfriend's children, as, for example, through provisions for spending money, attempts at disciplining them, and engaging in various forms of recreation and entertainment with them; (3) intermittent visits with family, since he may or may not take up a permanent residence with them; and (4) an open relationship. That is, the relationship between the quasi-father boyfriend and his girlfriend is not clandestine. Other members of her family may have full knowledge about their arrangement with each other. What rewards does the quasi-father obtain from this situation? According to Schulz, he obtains at least four assurances from his partner. First, he has the assurance that his food will be prepared for him. Second, his laundry will be done for him. Third, he has assurances of sexual gratification. And, fourth, he can expect familial companionship. Therefore, this type of relationship assures its participants both the instrumental and the expressive family functions.[20]

The *supportive biological father* has basically the same concern as the biological mother—support for the children even though both the mother and father do not entertain the probability of marriage to each other. Indeed, the man may already be married to someone else when the woman is impregnated or when the child is born. His support of his child or children is acknowledgment of paternity and an acceptance of its responsibilities, but neither the man nor the woman agrees to marriage. The duration of this support is uncertain and may or may not be sustained for a long period of time.[21]

The *supportive companion's* principal concern is having a good time with "a clean woman." On the other hand, the woman's primary wish is for support and reasonable companionship. This is a somewhat fragile relationship, but as Schulz cautions, it is not synonymous with prostitution. (A similar feature in white culture is the mistress.) Their relationship is not an impersonal business transaction, such as prostitution tends to be, but a mutual effort to obtain intimacy under severe economic and emotional difficulties. This type of relationship is characteristically found among men in their twenties and thirties and substantially younger unwed mothers. The older man may at first be perceived as someone who rescues the woman or girl from an extremely difficult situation. He provides her with a good time, emotional support, and spending money. He enjoys her companionship and sexual favors but does not desire family responsibility. Thus if and when a child is conceived as a result of their liaison, he abandons the woman and her offspring.[22] Undoubtedly, the supportive companion is the source of the current stereotype of the lower-class black male as a man of insatiable sexual appetite who exploits and deserts his childbearing woman and is either unwilling or incapable of serving instrumental parental functions.

The *pimp* is also the source of an exploitative image of the black male. Certainly, this image is perpetuated not only in popular novels but in black "sexploitation" movies and the theater as well. Schulz distinguishes, quite correctly, between the traditional and the more contemporary usages of the term "pimp." Classically, the term depicts a relationship in which a man lives off the earnings of one or more prostitutes who provide him with an elaborate life style, while he, in turn, provides them with police protection, bail money, if they are arrested, and some degree of social status in a subterranean life. Schulz employs the term to describe a stud or gigolo—a younger man who exploits well-financed, fading older women by providing sexual favors for them in return for a stylish life for himself. Although they are, in fact, "kept men," studs are not pimps in the classical or professional sense of the term.[23]

The role of the pimp, whether perceived in the classical or contemporary sense, appears to be glamorous. Impressionable ghetto blacks frequently wish to emulate pimps. These perceptions of pimps develop in a social context in which material acquisitions are highly prized and the legitimate avenues for achieving them are not equally accessible to ghetto black youths. They are impressed by the pimp's long "hog," or flashy automobile, and the excesses of his expensive clothing, called "threads" in black vernacular. They esteem the pimp's life style, at least as overtly manifested, as an easy way of "making it" in "the man's world." The pimp's employment, in their view, is legitimate as a way of making it, and making it quickly, with a minimum deferment of gratifications. Thus their heroes may be the "superflies" of the lower-class black community; the ghetto youth may come to idealize similar characters when they are portrayed in films. Thus the socialization that begins with the impressionable youth's own observations of objective reality is reinforced by the fantasies of the motion-picture world. However, the duration of the classical pimp's role is subject to extreme variation depending upon his prowess in managing his stable of prostitutes, on the one hand, and the degree to which the indiscretions of the stud or kept man will be tolerated by a woman who, on the other hand, feels that her powers of persuasion are dimming. Schulz claims that the classical pimp may in time become enamored of one of his prostitutes, marry her, and settle down to family life. But there is little reason to assume that the stud role is anything but transitory or that pimps in general have a real concern for their women. Men who play this role are likely to be peripatetic and transient and are not likely to marry women who have kept them.[24]

The research conducted by Schulz is important. Not only does he demonstrate the concern of lower-class black men for their women and their families, uneven though it may be, but his view is also clearly at variance with the orthodox sociological perspective advanced in the literature on family disorganization and revived in some of the more popular urban anthropological studies of the black underclass. The stereotype of the lower-class black stud as a veritable wellspring of raw sexuality, moving from bed to bed, leaving a flock of children in his path and abandoning them for support through public assistance is subjected to serious question here.

FAMILY FUNCTIONS

In other sections of this chapter we have referred to the capacity of black families to serve varied functions. We need now to specify and describe the different types of family functions. Billingsley, borrowing from Parsons and Bales, differentiates between instrumental and expressive functions in his analysis of black family life. The following discussion is based upon his insights and theoretical analysis of family functions in his provocative study *Black Families in White America*.[25]

The instrumental functions of the family facilitate and assure its maintenance as a physical and economic unit. They include such activities as providing for the economic well-being of family members and for physical and social sustenance. Instrumental functions also contribute to the stability of the family when meeting the basic needs of food, housing, clothing, and health care. The ability to meet such fundamental needs presumes access to such essentials as a dependable job and sufficient income, which constitute the fulcrum for performing instrumental family functions. Given the disadvantaged income and occupational structure in the black community, as compared to the white population, black families are predictably less effective in instrumental function performance. Here effectiveness depends upon conditions external to the black family structure—those uncertain opportunities in the larger social system.[26]

Expressive functions deal with emotional states—social relations and feelings *between* family members and their psychological well-being. It is in the realization of expressive functions that individual members come to share in what W.I. Thomas once labeled "a fulfillment of the four wishes." By that he meant that by virtue of membership in a reference group like the family the fundamental social desires for love and affection, a sense of belonging to a group, companionship and group acceptance, and self-recognition are met. This is precisely what black leaders like Reverend Jessie Jackson intend when they cajole blacks into repetitive recitations of "I am somebody," "I am important," "I am worthy," and "I am of value." Thus expressive functions are largely internal to the family system and depend upon the quality of reciprocal relationships among individual members of the family.

In some instances, as Billingsley observes, the lines between expressive and instrumental functions are blurred and indistinctive, as, for example, in sexual behavior, reproductive functioning, and socialization. Both instrumental and expressive functioning are involved in each process, as illustrated by the adherence of the majority of black families to the middle-class norm regarding pleasurable sex. That is, it is only through the institution of marriage that pleasurable sex is condoned or receives widespread social approbation.[27] Furthermore, even though an increasing number of unwed black mothers do keep their children rather than place them for adoption, the tendency to view such children as illegitimate still prevails and procreation by a married couple remains the norm rather than the exception. Idiosyncratic behavioral patterns that contradict this position may very well be class linked. If they are not class linked, they may instead represent a unique feature of black families and, perhaps, to use Hill's term, a "strength" of black families.[28]

Hill, in discussing family roles and functions, identifies five major strengths of black families: (1) strong kinship bonds as manifested in the capacity to absorb other individuals into the family structure and informal adoption, (2) a strong work orientation, (3) adaptability of family roles, (4) high achievement orientation, and (5) a religious orientation. These strengths account for the ability of black families to survive as going concerns. To provide support for his position Hill draws attention to observations such as the following: (1) the large-scale incorporation of minor children, elders, and subfamilies into one's family structure (this supports the notion of strong family bonds and provides evidence of techniques employed to perform both instrumental and expressive family functions); (2) the greater likelihood for black children rather than white children, born of unwed mothers, to remain within the family of procreation rather than to be adopted outside the family (in other words, some blacks may not view illegitimacy as socially stigmatizing as do some white families); (3) the employment of both husbands and wives in the black community (90 percent of the husbands and more than 66 percent of wives in all black families work, thus demonstrating a strong work orientation among black people); (4) high flexibility of black families in role performance and likelihood of an equalitarian authority structure.

Hill also shows how exchanges occur between husbands and wives in terms of traditional role expectations. These exchanges may be essentially role reversals structured by the social situation in order to get the job done.

Thus husbands may change diapers or cook or do heavy housework, depending upon social class affiliation. Wives may mow the lawn, clean the house, and repair things around the house. These exchanges and flexibility of roles may serve to keep the family intact when it is confronted with the crisis situations of involuntary family dismemberment.[29] They are also characteristic of egalitarian families. Many of Hill's observations are shared by other social scientists, notably Herbert Otto in his comments on the characteristics of a strong family.[30]

CONTROVERSIAL FAMILY ISSUES IN THE BLACK COMMUNITY

The black family in contemporary America is the subject of considerable controversy among academicians, activists, and bureaucrats. Although the controversy is somewhat amorphous in character, it focuses on several points: (1) divorce, (2) illegitimacy, (3) public welfare, and (4) the black matriarchy. These factors are essentially contravening variables, since they are believed by many to affect adversely family stability in general. Since constraints of space preclude a detailed treatment of each of these areas, the discussion that follows will be, at best, an introduction to the major issues involved in the controversy.

ILLEGITIMACY

Traditionally, illegitimacy in the United States is regarded as a black lower-class phenomenon and, therefore, as a strong measure of family disorganization. In this view the greater the proportion of children born outside the bonds of marriage, the greater the likelihood that the family is in a state of disarray. When we speak of the illegitimacy rate, we mean the number of illegitimate births per 1,000 unmarried women. This rate is much larger for blacks than it is for whites, even though in the ten-year period beginning in 1962, as the rates for blacks have shown a steady decline, the rates of illegitimacy in the white population have shown a steady increase in every age group. Between 1940 and 1961 the illegitimacy rates among black women almost tripled, but in the 1961–1968 period the rates for this group declined by as much as 14 percent. Significantly, during the same period the white illegitimacy rate tripled. Between 1940 and 1961 the black rate climbed from 35.6 to 98.3 while the white rate rose from 3.6 to 9.2. But between 1960 and 1968 as rates for black women declined to 86.6, the rates for whites increased to 13.2.[31]

The disparity in rates between the black and white populations may be explained by at least four factors: (1) a tendency for the proportion of illegitimacy to be underreported within the white population when compared to the black population (this situation may reflect better concealment patterns among whites as evidenced by the number who leave their communities during an illegitimate pregnancy); (2) greater knowledge of birth control and the wider use of contraceptives among the white population than among blacks; (3) greater utilization by white women of abortion to terminate unwanted illegitimate pregnancies, but greater incorporation of an illegitimate child in the black family; and (4) more children resulting from clandestine liaisons between a married person and a single person when legal separation and/or divorce expenses may be too prohibitive. Such persons may still legitimate the child by merely acknowledging paternity even though they are not married.[32] Of these four factors Hill points to the incorporation of the unwed mother and her child into the black family structure as singularly important.[33] He estimated in 1969 that more than 160,000 black babies born out of wedlock were absorbed into existing family structures. This suggests that black families have fewer reservations about accepting such children and are less inclined to condemn and ostracize the unwed mother and her child than within the white population. (It may also mean that some black families do not accept the external definition of illegitimacy as a cultural legal act.) Elizabeth Herzog, on the other hand, stresses the great similarity between blacks and whites on all factors when income is more nearly equal. If income is viewed as a major index of social class, then social class becomes much more powerfully associated with illegitimacy than does race or ethnicity.[34] Regardless, all things being equal, and given the adherence to societal norms as well as the disadvantaged economic position of the black population as a whole, high rates of illegitimacy appear to weaken the basic family structure. This may be especially the case when unwed mothers have no substantive means of either economic or psychological support.

DIVORCE

Prior to 1940 most studies in American sociology asserted that divorce was a phenomenon of the upper classes, whereas separation and desertion were more characteristic of the lower socioeconomic classes. However, findings of more contemporary sociologists, such as Pinkney,[35] Bernard,[36] Paul Glick and Arthur Norton[37] and J. Richard Udry[38] do not support this contention. Instead, their research supports the hypothesis that lower rates of divorce and separation are characteristic of the higher socioeco-omic classes, and, conversely, higher rates are found among persons of lower socioeconomic status. For example, Glick and Norton reported in their study of 28,000 households in 1967 that the chances for divorce were greater among blacks than among whites and that nearly one-half of the blacks who had married young experienced divorce. Divorces were less frequently found among men who married between the ages of 25 and 30 years, who were college graduates, and who had relatively high incomes.[39] These findings dispute Bernard's observation that the highest rates of divorce are found in middle- and upper-income blacks.[40] On the other hand, they seem to support the notion that desertion and separation are characteristically employed by lower-status blacks as a means of dissolving marriage. The divorce rates, however, have continued to increase with expanding urbanization so that now about a quarter of all marriages in the black population end in divorce. This increasing divorce rate points to the increasing stresses on the black family in its efforts to maintain intact families. It takes its toll on the ability of the divorced family to meet both instrumental and expressive needs of individual members and may have deleterious consequences on the psyches of both parents and children.

THE BLACK MATRIARCHY

In 1965 Moynihan asserted in his controversial report *The Negro Family: The Case for National Action*[41] that the black family was disintegrating at an alarming rate and was essentially pathological. At the root of this argument is that the black family is characterized by a high rate of illegitimacy, divorce, desertion, separation, and family instability, in general heightened by the absence of a husband-father and an ever-rising matriarchy in which black women are dominant authority figures. This argument further asserts that black women were decision makers by virtue of high participation in the work force and their capacity to earn a disproportionate share of family income. Thus, it is claimed, matriarchal structures are necessarily weak and disintegrating! According to Moynihan, the matriarchy itself is pathological, and its persistence suggested that the survival of the black family rested upon the ability of the family to produce a larger number of two-parent structures and to show a commensurate decrease in the number of black families on public welfare.

These assumptions can be disputed on four grounds. First, at the time of the Moynihan study in 1965 three-fifths of the black families were two-parent families—this study does not suggest, however, that matriarchy is more dominant than other forms of family structure. Indeed, as we have seen in earlier segments of this chapter, the equalitarian family type is far more pervasive in the black community than either the matriarchy or the patriarchy. Second, Lee Rainwater and William Yancy[42] and Beverly and Otis D. Duncan[43] have forcefully argued the case that the matriarchal family structure is not necessarily pathological. Rainwater and Yancy, like Billingsley and Hill, point to the presence of the extended family system and sets of emotional strengths among black mothers that may foster positive conditions rather than family instability. They also claim that a two-parent family in which the father is marginal to the family structure may be far less healthy and supportive than one headed by a capable and emotionally strong female. Third, Elizabeth Herzog and Hylan Lewis[44] maintain that there is no firm evidence to support the claim that the absence of a father contributes directly to pathological conditions or that it has adverse affects on family members, such as increasing delinquency and causing poor school achievement and confused sexual identification. Fourth, Moynihan failed to adequately explain all the facts that contribute to what is generally identified as instability and may have unintentionally implied that the victims of the situation are somehow blamable for their own conditions.* Similarly, he failed to see, as Schulz and others have pointed out, that women can make many different adaptive responses in the absence of a husband-father. Although receiving public assistance is not the most preferred adaptive response, nevertheless, it is one way of remedying the financial problem of distressed families.

THE WELFARE MYTH

In recent years a number of misconceptions have developed about public welfare as it relates to black people. So persuasive are the myths that the word "welfare" has now become a political code for antiblack sentiments, and the white population has been misled into believing that the myths are reality. Four misconceptions are especially at fault: First, there is and always has been a disproportionately large number of blacks on public relief. Second, the majority of people on public welfare are able-bodied, lazy, shiftless blacks. Third, black people do not wish to work but spend their time loafing. Fourth, black people have illegitimate children supported by public assistance. Each of these myths will now be briefly examined.

Blacks are relative newcomers to the public welfare system because of

* See William Ryan's *Blaming the Victim* (New York: Pantheon Books, 1970) for an explanation of this process.

the long-standing patterns of discrimination in many states that disallowed relief for large segments of the black population. Frances Fox Pivin and Richard Cloward maintain that blacks did not, for example, appear in significant proportions on the Aid to Families with Dependent Children (AFDC) rolls until 1948. Increases in the proportion of blacks receiving AFDC benefits had nothing to do with black family structure; rather they were a consequence of pressures exerted by the federal government, particularly on Southern states, to reduce discriminatory practices against blacks as well as of the migration of blacks to more liberal states.[45] Even these factors did not result in appreciable increases in the proportion of blacks receiving only this form of public assistance until after 1964.

More than 25 million Americans are officially below the poverty-income level. Of this number, approximately 15 million are receiving some form of public welfare. As of 1971, more than one-half of all these persons were white and 43 percent were black. The remaining recipients were Spanish, Orientals, and Indians. The high percentage of blacks on welfare is a consequence of more than a third of them (as compared to 13 percent of the white population) having incomes below the poverty level of $4,000 per year for a family of four. It should also be stressed that welfare recipients of all races are likely to be limited in marketable skills, have poor education, and be in poor health. Eight million of them are children under the age of sixteen; 2 million are aged; more than 1 million are disabled and blind; 3 million are mothers. In the state of Massachusetts, for example, according to the Massachusetts Public Welfare Council, three-fourths of the welfare recipients are either too old and disabled to work or are children. Some 50,000 recipients are mothers of children under the age of six, and 28,000 are mothers with dependent children over six.[46]

Although a larger proportion of the black population receives some form of welfare, this is offset by the higher proportion of whites who are recipients of Social Security benefits compared to the low numbers of black Social Security beneficiaries. Almost 24 million whites, compared to 2.7 million blacks, received Social Security benefits in 1971. About one-third of the white population below the low-income level received such benefits as compared to approximately one-fourth of the blacks in this income level. Thus with regard to Social Security benefits the inequities seem to hit blacks hardest while the benefits favor whites even at the low-income levels. Table 2-6 illustrates these points. This may be the result of persistent job discrimination, which has restricted blacks to low-paying occupations.

No reliable evidence supports the allegation that most welfare recipients are able-bodied men who do not wish to work. What evidence is available on this subject shows that less than 150,000 male public welfare recipients are classified as able bodied; however, the majority of these men do

TABLE 2-6.

Families and Unrelated Individuals Below the Low-Income Level in 1970 Receiving Public Assistance and Social Security Income, by Sex of Head
(*Numbers in thousands*)

Subject	All Families		Male Head[1]		Female Head[1]	
	Negro	White	Negro	White	Negro	White
Families						
Total	1,445	3,701	625	2,604	820	1,097
Receiving public assistance income	690	839	177	370	513	469
Percent	48	23	28	14	63	43
Receiving Social Security income	341	1,192	188	928	153	264
Percent	24	32	30	36	19	24
Unrelated Individuals						
Total	840	4,121	301	1,088	539	3,033
Receiving public assistance income	295	633	73	185	222	448
Percent	35	15	24	17	41	15
Receiving Social Security income	297	2,284	85	434	212	1,850
Percent	35	55	28	40	39	61

[1] For unrelated individuals, sex of individual.

SOURCE: U.S. Department of Commerce, Social and Economic Statistics Administration, Bureau of the Census.

wish to work and are enrolled in various government-sponsored training programs.

Nor is there valid evidence to support the notion that the majority of female welfare recipients are husbandless women who are constantly having children in order to increase their welfare earnings. Almost three-fifths of all the children in families on welfare are legitimate children. Seventy-three percent of welfare families have fewer than four children per family. Thirty percent of them have only a single child.

Thus no reason exists to believe that welfare is crippling the black population and forcing it to become increasingly pathological. Even though many are forced to become dependent upon welfare for survival, it is at best a temporary adaptive mechanism for people who are poverty stricken, infirm, and in need of financial support because of the loss of family members who provided the necessary instrumental functions. Nevertheless, the myths still persist in the face of objective data to the contrary. Table 2-7 shows some of the data.

If, on the other hand, the concept of welfare is extended beyond its traditional meaning, it becomes readily apparent that welfare comes in many forms. It is equally obvious that, collectively, the white American population receives far more federal benefits than does the black American population. For example, the white middle class receives a much greater share of Federal Housing Administration (FHA) loans than do blacks. Furthermore, the federal government has shown an unusual proclivity for subsidizing bankrupt corporations in the defense industry while simultaneously only granting, grudgingly, substantially smaller sums for the capitalization of minority businesses. These government-favored corporations are owned and controlled by the white middle and upper classes and are, indeed, the largest recipients of governmental welfare. Thus it is obvious that the amount of federal and local funds allocated for AFDC is in no way comparable to federal subsidization for middle- and upper-class whites in the United States.

TABLE 2-7.

Families Below the Low-Income Level Receiving Public Assistance in 1970

Families	Male Head		Female Head	
	White	Black	White	Black
Receiving public assistance income	370,000	177,000	469,000	583,000
Percent	14	28	43	63
Receiving SS income	928,000	188,000	264,000	153,000
Percent	36	30	24	19

SOURCE: U.S. Census, *General Social and Economic Characteristics*, 1971.

THE IMPACT OF URBANIZATION ON THE BLACK FAMILY

It was stated earlier that the black population in the United States is now predominantly urban. More than three-quarters of all American blacks live in cities. The process of urbanization among blacks, as in the case of the American population in general, occurred largely within the past century, since a century ago the United States was still quite fundamentally a rural nation. However, in the case of the black population, this transformation from rural dwellers to city dwellers had its most auspicious beginning at the end of the first decade of the twentieth century. It has continued at such an unabated pace that the trend now seems irreversible. As a process, the urbanization of American blacks occurred as America itself was transformed from an agricultural nation into an industrial one. Industrialization was accompanied by a population explosion in strategic areas, mainly from an influx of people from the farm to the city in search of a new life and higher standards of living. It also signaled basic changes in patterns of work and the development of a more complex division of labor. Thus even though the city was to become a profoundly unique experience for the migrant rural peasantry, black and white, its effect upon the black family would in time prove to be particularly notable.

At least two schools of thought prevail regarding the impact of urbanization on the black family. First is the deterioration theory as represented in the early works of Frazier[47] and the more recent but highly controversial arguments advanced by Moynihan.[48] The basic assumption that underlies the family deterioration theory is that urbanization has wreaked an almost uncontrollable disorganization upon the black family—a process stemming from the mass movement of a woefully unprepared sharecropping, tenant-farming, and unskilled population into a highly complex social structure. This lack of preparation for city life, coupled with the rapidity of their infiltration into urban settings, rendered blacks incapable of making satisfactory adjustments to urban complexities. Neither individuals nor families could cope with the myriad problems that confront the experienced urban dweller—problems of anonymity, personal isolation, limited primary group affiliations, impersonality, earning a living, finding suitable housing, obtaining basic health care, and establishing social bonds or developing a sense of group solidarity. Failing to make these adjustments, the family became disorganized, a condition most directly revealed by divorce, desertion, separation, illegitimacy, matriarchal family structures, sexual immorality or casual sexual relations, delinquency, criminality, high rates of unemployment, alienation, and general normlessness.

Frazier advanced this position in a 1939 prizewinning study, *The Negro Family in the United States*. As a point of clarification, it should be stressed that Frazier's analysis of what he called the disorganization of the Negro family was not intended to make black people culpable for their condition, as he defined it; rather, he was identifying those situations within urban social structure and the American experience that generated family deterioration. Of primary importance to him was the legacy of slavery, which, as a sustained institution, had numerous deleterious consequences for the black family. He saw in slavery and its consequences major structural divergencies from the normative patterns of American middle-class family life. These variations persisted through urbanization and were, in effect, viewed as atypical behavioral patterns. However, it is particularly significant that Frazier attributed a major responsibility for whatever disorganization he observed with black family structures to the pernicious elements of prejudice, discrimination, and white racism and not to callous blacks. These were the factors that accounted for large-scale unemployment and abject poverty, that fostered impoverished conditions, and that constituted the main impediments to the inclusion of blacks in the opportunity structure on an equal basis with the white population. Irrespective of these explanations, social scientists have often cited Frazier's position to support the general theory of black family disorganization. Almost as frequently as it has been cited, it has been quoted out of context and in such a manner as to support prevailing stereotypic and racist ideologies concerning black family blight.

Perhaps it is the persistence of misconceptions about black family life interfaced with intellectual racism that helps to explain the vituperative reactions among many practitioners and academicians to the publication of the Moynihan Report on the black family in 1965. In a way, Moynihan's analysis of the conditions of contemporary black families is similar to that of Frazier. Both give similar explanations of the so-called family disorganization or deterioration. Significantly, the Frazier-Moynihan perspective diverges in the level of consciousness with which racism, discrimination, and prejudice are viewed as contributing factors to the condition specified as disorganization. Frazier's position on this subject was clearer than Moynihan's. The contexts in which their publications appeared were quite dissimilar, however. For many American people Moynihan failed to specify clearly that Americans must devise effective means of first controlling prejudice and racism, which are the manifest springboards for discrimination, before any national effort of substantial credibility can be mounted to strengthen the black family. He did, however, stress the need to strengthen the role of the black male to halt further deterioration. The "tangle of pathology" which he describes, assuming that it has partial merit, is a function of inequities in the opportunity structure between blacks and whites—disparities so pervasive as to relegate blacks into an almost inescapable subordinate status. Moynihan does not sufficiently clarify this essential point.

A second school of thought maintained by Billingsley,[49] Hill,[50] Staples,[51] and others holds that many of the conditions characterized as disorganization may be viewed as either strengths or as new modes of adaption to untoward situations. It is also argued that the black matriarchy is a myth.[52] In this view the impact of urbanization on the black family is neither totally nor necessarily deleterious. It may not even be particularly dysfunctional as a process, but an ethos of racism permeating the nation and forcing blacks into a subordinate status can be quite detrimental to black family life. The fact that black families remain relatively organized around differentiated role-specific and role-general functions is a strength[53]; and the existence of extended family systems as a welfare family function is a significant adaptive response to urbanism.[54]

Regardless of the position or school of thought that one accepts, certain fundamental observations can be made concerning the urbanization of black families. First, as the earlier black population shifted from the farm to the city, they did not differ noticeably from earlier American immigrants except in terms of limited access to the opportunity structure and in the color of their skins. But these were profound differences, for they were to shape the character of the black family's experiences in the city. For example, being outside the opportunity structure placed them in a disadvantaged position within an increasingly complex labor force. Discriminatory practices prevented even the best trained men, with some notable exceptions, from obtaining high-salaried positions. Therefore, since they were largely laborers, occupational diversity was seriously curtailed, which, in turn, limited the income that could be earned legally. In many instances, unemployment led to poverty, which also engendered numerous personal problems.

Second, the isolated and impersonal conditions under which early black urban migrants existed, coupled with the freedom from powerful, if informal, structures of social control, permitted experimentation with social relationships between the sexes that would have generated severe social disapprobation in a rural setting. Thus urbanization fostered another interpretation of machismo or manhood—freedom to embrace a double standard of morality. Some may argue, as have Elliott Liebow[55] and Charles A. Valentine,[56] that this process is a sociopsychological response to failure as a man in an economic world in which the lower-class black male cannot earn his way and provide for his family as he basically desires. It is not an essential element in a culture of poverty. This is, of course, a point of continuing debate; however, there is general agreement that the urbanization of blacks is continually accompanied by increasing divorce rates. Even this observation does not solve the dilemma for protagonists of the two schools of thought described previously, inasmuch as those in the first school would perceive divorce as an index of disorganization, whereas those in the second school would undoubtedly view divorce as a mode of adaption that allows extrication from an intolerable situation.

Third, urbanization generated a transfer of several family functions to other institutional structures, either in part or in toto. Thus socialization is shared with educational institutions, protection with law enforcement agencies, and religious training with the established church, while recreational functions are dispersed among a wide array of secondary enterprises and voluntary associations, and economic functions are not now the exclusive responsibility of the family. The family is no longer primarily a producer but a consumer. But it is this transfer of economic functions that has facilitated increasing independence of women and removed many of them from the home onto the labor market.

One consequence of the independence of women is evident in the fourth and final observation—the breakdown of the traditional patriarchal family structure. As stated in the discussion of household patterns and authority structures among the black population, a shift from patriarchy to equalitarianism has occurred among black families. This transformation coincided with increasing urbanization and appears to be the most prevalent authority structure among present-day urban blacks in the United States.

In conclusion, it should be stressed that even though the black population continues to shift from the rural areas and small towns to the cities, we cannot assume that the migrant blacks are ignorant, unprepared peasants cluttering already overcrowded slums. More and more of them are moving from one large city to another and may be higher achievers than those blacks already residing in the cities into which they migrate. In general, intercity migrants tend to have obtained a higher amount of formal education and to be of higher occupational status than the black residents of their new cities.[57] It should also be stated that the problems of deviance that often correlate with urbanization will receive more attention in the final chapters of this book.

NOTES

1. For a discussion of the pathologies of black families cf. E. Franklin Frazier, *The Negro Family in the United States* (Chicago: University of Chicago Press, 1939); Alphonso Pinkney, *Black Americans* (Englewood Cliffs, N.J.: Prentice-Hall, 1969), Chap. 5; and Daniel P. Moynihan, *The Negro Family: The Case for National Action* (Washington, D.C.: United States Department of Labor, 1965).

2. John Hope Franklin, *From Slavery to Freedom* (New York: Alfred A. Knopf, 1948), p. 108.

3. *Ibid.*

4. *Ibid.*

5. Andrew Billingsley, *Black Families in White America* (Englewood Cliffs, N.J.: Prentice-Hall, 1968), pp. 143–144.

6. *Ibid., passim.*

7. Robert Staples, *The Black Family: Essays and Studies* (Belmont, Calif.: Wadsworth Publishing Company, 1971), pp. 149–159.

8. Robert Hill, *The Strengths of Black Families* (New York: Emerson Hall Publishers, Inc., 1972), p. 9.

9. David A. Schulz, "The Role of Boyfriend," *Coming Up Black: Patterns of Ghetto Socialization* (Englewood Cliffs, N.J.: Prentice-Hall, 1969), pp. 136–144.

10. Billingsley, *op. cit.*, pp. 18–25.

11. *Ibid.*

12. *U.S. 1970 Census of Population: General Social and Economic Characteristics* (Washington, D.C.: U.S. Department of Commerce, Bureau of the Census, June 1972), pp. 406, 417.

13. *The Social and Economic Status of the Black Population in the United States, 1971* (Washington, D.C.: U.S. Department of Commerce, Bureau of the Census, 1972), p. 126.

14. *Ibid.*

15. *Ibid.*

16. *Ibid.*, p. 131.

17. See *Social and Economic Status of Negroes in the United States, 1970* (Washington, D.C.: U.S. Department of Commerce, Bureau of the Census, 1971), pp. 110–111.

18. Schulz, *op. cit.*

19. *Ibid.*

20. *Ibid.*

21. *Ibid.*

22. *Ibid.*

23. *Ibid.*

24. *Ibid.*

25. Billingsley, *op. cit.*, p. 22.

26. *Ibid.*

27. *Ibid.*

28. Hill, *op. cit.*, pp. 5–36.

29. *Ibid.*

30. Herbert Otto, "What Is a Family?" *Marriage and Family Living*, 24 (February 1962), pp. 72–89.

31. *The Social and Economic Status of the Black Population in the United States, 1971, loc. cit.*, p. 111.

32. Elizabeth Herzog, "Is There a 'Breakdown' of the Negro Family?" *Social Work*, 2 (January 1966), pp. 3–10.

33. Hill, *op. cit.*

34. Herzog, *op. cit.*

35. Pinkney, *op. cit.*, Chap. 5.

36. Jessie Bernard, "Marital Stability and Patterns of Status Variables," *Journal of Marriage and the Family*, 28 (November 1966), pp. 421–439, and *American Community Behavior* (New York: Holt, Rinehart and Winston, 1949), p. 226.

37. Paul Glick and Arthur Norton, "Frequency, Duration, and Probability of Marriage and Divorce," *Journal of Marriage and the Family*, 33 (May 1971).

38. J. Richard Udry, "Marital Instability by Race, Sex, Education and Occupation Using 1960 Census Data," *American Journal of Sociology*, 72 (September 1966), pp. 203–209, and "Marital Instability by Race and Income Based on 1960 Census Data," *American Journal of Sociology*, 72 (May 1967), pp. 673–674.

39. Glick and Norton, *op. cit.*

40. Bernard, *op. cit.*, note 36.

41. Moynihan, *op. cit.*, pp. 6–9, 29–47, *passim*.

42. Lee Rainwater and William Yancy, *The Moynihan Report and the Politics of Controversy* (Cambridge, Mass.: The M.I.T. Press, 1967), p. 45.

43. Beverly Duncan and Otis D. Duncan, "Family Stability and Occupational Success," *Social Problems*, 16 (Winter 1969), pp. 273–285.

44. Elizabeth Herzog and Hylan Lewis, "Children in Poor Families: Myths and Realities," *American Journal of Orthopsychiatry*, 40 (April 1970), pp. 375–387.

45. Frances Fox Piven and Richard Cloward, *Regulating the Poor* (New York: Vintage Books, 1971), pp. 189–190.

46. *Boston Sunday Globe*, November 28, 1972, Section 6A.

47. Frazier, *op. cit.*

48. Moynihan, *op. cit.*

49. Billingsley, *op. cit.*

50. Hill, *op. cit.*

51. Staples, *op. cit.*

52. *Ibid.*

53. Hill, *op. cit.*

54. Staples, *op. cit.*

55. Elliott Liebow, *Talley's Corner: A Study of Negro Street Corner Men* (Boston: Little, Brown, 1966).

56. Charles A. Valentine, *Culture and Poverty: Critique and Counter-Proposals* (Chicago: University of Chicago Press, 1968).

57. Karl E. Tauber and Alma F. Tauber, *Negroes in Cities* (Chicago: Aldine Publishing Co., 1965), pp. 1–8.

3 | STRATIFICATION AND SOCIAL MOBILITY

Like all other social systems, the black community is characterized by some form of stratification. Differentiation of its members occurs according to certain criteria that serve to rank them into distinctive layers or various social strata. Though the roots of this system can be traced to slavery, its present dynamic character is a result of major transformations within our industrialized society. It is also evidence of increasing shifts from ascription to achievement as the basis for stratification and mobility. Both traditional socioeconomic status (SES) variables facilitate social differentiation and upward mobility as in the larger society; blackness, however, has played an increasingly important role in upward mobility within the black community in recent years. These observations will be elaborated next.

PERCEPTIONS OF SOCIAL CLASS

Contemporary views about social stratification draw upon the rich legacy provided by the seminal works of Karl Marx and Max Weber, so much so that when we think of social classes, we almost automatically fix in our minds concepts such as property, prestige, power, life styles, and economic base. These concepts are widely used in explications of social class by contemporary sociologists.

At the risk of oversimplification Marx's views may be briefly summarized as follows. Classes are groups of people, rather than specific individuals, who are united around commonly shared experiences in relationship to the means of production. The relationship to the means of production is dichotomized: Either people own these means (the bourgeoisie) or they sell their labor (the proletariat). The bourgeoisie is exceedingly powerful but limited in number, whereas the proletariat is considerably larger in size but limited in power. It is this disparity in the economic structure that forms the basis of all social classes and that determines one's place in the society as a whole. For Marx, then, economic position becomes the basis for quality of family life, prestige, status, and political power.

A second perspective on social class was provided by Weber, who, in effect, expanded and modified Marxian thought. For Weber three principal factors serve as the foundation of social stratification—the economic order, the social order, and the political order. These orders are generally interpreted as class, status or prestige, and power, respectively. Weber's use of the concept social order closely corresponds to the Marxian meaning of class; and it was, quite importantly, based upon the life chances and opportunities provided a person in terms of economic position. It should be clear that Weber stressed the independent nature of the three factors of class, status, and power even though they do intersect at crucial points within societies and subcommunities. By this is meant that the possibility of relatively powerless well-to-do and high-prestige relatively poor did exist within Weber's theoretical formulation. In fact, they exist in everyday life.

Both perspectives generated schools of thought among social scientists about the formation of social class[1] and, quite importantly, identified elements that should be specified when developing class distinctions. Thus the conceptual tools of property, power, prestige, and economic base are among the more common indicators of class position and determinants of mobility employed today.

Property refers to possessions and the implicit right to dispose of them as the owner sees fit. It is derived from group membership, exchanges of scarce values, capital investments, inheritance, and outright gifts, Its acquisition may be highly correlated with one's position in the economic, social, or political order.[2]

Although there are numerous conceptualizations of the term "power," for our purposes it may be viewed simply as the ability to control the decision-making apparatus and shared values of the social system. This ability may rest with one or more individuals, or it may be vested within certain groups under certain conditions. Group power, as perceived by Robert Bierstedt, may have its source in (1) numbers or the size of the group, (2) the degree of the group's social organization, and (3) the amount and types of resources available to the group.[3] Expanding upon Bierstedt's formulation,

Hubert Blalock suggested that a critical variable in the acquisition and maintenance of group power is the ability of the group to mobilize its resources over time until it reaches its goal.[4]

On the other hand, *individual* power may be derived from the roles performed by individuals (their institutional positions); implied or actuated force; the acquisition of property, which enables the individual to control the distribution of certain aspects of scarce resources; or from what Weber correctly called "charisma"—those personal qualities that permit certain people to influence, persuade, and charm others into complying with their wishes.[5] The sources of individual power are virtually identical to those that generate prestige or what Weber identified as social honor. However, it is imperative to stress the independent nature of variables such as prestige, power, and property, for the possession of one does not and should not imply the automatic possession of the other. Their independence of operation creates considerable status inconsistency in the American society— ranking high on one status dimension and low on another—and especially among black people in relation to the larger society. Regional and community variations may be missed entirely if categorical or uniform perceptions of power and prestige, for example, are taken as a norm in social class analysis. To illustrate, the amount of prestige awarded a college professor may be substantially greater in Walla Walla, Washington, a small college town, than would be accorded such a person in New York City. Moreover, the mere acquisition of property, for example, does not necessarily assure concomitant power and privilege. Some people in the United States, black and white, are more concerned with *how* one attains property or wealth than with the actual possession of it. Nevertheless, the acquisition of power, prestige, and property and a solid economic base may, as we shall see, facilitate upward mobility in the stratification system.

It is also possible for a discontinuity to arise between a person's objective class position and his subjective position in the social structure. By definition the objective class position refers to the real rank the person holds in a society according to some predetermined and somewhat universalistic criteria. The subjective class, on the other hand, refers to the rank the person feels or thinks he holds. The two may or may not be congruent. But the disparity between these two veiwpoints—how others see an individual and how the individual sees himself—often results in eccentric behavior among certain individuals.

ETHNIC STRATIFICATION

So far, we have stressed class as a fundamental basis for stratification in the America society. However, social class is only one of the two major systems of stratification in the United States. A second and equally powerful system is ethnic stratification.[6] This system by and large expresses where a particular group falls on a social distance scale, that is, how closely it approximates conventional norms and standards of social acceptability of the white Anglo-Saxon society in the United States. In every social distance scale ethnic groups, particularly the so-called new ethnics—blacks, Chicanos, Puerto Ricans, and Orientals to a lesser degree—are relegated to the bottom positions. European immigrants, including new European groups such as Italians, Jews, and Poles, rank above new minority ethnics in the eyes of most of the predominant society. Because of color, however, the newer ethnics have greater visibility, which helps to identify them and set them apart from white Anglo-Saxons. Their greater visibility may also function to restrict advancement within the opportunity structure and thereby retard upward mobility in a class system. Since they are set apart from the rest of the members of the larger society, however, and are excluded from full participation in that structure, they tend to develop a stratification system of their own, superimposed on and overlaid by the larger one.

The process of ethnic classification and subsequent stratification is more or less inescapable in a pluralistic society in which power is unequally distributed. Unequal access to scarce values and to goods and services by which they are identified, classified, and positioned within the social structure accompanies limitations of power. Whenever the color variable enters into the classification schema, it is almost axiomatic that the more closely a person or a group approximates whiteness, the higher his or its rank in the larger system. The same principle often obtains *within* some ethnic groups in their own stratification system. Color, therefore, has both a divisive and unifying effect. The dominant group uses it, on the one hand, to distinguish itself from subordinates or less favored individuals. Members of the subordinate group who approximate the dominant one in color employ it, on the other hand, in order to establish positions of privilege within the subordinate structure. Moreover, because all members of the subordinate group are lumped together, color becomes the unifying force in the face of externally imposed sanctions, categorical treatment, intergroup conflicts, and denials of access to highly prized scarce resources, goods, and services.

THE FORMATION OF
SOCIAL CLASSES IN THE
BLACK COMMUNITY

Chapter 1 showed how a stratification system formed among American blacks from the distinctions made between house servants and field hands during the period of slavery. House servants, for the most part, were mulatto offspring and the descendants of unions between white men and black slave women. During slavery, house servants were able to acquire a distinctive level of living that set them apart from the field hands. As we noted previously, they were also socialized into the cultural mandates and life styles of the white ruling class in a manner not available to other groups of slaves. The differences that emerged between house slaves and field hands were further widened because of the value placed upon white ancestry and the social status resulting from this value. The work done by house servants compared to that done by field hands also maximized distinctions based upon color and rank. The skills that house servants learned were predictably beneficial because they helped transform these slaves into freemen. Indeed, many house servants were manumitted; others were able to buy not only their own freedom but also the freedom of other members of their families. Through this process a class of free blacks became the founders of a propertied "aristocracy of color" among American blacks.

Black field hands, who either attempted to hold on to the rudiments of a rapidly disappearing culture or who desperately tried to accommodate to sketches of the new white culture, were forced to become America's underclass—the lumpen proletariat of society. Primarily unskilled and untrained, they worked with their hands, engaged in menial tasks, and supplied the brawn and labor necessary to build many of the physical structures of the American republic. They suffered the abuses of low status and low esteem. They were forced to internalize white perceptions of their value and to deny the worth of their color. Thus slavery produced a twofold class system among black Americans: an upper class based almost exclusively upon color and a lower class that consisted primarily of the sons and daughters of field hands.[7] It also originated a dual stratification system.

In time, as opportunities expanded through industrialization and shifted away from a paternalistic agricultural slavery system, stratification within the black population would somewhat parallel that of the larger American social structure. Earlier, black codes were promulgated to keep slaves in their place; later, varying legislation was enacted to restrict freemen and to subordinate them into a kind of caste arrangement in the American social structure. The post-emancipation period and particularly the post-Reconstruction period witnessed a proliferation of legal restraints aimed at preventing the emergence of an independent group of blacks[8]—all of which fostered a dual social structure and, inevitably, a parallel system of stratification. This observation supports the assertions by conflict theorists that social classes are man-made and subject to man-made change. The articulation of a *structure of privilege* versus a *structure of want,* for example, was indeed made by men who undoubtedly believed that their acts were rational. The mythical men of power not only created a system of inequality within the larger society and between the white members of that society and the black nonmembers; they also established a model that blacks would in time emulate for creating social differentiation among themselves.

Color. The color variable, often labeled "family background," persisted as the most important criterion for admission to the black upper class through most of the Reconstruction period and, in some circles, until the 1940s. The importance of the degree of color lightness in conferring higher status among blacks began to wane with expanding educational opportunities, which occurred during Reconstruction and afterwards. This process was stimulated by two major sources, the Freedmen's Bureau and white philanthropists.

The U.S. Congress established the Freedmen's Bureau in 1865 to provide economic, social, and educational rehabilitation for the newly emancipated slaves and refugees of the slavery period. Under its aegis some blacks were fed, clothed, and given medical treatment and other social services. The bureau also established schools that gave rise to a more literate class among the darker-skinned blacks and allowed many of them to lease land in order to get a head start toward economic betterment. The work of the Freedmen's Bureau only partially undermined the aristocracy of color. The same effect resulted from the work of the numerous philanthropic organizations, voluntary groups, and individuals who were concerned about the plight of the masses of black people. Institutions such as the American Missionary Association and religious bodies like the Methodist Episcopal Church, the Presbyterians, the Episcopalians, the Baptists, and, to a lesser degree, the Catholics founded institutions for the educational development of blacks. George Peabody, John D. Rockefeller, John F. Slater, Anna T. Jeanes, and Caroline Phelps-Stokes were among a fairly large aggregate of individuals who came forward with substantial financial aid to expand educational opportunities for black people. Over a period of three decades approximately 121 colleges and universities would be founded for educating the black masses. The establishment of black secondary schools, colleges, and universities increased the likelihood that darker-skinned members of the black population would become educated, which, in time, facilitated the erosion of the aristocracy of color.

Family Background. Family background was the second most important criterion for high status and upward mobility within the black community. The importance attached to one's family background, although diminished in broad significance since World War II through expanded economic and occupational opportunities, still persists in many segments of black social life. Regardless of the acquisition of wealth by the new black bourgeoisie[9] and the new black Anglo-Saxons,[10] admission to the pinnacle of the black social class structure is still a function of family name, social honor, and prestige. In several communities prestige continues to be accorded to persons whose families were respected in times past even though they themselves may have only modest means. Such families retain social honor for any number of reasons, including leadership roles in the community, positions held or services performed in the church, a lengthy history of unimpeachable character, relationships with white people, and respected personal attributes. In most instances, however, these preferred families have or once had considerable property, were never on welfare, kept their children out of trouble with white people and the law, and traditionally valued education. Today, these families often know each other because they have an extended and persistent network throughout the United States.

Education. Perhaps the one factor that emerged as the most potent instrument for effecting major changes in the class structure within the black community was educational attainment. Formal schooling especially helped to delineate a black middle class. This class was formed by people sufficiently literate to perform important roles and functions required within the larger social structure and within the black community. Originally, schoolteachers, undertakers, postmen, businessmen, insurance men, and real-estate workers comprised the black middle class. But the status of incumbents of these occupations varied from community to community and from region to region; often, though, some of these persons were included in the upper-class structure of the black society because of the convergence of a worthwhile occupation, a good family name, and the proper degree of education. What is of special importance here is that blacks, like many other low-status minority groups, placed a recognizably high value on educational attainment. So great was the value placed on educational achievement that black mothers were domestic servants to white people and fathers labored at low wages for white people in order to send their children to college and professional schools. Countless numbers of black young men and women deferred gratifications and sacrificed ordinary pleasures in order to raise money to go to college, often not knowing how they could afford to remain once admitted. Numerous black professional men and women of today did not come from well-to-do families that were able to support them throughout the period of college or professional training. But their eagerness to obtain an education moved them to work at service jobs for the white population to raise the necessary funds. Black students could be found working as waiters at country clubs or in the more genteel restaurants, as caddies, bellhops, and doormen in the larger hotels where tipping was generous, as janitors, laundrymen and women, cooks, domestic workers, part-time carpenters, bricklayers, and construction workers. Once education was attained, upward mobility within the black stratification system was considerably less difficult to attain.

As more black youth became educated and later as their economic positions improved, parents and brothers and sisters often shared in the benefits. Unfortunately, some who achieved success later spurned their hard-working mothers and fathers and others who had sacrificed in their behalf. These sons and daughters were, to put it bluntly, ashamed of their lowly origins; they often manufactured elaborate fabrications of family origins and falsehoods about their prestige and power within home communities. This pattern reflected a deeply rooted personal insecurity and an inability to express pride in achievements in the American tradition of the self-made man or woman. Many successful blacks today, however, do not shy away from knowledge of their humble backgrounds.

The importance of education as a cherished value within the black community can also be observed in the gross exaggerations of educational attainment and the importance attached to degrees obtained from certain institutions. Frazier once spoke of this situation in terms of the role of the black press in creating a make-believe world among black people.[11] Although present-day facts and more empirical investigations contradict much of what Frazier wrote in 1957, he was correct in his assertion that the black press frequently exaggerates the educational achievements of black people. The acquisition of a baccalaureate degree, especially from a prestigious predominantly white university, used to be reported as though it were a much higher degree. To some extent this is still true today. However, erroneous reporting has substantially lessened as a consequence of increasing sophistication and greater competence among black journalists. More attention and more coverage, though, are still given to graduates of predominantly white institutions than to graduates of predominantly black colleges and universities.

In general, then, it can be stated that at least until World War II the convergence of color, family background, and education formed the basic features of social stratification within the black community. The right combination of these elements differentiated various levels of social acceptability, status recognition, and special privilege observed within black communities throughout the United States. That system would undergo profound changes with improvements in the economic opportunities of black people and with the development of an expanded occupational structure that admitted an increasingly large and diverse group of blacks at the middle and upper ranges, both within the black community and the larger social structure, though to a far lesser degree. But these changes did not appreciably alter the subordinated status of the black social class system.

INDICES OF SOCIAL CLASS

What, then, are the measures of social class within the contemporary black community? In many respects the determination of social class among blacks is quite similar to that among whites. They differ in the degree to which some factors are more highly valued than others and, perhaps, *how* measures of social class are employed in daily life. Traditionally, sociologists associate class position with one's standing in relation to SES variables of occupation, education, and income. These variables are primary—possessing almost universal applicability. They are also associated with what we may now call secondary variables: family background, place of residence, status symbols, membership in formal and informal associations, voluntary groups, friendship cliques, church membership, and life styles. With the possible exception of church membership and family background, these factors are secondary in the sense that they are derived from the primary sources of class identity. In a society that is ethnically stratified, the factor of skin color becomes a further index of status and social class. Blackness may possibly supplant whiteness in the black community as a variable that defines class identity.

Within the black community all the foregoing determinants of social class function in social differentiation. It is the interplay among them that characterizes and distinguishes the system; however, primary variables are interrelated and often affect secondary outcomes. For example, the interplay of education and occupation has had a profound consequence on the amount of legitimate income received per year by black Americans, which, in turn, decidedly affects ability to attain status symbols and conspicuous life styles. *The crystallization and interaction of these variables in terms of role-sets and status rewards resulted in the elaboration of a class structure that is nonetheless definitive though imperfectly formed. However, the presence of such a system exemplifies the diversity within the community and destroys the myth of the black population as a monolithic homogeneous unit.*

SOCIAL STRATIFICATION WITHIN THE BLACK COMMUNITY TODAY

Two stratification subsystems prevail in the black community today: One is socially approved class, whereas the other has its roots in illegitimate structures such as the underworld of crime and vice. Our attention is focused primarily upon the former, although, paradigmatically, this subterranean underworld social structure can be superimposed onto the legitimate class structure in much the same way as the overall black stratification system can be superimposed onto the larger system within the American society. Figure 3-1 illustrates.

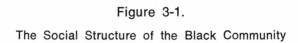

Figure 3-1.

The Social Structure of the Black Community

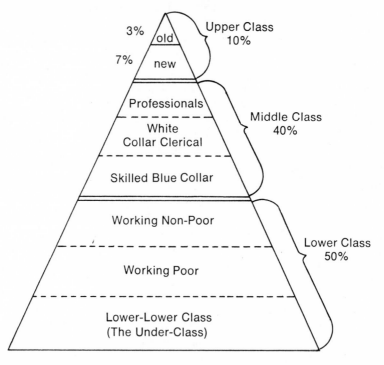

(Solid lines denote relatively stable divisions between classes whereas broken lines indicate that demarcations between substrata are often blurred.)

NOTE: The lower-class section of this pyramid is based upon the model presented by Andrew Billingsley, *Black Families In White America* (Englewood Cliffs, N.J.: Prentice-Hall, 1968) p. 123.

The legitimate social structure consists of three broad commonly accepted classes or strata: upper, middle, and lower. As indicated in Figure 3-1, each of the three broad social classes is further subdivided into two or more subclasses. The type of structure depicted in the figure demonstrates the immense variation in status and behavior characteristic of the black community. Some of the more extensive studies of the class structure within the black community were the earlier and relatively recent works of Frazier,[12] Horace Cayton and St. Clair Drake,[13] Gunnar Myrdal,[14] and Billingsley.[15] A systematic analysis of these studies would reveal changing determinants of class position, described previously, from one generation to another. The descriptions that follow depend heavily on insights gleaned from their contributions to this area of social life among black people.

THE UPPER CLASS

Regardless of the criteria used to assign social class position, the black upper classes are significantly smaller in size than all other social classes in the black community. Billingsley estimates that approximately 10 percent of the black population can accurately be classified this way.[16] If his claim is true, the proportion of blacks in the upper classes has only doubled in a 30-year period.[17] (Drake and Cayton claimed that only 5 percent of the black families in Chicago belonged to the upper classes.) However, the proportion of blacks achieving this status continues to increase as high educational attainments are made, occupational status and diversification are achieved, and real income rises.

The upper class is subdivided into two hierarchical strata: the old upper class and the newly arrived. The distinctions between the two substrata have created superordinate-subordinate boundaries between them. The old upper class includes persons with an enduring family name, high prestige, and respectable families. Its members are characterized by a long-established tradition of education, respectable occupations, dependable income, and unimpeachable reputations. Until the 1940s this group represented an aristocracy of color comprised particularly of those individuals whose families were descendants of free men and women who lived during the slavery period. Extremely color conscious, they often went to elaborate lengths to avoid interaction or social encounters with darker-skinned black people. They insisted upon physical segregation from their darker-skinned brethren and limited contacts with them. In some parts of Louisiana, for example, they established a separate elementary school system for themselves—apart from the already existing dual school system. Their marginality and existence as a third force in such communities that did not provide them with a high school system compelled them either to send their high-school- and college-age children to out-of-town schools or to schools where they could become *passé pou blanc* or *pasa blanche* ("passed for white") or to discontinue formal education at the grade school level. Those with a sufficient income chose the *pasa blanche* alternative, thereby losing a black identity and intermixing with the white population.

The color aristocrats formed a tenuously closed system strengthened by family and group restrictions against exogenous marriages to persons easily identified as black. This is still characteristic of many of these old families, who cling to memories of their glorious past when they were respected for their white ancestry. In time, however, this group was subjected to ridicule by less fortunate blacks and to abusive epithets such as "high yallar," "half-white bastards," and so on. Undeniably, this group received the benefits of special advantages because of the privileges associated with their color caste. A self-fulfilling prophecy prevailed, since those who were light skinned received higher education and the highly educated were in turn, likely to receive the better-paying jobs and be light skinned. This aristocracy of color was undermined, however, by factors mentioned earlier, and in time education, occupation, and income preempted the relative importance of color as the major attribute for upper-class identification.

The old upper class, comprising roughly 3 percent of the total number of black families, consists of persons in the following occupational groups: established physicians, surgeons, dentists, attorneys, judges, ambassadors and high-ranking government officials, wealthy bankers and insurance executives, college presidents and ministers of the larger, well-known churches. These are likely to be people whose families were able to provide them with what Billingsley calls "screens of opportunity"[18] when they were young which consisted of financial and emotional support, a legacy of achievement, and high motivation for success. As adults they, too, are able to support their families on a high plane.

Placing considerable value on marital stability, the old upper class tends to avoid divorces and separations and adheres to a strongly paternalistic family structure. They are often puritanical in public yet foster a double standard for men, since men are supposed to enjoy certain prerogatives not granted to women. They encourage excellence in manners and social intercourse and send their children to the better schools, often to private elementary and secondary schools as well as to private colleges and universities. Whereas their parents took pride in sending them to prestigious black colleges in the past (e.g., Howard, Fisk, Morehouse, Spelman, Talladega, Bennett, and Xavier), the sons and daughters of the old aristocracy now place a higher premium on having graduates of Harvard, Radcliffe, Princeton, Yale, Smith, Vassar, and Bryn Mawr. A few, motivated by loyalty and a commitment to blackness and to enhancing the opportunities for their children to find suitable marital partners from old families of the black professional class, still send their sons and daughters to prestigious black colleges and universities.

There is an extensive, nationwide network of social relationships among old upper-class families. The degree of familiarity among prominent black families may reinforce the stereotype among many white people that all educated blacks know each other. Although the stereotype is false, there is much truth in the claim that prominent black families, like the white elite, do attempt to maintain social intimacy with each other. Thus one often reads in the society sections of black publications such as *Jet* and *Ebony* or in the 214 black newspapers such as the *Amsterdam News, The Chicago Defender, The Los Angeles Sentinel*, the Cleveland *Call and Post*, the *Louisiana Weekly*, the *Pittsburgh Courier* and the *Norfolk Journal and Guide* not only about their jet-set social activities but about the social affairs of others who try to emulate them. But the relationships are not necessarily superficial and epicurean. If one is from North Carolina, for instance, and claims to be of old upper-class origins, one is expected to know the distinguished Spaulding family in much the same way as one who is from Georgia is expected to know the prestigious Dobbs family. Social interaction among the members of old upper-class families is facilitated by quick modes of transportation and comfortable financial situations. Thus it is not uncharacteristic for members of this group to travel great distances to attend a social function hosted by their counterparts in another city. Their children will travel from Atlanta and Charleston to Los Angeles or from San Francisco to New Orleans and Washington, D.C., to participate in the weddings of their friends, who will honeymoon, not at a black-owned motor lodge in Houston, but, probably, at an exclusive hotel in Honolulu, San Juan, Minorca, Paris, Rome, or London. Like their white counterparts, announcements of these activities are discreetly placed in the leading black publications and, occasionally, in the local daily—but rarely *The New York Times*.

The members of the old upper class are conspicuous consumers but stress good taste. Clothing is likely to be expensive, often specially designed and stylishly conservative; automobiles are selected for durability and are less ostentatious than those purchased by the new upper class; and residences are usually unpretentious structures set on sizable lots. Whether in the suburbs or in segregated areas of the city, their residences are likely to be located in the "more respectable" neighborhoods. Richly furnished, spacious rooms characterize these homes.

Their leisure-time activities are no longer centered on the playing of poker, as Frazier claimed,[19] if indeed that ever was their focal concern, but are highly diversified. There is, however, a network of bridge clubs that reveals who is admitted to class membership from time to time. They patronize the arts, enjoy the legitimate theatre, opera, and the local symphony. The musicians whose works they enjoy range from Bizet, Mozart,

Rachmaninoff, Chopin, Leontyne Price, Marion Anderson, to Duke Ellington. Entertainment is often done in the home, usually with members of cliques or to promote professional activities. Occasionally, members of the old upper class sponsor events or fund-raising activities for charitable purposes, and these benefits may take place either in their homes or in some reputable public place. In the Washington, D.C., area many old upper-class families, as well as the new upper class and professional middle class, take considerable pride in participating in the diplomatic cocktail circuit. The African embassies are especially open and hospitable to black Americans —reflecting mutual efforts to establish linkages and psychological identities with other black people. The diplomatic staffs of the nonblack embassies, on the other hand, do not differ appreciably from the upper echelons of the State Department and the federal government—in general, they often make an effort to assure only token integration at their social functions. For some blacks it is considered a privilege to be invited to socialize with functionaries of foreign nonblack governments and with high-level white government officials. These associations provide one mechanism for ensuring high social status.

In addition to these leisure-time activities, the old upper class travels a great deal, taking two or three vacation trips per year; a special colony of "black brahmins" goes to Cape Cod as do the upper-class blacks of the underworld. Many play golf and tennis and swim in their own pools, and ski. Others enjoy the spectator sports of football and basketball, and if it is a major social event, several will "turn out" for a prize fight. Although fraternities and sororities have diminished in social significance for them, the members of this class do join a variety of social clubs and voluntary associations or support major civil rights organizations such as the Links, the NAACP, the National Urban League, and similar predominantly black groups. They do not join white organizations because white organizations still engage in exclusionary practices that deny them equal access. Since there is considerable latent hostility in this class against white people, it is not likely that they would be eager to join them in social activities even if the opportunities were available. Cotillions in New York, New Orleans, and the San Francisco Bay area, for example, are still popular as a means of introducing their young to society, although, increasingly, the old upper-class families are sponsoring private coming-out parties for their daughters and abandoning the more public functions to the *nouveau riche* and social climbers.

The church has always played a significant role in the lives of black people; and the upper class is no exception. The members of this class are quite religious and committed to church membership. Not only do they tend to be members of Episcopalian, Congregational, and Presbyterian churches, but they also provide substantive financial support for them and attend services regularly. In many parts of the United States the old upper-class family members play prominent roles in the activities of these churches, serving on boards of deacons, as members of financial committees, and sponsors of charitable activities endorsed by the church. Affiliation with these churches is further evidence of this class' high status and of their differences from folk blacks. They enjoy the relatively quiet and unemotional services of the Congregationalists, Presbyterians, and Episcopalians. The Catholic church has increasingly attracted membership from the black upper classes. It was and continues to be the dominant church of the old aristocracy of color, particularly in Creole New Orleans, the southern portions of Louisiana, and the easternmost portions of Texas.

As a rule, the old upper class tends to be conservative on the issue of race relations, preferring not to be active participants in civil rights activities. They are also disposed toward biracial politics and bilateral agreements. They would rather provide financial support and ideas but avoid direct involvement. They are neither prone to the extremes of political radicalism nor disposed toward modern-day uncle tomism. However, their lack of involvement may reflect their desire to protect their privileged positions and their vested interest in maintaining the status quo.

With incomes ranging from $25,000 to $150,000 per year, the members of this class are in a position to support the style of life just described. Since so many of them are self-employed and are not dependent upon a fixed salary, they are in a better position to sustain this life style for a much longer period of time than are the new upper-class blacks. Thus there is a far greater degree of permanence attached to their social position.

THE NEW UPPER-CLASS
BLACKS

Although the members of this class may have higher incomes, which range from $15,000 to $1 million per year (made by mostly entertainers and shadies), they by no means parallel the old upper-class black family structure. Their income is transitory; that is, *it is not necessarily based upon secure occupations and high educational attainment.* They are, therefore, only able to sustain an upper-class life style for a relatively short period of time, depending upon the care with which their financial holdings are invested or upon the permanence of their occupations. The exception is found in those whose new class position is grounded on substantive educational achievements that have enabled them to move upward in the occupational structure and to earn substantial incomes either on their jobs, through investments, or through personal attributes.

This class provides evidence of the dynamic characteristics of the class structure within the black community. And in many ways, as in the case of the old upper class, the behavior of its members mirrors that of their counterparts in the white social class structure. The members are relatively new to prominence, fame, and money. Some have attained their positions through achievement rather than ascription, and some have managed to parlay special talents into financial success that enables them to purchase or literally buy upper-class status. Some, however, especially in the small towns of the South and in non-Southern communities where the black population is scarce, may also have the advantages of a notable family name and respectability. But most members of this class are reminiscent of the Horatio Alger rags-to-riches myth.

New upper-class members are likely to be relatively new to high political office and/or government office. They are self-made men and women who through hard work and ability to capitalize on opportunities have made it almost to the pinnacle of the black social structure, especially through benefits generated by the civil rights movement. Included in the new upper class are people such as Mayor Thomas Bradley of Los Angeles; a former mayor of Cleveland, Carl B. Stokes; his brother, Congressman Louis Stokes; Mayor Richard Hatcher of Gary, Indiana; Congressman Leroy Johnson of Atlanta, Georgia; and Mayor Johnny Ford of Tuskegee, Alabama. As a group, their meteoric rise can be attributed to educational achievement, present and past occupations, and charisma. Besides being comprised of politicians, congressmen, and state and local officials, *this class also includes a large array of entertainers, actors and actresses, and athletes. Their money is new, their incomes and social positions are transitory,* and they are less likely to have either middle- or upper-class origins. Although these professions enjoy a certain amount of prestige within some elements of the black community, the status conferred upon incumbents of such professions is highly selective. In this case status depends upon what services are performed for the welfare of less fortunate blacks, the leadership roles members of this class actually carry out, the extent of their commitment to civil rights activities, and whether or not their behavior conforms to idealized expectations of propriety and conventional norms. Thus it cannot be assumed that simply because a black actor earns in excess of a million dollars per year, or because an athlete is highly touted or a singer earns more money and is more widely known than a Detroit judge or a black college president, that the latter people are less important, less esteemed, or have lower prestige than any of the former. This is not the case in the black social world. Yet this erroneous assumption is often made by persons who do not understand the black social structure. In fact, the majority of the old upper-class black families and many of the established middle-class black families would not welcome into their families either entertainers, athletes, or actors who are not of similar class origins regardless of the amount of money these glamorous people make.

Billingsley cites evidence that shows that entertainers and athletes, male and female, are less likely to have old upper-class origins than are black professionals. He observed that 80 percent of the professional blacks have family origins in either the middle or upper classes. He also concludes, from his analysis of data drawn from *Current Biographies*, that 59 percent of the male and 50 percent of the female entertainers had old upper-class origins, whereas only one-eighth of the male athletes were originally from this class.[20] Achievement among this group is a question of special talent and the opportunities to capitalize upon those abilities. Thus, for example, as Billingsley correctly observed, tennis requires money to learn, play, and practice; therefore, it is primarily a sport of the middle and upper classes.[21] For this reason, as well as because of the greater resistance to professional tennis in general and reluctance of country clubs to allow blacks to become professionals at the sport, only two black people, Arthur Ashe and Althea Gibson, have advanced to national prominence in this field. This is not the case for other spectator sports such as baseball, football, and basketball. Since 1959, when Bill Russell first drew national acclaim for his prowess in basketball, black players have come to dominate this sport, perhaps more so than any other professional or amateur activity. Invariably, championship teams, whether in basketball, baseball, or football, particularly at the professional level, have a disproportionate number of black athletes. Professional sports is a major avenue through which young black men can use their special talents to rise in the social class structure—most especially in terms of life styles.

Similar breakthroughs, commensurate with the breakdown of racial and discriminatory barriers, have occurred in the entertainment world. The success of recording artists, television performers, and movie people illustrates the possibilities of emulating the life styles of persons in upper and middle classes regardless of class origins. But, at the same time, the tenuousness of their positions near the top of the social pyramid is likely to limit their staying power and make them highly vulnerable to downward mobility. The insecurity of this group in social behavior often reflects the precariousness of their position. However, some black athletes and entertainers are presently taking measures designed to safeguard and protect their social class status in the future. For example, the basketball star and coach Bill Russell is reported to own rubber plantations in Africa; James

Brown, a recording star of soul music, not only owns a recording company but two radio stations. Curtis Mayfield, who skyrocketed to national fame with his score of the black exploitation film *Super Fly*, owns Custom Records, a recording company. Smokey Robinson is a vice-president of the highly successful recording and promotions company, Motown. Other entertainers, such as Roberta Flack and Bill Cosby, are attempting to earn advanced graduate degrees to ensure second careers at a later time in life. Finally, other musicians, professional athletes, and entertainers also own restaurants and other business enterprises and have made what appears to be sound investments as a means of safeguarding their present social and economic status for the future.

The new upper class also includes a number of newly arrived physicians, lawyers, college professors, some business executives, and members of managerial groups. The likelihood of class permanence and/or movement to the top is substantially greater for this group than it is for entertainers, actors, and athletes. Many, in fact, are blessed with a middle-class origin, solid family names, and have originated from intact nuclear families. Several possess impeccable educational credentials and have impressive security and confidence in the presence of the old upper-class families. Indeed, according to much of the criteria, many of them are often indistinguishable from the old upper class.

The members of this class emulate the old upper class in life style as closely as possible. This effort to be like people at the top results in often exaggerated behavior. They are frequently among the most conspicuous consumers, wearing dazzling clothing, displaying a preference for expensive cars and for jewelry and furs. Their houses are usually lavishly furnished and located in the more expensive suburbs, wherever they have been able to break through the barriers of housing discrimination. Not infrequently, they will use the help of white friends to purchase houses for themselves in the more "exclusive" neighborhoods, especially when confronted with racial bigotry among real-estate personnel. Often, they are forced to pay prices far in excess of what a white person would pay for the same house. Occasionally, they are also victimized by excessive fees charged by black real-estate brokers who, using the rights of multiple listings and membership in real-estate associations, exploit the desire for owning a house in the "right" neighborhood. They also take inordinate pride in entertaining friends as well as friends of friends, taking special efforts to assure that announcements of these functions will be accompanied by excellent press coverage. Their entertainment practices are intended to be overt manifestations of success and high status; their purpose is to heighten social recognition and demonstrate their rights to belong to the upper class.

Members of the new upper class differ from those of the old upper class in the excessiveness of their social activity and with regard to the public nature of much of their behavior. They seem to be more tolerant of divorce and more permissive in the treatment of their children. Although they tend to join the same churches as the old upper-class families or may also hold membership in the better-known Methodist and Baptist churches, their commitment to organized religion may be questioned. They are less likely to engage in the more formalized leisure-time activities observed in the old families and less likely to have similar tastes in reading materials.

THE MIDDLE SOCIAL STRATA

The diversity in the social class structure of the black community is also reflected in the trichotomy of the black middle class: upper middle-class professionals, middle-class white-collar and clerical workers, and skilled blue-collar workers. These groups share in common high achievement motivation, a tradition of family stability, high religiosity, high regard for property ownership, a sustained history of political participation and activism, social striving, and consumption of durable goods. The subclasses differ in occupations, income, interracial attitudes, religious practices, educational attainment, and some aspects of political behavior. Because of these differences, and contrary to previous studies that treated this group as a more homogeneous class, the three substrata should be treated separately.

One of the weaknesses in Frazier's highly regarded and much acclaimed study, *Black Bourgeoisie*, is that it suffers from the pitfall common to most sociological studies at the time: the failure to make refinements in interpretations of social differentiation among black people. Thus he categorized all persons who are here identified as members of the old and new upper classes and the trichotomized middle classes as belonging to one relatively large bourgeoisie. Although that description may have been appropriate at one time (and this is a generous assumption) the exigencies of time and the salient changes in the socioeconomic conditions of blacks necessitate descriptions based upon more definitive demarcations. The black middle class is smaller than the lower classes but substantially larger than the black upper classes. Even with these observations in mind, it takes little more than common sense to recognize that the lines between each stratum within the middle classes, as well as those between the middle and upper classes, are often undefined. Harold Wilensky and Charles Lebeaux asserted that the lines between those employed in occupations identified as the upper working class and the lower middle class are blurred.[22] They were speaking about foremen, craftsmen, and high-paid operatives as opposed to clerks, salesmen, small entrepreneurs, and managers characteristic of the lower middle class. And they were referring largely to the overall American class structure rather than specifically to the black social class structure. Basically, though, the lines that separate the classes are not always distinct but are sufficiently formed to allow for certain types of classifications for analytical purposes.

THE MIDDLE-CLASS
BLACK PROFESSIONAL

The upper levels of the black middle class consist of those black professionals who have not yet qualified for admission to the new upper class. They are the teachers, social workers, white-collar employees, proprietors, managers and supervisors, accountants, lawyers who have not quite made it to the upper levels, as well as ministers of middle-range congregations. Their status, like that of many of those in the upper-class levels, is considerably higher than what it would be in the white community. Their occupations require a college education, which, coupled with family income, accords them a relatively high rank in the black social structure. Their incomes range from $13,000 to $15,000 per annum. In his study of black middle and blue-collar classes in the Catham community of Chicago Sidney Kronus found that the median personal income of the white-collar middle-class workers was $9,000, while their median family income was $15,000.[23]

Table 3-1 illustrates the distribution of blacks in standarized occupations. The paucity of blacks in the higher occupational levels becomes shockingly clear as this table is examined; it provides little comfort in observations that blacks have made notable progress in income and occupational advances during the past 25 years. If only 8 percent of the elementary and secondary schoolteachers in the United States are black and only 3 percent of the professional workers, 3 percent of the nation's engineers, 1 percent of the physicians, dentists, and related practitioners, and 3 percent of the clerical and kindred workers were black in 1971, then deprivations and inequities in the distribution of occupations and attendant incomes are obvious and, consequently, provide ample ammunition to dismantle arguments *against* affirmative action programs and compensatory hiring.

Upper middle-class professional families in the black community are likely to be stable and more equalitarian than patriarchal. Infidelity and illegitimacy are not condoned. The divorce rate is about 25 percent, and the average number of children per family is two. Males in this group prefer marriage partners of the same shade of color as themselves or somewhat lighter in complexion,[24] hence showing once again persistence of the aristocracy-of-color syndrome.

Religion for this group is more staid and serene when compared to observances in classes below it in the hierarchy. Their religious affiliations are with the Catholic, Methodist, Baptist, Episcopalian, and Presbyterian

TABLE 3-1.

Occupation of the Total and Negro Employed Population: 1970

(*Numbers in thousands*)

Occupation	Total	Negro	Percent Negro of Total
Total employed	76,554	7,361	10
Professional, technical, and kindred workers	11,349	611	5
Engineers	1,208	14	1
Physicians, dentists, and related practitioners	539	11	2
Health workers, except practitioners	1,205	101	8
Teachers, elementary and secondary schools	2,540	215	8
Other professional workers	5,857	270	5
Managers and administrators, except farm	6,371	170	3
Self-employed	1,164	36	3
Sales workers	5,443	167	3
Clerical and kindred workers	13,745	1,011	7
Craftsmen, foremen, and kindred workers	10,608	665	6
Mechanics and repairmen	2,444	142	6
Metal craftsmen, except mechanics and machinists	720	36	5
Construction craftsmen	1,940	150	8
Other craftsmen	5,505	337	6
Operatives, except transport	10,496	1,327	13
Transport equipment operatives	2,958	417	14
Truck drivers	1,380	185	13
Other transport equipment operatives	1,578	232	15
Laborers, except farm	3,427	688	20
Construction laborers	600	133	22
Freight, stock, and material handlers	1,347	219	16
Other laborers, except farm	1,479	336	23
Farmers and farm managers	1,426	43	3
Farm laborers and farm foremen	954	177	19
Service workers, except private household	8,625	1,475	17
Cleaning service workers	1,862	507	27
Food service workers	2,774	341	12
Health service workers	1,181	259	22
Personal service workers	1,154	125	11
Protective service workers	952	69	7
Private household workers	1,152	610	53

SOURCE: U.S. Department of Commerce, Social and Economic Statistics Administration, Bureau of the Census.

churches. As they moved up the social ladder, they in all probability changed their religious affiliations to those with higher prestige. Also, the character of the church may change as more members become middle class. In some instances, membership may be held in two churches as a means of accommodating both professional interests and social needs.[25] People in this group are social strivers who also emulate, as far as financial stability will permit, the life style of the members of the upper classes. This pattern of emulation extends to purchasing consumable goods and services, clothing, housing, and other evidence of the attainment of high social status. A high premium is placed on friendship cliques and on membership in service and Greek-letter organizations and voluntary associations. They also enjoy occasional theatre, both jazz and classical concerts, public lectures, and a relatively broad range of reading materials.

Politically, they tend to affiliate with the Democratic party or to classify themselves as independents. Although regional variations in this tendency may surface, by and large, blacks are not dissimilar from other ethnic groups in supporting one of their own people regardless of party affinities. Hence they can be counted on to vote. Having provided the major leadership for the civil rights movement, they can be characterized as political activists, picketing and demonstrating when needed. Membership in traditional organizations such as the NAACP, the National Urban League, and CORE has now extended to the Southern Christian Leadership Conference and to People United to Save Humanity (PUSH). But their children are likely to be enthralled with the militancy of Black Student Union and Afro-American societies.

The Middle Group. White-collar and clerical workers form the middle stratum of the black middle class. They can be grouped, occupationally, into clerical and kindred workers, sales workers, small entrepreneurs, and some entertainers who have yet to become established and recognized. Blacks comprise 3 percent of all sales workers and 7 percent of all clerical and kindred workers in the United States. Their salaries range from $9,000 to $13,000. Inasmuch as their life style and general behavior are not distinct from that of the professional middle-class group, we shall not dwell on this group.

SKILLED BLUE-COLLAR WORKERS

Blue-collar blacks are the skilled, stably employed craftsmen, foremen, mechanics, repairmen, metal craftsmen, construction craftsmen, and operatives. Their personal income range is from $7,500 to $12,000 per year.

Although their families are likely to be upwardly mobile, family background in the traditional sense and education are not the crucial variables for social advancement. This is not to imply that these people do not place a high premium on the education of their children. On the contrary, though they are less likely to be college graduates or to have attended college, they are willing to sacrifice themselves for the educational advancement of their children.

Blue-collar workers commonly stress family stability, which has held the marital dissolution rate to about 25 percent; thus 75 percent of these families are nucleated and intact. They tend on the average to have no more than two children per family and to be identical to the white-collar professionals in their color preferences among marriage partners.[26] They are more akin to the working poor and other lower classes than to the upper classes in their church preferences and religious activities. They belong to Baptist and some Methodist institutions that encourage emotional fulfillment and individual expression through active participation in religious services. Although almost half the members in this group are undoubtedly lifelong Baptists, if the men marry higher-status women, they may change to the religion of their wives. This tendency accounts for the increasing presence of Methodists, Catholics, and Congregationalists among this group.

The members of this stratum consume as much as money can buy and, like so many white Americans similarly classified, rely upon good credit ratings as a means of purchasing consumable goods. However, they are not able to save very much money, not only because of their consumption patterns but also because so much of their income is spent on meeting instrumental family needs: housing, food, clothing, and transportation. Color televisions, house parties, card playing, dances, night clubbing, bowling, and professional spectator sports are major forms of recreation. Whites in the same classification generally earn more money than blue-collar blacks, but it is likely that they spend proportionately less on recreation and less on instrumental needs and are, therefore, likely to save more for the future.

Politically, this group is likely to be Democratic and to have voted in the most recent national, local, and statewide elections. They do not tend to be as politically active in civil rights movements as the classes above them, and their support is comparatively uncertain and sporadic. Yet, blue-collar workers and blacks in the classes below them rage with bottled-up hostility against whites, which may account for their increasing attraction to separatist groups in the black liberation movement (see Chapter 9).

The middle classes, taken as a whole, are more disposed toward bilateral measures (e.g., many forms) of discipline for their children than are those in lower social strata. Thus they are less punitive and more inclined to employ persuasive approaches for eliciting obedience and conformity than to rely upon coercion and physical punishment. Yet they do demand respect for parental authority.

THE LOWER SOCIAL STRATA

The lower classes, constituting about 50 percent of the black population, include those classified as the working nonpoor, the working poor, and the lower-lower class, or underclass. They comprise the bulk of the black population by whatever measure employed. More than half of the American black families (53 percent in 1970) have family incomes below $7,000. Almost two-fifths have incomes below $5,000, and one-fifth of the black families do not earn $3,000 per year. The lower class is comprised of all these income groups.

The range of occupations within this group includes truck drivers, laborers of one kind or another, small-scale farmers, service workers, and private household workers. Blacks constitute more than half of all of America's private household workers (53 percent), more than one-fourth of the cleaning service workers, one-fifth of all the laborers, and 13 percent of the truck drivers. Thus black Americans continue to be overrepresented in the lower-paying occupations.

The majority are not receiving any form of public assistance; they are hard-working ordinary citizens. They are Ralph Ellison's invisible men in the sense that others refuse to see them and to recognize them for their values and their value to the total American community. They are the group most often studied by social scientists, misunderstood, and used as the basis for arrogant generalizations about the whole black community. The overwhelming majority of the black lower classes are people of integrity who basically and fundamentally want to survive in what they know to be an extremely difficult and hostile society. They have no great illusions about themselves or their personal accomplishments other than that they have survived, but they do have aspirations for their children. They, too, dream great dreams and even have high hopes of "making it" in the white man's world.

The Working Nonpoor. The working nonpoor are the top of the hierarchy in this strata. They are the semiskilled, steadily employed industrial workers. They comprise the largest portion of America's black truck drivers and other black transport-equipment operators. They are the 6 percent of the total number of craftsmen, foremen, and kindred workers, the 6 percent of the mechanics, and the 5 percent of the metal craftsmen listed in the

1970 population census as black. Yet these people are not likely to be included in the appropriate unions because of exclusionary practices that also limit the amount of personal incomes and fringe benefits that they can acquire for their families. By and large their wives work to supplement the family income and meet the instrumental needs of the family.

The majority of the families are intact; and more frequently than the families in classes above them their family structure may include subfamilies. They are members of the Baptist Church, lodges, the Elks, Masons, Ladies of the Sharon Star, and the Democratic party. Women in this group are active participants in and loyal supporters of the church, often attending church activities as many as five times per week. They are choir members, ushers, and fund raisers through raffles, fish frys, suppers, and potluck dinners. Their desire for status and recognition is often manifested in the type of automobile they purchase, how frequently cars are bought, and in their personal appearance at public functions. Friendship cliques are likely to be drawn from a circle of church members, the social and community clubs to which they belong, and the workplace. But the family is the most important element in the structure of their social relationships. The performance of affective family functions depends heavily upon kinship interactions. The working nonpoor are being drawn with increasing regularity into the ranks of political activists, black liberationists, and Black Muslims.

The Working Poor. These are irrefutably poor and borderline poverty people. Incomes of $3,000 to $5,000 per year just barely keep them hovering about the poverty line, and those who are able to avoid welfare take great pride in the fact that they are self-supporting. The families are more often nucleated and male headed. Employment is found predominantly in unskilled laboring occupations as farm laborers, migrant workers, service workers, porters, janitors, and domestic household workers. About one-third of all black families fall into this category, clearly the largest single class in the black stratification system. They have few amenities, except perhaps a television and occasionally a used automobile. Their continuing concern is with the day-to-day existence. The working poor are the disenchanted and disillusioned, alienated black Americans, who, like the underclass, see little progress and even fewer possibilities of breaking out of the throes of economic and social deprivation. Like the lumpen proletariat of the underclass, they achieved few economic and occupational gains from the civil rights movement, a fact that is the source of much of their pervasive frustration and disillusionment. Yet they want their children to succeed and still rest their hopes on education as the instrument for escape from poverty. More fundamentally, keeping their children "out of trouble" is a matter of great priority as a prelude to success.

The Lower-Lower Class, or Underclass. This group is at the very bottom of the black social structure and that of the general population as well. They are a wasteland of manpower and potential resources as depicted in Elliot Liebow's *Tally's Corner*. They rank lowest in income, occupational skills, employment, education, family stability, and the acquisition of status symbols. They earn less than $3,000 per year, often considerably less. The family head characteristically has a sixth-grade education or less. They are the laborers in the lumpen proletariat; they work at odd jobs, doing sporadic day work or serving as waitresses in low-paying cafés and bars. Migrant farm workers are also found here. The underclass constitutes the bulk of the welfare recipients within the black population. Suffering from the lowest life chances and minimal health care, they are inevitably condemned to delapidated housing in the urban slums and, quite frequently, to the concrete public-housing ghettos of the deteriorating inner cities of America. Abject resignation to insufferable conditions permeate lives compounded by a persistently nagging sense of despair, hopelessness, and frustration. Confronted with the stark reality that they are not likely to escape the ghetto, they show their machismo and their femininity through sexual expression. This, coupled with ignorance of and a disinclination to employ birth-control measures, accounts for families that average six to eight children. Most single-parent female-headed families are in this class. But, all types of family patterns are observable here: nuclear, extended, attenuated, and segmental.

Members of the underclass are folk blacks described by Charles S. Johnson. They are less likely to be assimilated into the mainstream of American life, not because they do not wish assimilation but because they are so far removed from it. (It is their life style that many, including some white radical intellectuals, romanticize as the authentically black experience in American life.) They have evolved a style of life, a unique culture as it were, as an adjustment to their status as economic, social, and political nonpersons. Their customs, beliefs, and values—which center on a fundamentalist religious perspective, just "making it" in the white man's world, sexual freedom, toleration of illegitimacy, trying to have a good time, and communication through the blues—all express a basic and compelling effort to adapt to a world that has excluded them. They are, therefore, the most vulnerable and unprotected among America's people—vulnerable to criminality and delinquency, to aggression and violence toward each other, to victimization by the underworld, to the stereotype of the "bad nigger," and to the lure of illegal means of achieving success.

Significantly, the black church plays an important part in their lives. Religion is an escape from the insurmountable problems of daily existence. Therefore, the shouting, dancing, and handclapping that is characteristic of the storefront churches, various religious sects, and of the fundamentalist groups provide opportunities for a kind of catharsis—a ventilation of feelings, emotions, and imaginative communication with others who share so much in common. The church also offers them social contacts, recreation, and an opportunity for leadership roles. Men and women can become pastors or ministers; there is little sex role conflict among the fundamentalist religions. Children are also often socialized into the possibilities of leadership through the church, and there are even a number of child-ministers in these institutions. The discontinuities of seemingly irreligious day-to-day activities are rationalized through expressions like "God is a forgiving being."

The underclass tends to use unilateral techniques in disciplining its children, relying upon the heavy hand of authority and physical punishment to coerce obedience and conformity.

THE SUBTERRANEANS

There is a subterranean class structure that exists in the black community about which little is known or has been written. This world of the shadies, a term used by Cayton and Drake[27] and Billingsley,[28] has, of course, its prototype in the white population, as Figure 3-2 shows, but our attention is directed to the black group. Impressionistic evidence suggests that this subterranean class structure can also be divided into three broad strata that parallel the legitimate system. Each system has social characteristics and mobility patterns similar to those found in the legitimate stratification system of America's blacks.

This extralegal group theoretically operates underground and is, of course, external to the legal structure. In the large cities of the United States it has a certain amount of control over organized vice, prostitution, gambling, narcotic trafficking, and various types of businesses that receive police protection. This control is only partial, since it is commonly held in the working class and lumpen proletariat black ghettoes that the man—that is, white people—actually controls organized crime in the black communities. The pimps, the pushers, the hustlers, and the vice lords are the fronts for white rulers who live in the suburbs and conduct legitimate businesses in the cities.

The upper class in this group consists of those "big-time" gamblers, racketeers, numbers kings, and shady businessmen who have made it to the top in terms of income and life style. They resemble the new upper class in their consumption patterns and overall life styles. They attempt to establish close social relationships with the new and old upper classes as well as with the middle classes, but with limited success even at the most superficial

Figure 3-2.

The Black Subterranean Class Structure: The World of Shadies and the Underworld

(Superimposed onto the Legitimate Black Social Structure)

Subterraneans   Legitimate Structure

Upper Class   Upper Class

Middle Class   Middle Class

Lower Class   Lower Class

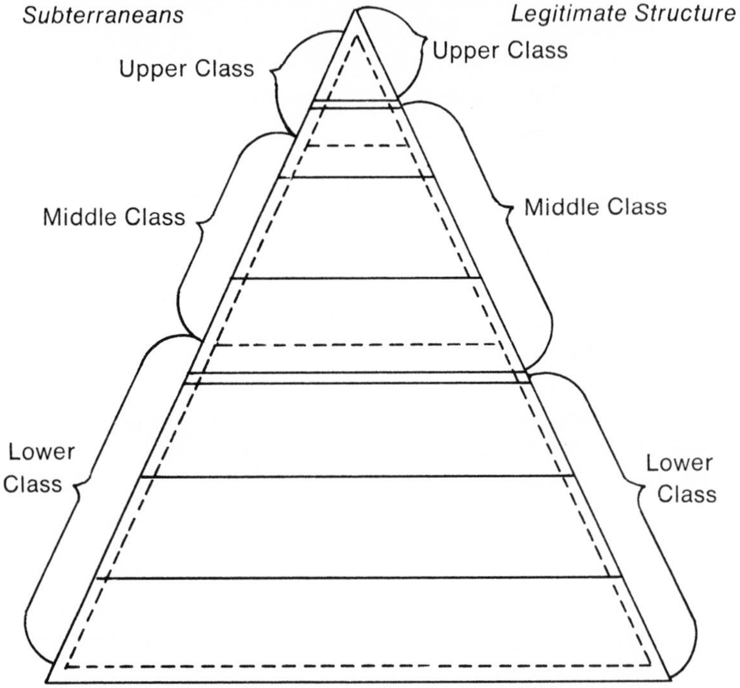

Broken lines denote Subterranean class structure and blurred divisions between classes.

NOTE: The upper and lower strata among Subterraneans are somewhat larger than the Legitimate upper and lower strata. But the middle-level Subterraneans are fewer in number than middle levels in the Legitimate black social structure.

level. They are concerned about their status in the community as well as the status of their children. Thus they attempt to conceal the nature of their work or refer only to the legitimate work with which they are associated. They may live in the same neighborhoods as upper-class black families, but, if their subterranean activities are known or suspected, they will be excluded from membership in the social circles of the upper and middle classes. Their money and stylish life do not enable them to gain entry into legitimate black society.

The middle class in this group is comprised of the more successful bookies, pimps, hustlers, call girls, and gamblers. The lower class is comprised of flunkies, junkies, and less successful prostitutes. They, too, follow the same life styles as their counterparts in the legitimate black stratification system. But the people in the middle and upper groups are perhaps more visible, for they frequent bars, restaurants, nightclubs, and other places that heighten their visible success. They drive long "hogs," wear expensive clothing and jewelry, and evoke the appearance of having "made it" without working. As was noted earlier, they become models for and are the source of considerable envy by lower-class black youths, who learn to regard their way of life as a means of escaping from poverty and living the good life.

MOBILITY PATTERNS AND ACHIEVEMENT

We have already inferred and suggested a number of factors affecting the probability of upward mobility or improvements in status and rank within the black community. In a society that is ethnically stratified, as is the American society, it is extremely difficult for minority groups to experience sustained upward mobility. This is historically and readily apparent for the major portion of the black population. No matter how successful they become as individuals or within the subsystem of stratification of the black population and no matter how successful they are in learning whatever is specified as American culture or in acquiring those characteristics attributed to the more refined and cultured whites, blacks still carry the physical signs of their biological inheritance, which give them a subordinate social status in the larger society. Only exceptional blacks can contradict or transcend that process and are tangentially accepted into the social world of high-status whites. Often this acceptance is a function of *reverse status conferring*, which blacks can bestow on some whites by their presence at white social functions. A case in point has been the competition for black militants at cocktail parties given by whites in various parts of the United States, who believe that their own status is enhanced by having the most extreme of the radical black revolutionaries in their homes. This type of shallow social activity has led such blacks to believe that their own self-importance has been heightened—a belief their admirers share.

Mobility also depends upon the acquisition of highly visible status symbols, which act as indicators to others of what the person has already achieved or believes he has achieved; that is, he shows he is economically successful whether or not he comes from an established, highly esteemed family. The display of status symbols and pecuniary gain may become crucially significant as determinants of how a person is treated and where the person is placed by others in the stratification schema. Thus wealth and property may generate prestige. The converse of this principle was illustrated in the case of the subterranean classes. It has also been suggested that, in some instances, high status may be found among those having excellent family backgrounds but limited wealth.

The factors of wealth, property, power, and prestige do behave independently and can exist separately and apart. By the same token, because an individual may rank higher on one of these dimensions, as, for example, higher on property than on prestige, some individuals find themselves in a state of status inconsistency.[29] This pattern influences the nature of their social participation and may lead status-inconsistent persons to feel undervalued in the stratification system. At a subjective level these people tend to rate themselves more highly than their objective position on an SES scale indicates. Thus some blacks feel rejected by a social world in which they subjectively believe they belong.

Marriage, a chance to use native intelligence, personal attributes, high achievement, and many other previously discussed factors all coalesce systematically to make the black society and its stratification system viable, dynamic, and somewhat open.

BLACKNESS AS A VALUE
IN STATUS AND MOBILITY

During the decade of the 1960s and perhaps at the apex of the new black revolution, another dimension to mobility and social acceptance emerged. We are speaking here of the concept blackness, which has no single meaning that can be easily explained. Blackness has several dimensions, including both color and a high level of consciousness of one's own identity. Symbolically, it is expressed in aspects of physical appearance such as the wearing of the Afro hairdo, dashikis, and African jewelry. It is also manifested in unique handshakes attributed to soul brothers and sisters, body English, and the manner in which blacks genuinely greet other black people. These external symbols are supposed to provide immediate identity as to "where people are coming from" and whether or not they are committed to a militant ideology. Perhaps of somewhat greater importance was the rhetoric of militancy couched in terms that communicated one speaker's determination to be himself and to "take no guff from either 'white honkies' or black 'uncle toms and oreos.' " These efforts sometimes bordered on the brink of absurdity, as, for example, the refusal of some "black blacks" to shake hands with a light-skinned black, who by virtue of his color is identified as an enemy. This determination to articulate one's own blackness and to communicate it to the outside world led to what may be called outblacking blacks or what George Napper has aptly called *Blacker Than Thou.*[30] Force or threats of intimidation and bodily harm were used to enforce conformity to newly defined black norms. One of the manifest consequences or payoffs of this orientation toward blackness was increasing access to shared values. This led, in turn, to access to more competitive resources (that is, better-paying jobs, higher incomes, and upward mobility in the stratification system). The more vocal individuals proclaimed their blackness, the more they gained control of certain jobs in the black community, whether trained for them or not, and others became "academic hustlers" in some of the more disreputable Afro-American studies programs. Responsibility was not infrequently abandoned for fear of reprisals from excessively militant blacks. The downfall of a few Afro-American programs, which, in fact, have as much legitimacy as a source of scientific inquiry as Slavic studies, Jewish studies, or American studies, can, in part, be attributed to this phenomenon. It may also be attributed to a shift in focus toward career-oriented curricula.

Blackness. The concept "blackness" has taken a curious route to social acceptability. It has wide acceptability among all but the traditionalists and die-hards of the aristocracy of color in the United States, who refute both its ideological meaning and its implications regarding biological heredity. This is particularly so, since the word "black" has had such a negative connotation in the English language. For instance, we use terms such as "black lie" to illustrate the worst form of mendacity, "black sheep" to suggest a social misfit, "blackmail" to mean extortion, and "black list" to mean the censure of a person for suspected nonconformity. The color black is associated with evil and most of the ethnophaulisms—derogatory terms directed against a group—are associated with the word "black." For many black children a dark color was a badge of inferiority, and, as young adults, until recently, they spent enormous sums of money attempting to erase that badge by the use of bleaching creams and hair processing. Even today, blacks are as conscious of color variation among themselves as whites are about theirs. Instead of differentiating their members on the basis of hair color, blacks differentiate among each other on the basis of varying hues of skin color. Thus one is very light, almost white, quite light, brown, medium, dark brown, dark, or very dark. These differentiations exist because they refer to external characteristics rather than to ideological positions or beliefs. As we shall see in subsequent chapters, one can be politically black and a biologically white-skinned black; this is further proof that how a person is treated is not necessarily a function of what he is, but how he is defined.

It should also be stressed that racism in America has a deleterious effect upon the self-images of many black children. Racism and discrimination can be devastating to those black children who are not supported by familial strengths and coping mechanisms. Indeed, the child comes to understand the forces of racism, segregation, and discrimination through the world of his family. His interaction with other family members affects his understanding of his identity and his self-realization. It is through his family, whether upper, middle, or lower class, that he comes to understand who he is and what he is becoming through the process of maturation. Thus it is the concept of what he learns during the socialization process that affects self-perceptions and identity. If he comes to see himself as a source of scorn and disparagement rather than a worthy human being, the black child will, of course, tend to internalize these negative definitions of himself. This is one condition that blackness as an ideology and as a source of pride seeks to correct. It attempts to provide an environment of personal worth and acceptance and to heighten one's self-esteem, self-evaluation, and higher aspirations for achievement. For blackness to be effective resocialization of parents is necessary in order to counteract those negative definitions that the black child still confronts through other socializing agents, most particularly the school. It should be noted that the position that the child's parents occupy within the class hierarchy will have a determining impact on any degree of success achieved. The relationships between social class and other life chances will be further elaborated in subsequent chapters.

IMPLICATIONS OF SOCIAL STRATIFICATION FOR BLACK UNITY

One consequence of a class structure within the black community is the possible isolation of the upper classes from the lower ones. Wherever this has occurred, evidence seems to indicate that intensified stresses, strains, and intragroup conflicts have ensued. What makes this situation crucial is that it portends structural, organizational, and philosophical divisions among groups who theoretically are bound together in the pursuit of a common goal—achieving status as first-class citizens in American society.

One of the manifestations of class-linked disunity is the tendency of members of the upper classes to blame the most obvious victims of racial bigotry, the black lower classes, for the present status of all black people. The black upper classes particularly blame the black lower classes for the failure of the latter to become fully incorporated, if not fully assimilated, as equals in the larger stratification system. Thus blaming the victim pervades this class and is often articulated in expressions such as "you (lower-class blacks) make it difficult for us (upper- and middle-class blacks)" or "if it weren't for you, our race would be much further ahead than it is now" or "I've got mine; now get yours!" In many ways persons who engage in this type of behavior mirror the raw prejudices and categorical treatment of blacks so pervasive among nonblack racial bigots. Therefore, a major problem emerges. Lower-class blacks maintain that whatever economic and social leverage black upper classes may possess is not adequately transformed into advantages for the black masses. Neither is that power used to substantially promote the social and political causes of the black population as a whole. On the contrary, they argue, the social, economic, and political advantages of the black middle and upper classes are used all too frequently to promote self-interest. Moreover, specific individuals relish the notion of being "a black first" without due appreciation for the possibilities of exploiting this advantage, however limited it may be, for the good of the black community. If these allegations are substantially true, this situation undoubtedly emanated from upper- and middle-class self-definitions as a separate and more privileged group whose status resulted from individual accomplishments rather than from any specific group quality.

The fact remains that lower classes are highly suspicious of middle- and upper-class blacks whose contributions to the larger black community are not well known. This suspicion often leads to generalizations concerning the interest of middle- and upper-class blacks in promoting broader interests than self, of substantive involvement in social action programs, and of demonstrated willingness to work in lower-income black neighborhoods. Suspicion is, furthermore, exacerbated by the role played by color, the residue of historical resentment and animosity among blacks of darker hues against lighter-skinned blacks. Another apparent consequence has been the lack of grassroots social action programs among lower-class blacks in the past. The prevailing mood of inaction, stimulated by the feeling of little or no support from the financially well-off, forced the less well-off to resign themselves to inaction and nonparticipation even in causes designed to bring relief to the black poor. These inconsistencies led to structural alterations in the civil rights movements and an articulation of new motivational techniques for broadening the basis of participation in the black liberation movement.

As we inferred earlier, an inordinate amount of financial resources seem to be allocated to status-seeking endeavors by affluent black people. This automatically reduces the total sum available for social welfare assistance to less fortunate blacks. A major dilemma faced by the middle- and upper-class blacks is: what is their responsibility to less advantaged blacks? How much of their resources can they or should they sacrifice for assisting those who, for whatever reason, have not become as fortunate as they?

Should they follow the model established by Jews, for example, by creating viable and extensive associations of black charities all consolidated under one single organization? Or should they continue already established mechanisms for assisting blacks who are in need of help such as voluntary organizations (for example, churches, fraternal organizations like the Elks and the Masons, private social clubs like the Links, fraternities, and sororities, and other formal institutions) as has been done in the past? Should they assume that their first responsibility is to their own families for guaranteeing their success and personal development, or should they disavow status rewards by making more substantive financial contributions to the less well-off blacks in the anticipation that the latter group will be brought into the mainstream of American society?

Any course taken regarding assistance to other blacks or pertaining to an ideological position may be interpreted as a reflection of class interest or promoting selfish interests. A given course may result in one's being labeled at once a tom, a traitor, an oreo, or a black bourgie. There is no simple all-encompassing response to these questions. Implicit in them is the agonizing dilemma that confronts the successful black person in America today.

NOTES

1. For varying dimensions of social class and theoretical formulations cf.: Karl Marx, *Capital*, Max Eastman (ed.) (New York: Modern Library, 1968); *The Communist Manifesto* (Chicago: Regnery, 1969); *Pre-Capitalist Economic Formations*, Eric Hobsbawm (ed.), O. Jack Cohen (tr.) (New York: International Publishers, 1921); and Max Weber, *The Protestant Ethic and the Spirit of Capitalism*, Talcott Parsons (tr.) (New York: Scribner, 1930); *The Theory of Social and Economic Organization*, A. M. Henderson and Talcott Parsons (trs.) (Glencoe, Ill.: The Free Press, 1947). The functionalist aspect is explained by Kingsley Davis and Wilbert E. Moore, "Some Principles of Stratification," *American Sociological Review*, 10 (1945), pp. 242–249. The conflict school is elaborated in Ralf Dahrendorf, *Class and Class Conflict in Industrial Society* (Stanford, Calif.: Stanford University Press, 1959).

2. Roger G. Emblen, *Society Today*, 2nd ed. (Del Mar, Calif.: CRM Books, 1973), pp. 196–198.

3. Robert Bierstedt, "An Analysis of Social Power," *American Sociological Review*, 15 (December 1950), pp. 730–738.

4. Hubert M. Blalock, Jr., "A Power Analysis of Racial Discrimination," *Social Forces*, 39 (1960), pp. 53–69, and *Toward a General Theory of Inter-Group Relations* (New York: Wiley & Sons, 1967).

5. Emblen, *op. cit.*, p. 198.

6. T. Shibutani and L. M. Kwan, *Ethnic Stratification: A Comparative Approach* (New York: The Macmillan Company, 1972), pp. 33–34.

7. Gunnar Myrdal, *An American Dilemma* (New York: Harper & Row, 1944), Chap. 32 and p. 689.

8. *Ibid.* Also see C. Van Woodward, *The Strange Career of Jim Crow* (New York: Oxford University Press, 1957).

9. See E. Franklin Frazier, *Black Bourgeoisie* (New York: The Free Press of Glencoe, 1957), for a discussion of the black middle class.

10. Nathan Hare, *The Black Anglo-Saxons* (New York: Macmillan, 1970).

11. Frazier, *op. cit.*, Chap. 3.

12. Cf. Frazier, *ibid.*, and *The Negro Family in the United States*, rev. ed. (New York: The Macmillan Company, 1957).

13. Horace Cayton and St. Clair Drake, *Black Metropolis: A Study of Negro Life in a Northern City* (New York: Harper & Row, 1945).

14. Myrdal, *op. cit.*

15. Andrew Billingsley, *Black Families in White America* (Englewood Cliffs, N.J.: Prentice-Hall, 1968).

16. *Ibid.*, p. 123.

17. Cayton and Drake, *op. cit.*, Vol. II, p. 522.

18. Billingsley, *op. cit.*, p. 129.

19. E. Franklin Frazier, *Black Bourgeoisie*, rev. ed. (New York: The Free Press of Glencoe, 1961), Chap. 9.

20. Billingsley, *op. cit.*

21. *Ibid.*

22. Harold Wilensky and Charles Lebeaux, *Industrial Society and Social Welfare* (New York: Russell Sage Foundation, 1958), pp. xxvi–xxvii.

23. Sidney Kronus, "Some Neglected Areas of Negro Class Comparisons," in Edgar Epps, (ed.), *Race Relations* (Cambridge, Mass.: Winthrop Publishers, 1973), pp. 236–249.

24. *Ibid.*, p. 241.

25. Cayton and Drake, *op. cit.*

26. Kronus, *op. cit.*

27. Cayton and Drake, *op. cit.*, p. 524.

28. Billingsley, *op. cit.*, pp. 138–140.

29. Cf. Gehard Lenski, *Power and Privilege:A Theory of Stratification* (New York: McGraw-Hill, 1966), for an elaboration of status inconsistency theory.

30. George Napper, *Blacker Than Thou: The Struggle for Campus Unity* (Grand Rapids, Mich.: William B. Eerdmans Publishing Company, 1973).

4 | CONTEMPORARY ISSUES IN EDUCATION

The black population has, for more than a century, focused on achieving equality primarily through high educational attainment. This is because blacks strongly believe that education is at the cutting edge of broad social changes and is the most effective route to upward mobility. To achieve this goal blacks have employed a variety of adaptive techniques and strategies during this period of time including accommodation to segregation, accepting benefits from white philanthropists and philanthropic organizations, aggressive litigation, and militancy. Although the historical underpinnings of present conditions are extremely important, the primary focus of this chapter is on contemporary issues in education affecting the black community.

SEGREGATION IN THE PRE–1954 PERIOD

The education of blacks has always been subjected to the largess of the white population. This principle prevailed through the period of slavery, when sympathetic whites violated restrictive codes against teaching rudimentary educational skills to slaves; religious groups in the North and Middle Atlantic states made efforts to formalize the inclusion of blacks in integrated school systems prior to the Civil War; the Freedmen's Bureau, created in 1865, also had educational goals, and under its auspices federally supported Howard University was established in Washington, D.C.; and, finally, enormous financial and manpower support was provided by philanthropic organizations and individuals as was mentioned in Chapter 3. As a direct consequence of these efforts, coupled with the momentum given to education by "black reconstructionists" (these were largely the black elected officials in Congress and state and local governments), by 1880 more than 700,000 black children were enrolled in school in ten Southern states and almost a million by the turn of the century.[1] Blacks seemed headed toward full incorporation into the educational structure of American society.

Plessy v. *Ferguson.* Undoubtedly, the most serious blow to this effort was the momentous decision rendered in the *Plessy* v. *Ferguson* Supreme Court case of 1896. Applied first to public transportation, it enunciated the principle of "separate but equal," which had implications extending far beyond public conveyances into the entire institutional structure of American society. This decision justified racial segregation, legitimated educational apartheid and institutional duality, and re-established the traditions of white supremacy with black inferiority and structured privilege based upon color.

Plessy v. *Ferguson* resulted in a dual system that was indeed separate but manifestly unequal. Inequalities occurred, for example, when new facilities were constructed for white students, while black students inherited the deteriorating schools vacated by whites or remained in dilapidated, often overcrowded, and sometimes widely dispersed schools. Black students often had to walk 15 to 20 miles to schools while buses passed them en route, transporting white pupils to school. Inequities also occurred in the availability of educational resources (for instance, textbooks, supplemental reading materials, libraries, musical instruments, laboratories, and physical education facilities), some of which were transferred to black schools after whites had discarded them or were either outdated, underallocated, or totally absent. The only exceptions to the inequities came when white benefactors and concerned blacks were able to raise monies to acquire educational resources. How many black children learned the rudiments of physics without ever experiencing the pleasures of seeing electricity or mechanics demonstrated in a classroom? How many learned the foundations of chemistry without ever seeing a test tube or a Bunsen burner?

As a further consequence of *Plessy* v. *Ferguson*, the dual educational system often led to separate curricula for blacks and whites constructed to maintain a system of segregation and patterned superordinate-subordinate relations between the races. Hence whites were generally offered a college-preparatory curriculum, whereas blacks were given a less well developed liberal arts curriculum adequate for their admission to predominantly black colleges or to industrial/vocational education in which blacks were to acquire skills required to serve mainly the white community. Industrial arts education for blacks was rationalized in the North on the basis of notions about the inability of blacks to handle a rigorous academic curriculum or on the futility of such offerings to blacks, since they were unlikely to be admitted to colleges anyway. Often, Northern blacks received college-preparatory training only after insisting upon it as an inalienable right. In both the North and the South, less sums of money were expended by school systems on the education of black children. In some Southern states the amounts expended per black child varied from one-fifth to one-third of the amount for white children,[2] and worsened to one-seventh before substantial improvements would be forthcoming. Inequalities in educational expenditures would continue, though not with the same magnitude, in the North[3] into the late 1960s and especially in those 30 states containing three-fifths of all black public school students.[4] Financial inequities also extended to the lower salaries paid to black teachers despite the heavier workloads demanded of them. It was not until 1940 in the U. S. Supreme Court case of *Alston* v. *School Board of the City of Norfolk*, that black teachers were granted relief from salary inequities and not until 1954 that salaries of black teachers approached parity with those of white teachers.

Corrective Steps. Philanthropists and philanthropic organizations made the first frontal attacks against educational inequalities and took major steps toward ameliorating the conditions created by *Plessy* v. *Ferguson*. Hence through the efforts of foundations such as that of George Peabody, John F. Slater, Anna T. Jeanes, Julius Rosenwald, Phelps Stokes, Andrew Carnegie, and the Dukes and Du Ponts, education for blacks immeasurably improved. The foundations sponsored teacher-training programs, expanded education into neglected rural areas, constructed school buildings and libraries, and provided educational resources for black secondary schools and colleges, thus creating a significant force of highly trained blacks despite enforced segregation. Their efforts stimulated public school attendance by blacks so much so that the number of black pupils doubled between 1900 and 1940 (from 1 million to 2,698,901, or 6.4 percent of school-age children) and reached 5 million by 1950. An irreversible trend had been established in black education.[5]

In the five-year period prior to 1954 several states had also taken corrective steps to improve the quality of education, school buildings, and other facilities for black children. The primary purpose of this flurry of activity was to refute the claims argued increasingly before the various courts by the NAACP that segregated schools were universally unequal. White officials hoped to convince the courts that new schools, libraries, and science laboratories demonstrated their commitment to improvements in education for black people, but in an apartheid structure.

The NAACP maintained a relentless pressure to force social change by attacking segregated educational institutions, which were probably the most sacred segregationist institutions within the white community except possibly the family and finance.[6] To test the constitutionality of segregation the NAACP selected cases that were representative not only of geographical regions but also of the persistent problems stemming from the separate-but-equal decision. A brilliant cadre of black lawyers, including Thurgood Marshall, now a justice of the U. S. Supreme Court, and James W. Nabritt, argued these five cases: *Brown* v. *Board of Education of Topeka, Kansas*, *Briggs* v. *Elliot* (South Carolina), *Davis* v. *County School Board of Prince Edward County* (Virginia), *Gebhart* v. *Belton* (Delaware), and *Bolling* v. *Sharpe* (District of Columbia). Armed with voluminous and convincing evidence from social research, they persuaded the Supreme Court to respond favorably. In the lead case, *Brown* v. *Board of Education of Topeka, Kansas*, the Court decreed that the segregation of black and white children was unconstitutional and that the separate-but-equal doctrine did not apply to education. No other decision of the Supreme Court since *Plessy* v. *Ferguson* has had the impact of the *Brown* case nor carried with it such great potential for both positive change and racial conflict.

Predictably, reactions to the 1954 decision were mixed. The white South was stunned, angered, and somewhat apoplectic. White Southerners were psychologically unprepared for this revolutionary decision. They could envision the long-range effects that the destruction of segregation in education would portend for the survival of white privilege and power. In short, the decision had dealt the "Southern way of life" a death blow. The white North applauded the outcome of the case not only because it approved the decision but also because the case focused attention specifically in someone else's backyard. The decision was greeted as a momentous victory for and by the black community of the United States. For the first time many black people had a spark of hope that first-class citizenship was a possibility. Not all black people were enthusiastic, however, especially those who had for so long profited by the maintenance of dual structures and parallel institutions. Several persons in this group who were motivated by personal aggrandizement viewed the 1954 Supreme Court decision with almost as much animus as did the rank-and-file Southern white person who saw Southern culture crumbling. Indeed, Uncle Tom college presidents admonished "their" black students against applying for admission to the bastions of white supremacy —the state universities—for to do so, they cautioned, "would only cause trouble" and, besides, "we have our own colleges right here." They *feared* integration and desegregation because they implied a threat against personal survival.

The white South decided that it would never dismantle white educational privilege and control. It embarked upon a campaign to circumvent the Supreme Court's decision of 1954 and the stipulation to desegregate "with all deliberate speed," which was decreed by the Court in 1955. Hence, immediately after the 1954 decision, the South evolved a number of delaying tactics for noncompliance. Among them were: (1) nullification and interposition in Virginia, (2) massive resistance throughout the South, (3) legal maneuvers, (4) threats against and intimidation of blacks and white sympathizers, (5) resistance to desegregation by white Southern congressmen as reflected in the *Southern Manifesto*,[7] (6) violence against integrationists and their property, (7) personal intervention by respected state officials who attempted to block the entry of black children into previously all-white schools, (8) the closing down of schools to prevent desegregation, and (9) the use of state funds to establish private schools for whites.

INTEGRATION AND DESEGREGATION: POST–1954

Because of the success of the nine strategies of noncompliance, integration and desegregation proceeded at an extremely slow pace. For a while it appeared that the more resistant elements in the Southern white community had won the struggle to preserve their dual system. By 1957 in Arkansas, for example, where Little Rock had become a symbol of both white resistance and federal intervention, slightly more than 100 of the 100,000 school-age black children were integrated into the 422 school districts. Three years later the situation had not shown measurable improvement. Furthermore, no school integration had commenced in five Deep South states: Alabama, Georgia, Louisiana, Mississippi, and South Carolina. In four states—Arkansas, Florida, Virginia, and North Carolina—mere token integration had occurred—only 500 out of 800,000 black pupils. In 1960 only West Virginia and the District of Columbia could rightly claim that they had achieved integration. Reasonable success occurred in the border states of Oklahoma, Missouri, Maryland, Delaware, and Kentucky. By 1960 only 6 percent of the black children in the South were attending desegregated schools. It was apparent that the doctrine of gradualism that had emanated from the with-all-deliberate-speed principle was a major impediment to change. This is probably why there were approximately 60 cases protesting continuing school segregation pending court resolution at the end of the 1960 school year.

The pendulum began to swing toward increasing desegregation late in 1960, however. Several factors combined to account for a shift of sentiment: (1) There was national sympathy toward the student sit-in movement and Dr. Martin Luther King's passive-resistance strategies. (2) The nation literally convulsed at the sight of white Southern brutality and raw violence directed at the CORE-sponsored Freedom Riders throughout the South, particularly in Alabama. (3) A sense of moral outrage arose against the ugly faces of bigotry expressed by Southern whites with each effort to desegregate a school. (4) In Washington, D. C., there was a growing concern with the nation's image abroad, especially in the newly independent African states and in Europe. (5) Finally, the election of President John F. Kennedy, whose liberalism or sympathy was taken for granted, created a high degree of optimism among blacks and their supporters. These factors accelerated the pace of the civil rights movement, which began, in turn, a continuing process of profound social change.

The U. S. Civil Rights Commission, established in 1957, compiled massive data on school desegregation, school by school, city by city, district by district, and state by state. The work of the commission, the accelerated pressure of the civil rights movement, a Justice Department oriented toward the enforcement of federal laws, and the death of President Kennedy created an atmosphere in which Congress seemed to have no choice but to enact the strong Civil Rights Act in 1964. This act, along with the Elementary and Secondary Schools Act of 1965 began to undermine the segregation forces and to erode resistance to compliance with the law. Congress had empowered the Office of Education of the Department of Health, Education, and Welfare to cut off funds from any school that refused to comply with desegregation regulations. Several school districts, faced with the dilemma of choosing between desegregation or reduced funds for segregated school programs opted for the former. Thus by 1968 there was substantial movement toward compliance with desegregation mandates. Still, more than two-thirds (68 percent) of black children were attending all-black schools in 11 Deep South states, and 12.3 percent of the black children (57.7 percent) were attending schools that were 80 percent or more black. Politicians who did not seem to favor desegregation would assert in 1970, however, that 97 percent of the *school districts* were desegregated. This was a misleading statement based on a curious fact: For a school district to be classified as desegregated, only one black student need be enrolled. Therefore, statistics on district desegregation are relatively meaningless when they do not tell us the proportion of black pupils and white pupils who are regularly attending school with each other. Nevertheless, one cannot deny that considerable school desegregation resulted in the 1960s, particularly in the South.

By the mid-1960s the battle over school integration and desegregation began to shift to the Northern and Western states as did the civil rights movement in general. It was spurred by racial unrest and urban riots. De jure segregation was illegal, but little had been done to attack the massive problems of de facto segregated schools found in the non-Southern areas. The major condition that fostered de facto school segregation in the North and West was in the housing distribution of these areas. As a result of a long tradition of establishing neighborhood areas according to race and ethnicity, almost all of the larger cities outside the South had clearly defined black and white areas. The migration and concentration of blacks in the inner cities of the United States and the flight of the white population to the suburban rings around the cities, as we saw earlier, had created enormous problems of racial separateness in these communities. Investigations into the conditions of inner-city schools pointed to the similarities between Southern-style de jure segregation and Northern-style de facto segregation—black and white pupils were still separate and unequal. These conditions also reveal the extent to which resegregation had occurred.

DYSFUNCTIONAL CONSEQUENCES OF DESEGREGATION

Resegregation. One of the major dysfunctions of desegregation and of the failure to eradicate the original patterns of segregation is that of school resegregation; that is, segregation in schools or districts following their desegregation. Although the inmigration and outmigration patterns in urban communities account for much resegregation, they are not totally responsible. But the inescapable conclusion is that the larger urban communities of the United States are becoming increasingly black and poor. That the school systems are rapidly achieving a black majority can be illustrated by the following examples: (1) In 1958 Atlanta, Georgia, operated a segregated school system in which 70 percent of the schoolchildren were white and 30 percent were black. In 1973 Atlanta had some 96,000 schoolchildren, 80 percent of whom were black and only 20 percent of whom were white. (2) Washington, D.C., has a school-age population of 178,000 persons, and 86 percent of them are black. Yet in the surrounding urban communities of Maryland and Virginia the school-age population is more than 80 percent white. (3) In Richmond, Virginia, the proportion of black school-age children in the public school system is in excess of 70 percent and is increasing year by year. (4) Chicago's school population is in excess of 850,000, and already 43 percent black. But what is significant about Chicago is that so many of its schools are either totally black or have a black majority. In 1973, for example, of Chicago's 551 elementary schools, 142 of them were all black; 267 were 95 percent black. By comparison, 9 elementary schools were all white, and 75 were more than 85 percent white. Among the 73 high schools in Chicago none were all white, but clearly a dozen were all black and 26 were 95 percent or more black. (5) Boston has 97,000 school-age children, one-third of whom are black, but they are contained in the predominantly black communities of Roxbury, Dorchester, and Mattapan. This racial isolation led the Department of Health, Education, and Welfare to charge Boston with operating a dual system of education, in both 1972 and 1974. The Boston school system is not too dissimilar from that of Denver, Colorado, which has been charged with deliberately gerrymandering school districts so as to create a segregated school system. These examples illustrate how resegregation has occurred, and they show the magnitude of the desegregation problem.

Often, where schools have desegregated, a pattern of *within school resegregation* can be observed. For example, some schools employ the technique of ability grouping of students, resulting in the separation of white students from black students. Portable classrooms are also used to segregate students; some students are segregated in libraries, on playgrounds, and in cafeterias. Some schools employ feeder patterns and controlled transfer policies to accomplish racial isolation. In the case of feeder patterns movement from grade schools to junior and senior high schools is devised so that white students enter certain schools that will remain predominantly white and black students enter schools destined to remain exclusively black.

Displacements. In many instances displacements, demotions, and loss of jobs by black teachers occurred as a consequence of desegregation. In June 1973 the National Urban League, the National Education Association, the Southern Regional Council, and the Southern Center for Studies in Public Policy sent representatives to Atlanta for a special conference on employment displacement resulting from school desegregation. They reported that, in the 17 Southern and border states, approximately 6,000 black teachers and principals lost their jobs as a result of school mergers. Several thousand more were demoted, and the administrators in these states either hired or transferred approximately 25,000 white educators for positions that blacks should have filled. This represented a loss of about a quarter of a billion dollars in salaries for the black community.[8]

The major educational associations of the United States have also reported from time to time cases of demotion of black school principals to assistant principals—and of their being replaced by less competent white persons at desegregated schools. In some instances of demotion black principals were given heavy teaching assignments, janitorial duties, and no administrative responsibilities. Early in the desegregation period, especially in the late fifties and early sixties, the firing of black teachers and the failure of schools to renew their contracts were common. Funds for compensatory educational programs for black children were diverted to activities other than the original purposes for which the funds were intended.

One-fourth of the South's public school pupils are black, but only one-fifth of its teachers are black. There most black teachers are assigned to relatively poor areas of towns, cities, and rural communities. But, under the provisions of Title 1 of the 1965 Elementary and Secondary Education Act, the federal government can make funds available for the hiring of teachers in depressed areas. Already more than 15,000 teachers, a majority of them black, have been hired under the provisions of this act. Even this number, though, has not been sufficient to raise the levels of black-white teacher ratios as ordered by the courts. To accomplish this task, according to the participants in the Atlanta Conference, the proportion of black teachers required in 17 Southern and border states would have to be raised from a low of 12 percent in Alabama to a high of 37 percent in Missouri.[9]

Unfair discriminatory practices in teacher assignments are still prevalent in many areas of the North. Urban black schools still have a disproportionately high number of less well-prepared and less experienced teachers. A frequent pattern is to assign the more experienced and, often, better-prepared white teachers to the more prestigious and predominantly white schools. The less well-prepared white teachers are sent to the inner cities, often under the inducement of receiving "combat pay"—that is, extra money incentives—for teaching in ghetto schools. In many inner-city schools, many teachers do not live in the neighborhood and thus have little or no appreciation of the types of problems encountered by students whose major preoccupations are with day-to-day survival. Many are insensitive to cultural differences in their students based upon social class structure and different opportunity patterns. This insensitivity is usually reflected in their belief systems concerning the educability of the students. Many, for instance, communicate to their students, especially to black students, negative perceptions of the students' ability to learn, and these students, sensing this, respond by not demonstrating evidence of having learned.[10] Worse yet, this kind of teacher insensitivity is not confined to the inner city schools. It is also found among other types of authority figures, including some policemen and social workers. Given the already deeply ingrained problems of identity crisis resulting from inequalities, we cannot fail to note how the negative attitudes that some teachers communicate to some of their students accelerate the psychological damages suffered by so many inner-city students.

During 1973 and 1974, several cities have made serious efforts to alter the distribution pattern of teachers in their public school systems so as to create more realistic ratios of black-white teachers in the schools. Among them is New Orleans, a city that a decade ago had achieved a national reputation for bigotry because of its resistance to desegregating the McDonough 19 and William Frantz schools. On July 10, 1972, the New Orleans school board adopted a policy of assigning teachers in such a way that each school in the district is 50 percent black and 50 percent white, with a 10 percent variance at the elementary level and a 5 percent tolerance at the high school level. The order became effective as of that date, and principals and other administrators were to proceed to implement the new policy in time for that fall's classes.[11]

In the New Orleans system 63 percent of the elementary school teachers and 51 percent of the high school teachers were black when the "50-50" policy was promulgated. That is, 37 percent of the elementary school teachers and 49 percent of the high school teachers were white. In order to implement the 50-50 policy, 831 teachers (501 black and 330 white) were transferred. There were no mass resignations. In fact, of the 49 teachers who resigned subsequent to the mandate, only a handful did so to avoid faculty desegregation. One should not infer from this that the 50-50 policy and the transfer of more than 800 teachers was greeted with uniform enthusiasm. Some teachers complained about having to ride across the Mississippi River to Algiers; others wanted to remain in the more prestigious and progressive schools. Others had trepidations about working under the supervision of black principals because of their reputation for "being harder on teachers," and some feared attending school functions in certain high-crime areas after school hours.[12] Nevertheless, the plan went into effect as ordered and without major or serious consequences during its first year of operation. And it was carried out by a firm school board that had already warned teachers either to accept assignments or to leave the system.

POSITIVE ASPECTS OF
INTEGRATION

In order to understand the goals of integration we must make a critical distinction between terms, especially since the concepts integration and desegregation are often used interchangeably. Actually the two terms are not synonymous. *Desegregation* is the removal from the social structure of legal and social barriers based upon racial and ethnic discrimination against a group. Implicit in desegregation is the conscious and systematic elimination of segregation in the society and the simultaneous realization of constitutional entitlements of citizenship.[13] This is basically a structural process and may or may not be accompanied by changes in the subjective perceptions or attitudes of individuals. *Integration* is, on the other hand, according to Clark, subjective and refers to attitudinal change in the hearts and minds of men and women.[14] It suggests the elimination of the sociopsychological barriers of interracial contact such as stereotypes, fears, and prejudices.

Desegregation, it was believed, would eradicate institutionalized segregation. The concern was not with changing the hearts and minds of segregationists; rather, it was an effort to respect the constitutional prerogatives of dispossessed people and to assure them legal protection and the preservation of their rights. An even broader extension of the implications of desegregation was the optimistic belief in the possibility that children of different racial and ethnic characteristics would, at a more personal and subjective level, rise above the prejudices of their parents and forebears.

Advocates of integration maintain, however, that it is only through an integrated society that people can learn to respect one another's differences and to appreciate the vitality of diversity. Through integration as a process, they believe, people come to share understandings and to learn firsthand of cultural variation without denigrating or disparaging these differences. Integration, then, would involve the systematic elimination of racial animosity and ethnic prejudice as individuals come to understand how stereotypes and false assumptions about each other are truly inapplicable. Thus the path toward cultural, structural, civic, and other dimensions of assimilation would be more easily traversed if desired. In a word, this is the orthodox American goal—the merging of all parts into an integrated whole that is by definition better than the sum of its parts. As we shall see in Chapter 10, this view has come under serious challenge by those who question the very legitimacy of the goal, let alone the improbability of achieving an integrated society. Nevertheless, the quest for integration has persisted as the major underpinning of the black struggle in America, which also stresses cultural pluralism and separatism as alternatives to assimilation. These are predictable responses to a process that has always been one way—from black to white.

But, more recently, integration has even broader implications! At issue is not only the question of equality of opportunity but also the actual realization of that opportunity. Why? Blacks and whites of liberal persuasion have come to realize that minority group individuals can share the same opportunity as whites to education and that some who may be much better prepared for jobs than others are *never* hired; they may not be promoted, and they may not be retained once they are hired. In a truly integrated society, though, the promise of opportunity is expanded into the achievement of results. There would be minority group members in high adminis-trative positions of the school system—school superintendents, heads of boards of education, school principals of desegregated schools, or holders of other positions that involve invaluable contributions to the decision-making process. Presidents, chancellors, deans, and departmental chairpersons of desegregated institutions of higher learning would be black or of other racial or ethnic origins. As a result, black schoolchildren would be able to see them as role models and white schoolchildren would be able to begin the process of destroying false images and negative stereotypes of minority group members. The psychological impairments created by inferior status and the problems of limited achievement motivation could be gradually ameliorated. It is assumed, of course, that the system would treat minorities *and* majorities on the basis of objective opportunities for equal training and the achievement of job experience.

TABLE 4-1.

Percent High School Dropouts Among Persons 14 to 19 Years Old, by Sex and Age: 1970 and 1971

Age	1970				1971			
	Black		White		Black		White	
	Male	Female	Male	Female	Male	Female	Male	Female
Total, 14 to 19 years	15.9	13.3	6.7	8.1	11.6	10.5	6.9	7.8
14 years old	0.9	2.9	1.4	1.1	0.9	0.4	1.0	1.1
15 years old	3.3	2.7	2.0	2.4	3.8	1.5	1.1	1.9
16 years old	10.9	11.1	5.0	6.7	7.2	4.2	5.3	6.2
17 years old	16.0	13.7	7.6	10.2	11.8	15.2	7.6	11.0
18 years old	29.8	27.8	13.6	14.1	22.7	20.8	12.8	13.6
19 years old	44.1	25.8	12.9	15.7	29.3	24.6	15.9	14.0

Note: Dropouts are persons who are not enrolled in school and who are not high school graduates.

SOURCE: U.S. Department of Commerce, Social and Economic Statistics Administration, Bureau of the Census.

What, then, have been the accomplishments since the major efforts toward desegregation were initiated? Using 1965 as a benchmark, a year after the Civil Rights Act, which used the promise of cutting off funds as a lever to promote compliance, we can point to a number of significant though not always dramatic changes and achievements. There have been noticeable improvements in the number of young black adults enrolled in school. The number of children attending school who were of the compulsory ages of 6 to 15 years was maintained at 99 percent between 1965 and 1971. The number of black three- and four-year-olds attending nursery school or kindergarten rose from 12 percent in 1965 to 21 percent in 1971. The latter figure was precisely the same as the white population. The proportion of black five-year-olds attending school increased from 59 percent in 1965 to 81 percent in 1971. The most dramatic increase in the proportion of blacks attending schools between 1965 and 1971 was in the 20-to-24 age bracket, in which the percentage doubled from 9 to 18. Despite the successes in enrollments, however, black children were still twice as likely as white children to drop out of school, and they were more likely to be below the modal grades for children of their age. In 1971 the black male high school dropout rate of 11.6 for children between the ages of 14 and 19 was almost double that (6.9) for white males. The black and white female high school dropout rates were 10.5 and 7.8, respectively.[15] Only about

TABLE 4-2.

Percent of Enrolled Persons 14 to 17 Years Old in and Below Modal Grade by Age: 1971

Subject	Negro		White	
	Male	Female	Male	Female
In Modal Grade[1]				
Total, 14 to 17 years old	44.3	52.1	65.5	72.1
14 years old	53.3	56.7	67.9	72.4
15 years old	43.9	54.9	63.3	70.7
16 years old	38.2	51.9	64.1	69.3
17 years old	39.7	41.7	66.8	76.5
Two or More Years Below Mode				
Total, 14 to 17 years old	14.3	9.7	5.4	3.1
14 years old	11.5	6.9	3.9	3.9
15 years old	11.8	7.8	4.6	3.4
16 years old	13.3	5.6	5.8	2.5
17 years old	22.0	22.5	7.0	2.4

[1] Modal grades are: 14 year olds, high school 1; 15 year olds, high school 2; 16 year olds, high school 3; 17 year olds, high school 4.

SOURCE: U.S. Department of Commerce, Social and Economic Statistics Administration, Bureau of the Census.

half of the black children, compared to no more than two-thirds of the white children of the United States, were enrolled in their modal grades in 1971.[16] Tables 4-1 and 4-2 illustrate these facts. Also notable is the fact that almost three-fifths of black people between the ages of 25 and 29 had completed high school by 1971.

CONTEMPORARY ISSUES IN PUBLIC SCHOOL EDUCATION

Busing. By far the most volatile and politically divisive issue in public school education today is that of busing. The issue was of such national concern that President Nixon used it as a keynote in his campaign for re-election in 1972, and hundreds of other aspirants for elective political office in the United States have used it as well. President Nixon again "fanned its flames" when he was caught up in the Watergate scandal and low-popularity ratings in the public-opinion polls; in a nationwide radio address on March 21, 1974, he called for antibusing legislation. Importantly, the persuasive force of moral leadership invested in the President was withdrawn from busing as one of many techniques for achieving desegregated schools. In effect, the President revealed himself to be in the same camp as the strongest advocates of racial apartheid in America's public schools.

The entire issue of public school education in urban areas involves several harsh but complicated realities. As cities become blacker and poorer, for instance, they correspondingly lose a viable tax base. Traditionally, taxes have supported public schools; but when the owners of property and revenue producing businesses move to suburbia, the funding sources steadily decline. Concomitantly, property taxes in the cities steadily climb, thereby draining resources of propertied persons who do remain within cities. The refusal of most state legislators to relieve the situation reflects their characteristically antiurban stance and minimizes the probability of equal education. Thus suspicion is heightened that whites who control the power resources are not inclined to provide a quality education to an all-black school system whether it is administrated by blacks or whites. Nevertheless, the courts will be compelled to resolve a basic constitutional question: can busing be constitutionally upheld as a tool to protect the rights of black children to desegregated education and essentially a unitary school system? Given the conservative bent of the Supreme Court during Nixon's presidency and President Ford's administration, busing advocates need not be optimistic.

On what basis can busing be justified? Proponents of busing claim that it is a viable and necessary technique to achieve the mandate of desegregation in public schools. They argue that because of systematized patterns of circumvention by the various boards of education and white flight the goal of a nationwide desegregated school system cannot be achieved without some form of busing. They also observe that busing is not a new experience for the school systems of America; literally, hundreds of thousands of children are bused to school each day. The majority of them are bused not to achieve desegregation but to maintain a segregated school system. Less than 2 percent are bused for desegregation purposes. Opponents of busing in reality do not question the principle of busing, but they quite fundamentally reject the principle of desegregated schools. As Father Hesburgh of Notre Dame University once commented, "it's what's at the end of the line" that opponents to busing oppose.

Advocates of busing claim that busing facilitates the ultimate goals of an integrated society by encouraging individuals to learn about themselves and others through formal and informal patterns of social interaction; a better quality of education will be protected in a school system where whites are present in large numbers, especially if they are from middle- and upper-class homes; the intermixture of pupils across racial, ethnic, and social class lines is likely to improve the academic performance and heighten achievement motivation in all the students in desegregated schools. As a further consequence, they expect that reading scores and the whole range of academic skills will improve through provisions for better facilities and for competent teachers interested in every facet of the learning and teaching process.

Social science research has provided findings that may be used either to support busing or to oppose it. The highly respected and often much maligned Coleman Report[17] concluded that student achievement was superior in integrated schools and that the background of a pupil's classmates was a major variable affecting success in school. Achievement is also highly related to the availability and utilization of certain types of facilities and supplies such as chemistry and physics laboratories, language laboratories, textbooks, and libraries. Not infrequently, severe shortages of achievement-related facilities exist in black ghetto schools.[18] These findings also explain why some black parents encourage busing to suburban schools where these facilities and equipment are more plentiful. One of the more successful efforts toward this end is the program being carried out by the Metropolitan Council for Educational Opportunities (METCO) in Boston, which buses approximately 1,900 black students to 31 predominantly white suburban communities. Yet in the fall of 1974, federal officials and state and local police were required to enforce a federal mandate to use busing for school desegregation (see discussion below).

Recent support for some of Coleman's basic conclusions was found in a seven-year study by the International Association for the Evaluation of International Achievement. This study involved about 258,000 students and 50,000 teachers working in 9,700 schools of 19 different countries. It supported Coleman's claim concerning the primacy of the home environment in achievement but also concluded that (1) mass education has neither a deleterious effect nor lowers standards for gifted children, and (2) inequality is both created and perpetuated by elitist schools.[19] This study also refutes the assertions made by Christopher Jencks that school desegregation, compensatory education, and other related factors have not proved effective in reducing inequalities of cognitive skills or academic success in general.[20]

Opposition. The range of opposition to school busing encompasses a curious mixture of true bigots and parents who are genuinely concerned about their children's welfare and the quality of education they are likely to receive if busing occurs. The opposition also includes those persons who are committed to the concept of neighborhood schools and community control over education. Some are white; others are black.

Other opponents include fair-weather liberal social scientists who mask their opposition behind thinly veiled racist interpretations of highly suspect research, self-serving academic opportunists seeking national publicity, and militant blacks (and their white radical cohorts) committed to educational separatism. The true bigots resist busing because of their commitment to segregation and the maintenance of white privilege and black subordination. Like their predecessors in Clinton, Tennessee, and Little Rock, Arkansas, many of the more extreme opponents are inclined to use violence in order to prevent busing for desegregation purposes. This proclivity was implicit in the charges brought against five former members of the Ku Klux Klan for burning school buses at Pontiac, Michigan, in 1971; buses were burned in Denver, Colorado; white men attacked black children in Lamar, South Carolina; and in 1972 violence and abuse were directed at black schoolchildren in the Canarsie school district of Brooklyn, New York, replicating the deeply rooted bigotry of Selma, Alabama, during the 1960s; the hatred in the faces and on the signs carried by people who stormed the office of Governor Sargent of Massachusetts in Boston during the spring of 1973 and who attacked buses and black men in South Boston in 1974 duplicated almost verbatim the animosities and fears expressed in Little Rock in 1957.

Opponents to busing formed various antibusing groups such as the Concerned Citizens of Canarsie, the Canarsie Chapter of the Italian-American Civil Rights League, and the Concerned Parents Association in Charlotte, North Carolina. Similar groups, some comprised of as many as 20,000 to 25,000 people, organized in Boston to protest "forced" busing and to "protect" neighborhood schools and marched to the state house, as, for example, on April 3, 1974. Voters in some communities, such as New York City, Dayton, Ohio, and Pasadena, California, either resisted the efforts of superintendents and school boards favoring increased desegregation, forced them to resign, or defeated them at the polls. Others elected school committee members who seemed less inclined to implement desegregation plans calling for racial balance or those who favored maintenance of the status quo. Some voters have effectively excluded minority members from the school committee or board of education both prior to and since the advent of the *Brown* case. Boston, for example, has never elected a black person to its powerful school committee. This is in stark contrast to Southern cities like Atlanta, where the chairman of the board of education has been black, and Durham, North Carolina, which has had black school board members for several years.

Boston illustrates a complex of many different issues in addition to that of general resistance to busing. Massachusetts was the first state in the United States to pass a racial imbalance law (1965). New York and Connecticut followed suit, and several cities in the latter two states have made substantial progress toward implementing their racial imbalance laws. The Boston school system is more segregated, however, than it was when the racial imbalance law was first enacted. Significantly, in Boston, a city traditionally regarded as liberal by outsiders, several major gains have come to the city since a provision for racial imbalance was incorporated into the legal statutes. For example, without advancing much toward desegregation, the city of Boston was able to obtain ten new school facilities in three years and millions of dollars in state aid to support a number of innovative programs, some of which involved limited busing to suburbs, including METCO and Operation Exodus.* Curiously, Boston was the springboard for massive antibusing sentiments in Massachusetts during 1971-74 period. This contradiction of the liberal ethic may be partially explained by the rigid ethnic segregation in Boston's communities, which is connected with the desire to protect the ethnic character of "neighborhood" schools. Incipient racism, which only required a critical incident to force it to the surface may also explain the situation. Where the two factors intersect is difficult to ascertain. What is evident, however, is that Boston is in the forefront of the reactionary movement to repeal or blunt the effect of the racial imbalance law. The Boston school committee has been the major impediment to implementing it. Vociferous citizens of Boston forced the introduction of proposals into the Massachusetts legislature during the spring of 1973 that would (1) repeal outright the racial imbalance law, (2) change the defini-

---

* Operation Exodus is a voluntary program involving the busing of black ghetto children to suburban or predominantly white schools.

tion of racial imbalance from schools having 50 percent nonwhites to schools that are 70 percent black, (3) prevent school busing without parental consent, and (4) require a referendum on changing school districts, which, would in effect, retain neighborhood schools and limit the amount of desegregation substantially. The Massachusetts legislature capitulated to political expediency and bigotry by enacting two pieces of legislation that would accomplish these four goals. It forwarded the legislation to the Supreme Judiciary Court, the state's highest court, for a determination of constitutionality *before* presenting it to the governor for his signature or veto. The governor's veto of legislation permitting busing only by parental consent was upheld.

A similar effort to block busing was mounted in the legislature in 1974. The governor countered with his own plan for desegregation, which effectively placed the major responsibility for school desegregation on the black population. His plan would have permitted the payment of $500 to each urban and suburban white school for each black pupil accepted from a predominantly black school. The black legislative caucus of the Massachusetts legislature called this offer a bounty, and some said that the governor had capitulated to racism and bigotry for political expediency during an election year. (But he was defeated in his reelection bid in November 1974.) Shortly thereafter (June 1974), U.S. District Judge W. Arthur Garrity issued a long-awaited decision in a case sponsored by the NAACP. He found that Boston operated a deliberately segregated and dual school system and he ordered Boston to desegregate its school system by September 1974.

Predictably, the Massachusetts state legislature and the governor finally capitulated to the endless but well-orchestrated attack against compulsory busing for desegregation by enacting a voluntary integration plan for the city of Boston. Governor Francis W. Sargent signed this new law on July 26, 1974. Consequently, the state board of education no longer has the authority to redraw school districts and order busing. The responsibility for implementing desegregation plans is left entirely to cities and towns of the commonwealth. In effect, after nine years of bitter struggle, the Massachusetts racial imbalance law was revoked without ever being implemented. But it was opposition to Judge Garrity's order to desegregate that resulted in extensive violence in Boston in the fall of 1974.

White antagonists to school busing also express a mixed bag of fears and objections. Busing their children into black ghetto schools, they argue, means exposing their children to lowered standards, to an inferior quality of education, and to black children allegedly behind them in reading and verbal skills. This contention has its roots in the long-established claim that predominantly black schools are inferior. They do not feel that they should shoulder the blame for this situation or for what their forefathers did or failed to do. Others insist that busing makes the schools inaccessible in emergency situations. Some express fear of children's being transferred into strange neighborhoods and fear for their safety and welfare.

Curiously, white antibusing proponents of this view seem to feel that blacks have no justification to fear physical abuse and attacks when they are bused into predominantly white schools and neighborhoods. Evidence cited earlier does not support this view of non-violence.

Attitudes of Children. Both black and white children have mixed attitudes toward busing. Some black students resent the closing of their schools and the traditionally one-way busing in which they are required to move from their homes to predominantly white areas; some have expressed feelings of loneliness and isolation in white schools; some have become frustrated by their inability to compete successfully with the intellectual breadth of some of the better-prepared white students in middle-class areas; some resent being disciplined by white administrators and teachers and often point to the inequalities of the structure of discipline and academic expectations between the two races. White students who oppose busing claim inequalities in discipline, maintaining that white administrators are more permissive toward blacks; and some express fear of black students from ghetto neighborhoods and are conscious of their inability to adjust to different life styles. But the evidence regarding different attitudes of black and white students toward busing is often contradictory and needs further explanation through systematic study. Further inquiry is especially needed, since some reports indicate that the majority of white and black students have positive interrelations in desegregated schools whether they are bused to them or not.

Black Opposition. The black community has not reached a consensus on the issue of busing. Some black groups oppose it on educational grounds, while others denounce it mainly for ideological reasons. The black middle class in Atlanta, for example, seems lukewarm on the busing issue mainly because through parallel institutions they have developed a school system for blacks that is in many ways superior to that offered to whites. Their fear is that busing their children out of the neighborhoods will put them into classes with students who are behind the black children in reading and verbal skills and will subject them to lowered standards of education in general. (Moreover, the NAACP suspended its Atlanta chapter in 1973 for agreeing to maintain school segregation in exchange for administrative positions.) CORE, on the other hand, essentially takes an ideological position in opposing busing, though many of its objectives are educational. Its views are representative of those widely held among black militants. Its opposition to busing to achieve desegregation rests upon the following six claims: (1)

Busing destroys the concept of neighborhood schools, and thus (2) it undermines the possibilities of community control through which blacks are seeking hegemony over their own destinies. (3) Busing gives credence to the racist notion that blacks can only learn in the presence of whites, since they are by nature inferior to whites. (4) Busing would have deleterious effects on black children who would continue to be transported into strange and hostile neighborhoods outside their friendly communities, with alienation and personality defects as the primary outcomes. (5) Busing has no massive support in the black community. And (6) blacks have no special desire to embrace the inconveniences of busing to integrate with white people who have all too often demonstrated their contempt for blacks and their lack of desire for meaningful interaction with blacks. Thus CORE, in a dramatic shift from its posture during earlier days of the civil rights movement, joined hands with the Nixon administration and Virginia against the NAACP and the board of education in the Richmond case, which sought the implementation of metropolitanization* by busing for desegregation.

Several cases are pending in various district and appellate or circuit courts that focus on some aspects of busing. For example, cases are pending that affect busing plans in cities such as Atlanta, Boston, Chattanooga, Chicago, Buffalo, Dayton, Detroit, Durham, Grand Rapids, Hartford, Indianapolis, Louisville, and Wilmington (North Carolina). They range from metropolitanization to gerrymandering. In 1973 clarification of the metropolitanization concept as a vehicle for desegregation through busing across city and county lines was expected in the Richmond, Virginia, case. As a solution to the busing problem, the NAACP and the board of education of the city of Richmond had proposed enlarging the geographical boundaries of the school district to encompass inner-city black schools and suburban white schools. This was a direct attack on the problems of increasing numbers of blacks in the city school systems and increasing numbers of whites in the suburban schools, or, in effect, resegregation. However, the Supreme Court reached an impasse in a 4-to-4 deadlock, with Justice Powell abstaining, which delayed resolving the issue. The Sixth Circuit U.S. Court of Appeals by a 6-to-3 vote returned a similar case in Detroit to the lower courts and thereby permitted delays of two-way busing until all 52 suburban districts had a chance to file an appeal. In effect, this decision substantiated the principle of metropolitanization. But the Supreme Court kept the Detroit case, also known as *Bradley* v. *Milliken*, under review. On July 25, 1974, by a split 5-to-4 decision, the U.S. Supreme Court revoked the

---

* Metropolitanization refers to a proposed plan whereby the city and suburbs are incorporated as a single unit that permits two-way busing within the parameters of this large unit.

lower court's order to employ the metropolitanization concept of busing to assure a desegregated school system. By invalidating these plans, the Court restricted busing to city limits and disavowed interdistrict busing (from the cities to and from surrounding suburbs) as an acceptable remedy for rectifying unconstitutional denials to black schoolchildren. Justice Thurgood Marshall, in a stinging dissent, said that the narrow majority decision was "a giant step backward." Others saw the decision as a retreat from judicial commitments to end segregation, and some anticipated an increasing apartheid through an accelerated white exodus to the suburbs. Nevertheless, the issue of metropolitanization is not dead. It is likely to surface again when the plaintiffs can establish a clearer relationship between deliberately segregated housing patterns and school segregation.

On June 21, 1973, the U.S. Supreme Court in the *Denver* case warned all cities of the United States that gerrymandering school districts so as to recreate segregated school communities was illegal and constitutionally intolerable. On April 8, 1974, Tenth Circuit Court Judge William E. Doyle ordered Denver to integrate its 70,000 schoolchildren by fall 1974 by redrawing boundaries, pairing racial groups, and creating school mergers and greater racial balance in the schools. Other school districts, such as Charlotte-Mecklenburg and one of the first cities to voluntarily desegregate through busing, Berkeley, California, have employed busing with particular success and minimal strife once a firm position was taken.

The successes in school busing have not deterred its antagonists from pursuing their steadfast efforts to oppose it. Metropolitanization has been countered with plans to splinter school districts, as in Houston. The withholding of funds by the Department of Health, Education, and Welfare to force compliance is met with recalcitrance and subterfuge by antibusing school committees and by the enactment of state legislation—all of which inevitably results in protracted court battles. Efforts to enact an antibusing measure failed in the U.S. Congress during 1972. But by mid-1973 nine states had approved an amendment to the Federal Constitution to prohibit busing for desegregation purposes. Further impetus came when the House overwhelmingly endorsed an antibusing law as a rider to the education bill of 1974. Confronting these developments are the pairing plans, METCO programs, and the stress on equality of education through equitable financial support. The fact remains that despite the achieved progress toward school desegregation in some cities and states, the North still lags considerably behind the South in abolishing a segregated school system. The reluctance of the North, combined with insensitivity of many white persons who control the city school systems, compelled many black persons to turn to community control as a remedy to the problem of racial apartheid in the United States.

COMMUNITY CONTROL

Community control is to be distinguished from decentralization. *Decentralization* refers to the shifting of operating and administrative control over limited aspects of the school system to district or community boards of education. These boards are not completely autonomous, since city-wide boards of education control most of their funds.

In community control, decentralization exists but its major underpinning is an ideological posture. Operationally, the term means control over all institutions and resources within a given territorial community by its members for their benefit. As it pertains to the black community, community control is based upon what Roy Innis of CORE calls "enlightened self-interest"[21] and the claim that schools that were previously white controlled and administered have caused the miseducation of black youths. Whites, it is argued, have prevented self-determination among blacks, and they have perpetuated notions of black inferiority and distorted self-concepts not only among black students but the American population as a whole. They have also denied the existence of a black culture and minimized the uniquely varied roles performed by blacks in American life. Community control advocates insist that the curricula of white-controlled schools are not relevant to black life. Under community control, however, blacks would neither be coopted by a white power structure for personal gain nor be tools of white racism. The primary goal of blacks would be the control of the decision-making process affecting the quality of their lives and the education of their children. In other words, they would have absolute sovereignty over the formal education of black children and the right to use the school as an instrument for institution building and the attainment of nationalistic goals. To achieve these ends school districts would be drawn so as to reflect the neighborhood patterns of population dominance and subordination throughout the city and alternative schools would be established.

Also implicit in community control are the rights to: (1) hire and dismiss administrators, teachers, and supporting personnel of community schools, (2) control financial resources and expenditures, (3) gear the curriculum so as to more adequately socialize black children in a black value system, and (4) rectify, through black control, the educational and societal disabilities of the past.[22]

The issue of community control was the battleground and rallying cry in the prolonged Ocean Hill-Brownsville conflict of 1968 involving P.S. 201 and District 23 in New York City.[23] Resolution of the central issues of school control, which had polarized a predominantly Jewish teaching force and administration from a predominantly black population, resulted in the establishment of decentralized school boards. Under this plan New York City agreed to create semiautonomous school boards for each of 31 elementary school districts reporting to one central board of education for the city of New York. The underlying assumption of this plan was that greater community voice in school affairs and greater community participation in the decision-making process would restore confidence in the public schools and substantially improve the overall quality of education in city-operated schools. It was also a response to the allegations made by ghetto parents that the school had failed their children through poor education and unfulfilled promises.

Reports on decentralization and community control in New York City vary from one extreme to another. In recent years adversaries seem to have been more loudspoken than supporters. Some claim that decentralization and community control have had "disastrous effects on the performance of children" and that the basic issue of teaching children to read, write, and learn has become subordinated to racial politics.[24] Others have charged persons involved in key positions in some school districts with incompetency, the misappropriation of funds, and causing increased polarization between the races. Whether these charges can be substantiated or not is a moot issue and belies another more fundamental reality: Reading scores in New York City have been falling steadily since about 1965, five years before the decentralization plan went into effect. Thus the central issue is not whether the schools are in the hands of an all-black or a racially heterogeneous group, but how to improve the quality of urban education and make it more relevant for a rapidly changing and highly complex society. Concrete steps—such as a redistribution of financial resources, radical alterations in the curriculum and the pedagogical process, the assigning of more experienced teachers sensitive to the needs of underprivileged and poverty-stricken communities, and the strengthening of all the educational resources of the urban community—are imperatives for educational enrichment and for meeting the crises of urban education.

This is precisely what the black community has been trying to do during the past ten years: attempting to establish accountability and alternative models to sterile, irrelevant education in public schools through a variety of innovative community schools. Even in the face of discriminatory actions and often with limited financial support, success has been achieved in a number of community-based institutions. Among the more successful programs are the Massachusetts Experimental School System, and community schools in the Roxbury, Highland Park, and St. Josephs districts of Boston. In addition, the black community has been instrumental in facilitating the Model Cities Higher Education Program.

Street Academies. One of the earlier forms of alternative schools was the advent of street academies in the 1960s. These storefront facilities, scattered in cities across the country such as New York, Washington, Cleveland, and Oakland, California, are an innovative response to the high school dropout problem among urban black youth. Students, unable to complete the regular high school program or who felt that it was irrelevant to their needs, are encouraged to return to an informal but academically rigorous atmosphere for the remainder of high school training. Although varying from city to city, the attrition rate in the street academies is as low as 2 percent in cities having outstanding programs. Many of the graduates of these schools have continued to collegiate and graduate education; some have completed college work with distinction and won substantial fellowships for graduate and professional training. Almost 500 street academy graduates were in higher education in 1973 and another 500 were involved in career-oriented positions or training programs. Undoubtedly, Harlem Prep is the most highly regarded institution of this kind. Despite its notable successes, however, Harlem Prep encountered funding difficulties and would have closed had it not become incorporated into the New York City school system in 1973.

Even with these steps, the most effective educational improvements can only result from transforming home conditions within the black community so as to give children the motivation for achievement. Moreover, attitudinal transformations may also be necessary. For example, some elements in the black community will have to confront the traditional viewpoints about learning: Is learning only something for girls or should boys be concerned with it too? Is it unmasculine to be intelligent and to show interest in educational achievement? While this attitude is not confined only to the black community, it is endemic to practically all the lower and working classes in the United States. Even if this attitude changes, the income levels of the people who hold it will have to rise to enable the financially less well-off to purchase those learning aids that can facilitate a head start in the home prior to admission to nursery and grade schools. There is much merit in taking seriously sociological evidence that the home environment is of primary importance in academic achievement.

HIGHER EDUCATION

Black Colleges in Transition. Much of what has been said earlier concerning the legal mandates for desegregation at the elementary and secondary school levels is also germane for experiences at the college and university levels. However, the desegregation efforts pertaining to graduate and professional schools began much sooner. Black colleges had come into existence during the mid-nineteenth century as a response to segregation and discrimination. The first to be founded were Wilberforce University in Ohio and Lincoln University in Pennsylvania before the end of the Civil War. Both were established to "Christianize" and educate blacks in a liberal education, and both had integrated faculties from their inception.

Most of the 123 black colleges and universities founded since then are located in the South, and they served an almost exclusively black student body. At the beginning the majority offered the equivalent of a good secondary school education. Subsequently, they evolved along the classical model of white liberal arts colleges. Originally serving a variety of purposes, some catered to an elitist social class while others attempted to democratize higher education. Some were better financed and better staffed, offering a more rigorous curriculum that exacted higher standards. Others, on the other hand, did not uphold such rigorous and high academic standards. Because of serious problems which will be described presently that beset them from the outset, it is a tribute to their tenacity that they have continued for more than a century. Those philanthropic organizations that were instrumental in developing primary and secondary education for blacks played a major role in ensuring the survival of black colleges.

Functions. Black colleges provided opportunities for higher education throughout the period of de jure segregation; they served a clientele that could not be admitted to institutions serving whites, though those same institutions were supported by taxes paid by blacks; they offered blacks a chance for achievement when no one else would; they trained more than 80 percent of all black college graduates and in the process were responsible for the development of significant leadership forces in the black community. Furthermore, they came to be the source of considerable community pride, symbols of racial advancements, and part and parcel of the social mobility structure within the black community. Their very existence served as a continuing reminder of the intellectual acumen among black people and their teachers were visible role models worthy of emulation.

Problems. Yet, from the beginning, black colleges were plagued with essentially two types of problems, affective and organizational. Affective problems included those that emanated from social control and interpersonal relationships. Organizational problems were a function of management and the administrative structure of the institutions.

Organizational problems were also expressions of the role perceptions that the college or university president had of himself. He had inherited a model of administration from his white predecessors, but in the process of emulating them he tended to exaggerate their behavior. This development, combined with his suspicions of underlings, led him inevitably to a type of "vest-pocket administration" characterized by presidential autonomy, secrecy, and the inability to delegate authority or decentralize the decision-making structure. In many cases his limited knowledge of finance exacerbated financial problems endemic in black colleges. These institutions were almost always in financial straits, struggling to survive, not knowing whether they would close before the year was over or even if teachers could be paid from month to month. Financial problems placed numerous constraints on the acquisition of educational resources and the ability to hire competent staff, which inevitably affected accreditation. Construction of new buildings was always in doubt and often delayed. The curriculum varied from one institution to another, but not infrequently teachers were required to be experts in several different fields and to teach as many as fifteen to twenty semester hours. Although the heavy teaching loads were prevalent at several institutions, they did not occur at all of them. Nevertheless, this environment could hardly generate a high rate of scholarly productivity. Thus we must conclude that prior to World War II high scholarly productivity may have been neither encouraged nor adequately rewarded except at noted centers of scholarly activity such as Howard University and Fisk University.

Affective problems covered a wide range of activities regulated by a deeply entrenched but highly exaggerated Puritan ethic. A rigid conceptualization of morality, which also prevailed at small sectarian white colleges, encompassed all aspects of social life in many black colleges. This included proscriptions against face-to-face dancing between the sexes, restrictions against unsupervised dating, regulations against card playing and various recreational games, smoking in public, drinking alcoholic beverages, and faculty-student social relations. A morbid fear of premarital pregnancy prevailed, and when it occurred, both the father and expectant mother were expelled. Similarly, a paternalistic orientation governed behavior between faculty and administrators.

This host of problems in no way denies the good fortune that the black colleges have had in attracting a cadre of dedicated, diligent, and perservering teachers and a few excellent administrators. They still do attract such lights. These are men and women who have devoted themselves to teaching and research under the most difficult educational conditions. Their work and the successes of their students substantiate the claim that less well-known institutions can train outstanding students and successful adults just as the more prestigious ones can. Both outstanding and poor students graduate from black colleges just as outstanding and poor students graduate from predominantly white institutions. That four-fifths of all black college graduates and holders of professional degrees received their undergraduate training at predominantly black colleges and universities is more than sufficient evidence of the value of these. institutions. Moreover, black college graduates, natives of the South, now provide most of the professional black men and women who hold positions of importance both in and outside the South. They are the physicians and surgeons, the attorneys, the social scientists, the heads of academic departments in white universities, the successful business people, the accountants, and the engineers.

The proportion of successful and educated blacks who are of Southern origin is far greater than those of Northern birth. One explanation for this development lies in the high motivation of Southern blacks to use education as a vehicle for upward mobility and for survival in a highly segregated society. Southern blacks were also exposed to a larger array of educated role models than were Northern urban blacks, who, because of social class barriers and institutionalized discrimination, were isolated from successful and achieving blacks. A further explanation is that Southern black colleges were more accessible to college-age blacks and would admit them without regard for a quota system. In other words, despite the deprivations of income and allegedly inferior schools, black college students in the South were better able to seize educational opportunities and they did so in greater numbers. Perhaps, of even greater importance, they had black teachers who encouraged them to maximize their potential, to pursue a college education, and to achieve high goals commensurate with their abilities. Black urban youths in the North rarely experienced such concern from their high school teachers.

But discrimination and segregation set boundaries or limits on what black students could achieve in professional education and graduate training particularly in the South and in the border states. This situation was also true in the North, where admission quotas were enacted. Blacks seeking postcollegiate training found it necessary to "go North" if they could afford the financial burden. Few ever received monetary support from Northern and Western institutions, which again served as an impediment to educational attainment.

To combat discrimination in higher education the NAACP embarked upon a plan to alter the structure of university admission patterns. The basic goal was to open the doors of graduate and professional schools in the Southern and border states to black college graduates. The first successful test case came in 1938 when the U.S. Supreme Court decided in *Missouri ex rel. Gaines* v. *Canada* that the University of Missouri must admit Lloyd Gaines to its school of law. This was a milestone achievement, since many states had required blacks to accept out-of-state tuition grants to finance postcollegiate education rather than admit them to their all-white universities. Gaines was not required to accept this type of grant. Another major breakthrough occurred in 1946 when Ada Lois Sipuel applied for admission to the school of law at the University of Oklahoma. The state of Oklahoma was not inclined to establish separate law schools for black students, as had several Southern states. Rather, despite the ruling in the Gaines case, the state attempted to force her to accept an out-of-state tuition grant. She refused, and, finally, in 1948, the University of Oklahoma was required to admit Ada Sipuel.

Two other cases pertaining to graduate education were significant in this earlier period: the *Sweatt* case in Texas and the *McLauren* case in Oklahoma. In the Texas case Herman M. Sweatt, a mail carrier, had applied for admission to the University of Texas Law School. Texas quickly established a makeshift law school for blacks in four basement offices as a pretense at separate-but-equal facilities. However, this facility did not contain adequate libraries, moot courts, faculty, and other educational resources available at the University of Texas. The U.S. Supreme Court ordered Sweatt's admission to the University of Texas in 1950 on the grounds that the black law school did not approximate equality with the university's law school. The *McLauren* case in Oklahoma dealt with the issue of segregation within schools that had already been desegregated. The Graduate School of Education at the University of Oklahoma had admitted G. W. McLauren but had segregated him from his classmates. He was placed in an anteroom that adjoined the main classroom and was segregated in the dining room. Finally, he was admitted to class but segregated by a rope barrier. In 1950 the Supreme Court ruled that "substantial equality" was not provided by these arrangements and, therefore, McLauren had to be integrated in all facilities of the university. These four decisions also paved the way for the U.S. Supreme Court's favorable ruling in the 1954 *Brown* case.

In the main, the decisions reached by the Supreme Court regarding elementary and secondary education and the Civil Rights Act of 1964 have also had an impact on changes in higher education. The order issued June 12, 1973, by the U.S. District Court of Appeals for the District of Columbia, which enforces desegregation in 17 states, has profound implications for higher education as well as public schools in general. This order required the Department of Health, Education, and Welfare to discontinue providing funds to institutions that were in violation of the 1964 Civil Rights Act. HEW was also told to enforce compliance from 10 college systems in addition to some 200 elementary and secondary schools. Pennsylvania was the only Northern state included in this order; however, the mandate has far-reaching implications for institutions in other states that have not moved forward in desegregating faculties and student bodies. Florida was the first of the states cited to respond. In late June 1973 the Florida board of regents agreed to a five-year plan for accelerating faculty and student deseg-regation at eight of its nine state universities, which were predominantly white. The University of Florida agreed to obtain 321 additional black faculty members and 4,576 black students, but under the threat of loss of federal funds if it did not desegregate both faculty and student body.

Enrollment Patterns. By virtue of federal support, favorable decisions from the U.S. Supreme Court, and a broad range of responses by predominantly white institutions following the assassination of Dr. Martin Luther King, major changes have occurred in the enrollment patterns of black students in colleges and universities. In 1960 black colleges enrolled more than half of all black college students in the United States. As early as 1964, and certainly by 1970, only one-third of the 400,000 black college students were attending black institutions.[25] By 1972-1973, however, fully three quarters of the 727,000 black college students were enrolled in nonblack institutions outside the South. Forty percent of them were in junior colleges, approximately 35 to 40 percent were in traditionally white colleges and universities, and about 25 percent remained in the traditionally black colleges. Table 4-3 points to the dramatic increase in black student enrollment in colleges between 1965 and 1971. An examination of this table reveals that the proportion of young blacks of college age actually enrolled in college increased from 10 percent in 1965 to 18 percent in 1971.[26] But this is still substantially lower than the proportion of white college enrollees. Black graduate school enrollment is much more critical. Only 1.72 percent of graduate enrollees are black, and of all the Ph.D.s granted between 1964 and 1968 less than 1 percent went to blacks—clearly a horrendous predicament.

TABLE 4-3.

College Enrollment of Persons 18 to 24 Years Old, by Sex: 1965 and 1971

(*Numbers in thousands*)

	1965			1971		
	Total,	Enrolled in College		Total,	Enrolled in College	
Sex and race	18 to 24 Years Old	Number	Percent of Total	18 to 24 Years Old	Number	Percent of Total
Negro	2,041	210	10	2,866	522	18
Male	935	99	11	1,318	262	20
Female	1,106	111	10	1,547	259	17
White	16,505	4,213	26	20,533	5,594	27
Male	7,641	2,593	34	9,653	3,284	34
Female	8,864	1,620	18	10,880	2,310	21

SOURCE: U.S. Department of Commerce, Social and Economic Statistics Administration, Bureau of the Census.

A crucial observation is that the majority of black college students come from low-income homes. Approximately three-fifths of all black college students come from families whose annual incomes are lower than $7,500, and 11 percent come from families whose incomes are lower than $3,000 per year. Thus most black college students require financial aid in order to remain in school once they are admitted. It is this failure to supply needed financial assistance beyond the sophomore year that accounts for a substantial portion of the high dropout rate among black college students in predominantly white institutions. Obviously, other explanations also account for the high dropout rate, such as: (1) lack of preparation for a rigorous college program, (2) failure of institutions to provide assistance for tutorial programs and supportive services once blacks are admitted, (3) failure of some students to take seriously the requirements of college, (4) lack of self-discipline for academic study, (5) the racial prejudice of white instructors who are bent upon exacting higher standards for black students than they require of white students, and (6) a new form of academic paternalism that permits high grades for less-than-adequate performance. But limited income probably takes the most heavy toll, since worry over how to pay tuition, room and board, and to purchase books interferes with the normal process of academic training.

BLACK STUDENTS IN
WHITE COLLEGES

The problems just listed confront black students in general and are somewhat more acute for those blacks who are enrolled in predominantly white colleges. They are exacerbated by the belief that white institutions only mirror the prejudices and discrimination of the larger society. Many black students, for example, resent the prevailing tokenism in the recruitment of black students and black faculty in white institutions. They are now demanding a precise recruitment program that will result in a critical mass of black people at white institutions. Furthermore, in the late 1960s, a consistent complaint was the lack of sensitivity to and the incorporation of the black experience in the overall university milieu and in the curriculum of most American institutions. This feeling precipitated the black studies movement and led to the establishment of programs in black studies or Afro-American studies having mixed success in several hundred colleges—black and white—throughout the country. Some blacks also established Afro-American cultural centers and black living quarters. Black students are involved in day-to-day confrontations with faculty who allegedly grade them lower than whites and do not provide them with opportunities for make-up work on the same basis as for white students. By the same token, some black students feel victimized by those excessively liberal white faculty members who with a kind of paternalism wish to protect them from injustices.

Participation in communal activities at black cultural centers and Afro houses and in the affairs of the black community in which the white college is located occasionally relieve the inadequacy of social life. Dating poses other problems and anxieties. This is especially true for black females who often feel abandoned by black brothers for white females. The pain of rejection is all the more acute when the black male is or has been outspoken on black liberation and black power and vociferous in his claim that "black is beautiful." When black college women see these men sporting the external symbols of being black—the wearing of an Afro hair style and dashikis or African jewelry and using the raised clenched fist, while they walk arms locked with a white female—many conclude that these men are hypocrites who espouse only rhetoric. Black men who date across racial lines make the case that their personal lives must be separated from their ideological postures. The two are not necessarily coterminous.[27] Others rationalize interracial dating in economic terms, claiming that white women are freer with their money—that is, more willing to share it with them than are black females. Still others secretly explain that they are only establishing linkages whereby white male racism can be managed through their association with white women.

Not all the dissatisfaction has come from poverty-stricken or low-income black students. Thomas Sowell, a black economist, charges that many white colleges have overlooked the needs of the black middle class in their rush to enroll "authentic ghetto types" and have failed to reward the former group of deserving students for high academic achievement by not granting them the fellowships, scholarships, and financial aid they need. In admission policies regarding the authentic ghetto type, he maintains that such institutions have given greater weight to factors such as political disposition, ideological stance, and the degree of social alienation rather than to evidence of strong academic achievement. He also claims that one of the direct consequences of rejecting black middle-class students is a reinforcement of old stereotypes about black inferiority and about the lower possibilities of educating black students, especially when poorly trained students who should never have been admitted at all fail.[28]

The black middle-class student, whether enrolled in a predominantly black college or a traditionally white institution, is caught in a dilemma—an identity crisis. This problem stems from a sense of estrangement, arising on the one hand from alienation to the experiences of the black ghetto and on the other hand from the desire to be authenticated as truly and unequivocably black. To be black for many of them is to engage in behavior that is contradictory to all they learned in middle-class socialization. They had been taught and trained to behave according to mainstream normative structures. To be black also means rejecting an internalized value system that is at variance with the value system alleged to be more representative and authentically black (e.g., rejection of a commitment to punctuality, time; rejection of the ethic of work that assumes an inherent goodness of hard work; rejection of study skills as acceptable routes for academic success). Occasionally, these values defy articulation by some advocates of blackness, except that they do not wish to become slaves to the white man's world and to the acquisition of material wealth as have their parents in many cases. But their parents wish to encourage black identity and racial pride and simultaneously persuade them to train themselves for competitive positions in a desegregated and highly individualized social structure. Other students see no inconsistency in their rejection of white values, their commitment to a black identity, and their preparation for work in either the mainstream or the black community. For them being a member of the black middle class poses no major problems, and many fully expect to share in the future leadership of the black community.

Clearly, all black students merely by virtue of their enrollment in a predominantly white university or college do not experience the types of problems described here. A significant number of students who entered college through Upward Bound Programs as well as those who are of middle-class origins have successfully completed college and graduate or professional training. The roster of honor students among them increases year by year, and the number who have successfully integrated into the mainstream of college life is also on the upswing. This is evidenced by the numerous black student-body presidents; editors of yearbooks, reviews, and school papers; campus journalists; participants in student government; members of departmental clubs and other honor societies. Black athletes, too, are coming to realize their participation in college athletics involves a quid pro quo or a situation of exchange by which they contribute their athletic ability in return for a quality education usable when they leave college and sometimes convertible into lucrative professional contracts.

MANPOWER PROBLEMS

Even with the increasing black student enrollments in undergraduate colleges and universities, a serious manpower shortage of trained black people exists. Chapter 6 will elaborate on this point; however, it is worthy of preliminary examination here. Prior to the 1954 Supreme Court decision, segregation and discriminatory practices dissuaded black college students from pursuing careers in fields other than teaching and the ministry. A few went into medicine, mainly at either Howard University or Meharry Medical College, and still fewer enrolled in law schools. A small number were encouraged to obtain the doctorate degree—a Ph.D. or a Ed.D. As a result, the mushrooming demands for black holders of the Ph.D. at both black colleges and white institutions have created a critical shortage of black professors throughout the United States. The universities are not producing a sufficient number of black Ph.D.s to even approach the demand. Many black colleges struggle to attract and hold black Ph.D.s who now have opportunities to work in white institutions. In some instances, though the evidence is far from complete, black faculty are in a favorable position to attain excellent salaries and good positions in colleges and universities. This has caused a degree of trepidation among some administrators who are afraid of the white faculty's feeling that it is the victim of so-called reverse discrimination. Others are able to explain what appears to be inflated salaries in some cases on the grounds of special talents and resources that a black faculty member brings to the university situation. In reality, many black college professors, like white women, are frequently underpaid and highly exploited. Nevertheless, the shortages are likely to become even more acute unless the graduate and professional schools undertake a massive recruitment effort and broaden the base of financial support that will encourage blacks to go beyond the baccalaureate degree. Some foundations, such as Ford, Rockefeller, Russell Sage, and John Hay Whitney, in addition to the Links and the Elks in the black community, have an established tradition of assisting black graduate students.

There is a grave danger that financial support for black college and graduate students is on the decline, however. Cutbacks in government financing of educational programs will have a decidedly negative impact on black student enrollment and staying power in college and graduate schools. Increasing evidence suggests waning direct support for black students at several white universities and colleges. As their boards of trustees order budgetary restraints and as the emotional commitment to assist black students evaporates, black enrollments decline. Moreover, some middle-class white students feel that blacks are gaining at their expense, and white faculty who represent their interests ask for more financial aid for both working-class and middle-class white students. They share the hard-hat view that blacks have gotten too much too soon and much too easily. Nevertheless, it is absolutely certain that black students are still grossly underrepresented in higher education despite the improvements of the 1960s.

Militancy. In recent years, especially since 1960, black colleges have found themselves embroiled in demands for major social changes. Black students in black colleges were the first to attack institutionalized discrimination and segregation in mass society. They seemed to have been dormant for a while thereafter, but then they shifted their attention internally toward the black institutions themselves. They were outraged at the oppressive paternalism of the college administrations, at the administrations' perception of them as irresponsible children who could be easily manipulated and controlled, at their lack of voice in the decision-making apparatus of their institutions, and, indeed, at their lack of participation in most matters of direct concern to them.

Therefore, they began to demand relevance in the curriculum, a better-trained faculty, improvements in dormitory life, improvements in the quality of food, and substantive changes in their social life. They also demanded better libraries and improved educational resources and the firing of faculty and administrators who regarded their demands as unwarranted intrusions by people who had no rights other than those granted by the administration. These students began to view such faculty as white folks with black faces and just as repressive as white people in the larger society. Uprisings at black colleges in the middle and late 1960s and early 1970s challenged the fundamental authority structure of the colleges and the slave mentality that prevailed at several institutions. Unmistakably, the disruptions and threats of disruptions did effect change, thus providing evidence of the transferability of tactics and strategies learned in the civil rights and black liberation movements to the world of higher learning.

But black colleges changed also because they simply had to change in order to survive. They had to improve the quality of the faculty, instructional facilities, and resources to compete with the white institutions that were robbing them of faculty and students. They had to make salaries more competitive, and to create a more democratic, less paternalistic atmosphere if they were to survive. Thus private institutions, through the United Negro College Fund, for example, appealed for massive financial support for meeting the challenges of the 1970s. The response continues to be positive, and the 41 institutions receiving support from the fund are viable educational enterprises today.

It may be that few Americans understand the tremendous role that the United Negro College Fund (UNCF) has played in the education of black youths since its founding in 1943. The Fund was organized as a response to shrinking financial contributions from white philanthropists and to the recognition among black educators that blacks must assume a greater responsibility for the education of black youths. It was started by several black college presidents organized under the leadership of Dr. Frederick D. Patterson, who was then President of Tuskegee Institute, who decided to pool their fund-raising resources in order to assure operational expenses and to improve faculty salaries as well as educational facilities. Since then the UNCF has raised over $150 million; in 1974 alone, its goal was to raise $15 million for its participating colleges and universities. Beginning with 27 predominantly black colleges, whose total enrollment was about 12,000 students, the UNCF expanded over the next thirty years to include 41 colleges with a total enrollment of approximately 46,000 students. Its efforts have resulted in both the continued survival of many black colleges and in furthering the education of individual black college students.

Had it not been for the work of the UNCF, it is clear that many black youths would never have received a college education, and the nation would have been deprived of a large segment of the educated black leaders and black intellectuals. This group of Fund-aided people includes three-fourths of all blacks holding doctorate degrees, more than four-fifths of black physicians, three-fourths of black officers in the armed services, and four-fifths of black federal judges.*[29]

An even more compelling explanation for changes in traditionally black colleges was the threat of mergers with formerly all-white institutions in or near where the black colleges were located. Such threats were the concern of, among others, Florida A & M University, Delaware State College, Tennessee State A & I University, and Morgan State College. West Virginia State College is now 50 percent white, Delaware State at Dover 40 percent white, and Bluefield State in West Virginia 80 percent white. Maryland State College has now been incorporated into the University of Maryland Eastern Shore. The public black institutions in North Carolina are part of the state college and university system, and Arkansas AM & N has now merged with the University of Arkansas. Following a 1972 election in Fort Valley, Georgia, in which black students voted in a large number of blacks into important local elective positions, the white citizens petitioned for the merger of three black state colleges at Fort Valley, Savannah, and Albany with the white state colleges in order to minimize black control of local government.

A final issue confronting black institutions concerns the development of what Stephen Henderson calls an authentic black university.[30] He sees such a university as a departure, dictated by liberation, from the traditional, white-oriented education toward a search for a sense of direction in which blacks learn to serve black people rather than white colonizers. He envisions this university as "unashamedly political" in the creation of new conceptual themes and dogma about black people and their experiences. It requires a thorough knowledge of the white world and its institutions and how that world has employed its power to contain and dominate black

---

* A list of all 123 black colleges, private and public, can be found in the *Negro Almanac*.

people. The creation of a new black university along these lines, it is argued, is vital for black survival in the twentieth century. Others have called for mergers of black colleges, particularly church-related ones, for creating greater viability, while still others plead for the establishment of high-prestige black universities capable of being truly great intellectual centers.

No matter what the resolution of this issue is, the conditions that have created and justified black colleges and universities remain with us in one form or another, and their need continues to be compelling.

NOTES

1. John Hope Franklin, *From Slavery to Freedom* (New York: Alfred A. Knopf, 1952), pp. 303–305.

2. Gunnar Myrdal, *An American Dilemma* (New York: Harper & Row, 1944), pp. 337–341.

3. *Report of the National Advisory Commission of Civil Disorders* (New York: Bantam Books, 1968), p. 434.

4. Robert R. Wheeler, "Public Schools, Public Policy, Public Problems: Some Observations and Suggestions," *Proceedings of the National Policy Conference on Education for Blacks* (Washington, D. C.: The Congressional Black Caucus, 1972), pp. 103–113.

5. Myrdal, *op. cit.*, p. 942.

6. The pattern of segregation in higher education had already been interrupted by virtue of a series of NAACP successes in gaining admission of black students into previously all-white graduate and professional schools in Southern and border states.

7. *The Southern Manifesto* was a statement of defiance against the U.S. Supreme Court's 1954 school desegregation decision, signed by 19 senators and 77 representatives. It also was an effort to reinvoke the principle of states' rights in the field of education.

8. Reported in *The New York Times*, June 3, 1973, p. 26.

9. *Ibid.*

10. Among the scholars who have addressed this issue and reached similar conclusions are Kenneth B. Clark, *Dark Ghetto* (New York: Harper & Row, 1965), Chap. 6; Robert Rosenthal and Lenora Jacobson, *Pygmalion in the Classroom: Teachers' Expectations and Pupils' Intellectual Development* (New York: Holt, Rinehart and Winston, 1968).

11. *New Orleans States Item*, August 31, 1972, p. 1.

12. *Ibid.*

13. James W. Vander Zanden, *American Minority Relations* (New York: Ronald Press, 1966), pp. 9–10.

14. Kenneth B. Clark, "Desegregation: The Role of the Social Sciences," *Teachers College Record*, 63 (1960), pp. 16–171.

15. *The Social and Economic Status of the Black Population in the United States, 1971*, U.S. Department of Commerce, Bureau of the Census, Current Population Reports, Series P-23, No. 42 (Washington, D.C.: Government Printing Office, July 1972), p. 81.

16. *Ibid.*

17. James S. Coleman, *Equality of Educational Opportunity* (Washington, D.C.: Department of Health, Education, and Welfare, U.S. Printing Office, 1967).

18. *Ibid.*, pp. 21–25.

19. *The New York Times*, May 27, 1973, p. E-9.

20. See Christopher Jencks, *Inequality* (New York: Basic Books, 1973); also see Howard F. Taylor, "Playing the Dozens with Path Analysis: Methodological Pitfalls," in Jencks et al., "Inequality," *Sociology of Education*, 46:4 (Fall 1973), pp. 433–450, for a critical discussion of Jencks' position.

21. *Proceedings of the National Policy Conference on the Education of Blacks* (Washington, D.C.: The Congressional Black Caucus, 1972), p. 133.

22. *Ibid.*, pp. 129–146.

23. See various issues of *Commentary* magazine during 1968 and *ibid.* for a description of the issues related to the Ocean Hill-Brownsville crisis.

24. See *The New York Times*, December 3, 1972, and March 18, 1973, *New York Times Magazine*, pp. 14ff, for interview with Kenneth B. Clark.

25. Fred E. Crossland, *Minority Access to College* (New York: Schocken Books, 1970).

26. *The Social and Economic Status of the Black Population in the United States, 1971, loc. cit.*, p. 85.

27. Cf. Charles V. Willie and Arline S. McCord, *Black Students at White Colleges* (Columbus, Ohio: Charles E. Merrill Publishing Co., 1970), and Harry Edwards, *Black Students* (New York: The Free Press, 1970), for provocative and insightful discussions of black college students, their self-perceptions, problems, and strategies for social change.

28. Thomas Sowell, *Black Education: Myths and Tragedies* (New York: McKay Publishing Co., 1973).

29. Charlayne Hunter, "Negro College Fund, a Success at Thirty, Running Harder Now," *New York Times*, October 18, 1974, p. 43.

30. Stephen Henderson, "Toward the Black University," *Ebony*, 25 (September 1970), pp. 108–116.

5 | HOUSING: THE GHETTOIZATION OF BLACKS

The issues of housing and residential segregation in the United States crystallize in microcosm the problems of segregation, discrimination, and injustice afflicting American life in general. Segregation in housing has far-reaching implications for behavior in a number of social institutions and daily behavior. It is reasonable to believe, for example, that school desegregation would be far more easily accomplished if housing were desegregated. Historical evidence shows us that this goal will continue to be difficult to attain, however. One of the most fundamental reasons for this difficulty is that housing patterns reflect the internal colonialism by which the powerful and privileged control the movements of the subordinate and less powerful. The reader is reminded that this concept is used to describe the control and manipulation of institutional life of a people by an external group.

INTERNAL COLONIALISM AND BLACK GHETTOIZATION

It can be argued that the present structure of housing patterns, which cordons off blacks from others in the larger community, is tantamount to an internal colony. Not only are blacks and whites physically separated from each other, but a white population residing outside the territorial communities assigned to blacks owns, administers, and controls black resources, particularly land and property on which blacks reside, as well as many aspects of institutional life among the black population. Bankers and money lenders, mortgagers, captains of real estate, and the barons of federal and local governments own and control these properties. Housing has been the instrument for both separating the races physically and establishing the political supremacy of a dominant group. It both specifies and maintains racial territories as well as protects those boundaries deemed necessary for socioeconomic containment. Because the possession of housing is equated with the possession of power, there has been a persistent rapaciousness in acquiring it. The ownership of vast quantities of housing property has meant immense wealth, economic and political power, and social control.

One consequence is that through a historical process of migration and population shifts blacks became concentrated into identifiable geographical areas called ghettos. As we shall see, ghettoization and domestic control by forces external to the black community occurred simultaneously through mutual facilitation. As we noted previously, the majority of the black population were originally concentrated in rural areas of the South. Even though the races coexisted in close proximity to each other in the rural South immediately after emancipation, a pattern of racial separation followed on the heels of the decision rendered in the *Plessy* case. Territorial boundaries further separating the races, legitimating white control over land and related resources, soon followed. In general, whites controlled the land that blacks worked; few blacks ever achieved recognition as members of the landed aristocracy. White control over land and resources in the rural South placed limitations upon resource utilization by blacks and manipulated their movement from one area to another.

The subordinate status of blacks became even more apparent as they moved from isolated farms into urban communities because in the cities they were confined to specific geographical areas that even more sharply separated them from the white population. As blacks moved from farm to city and from Southern city to Northern urban communities, the emergent ecological pattern was one of increasing geographical concentration or racial clustering rather than dispersion. In most instances the teeming millions who moved from the South to the North between 1915 and 1970 ended up in the central zones of cities and have remained there. This situation contrasts with that of whites, who may have begun their urban experience in virtually the same geographical area but were able to redistribute themselves into the ever-widening periphery of the city and, finally, into resegregated suburban communities. It was this process of migration followed by concentration and aggressive confinement of blacks into more or less self-contained residential areas that resulted in the establishment of black ghettos. The ghettos assumed a special ambience or character of their own. More important, for the moment, blacks did not have control over their ghettos, except in a most superficial way, although it may have appeared otherwise. The reason for this was because the land, buildings, and financial power were not in black hands to any appreciable degree. An almost invisible white power structure that sought to contain blacks by restricting their movement and limit their access to scarce resources, on terms that they dictated, controlled the land, its use, and its dwellings. Exploitation undergirded by racism is thus a basic condition of containment in the ghetto. In Northern cities, as had happened in the South, blacks again found themselves ruled by an external group, the domestic colonizers.

Housing patterns assumed the characteristics of domestic colonialism: (1) when the white population realized that it could physically separate the blacks without violent resistance and that this physical separation could form the essential elements of social boundaries between them, (2) when whites, as the dominant group, began to exploit their control over the housing market among blacks for their own financial and social purposes, (3) when they could deny access to better housing to those blacks who had sufficient income to purchase housing in white neighborhoods, (4) when whites established their control over the movement of blacks from one area to another, and (5) when they understood that they could translate their political dominance into administrative control over all other forms of institutional life among black people.

Although residential segregation supported boundaries already assumed to exist between the races, resulting invidious distinctions in the quality of housing had the added effect of establishing *intragroup* boundaries among blacks of different social classes or socioeconomic status. As pointed out in Chapter 3, where one lives often defines how one is perceived by others and how one is viewed defines, in turn, social status in the community. Thus as whites vacated the "better areas" of the rising black ghetto, the more economically better-off and higher-status blacks invaded and succeeded them. This process accentuated differences among the various strata within the black social class system. Just as physical isolation of better-off whites was equivalent to social isolation of the white middle class from "poor white trash," a similar pattern of behavior emerged among blacks. The more economically and socially advantaged blacks anxiously established physical boundary lines between themselves and those considered beneath them in social status, thereby restricting social contacts, except on their own terms. Thus the Baldwin Hills of Los Angeles was socially distant from Watts; the early Gold Coast of Cleveland was spatially and socially separated from the Scoville-Central Avenue crowd; and the blacks in the far northwest of Washington, D.C., were far removed from those blacks residing in areas close to the Capitol. Although these boundaries are maintained and controlled by devices that originated in the external community, class conscious blacks often seek physical separation through housing as an instrument for reaffirming social distance between the haves and the have-nots. Thus housing discrimination provides further evidence of the interrelatedness of race and class in understanding the ramifications of both intragroup and intergroup behavior.

Although intragroup social boundary systems are of special interest in a study of the black community, the impact of racial separation through housing segregation has a far greater effect on the day-to-day life experiences of black people. Segregation in housing and the impregnable boundaries established through this process victimize blacks in education, in occupations and access to their jobs, in hospitals and medical facilities, and in other necessities of social life. The majority are forced to live under debilitating conditions within a social environment that, as persons outside the community observe, confirms stereotypes and negative perceptions attributed to the black population as a whole.

Nowhere has the housing crisis of the 1970s been more evident than in the quality of housing offered to the black population. We should recall that the vision of the good life in America is supposed to be intertwined with the ownership of single-family homes. This view is considered a normal expectation, if not a God-given right of all Americans, irrespective of race, color, or creed. An extension of it is the assumption that the single-family home or whatever housing the family has should be in a "decent" neighborhood. Although standards of decency vary from region to region and from class to class, an acceptable dwelling has certain attributes in common: (1) good physical condition—that is, the dwelling is not dilapidated; (2) the presence of hot running water and a private bath; and (3) adequate space—that is, there is no overcrowding.[1] A dwelling that does not meet these minimal conditions becomes suspect. Moreover, the dwelling should be in a neighborhood of adequately well-maintained housing that is relatively clean and free of litter.

Homeownership. According to the latest census data, slightly more than two-fifths of all black Americans (42 percent) own their own homes in contrast to almost two-thirds of whites who own theirs. The 4 percent increase in black homeownership observed from 1960 to 1970 does not depict notable progress during a period often described as a decade of unparalleled progress for black Americans. Regionally, a far greater proportion of Southern blacks (47 percent) own their homes than blacks in any other part of the nation. Because of benign racism and ingrained self-sufficiency the Northeast, which traditionally has enjoyed the reputation of liberalism, lags behind all other sections in black homeownership (29 percent). The West (40 percent) and the North Central states (42 percent) approximate the national average of black homeownership. This description suggests that we need to know more about the quality of the houses owned by blacks and about the people who rent either privately owned apartments or public housing of one form or another, many of whom are at the mercy of rapacious landlords.

The relationship among employment, income, and housing is obvious in the disparities of homeownership among various segments of urban communities. In the central city where the unemployment rate and poverty level are the highest, and land space is limited, proportionately fewer people own their own homes and significantly more persons rent. In contrast, in areas outside the central cities, where not only more people are employed but also at higher salaries and in more prestigious occupations, homeownership is considerably more widespread and fewer people rent. Thus about one-third of all central-city blacks live in self-owned dwellings, whereas more than half of black suburbanites, or those living outside the central cities, own their homes. By contrast, almost two-thirds of central-city whites and approximately three-fourths of the white suburbanites own their homes. Disparities between the two groups in homeownership are inextricably intertwined with both race and economic conditions. If the black poor are unable to find suitable employment and if they are compelled to work at poverty-level wages, they are neither likely to save sufficient money to pay for single-family dwellings nor to rent in the more desirable areas. In effect, the black poor are condemned to either substandard housing or to public housing, which in many cities is the epitome of economic and social degradation.

Plumbing. Owning a house does not necessarily mean that housing is adequate any more than renting means that the dwelling is automatically undesirable. In 1970 blacks occupied less than 10 percent of all occupied housing in the United States although they constituted almost 12 percent of the total population of the country. These black-occupied housing units constituted more than a quarter (27.6 percent) of all housing units in the United States having incomplete or substandard plumbing. This situation was a slight deterioration from the plumbing conditions existing a decade earlier. Then, as now, a disproportionately large number of black people were living in dwellings devoid of the basic plumbing facilities normally expected of American families irrespective of race or ethnicity, that is, a bathtub solely for occupants' use and a toilet that is functional (flushes). More than a million housing units occupied by blacks had plumbing inadequacies in 1970. Moreover, the higher the income, the more likely are persons to live in units in which the plumbing is complete. Similarly, housing units of greater financial values are more likely to contain complete plumbing units than houses of relatively low value.

Overcrowding. This is another characteristic of black-occupied housing units. According to Department of Health, Education and Welfare standards, a unit is overcrowded when more than one person occupies a single room. By this measure approximately one-fifth of all black housing units are overcrowded in comparison to 7 percent of white housing units. Excessive crowding is particularly characteristic of rented dwellings, which contain sometimes double the number of persons per room than in owner-occupied dwellings. The stress on one person per room as the measure of overcrowding may somewhat obscure the problem, however, for it is a statistical average or a mean that in no way communicates the severe conditions of room density experienced by some poor black families in both rural and urban areas. It gives no indication of the hundreds of thousands of families living in dwellings with three or more persons sleeping in one room, for instance.

Physical Conditions. The conditions of housing for the black population vary with socioeconomic class or more specifically with the amount of income. Fully two-thirds of all urban blacks are restricted to housing that does not meet required federal standards. The middle and upper classes have managed to overcome some limitations imposed by discrimination and racial isolation. Therefore, they are in a more favorable financial position for locating high-quality housing. If by chance they are behind the barriers of the ghetto wall, they live in the best housing available within the segregated black community. If they have managed to move into desegregated neighborhoods, their housing is equal to if not superior to that of their white neighbors, but they have been required, in all probability, to pay more for what they obtained than a white person would have had to pay for the same quality of housing.

By contrast, blacks at the lower end of the income and socioeconomic structure are not so fortunate. Houses range downward from a modest condition to a dilapidated one that defies belief—the last are usually houses worn by years of poor maintenance and progressive deterioration. The exteriors of these dwellings are commonly in a state of disrepair or in need of paint; roofing and windows beg replacement; siding, steps, and parts of front porches are often missing; the interiors violate most existing health and sanitation codes; peeling plaster, holes in ceilings, and broken floors may serve as points of entry for rats with voracious appetites, which, if unsatisfied, attack the human occupants of such dwellings. If plumbing is present, it may or may not be functioning properly. Sewage often backs up and overflows sometimes into the kitchen sink. Unscrupulous and rapacious landlords refuse to make necessary repairs because they feel repair costs will necessarily inflate rents in an already overpriced dwelling; they also realize that given the continuing pressure for housing generated by increasing immigration to the city, a seriously dilapidated unit will not remain vacant too long. Poverty-stricken homeowners may not have sufficient money to pay for basic repairs; so many families attempt to repair facilities themselves or to use the services of friends whenever possible. Of course, immense variations characterize the black community, so much so that even on a single street it is possible to move from the extreme of dilapidation to dwellings of superior quality.

Public Housing. The conditions under which blacks are forced to live, especially those at the lower echelons of the socioeconomic spectrum, are far worse in public housing. Sixty percent of public housing occupants in the United States are the poorer segments of the black population. This national average may be somewhat misleading, though, since in some cities the proportion of blacks occupying public housing is considerably larger and approaches 100 percent. In others the proportion may be substantially less. Over the years, in contrast with its beginnings, public housing has become identified with the black poor. Whether black or white, standards and conditions are so far below the norm as to invite serious attention. But the conditions, across the country and city by city, are worse when these dwellings are occupied by blacks. A few illustrations may make the point explicit.

Perhaps the classical case of public housing deprivations is the Pruitt-Igoe public housing development in St. Louis. Built almost two decades ago and winner of an architectural design award in 1958, the project deteriorated so rapidly and uncontrollably that a decision was made to destroy it entirely in 1973. This "monster," as it came to be known, consisted of about 33 buildings of 11 stories containing 2, 567 units. At first the project was racially integrated. Poverty-stricken blacks, who moved up from the South, without jobs and with limited incomes, were finally forced onto public welfare and moved to Pruitt-Igoe. Simultaneously, whites steadily moved out. As this change was occurring, maintenance suffered, administration worsened, and security all but vanished. In time, Pruitt-Igoe became a symbol of public housing failure rife with crime, drug abuse, deviant behavior, physical attacks, sexual assaults in hallways, elevators, and on project grounds, broken windows, serious plumbing and water problems, excrement in elevators, and a sense of fear, disaffection and rejection by its inhabitants. Because of these and similar conditions in other public housing a stigma became attached to public housing residents. This stigma is so powerful that once a person is identified as a project occupant he or she may very well be perceived as a drug user, a dope pusher, a rapist, an unwed mother on welfare, a good-for-nothing derelict, or a social and economic parasite.

The conditions of Pruitt-Igoe were not peculiar to that project alone. They are repeated again and again all across the country. They exist at Columbia Point in Boston, at the 1,206-unit Stella Wright Project in Newark, New Jersey, at the 3,600-unit Cabrini Green Project in Chicago, and at several projects housing literally thousands of blacks and Puerto Ricans in New York City. Similar situations exist in Oakland, Cleveland, and Detroit. Too many people regard projects as urban jungles and concrete ghettos, and whether they are occupied by blacks or whites, the negative perceptions persist. However, the racist structure of the American society guarantees far more attention, better maintenance and repair systems, better security, more frequent garbage pickups, and improved conditions or facilities in public housing when a significant proportion of the occupants are white. Similarly, more systematic care is provided for the upkeep of any community where whites are in the majority in contrast to the types and range of services provided to predominantly minority, especially black and poor, areas. But the human tragedy perpetrated by these distinctions, invidious as they are, lies more poignantly in the distortions of the spirit and self-concept among people who devalue themselves because they have internalized demeaning negative perceptions projected upon them by others.

Facilities. Not only the types of dwellings people occupy but also the range of facilities contained in them reflect income inequities. Thus if the median income of blacks is nationally less than two-thirds that of the white population, blacks would not likely have sufficient funds to match whites in their ability to purchase consumable goods and amenities. Almost three-quarters of all white American households contain a clothes washer and dryer. But only one-eighth of black households contain a clothes dryer and slightly more than one-half (51 percent) have any type of washing machine available. More than twice the number of white households possess some form of air conditioning, and four times as many of them contain central air conditioning systems.

The greater capacity of whites to purchase amenities extends further to their ability to own two or more houses—for almost 2 million Americans, most of them white, own a second home. This occurs at a time when one-sixth of the American population, disproportionately black, do not have decent houses to live in.[2]

Territoriality and Sense of Community. Despite negative dimensions of racial isolation and the impediments of segregation and discrimination, blacks living in and among themselves have reaped a positive benefit—the development of a sense of community. Territorial confinement required adjustments and institutional arrangements to meet human needs. It also highlighted a need for mutual support and the sharing of limited resources as a means of survival. It fostered constructions of institutional arrangements for expressive and instrumental needs; it facilitated social participation, which in turn hastened intracommunity incorporation as well as a sense of corporate identity; it helped establish mechanisms for social control to

assure general conformity to community expectations; and it created a segregated community that produced its own leadership structure with the specific mission of creating ingroup solidarity or group cohesion and of pre-
paring the black population for requirements demanded for gaining equal
access to shared values of the larger society.

Residential Mobility. Thousands of black people change their place of
residence one or more times during the course of the year. (See Chapter 1
for a discussion of push-and-pull factors.) Blacks in rural areas rarely move
from one rural area to another. They are, however, frequently disposed
toward abandoning the farm for the city. The most observed pattern until
recently showed rural Southern blacks moving to the nearest Southern city
of some size, which was then used as a way station prior to the final move
away from the South altogether for points in the North and West. Although
the areas outside the South continue to receive a number of blacks, as evidenced by the migration of 305,000 blacks to the North between 1965 and
1970 and of 150,000 blacks to the West during the same period, the large
Southern cities are also receiving blacks in disproportionately large
numbers.[3] Only one Southern city, Birmingham, Alabama, experienced a
population loss of blacks during the 1960s. The racial turbulence that characterized Birmingham during that period probably accounts for the population decrease there. Simultaneously, Deep South and border cities such as
Houston, Dallas, Atlanta, New Orleans, St. Louis, Memphis, Richmond,
and Jacksonville, Florida, experienced a high influx of blacks primarily
from rural areas. The South has more than 15 million substandard houses,
many of them occupied by rural blacks. Their exodus into nearby cities may
be partially explained by their search for better sustenance and housing.
Because of improving economic and social conditions and opportunities for
significantly better housing in some of these cities, despite a residue of discrimination that persists, this trend seems to suggest that these cities are
likely to retain a sizable black population for some time in the future and
thus slow the process of black outmigration from the Southern and border
states. Moreover, even though evidence of a significant reverse pattern of
migration is almost circumstantial, it does exist. That is, many blacks, disillusioned by unfulfilled promises of a better quality of life in the North and
West, are returning to the South. Others are returning for political and ideological reasons such as a desire to work in a predominantly black social
milieu and for a largely black constituency. Some black professors, for
example, are giving up their positions in predominantly white Northern universities to return to work with and for black institutions.* The extent to
which this reverse pattern exists is yet to be empirically investigated.

---

* An example of this trend is provided by Professor C. Eric Lincoln, a distinguished sociologist who after many years of working in predominantly white institutions such as Union Theological Seminary moved to Fisk University in 1973.

Intraurban Patterns. A 1971 report of a national survey on residential mobility provides substantial data on patterns of residential mobility of blacks in urban areas. Ronald J. McAllister and his associates studied both residential mobility patterns and residential preferences in 43 metropolitan areas across the country. They reported that 10 percent more blacks than whites changed their place of residence during the survey period. More than 50 percent of the black households changed residences between 1966 and 1969. Over 95 percent of those blacks who moved remained within the same city. When the variable of "retrospective mobility" was examined, McAllister reported that blacks still tended to change places of residence within the same city or town and to shun long-distance moving. Moreover, they tended to move within the same neighborhood (41 percent). Renters are also more likely to be residentially mobile than are homeowners. For example, approximately 70 percent of the renter respondents in contrast to 25 percent of the homeowners changed places of residence. Because of discrepancies in tenure status between blacks and whites, blacks, then, are more likely to be more residentially mobile than are whites.[4]

The McAllister data also showed that approximately one-fifth of mobile blacks were forced to move in contrast to about 6 percent of white movers. Being forced to move, he found, subsumes such factors as the destruction of the residential unit, eviction, or the takeover of the property though eminent domain.[5] This finding is important in supporting other empirical studies that show that a substantial number of blacks are evicted from homes during the course of a year in addition to those who suffer serious residential dislocation from the ruse of urban renewal. In other words, their houses are destroyed; they are forced to leave, almost never to return to new dwellings constructed at the site where their former homes once stood. Blacks also move, however, to escape overcrowded conditions or because they purchase new homes or because they want to be close to their jobs.

Although the number of blacks who moved into suburbia almost doubled during the decade of the 1960s, the proportion of blacks in the suburbs remained about the same in 1970 as it was in 1960—approximately 4.5 percent of the total number of suburban residents. However, physical integration into suburban communities does not in and of itself lead to social integration into such communities. Thus residentially mobile blacks who move into predominantly white areas may or may not experience positive interaction with whites. In fact, they may not have any social interaction at all and may be residentially segregated in white communities. Racial considerations aside, most city dwellers see no "imperative obligation" to be sociable with one another. As a rule, they associate with one another either because they like each other or because of some mutual benefit. Thus neighborliness in an urban context takes on a decidedly different meaning than in a small town or rural community, where neighborhood friendship usually is so highly valued. One explanation for this phenomenon lies in the decreasing interdependence of people on one another as they move into urban communities where they can purchase so many requirements of human existence, technological and social.[6]

Advocates of the contact theory in race relations assume that physical integration will eventually lead to social integration and, subsequently, to a reduction of prejudice. Whether or not housing integration per se substantiates this theory may be questionable. However, it does appear that positive interaction between the races is largely a function of the types of dwellings and neighborhoods within which social contact occurs. Differences in the nature of contact may be far greater in public housing than that observed in neighborhoods characterized by private single-family houses. Residents of public housing are likely to be low-income groups and persons of low social status. Competition among them for scarce commodities, jobs, and social status is likely to be sufficiently keen so as to heighten racial animosities. In public housing blacks and whites may initially coexist in disharmonious relationships to one another. But everyone is virtually in the same pot together. With limited incomes and occupational constraints, they are not likely to escape one another for a while. They are forced by circumstances and close proximity to get along.[7] This view presupposes that contact will, of course, be of considerable duration and, further, that blacks and whites are in relatively the same proportions in a given housing project. It does not take into full consideration the probable white exodus from housing projects in which the proportion of blacks reaches a "tipping point," to other projects in which they will be in the majority. However, the basic premise that, in general, social interaction in a public housing project by virtue of day-to-day contact is at a much higher level than in single-family housing residential areas seems warranted. By virtue of the higher levels of interaction, previously negative perceptions are not confirmed, and people tend to make more realistic and relatively unprejudiced assessments of one another.

The situation in single-family neighborhoods, particularly suburban areas, may be decidedly different. The lack of neighborliness probably reaches its apex in many suburban communities, where privacy is highly valued. There is reason to suspect, however, that here, too, the physical interaction of blacks is less likely to lead to their social integration than would be the case for whites. In a Connecticut study reported by Henry Stetler,[8] whites in close proximity to blacks in suburban communities seldom interacted with them. In fact, half of the whites residing next door to blacks seldom interacted with them, and three-quarters of those whites living three doors away from blacks had few social encounters with them. This study also revealed that four-fifths of white neighbors of black people did not engage in any form of activity with blacks in the community, and only one-quarter of them had social relations with blacks inside their homes. Undoubtedly, the initial perceptions and belief systems that whites and blacks have of each other prior to the physical integration of neighborhoods will in a large measure condition them for subsequent social interaction and, possibly, social integration. Social integration of blacks with whites may also be fostered if there is equality or superiority of blacks in terms of socioeconomic status relative to whites in their new neighborhoods. Such upwardly mobile blacks tend to be better educated, to own their homes,[9] and to have relatively higher incomes than their new white neighbors. Perhaps this last fact alone makes them more acceptable. Although there may be merit in this assumption, other factors may also be important. For example, recent sociological research in this area suggests that the degree of cosmopolitanism possessed by the white person may be positively associated with a predisposition toward social integration with blacks who move into predominantly white areas. Cosmopolitanism is a multivariate concept, including such dimensions as high culture or aesthetic appreciation, liberal political beliefs, and a more universalistic perception of life—thinking that is not constrained by community context. Thus the conclusion is that the higher the degree of cosmopolitanism among white neighbors, the more tolerant they appear to be concerning social integration with blacks.[10] However, the predominant evidence suggests that even as blacks change their residences outward into the suburban ring, they are not likely to be physically integrated into predominantly white neighborhoods in appreciable numbers. Few whites may even know of the presence of blacks in the community. On the other hand, a resegregation of blacks into identifiable black sections of the suburban community, may heighten visibility as well as social boundaries. In the latter instance social contact between the races will be minimal at best. And the pattern of racial separation continues to persist. At this juncture a major point should be reiterated. It is highly doubtful that the motivation of blacks for housing integration or desegregation is social integration with whites. But the majority of black Americans do wish to obliterate discriminatory *behavior* of white Americans so that blacks, too, can have equal access to decent housing.

TECHNIQUES OF DISCRIMINATION IN HOUSING

Discrimination in housing is a major social problem. It is deeply ingrained in American life and exacerbates already strained relations between the races. And it is the most basic manifestation of racial apartheid.

in the United States. Over time several techniques of discrimination that effectively barred blacks from having access to decent housing were institutionalized. These techniques will be discussed next.

Government Policy. Historically, the federal government has been the major perpetrator of housing discrimination. The historical antecedent for present-day conditions and inequities can be found in policy mandates promulgated by federal and local agencies, as well as in a policy of calculated inaction or "benign neglect." It should be noted that restrictive covenants, which will be discussed in greater detail shortly, preceded the Federal Housing Administration (FHA) by several years. But the government set the original standards that began and fostered residential segregation that effectively prevented blacks from having equal access with whites to decent housing. How did this situation become so pervasive in American communities? Beginning in the early 1930s, when this nation was deeply entrenched in a dehumanizing economic depression, the federal government embarked on a housing program designed to bring relief and to improve the quality of housing mainly for white Americans. It embarked on a program predicated on the assumption that Americans had the right to own single-family dwellings. This was the theme that emerged from the President's Conference on Homebuilding and Home Ownership in 1932, which, in turn, led to federal intervention in financing single-family homes by a number of new methods, among them: (1) the amortization of long-range mortgages, (2) provisions for federal insurances of home mortgages, and (3) assistance in securing housing credit needed over a relatively long period of time.[11]

The federal program led to the establishment of specific agencies that further stimulated the development of private dwellings, particularly for white Americans. Foremost among the agencies created during the New Deal period were: (1) the FHA, established as a requirement of the National Housing Act of 1934; (2) the Federal Home Loan Bank System, established in 1932; (3) the Home Owner's Loan Corporation; and (4) the Federal Farm Mortgage Corporation. The policies of the FHA were discriminatory from its inception. Beginning in 1935, for example, its handbooks dissuaded residential integration by discouraging the granting of mortgages for houses that were not in racially separate areas of the community. The FHA had redlined many neighborhoods, separating black and white residential areas from each other for the purpose of determining eligibility for FHA home mortages. Banks, insurance companies, and private lenders were willing accomplices in the process of redlining and segregating residential areas, basing their refusal to invest in home mortgages for blacks on articulated FHA policies.[12] The policies of federal agencies not only perpetuated housing segregation with federal approbation but also encouraged the state and local levels to engage in practices that proved to be substantially more blatant and divisive. Thus the state and local agencies implemented legal restraints that, among other things, established residential zoning as a legitimate technique for maintaining and enforcing racial separation. Some enforced block-by-block segregation, while others vehemently and aggressively implemented restrictive covenants. The all-white National Association of Real Estate Boards, which throughout most of its 65 years of existence has barred black people, enthusiastically endorsed this approach.

The FHA policies during the 1930s and 1940s did not completely satisfy its administrators, who seemed bent on creating and institutionalizing differences in the quality of housing for blacks and whites. Following the promulgation of the United States Housing Act of 1937, for example, the construction of public housing was to serve as a major instrument for combating the last stages of a lingering economic depression. Initially, housing units that were constructed housed the white population for the most part and admitted relatively few blacks. Public housing was, therefore, originally addressed to the needs of poor whites, but today it is assumed that public housing is mainly to house poor blacks. In some cities, as was previously stated, this is quite true. For example, 50 of Chicago's 54 housing projects are more than 99 percent black. In the remaining four, however, the black proportion does not reach one-twelfth of the total number of residents.[13] Consider the fact, though, that in the years since 1937, federally subsidized public housing agencies constructed only about a million units.

But, in approximately the same period of time, by virtue of guarantees under FHA insurance, more than *10 million* units have been constructed for middle- and upper-income groups—largely white. Immediately after the end of World War II, even when the official policy of refusing to finance unsegregated housing was abrogated in 1949, the FHA continued to give preference to the financing of single-family dwellings in the growing white suburban ring. Not only did the FHA turn a deaf ear on housing for people whose earnings were below national median family incomes and for the elderly poor, but it did little to facilitate the construction of public houses for such groups. Even more amazingly, it encouraged the white exodus from the inner cities to the suburbs. One consequence of this is that not even 2 percent of all housing starts are in the area of public housing.

The policies of the various federal agencies helped to systematize many damaging stereotypes concerning the incorporation of the black population into residential neighborhoods and to institutionalize all forms of racial segregation in housing. Myths were used to rationalize housing discrimination, and for a significant number of white homeowners and for black middle-class social climbers the myths assumed an aura of reality. One of these more widely held beliefs is that property value automatically depreciates once blacks move into a neighborhood. A series of sound and thoroughly systematic studies, beginning with the classical works of Luigi Laurenti,[14] has failed to verify this assumption. Again, blacks who desegregate a white neighborhood are in the main economically much better off than their new white neighbors. They are not the equivalents of the European white ethnic immigrant family who buys a home. In the latter case, *all* members of the household—husband, wife, and children—participate to make the purchase of the new house a cooperative venture. In the case of blacks the purchasing of a house as well as its maintenance are a collaborative effort of only the husband and wife at best.

It is often assumed, particularly in the inner city, that black movement into a given dwelling is followed by housing deterioration. But this argument fails to take into consideration the already seriously deteriorating conditions of these dwellings when blacks inherited them from the white middle and working classes. Often, to make them salable these houses have been given cosmetic treatments that hide their basic dilapidation until the sale is completed. Thus the filtering process by which the more economically advantaged groups vacate homes in one area as they obtain newer ones in other areas does not necessarily mean that blacks obtain houses of substantially high quality. When people who have limited incomes for repair and maintenance purchase houses in filtered areas, the process of deterioration already begun will proceed, like a kind of self-fulfilling prophecy, to its predictable end.

The Real-Estate System. The chicanery of the real-estate institution has also prevented blacks from attaining equal access to decent housing. On a more formal level, real-estate boards, which are controlled by whites followed a code of segregation and racial separation during the 1930s, 1940s, and 1950s. There were no black realtors, or at least they were not in sufficient numbers, until the end of World War II. Even then, they were not members of the National Association of Real Estate Boards, which controlled and monopolized the housing market. Because of this few blacks were approved for showing and selling houses to black people; those who were approved could not use the registered term "realtor," which was reserved for white entrepreneurs in real estate. Blacks then coined their own term to describe their activities in real estate, and black realtors became known as realtists when they formed the National Association of Real Estate Brokers in 1947.[15] Meanwhile, white realtors either refused to show houses to potential black buyers, or claimed that the house had just been purchased; or when finally forced to show a house to black buyers, they would often inflate its price beyond the reach of the buyer, or they would handle the transaction in such a manner as to insult the intelligence of the buyer. These practices all too frequently forced blacks to withdraw from seeking housing in "all-white areas" and to make a painful retreat to the ghetto.

Not infrequently, real-estate associations and some firms were in collusion with neighborhood associations, banks, mortgage firms, and lending agencies. Neighborhood associations entered into agreements with some real-estate agencies guaranteeing them the prerogative of approving a potential buyer in their neighborhood before completing the final agreement to purchase. Some of these associations went so far as to assign a ranking system by which points were awarded potential buyers on the basis of color, education, income, occupation, and general desirability. These agreements effectively excluded blacks as well as other ethnic minorities considered as "undesirables." Moreover, having been told that blacks were not acceptable to the members of the neighborhood association or, primarily, its leadership structure, blacks would occasionally be gently dissuaded from pursuing the issue any further on the pretext that "they would not be happy in such an incompatible area." Banks and mortgage and lending agencies refused to grant mortgages or to provide financial assistance needed to complete the deal if, indeed, blacks had managed to get that far in the transaction. Occasionally, they rationalized their refusals with claims of potential loss of white business—whites threatened to take their business elsewhere if blacks were permitted to obtain mortgages and to purchase houses. Appraisals were distorted, values inflated, and blacks were declared ineligible for loans.

Real-estate agents also drew upon other discriminatory techniques designed to dissuade blacks from a course of residential desegregation or from the pursuit of adequate housing. Thus blacks were steered away from housing units situated in predominantly white areas to areas that were largely black or already physically integrated. This was often done on the pretext of group compatibility. Others used the common practice of *block-busting*, which generated panic selling by white residents. Unscrupulous realtors would suggest to white homeowners that, following the entry of sometimes a single black family into one block, the entire block would be "going black." Fueled with the fears and myths of property depreciation, whites were admonished to "sell now" or later suffer a great financial loss. Many chose to sell and often at low costs. Block by block, this process systematically accomplished white removal and replacement by blacks who purchased these houses at hugely inflated prices. Realtors thereby reaped excessive profits from expanding the black ghetto and driving a wedge between the races.

Zoning Laws. When these techniques failed in their effectiveness, and sometimes they were unsuccessful deterrents, state and local officials resorted to zoning for exclusionary purposes. Historically, zoning is an antecedent practice to a number of techniques presently in use to oppose neighborhood desegregation. It first came to the attention of the United States Supreme Court in the case of *Buchanan* v. *Worley* (1917). Louisville, Kentucky, had a statute that forbade incursion of members of one race into an area chiefly occupied by members of another race. The Supreme Court rejected this statute. Then, in 1927, New Orleans (in *Harmon* v. *Tyler*) attempted to exclude members of one race from an area chiefly occupied by members of another race without obtaining the latter's consent. In 1930 zoning was again tested in the case of the *City of Richmond* v. *Deans* because it had been used as a means of supporting the ban against interracial marriages. Under this mandate a person could not buy in an area where the majority of the residents were persons he could not legally marry.[16] In both the *Harmon* and *Richmond* cases the U.S. Supreme Court reaffirmed and extended its decision reached in the *Buchanan* case.

Today, zoning laws are much subtler than those laws enacted prior to the advent of World War II. Zoning advocates attempt to circumvent racial considerations in their construction. But it is generally conceded that exclusions by race are the basic underpinnings of many zoning statutes or regulations regardless of how subtly they are hidden. Equally fundamental is the use of zoning ordinances in the basic struggle of control over land and its use. Zoning may be used for both exclusionary purposes and to determine how land may be best used for maximum benefit of the community; but when housing is the issue, zoning is used exclusively to restrict entry of certain groups of people into a community and to determine where they shall be contained. Some zoning ordinances impose restrictions on lot size, as in East Haddam, Connecticut, which in 1967 implemented a proposal establishing minimum lot sizes of one or two acres of land. In the prestigious North Plains area the minimum lot size was set at four acres. The Supreme Court had already ruled that the efforts of Sharon, Massachusetts, in 1964 to rezone residential areas into four-acre lots were unconstitutional. Others establish acceptable footage requirements for new buildings and rigidly apply them to blacks but relax them for whites who wish to construct in the same area; or they bar apartments, public housing, multifamily dwellings, and cooperatives. Some set aside land for industrial use so as to restrict the amount of residential land that might be available for housing unwelcomed people. Similarly, municipalities have condemned land after learning that blacks would soon be occupying those areas.[17] The net effect of zoning regulations has been to continue denying blacks an opportunity to move into suburbia and, therefore, to confine them to restricted residential areas within the city boundaries.

Restrictive Covenants. At the same time that zoning laws were becoming institutionalized, another devious method of racial exclusion was applied to prevent residential desegregation. These were called restrictive covenants, which are agreements in the purchase contract that a given piece of property will not be sold to certain categories of people. These contracts were to exist from 50 years to perpetuity and barred sale to such groups as blacks, Jews, Arabs, Armenians, Italians, Koreans, Asian Americans, American Indians, Spanish-speaking Americans, Greeks, and others. Clearly, their intent was to exclude swarthy-complexioned Americans and, more forcefully, in some areas to extirpate blacks from certain residential areas. Many white Americans who shared similar sentiments knowingly and willingly endorsed this practice by including such clauses in their property contracts. In 1948, however, in the case of *Shelly* v. *Kraemer*, the U.S. Supreme Court stated that restrictive covenants were unenforceable. Subsequently the so-called Van Sweringen covenant arose, which forbids the sale of property without consent of its original owner. Other variations of this covenant prevent the sale of property without consent of club members where neighborhood recreational facilities are involved, or the occupant may be expected to lease the land for 99 years without the possibility of transferring the property to another party.[18] When some real-estate brokers began to disregard restrictive covenants following the decision reached in the *Shelly* case, persons adhering to the covenants sued them. Thus in the case of *Barrows* v. *Jackson* of 1953—which was sponsored, as were all the previously mentioned Supreme Court cases, by the Legal Defense and Education Fund of the NAACP—the Court concluded that damages could not be exacted from persons who had violated restrictive covenants. To award damages, the court concluded, would be tantamount to acknowledging their enforceability.

Violence. A further deterrent to the physical integration of blacks and whites is the penchant of whites to resort to numerous forms of violence against invading blacks. When a black dentist in Cleveland attempted to move into the Forest Hills section of Cleveland Heights, Ohio, a few years ago, his house was firebombed. He was left unmolested only after receiving police protection and after it became clear that he and his family would not be driven away. Similar episodes of physical attacks against black families are repeated again and again all across the country.

The attempts to construct Kawaida Towers in Newark, in 1972–1974, and of blacks to gain entry into the Forest Hills section of Queens in New York City illustrate the convergence of fear, myths, prejudice, and interracial or ethnic conflict involved in the physical integration of blacks into housing areas where whites are in the majority. The Kawaida Towers project is a proposed 16-story 210-unit apartment building in Newark, under the sponsorship of a Pan African organization headed by an avowed black nationalist, playwright Imamu Amira Baraka (Leroi Jones). It is to be located in the vicinity of both two-family homes and apartment buildings in the predominantly Italian-American north ward. The Italian members of the adjacent community expressed the typical fears commonly voiced about black intrusion into white areas: depreciated property values, increased crime rates, endangerment by blacks to the safety of other people, the inevitability of a slum if blacks moved in, and the increasing pressure on an already overcrowded condition in the neighborhood schools. They attempted to block construction of the Kawaida Towers and set the stage for a verbal and sometimes physical battle.

The Forest Hills section of Queens proposed for scatter-site three 24-story towers containing 840 units of public housing for low-income groups was occupied primarily by middle-class American Jews. Fears of inundation by hordes of welfare families were expressed by these long-established residents, even though 40 percent of the housing units would be reserved for the elderly poor, both black and white, some of whom would come from the Forest Hill area. After a number of verbal battles and confrontations, the issue was finally "resolved" by reducing the number of units to 432 apartments, which would house approximately 1,300 people, an almost 50 percent reduction in the original number planned for the project.

The pattern emerging from these two illustrations seems to suggest that in the redistribution of low-income blacks from one area to another when the new site selected is contiguous to another ethnic or racial minority area, these minority groups frequently reveal the degree to which they have internalized the prejudices and the fears of the dominant group to which they now belong. They, too, will resort to traditional practices to protect their property and rights, which they regard as inviolable.

As a consequence of the pernicious forms of discrimination and exclusionary practices described here, most American cities have become almost incurably segregated. Blacks and whites are so separated that, according to studies by Taeuber and Taeuber,[19] adequate integration in housing would demand 88 percent of the black population to move from their present blocks to white blocks. This is, of course, a most formidable task and one that is not likely to be accomplished in the foreseeable future. Some cities are more segregated than others and require substantially greater dispersion of blacks on a block-by-block basis to achieve random patterns of residential integration. Pierre DeVise claimed in a 1971 study that Chicago is the most residentially segregated city in the United States.[20] Among the 20 most rigidly segregated cities in the United States only two Southern cities, Dallas and Houston (significantly, these are rather new cities), are included among the first 10. The remainder are Northern cities: Chicago, Indianapolis, Milwaukee, Dallas, St. Louis, Cleveland, Detroit, Baltimore, Houston, and Philadelphia. The next ten most segregated American cities in this order are: Boston, Memphis, Phoenix, New Orleans, San Antonio, San Diego, Washington, D.C., New York, Los Angeles, and San Francisco.

Urban Renewal. The U.S. Congress authorized a program of slum clearance in Title I of the Housing Act of 1949, which was again expanded in 1954. The original intent of this program was to clear slum land, redevelop it, and render it more habitable for former occupants. In time, because of the abysmal failure of the program and the disproportionate dislocations of urban blacks, urban renewal became synonymous with "black removal." Few public housing projects, for example, were constructed on land vacated by the largely nonwhite urban poor. The $1 billion appropriated for slum clearance and relocation of displaced families rarely aided blacks removed from their homes. Instead, blacks were shifted from one area to another. Even when new housing was constructed on land they had previously occupied, rents usually became too prohibitive to permit them to return to their original communities. In other instances high-rise governmental centers replaced houses previously occupied by black people. In some instances local agencies were unable to build anything because of a shortage of funds or because they had to scuttle poorly conceived redevelopment programs. Consequently, in several cities one can observe vacant block after vacant block in extremely expensive land areas and abandoned buildings condemned for urban renewal but never razed.

Black Resistance to Desegregation. Another explanation for the failure of physical desegregation of housing lies in unavailability of blacks willing to desegregate. Many blacks believe that residential relocation severs established community ties and fragments institutions; more and more black people have become increasingly inured to white resistance and discriminatory patterns of behavior and now question the value of the desegregation effort. Still other blacks feel an intense need for blacks to remain in identifiable neighborhoods set off by a clearly defined territorial demarcation within which the right of self-determination, community control, and the development of black institutions can be assured. They envision the racial ghetto as a promise of a strong power base for black people from which they can launch an all-out assault against a system that has perpetually denied them open admission as equals. Blacks in this group prefer to invest their time and energy in a continung process of institution building and the strengthening of a black value system that can effectively impart a new sense of self-worth to black people. They reject the notion that blacks can only be free if they cavort with people of another race or if they are physically integrated with them. They do not believe that the myriad problems of the racial ghetto are insurmountable; they feel certain that with sufficient financial assistance black people have the talent and the technological know-how to solve these problems. Blacks who refuse to move from the black ghetto realize that the ghetto is a bitter and sometimes truculent place. It is diverse, excitingly viable, and it belongs to blacks who are determined to extricate its control from white bankers, mortgagers, realtors, and other members of the power structure who originally seized control of it and relegated blacks to a colonial status. The unanswered and difficult question is: To what degree can blacks succeed in this enterprise?

LEGISLATION AND CHANGE

Just as the federal government has traditionally been responsible for so, deeply embedding residential segregation in American life, it has also been instrumental in effectuating changes in the quality of housing available to blacks and other minorities. Beginning in 1962 a number of decrees, pieces of legislation, and Supreme Court decisions have improved housing available to blacks.

The first major crack in the wall of housing segregation occurred when President Kennedy issued Executive Order 11063, which prohibited discrimination in federally assisted housing. By this time approximately 17 states and some 56 municipalities had enacted antidiscriminatory legislation in housing. However, this order was not all-inclusive and covered only 13 percent of housing not previously covered by existing local or state statutes and only 23 percent of new housing starts.[21] Persons who violated the terms of the presidential order were subject to contract termination and to refusal of further governmental aid. By 1965, 20 states and the District of Columbia had enacted antidiscriminatory housing legislation covering some 80 million Americans.[22]

Although the Civil Rights Act of 1964 forbade segregation and discrimination in any program using federal funds, it had limited effectiveness because the act was not enforced widely enough. Pressure continued for a stronger law granting extensive enforcement authority. Some observers claimed that such a law was not approved by Congress in 1966 because of the direct action Dr. King and the Southern Christian Leadership Conference mounted through incursions into the white neighborhoods of metropolitan Chicago. If that is so, it is an ironical twist of history that his assassination may have been the prime mover in persuading Congress to enact a strong antidiscrimination bill in the Civil Rights Act of 1968, approved two weeks following his death. The crucial section pertaining specifically to housing was Title VIII of the act, which became effective in 1970. Under its terms, prohibitions against discrimination covered approximately 80 percent of the nation's housing, excluding only the 20 percent that fell in the category of privately owned two-to-four dwelling units. Enforcement was theoretically assured by a tortuous time-consuming process of complaint filing, investigation, persuasion for compliance, opportunities for relief, and the right of the U. S. Attorney General to intercede by taking court action to assure compliance and relief. Damages of up to $1,000 could be collected once discrimination had been proved. If the complainant persisted and had the time to pursue this unwieldy process, and assuming that he won the case, the house or the apartment could be sold or leased to him. Often, because the process is lengthy, persons in need of legal assistance give up in exasperation. Consequently many violators go unpunished, and illegal practices continue only slightly abated.

Finally, the Housing and Urban Development Act of 1968 (considered by President Johnson as a major breakthrough in meeting the problems of the poor), followed by similar acts in 1969 and 1970, was designed either to create or to rehabilitate some 26 million housing units over a ten-year period. This included about 6 million federally subsidized dwellings as a response to the specific needs of the poorer elements in the Johnson administration's Great Society. Included in this program were low-rent housing owned by the government, urban renewal, the development of wholly new cities, and the famous sections 235 and 236, which were essentially subsidy programs permitting the government to assume all interest costs in excess of 1 percent charged by the lender for home buyers and renters, respectively. The implementation of these sections resulted in an increase from 156,000 to 390,000 of subsidized units between 1968 and 1971; the majority were located in the central city.

Although these acts did permit a significant number of new housing starts, they also raised the level of expectations among literally thousands of urban blacks for new housing that never came their way. Further, it set the stage for victimization of blacks by money-hungry investors, bankers, mortgagers, and realtors. Unaccustomed to the intricacies of home purchasing, many unsophisticated inner-city blacks fell prey to unscrupulous speculators and incompetent FHA staff and inspectors who were easy marks for bribes. A typical devious practice was for speculators to purchase old homes and dress them up with superficial repairs in order to enhance their marketability. An FHA appraiser would assign them an inflated value, and unsuspecting buyers would be totally unaware of the hidden defects until later. The defective wiring, inadequate plumbing, and leaky roofs were so costly to repair that some recent homeowners, who had invested comparatively little, simply decided to abandon the dwellings rather than assume the exorbitant repair costs. After these defaults the abandoned property was returned to the federal government.[23] In the sale of rental property similar experiences were reported. The developers paid little attention to the needs and demands of tenants. As a result, many tenants walked away from their dwellings. In Detroit alone an estimated 10,000 houses have been abandoned, and the Department of Housing and Urban Development now owns more than 7,500 single-family units and possibly some 50,000 homes throughout the country through foreclosures. Moreover, if foreclosures and defaults are combined, the federal government could possibly hold almost 240,000 subsidized housing units in the foreseeable future.[24] One experimental method of attacking the problems of defaults and foreclosures is to lease with an option to buy the property. Another technique for reclaiming abandoned developments is through urban homesteading, in which dwellings are purchased for as little as $1 as an incentive to return people to vacated urban areas.

PROTEST ORGANIZATIONS

Earlier, we stated that the proportion of blacks who moved into suburbia doubled during the decade of the 1960s but that their relative percentages of the total suburban population did not change during that period. We further explained that this situation was a direct result of the steady exodus of the white population from the city largely with the direct assistance of federal loans and FHA programs and because of whites' ability to obtain much needed financial guidance and assistance from banks, mortgage firms, and other lending institutions. However, the great outflow of the white population should not be permitted to obscure the significance of the number of American blacks who have managed to move into more desirable areas of both the city and the suburbs as a consequence of enforcement (although of questionable effectiveness most times) of legislation enacted during the time of the Great Society.

Open housing was neither a spontaneous occurrence nor the work of a single racial group. The battle for open occupancy of apartments and single-family homes assumed the characteristics of a social movement as is well documented by Juliet Saltman in *Open Housing as a Social Movement*.[25] As such, it involved a huge cast of characters and organizations cutting across all racial and ethnic lines. The effort involved the combined work of the National Committee Against Discrimination in Housing (NCDH), the tireless, sustained, and largely legal efforts of the NAACP, the "dwell-in movement"* sponsored by CORE during the early 1960s, and the Operation Equality Program sponsored by the National Urban League during the latter part of the 1960s and into the 1970s.

Collectively, these organizations attacked problems of unfairness in pricing, purchasing, and the previously discussed strategies and techniques

---

* Dwell-ins were a form of sit-in which involved prolonged occupation of a real-estate salesman's office in order to prevent discrimination in the sale of housing.

used to circumvent open housing. They lobbied with both major political parties at local and state levels, attempting to persuade governmental and political bodies to enact open-housing legislation; systematically, they attacked racial quotas of the FHA and urged appointment of intergroup experts to deal with the problems related to physical integration of blacks into previously all-white residential communities. Suits were initiated to control the unjust dimensions of urban renewal, to stop serious dislocation and displacement of the poor, and to protect tenants' rights. (For example, the ruling in the 1969 case of *Thorpe* v. *Housing Authority of Durham, North Carolina,* prohibited landlords and other housing authorities from evicting occupants without fair notice or the possibility of arranging a hearing if warranted. Significantly, this decision affected almost 205 million low-rent tenants in public housing at the time.) Conciliation, moral suasion, and direct confrontation strategies were also employed in order to improve housing for blacks and other dispossessed groups.[26]

In addition to the aforementioned groups, it is important to note that throughout the past two decades, especially, countless individuals and local fair housing organizations were instrumental in effecting change as part of a national movement against segregation in housing and for the opening up of decent housing to the black community.

BLACKS IN REAL ESTATE

Today, blacks control about 2 percent of the $39 billion housing market. Although this is a paltry sum of money in view of the numbers of blacks in the American population, it is, however, a significant improvement over the position blacks occupied in real estate prior to the 1960s. One explanation for this limited success lies in the formation and subsequent work of the 6,000-member National Association of Real Estate Brokers. This organization, organized in 1947, was the stimulus for the development of major black-owned mortgage firms and institutions such as United Mortgage Bankers of America, formed when the all-white Mortgage Bankers of America was inaccessible to blacks. The black association of real-estate boards also established a series of auxiliary agencies necessary for real-estate operation and management. Thus various specialists established themselves, including black developers, appraisers, brokers, and managers. Today blacks are involved in property management, mortgage banking, and the buying and selling of real estate. No American city with a fair-sized black population is without black-owned real-estate firms serving the needs of the black community. In addition there are some 22 black-owned mortgage banking institutions in the United States. But blacks are still in the incipient stages of real-estate activity. Notwithstanding, they have begun to move aggressively in this field and to maximize their resources through cooperation, consolidation, and reciprocal relationships. Their position remains somewhat uncertain, however, since so much of the business conducted by blacks is tied to the federal government. Consequently, black realtors continually fight against racism for a better distribution of wealth and income among blacks and for a more aggressive housing development program under both federal and private sponsorship.[27]

Stimulated by the housing legislation of the late 1960s, the federal government approved funds for the establishment of several new towns. Among the first ten approved was a $14-million loan (actually, the right to issue government-backed bonds in that amount) to Floyd McKissick, former National Director of CORE. McKissick's new town, called Soul City, is located ten miles south of the Virginia border near the triangle cities of Durham, Raleigh, and Chapel Hill, North Carolina. This will be a kind of "free-standing town" in the sense that it is to be a self-contained community. Soul City, North Carolina, is so far the only complete community planned by a black developer that is backed by the Housing and Urban Development Department. This is a major undertaking calling for the investment of considerable capital outlay and government investment as well as the utilization of an array of black professionals, who are in short supply (for example, specialists in mining, soil analysis, sanitary engineering, and planning and development—these are areas in which the numbers of blacks are minimal). The response of black people to Soul City is predictably mixed. Some applaud McKissick for his entrepreneurial stewardship, while others regard his association with the Nixon administration as something approaching turncoat behavior, especially given his militance in the civil rights movement.

POLICY COMMITMENTS

The Kerner Commission sponsored during President Johnson's administration suggested a number of basic strategies for attacking the housing problem. Among its more salient imperatives were a demand for more decent housing in all sectors, public and private, and an enforcement of all open-housing laws. The very fact that the housing problem reached such gigantic dimensions during the 1970s is telling proof of the failure of existing legislation, a failure that is not indicative of poor laws necessarily but of a lack of will to enforce them. Housing is a victim of political expediency and reflects the magnitude of racism and the lack of commitment by public and private sectors in bringing relief to an appalling condition. New policies must be formulated to confront head-on the issues of interest rates, housing supplements, and the quagmire of public outlays.

NOTES

1. Nathan Glazer, "Housing Problems and Housing Policies," *The Public Interest* (Spring 1967), pp. 21–51.

2. Joseph P. Fried, *Housing Crisis USA* (Baltimore: Penguin Books, 1971), p. 21.

3. *The Social and Economic Status of the Black Population in the United States, 1971*, U.S. Department of Commerce, Bureau of the Census, Current Population Reports, Series P-23, No. 42 (Washington, D.C.: Government Printing Office, 1972), p. 97.

4. Ronald J. McAllister, et al., "Residential Mobility of Blacks and Whites: A National Longitudinal Study," *American Journal of Sociology*, 77 (November 1971), pp. 448–453.

5. *Ibid.*, p. 453.

6. Rudolf Heberle, "The Normative Element in the Neighborhood Relations," *Pacific Sociological Review* (Spring 1960), p. 79.

7. Carolyn R. Zeul and Craig R. Humphrey, "The Integration of Suburban Blacks in Suburban Neighborhoods: A Reexamination of the Contact Hypotheses," *Social Problems*, 8 (Spring 1971), pp. 462–474.

8. Henry Stetler, *Racial Integration in Private Interracial Neighborhoods in Connecticut* (Hartford, Conn.: Commission on Human Rights, 1957).

9. Karl E. Taeuber and Alma Taeuber, *Negroes in Cities* (Chicago: Aldine, 1965), pp. 155–165.

10. Zeul and Humphrey, *op. cit.*, p. 472.

11. Glazer, *op. cit.*

12. Monroe W. Karmen, "Government Programs," *Black Enterprise*, 3 (August 1972), p. 22.

13. Robert E. Forman, *Black Ghettos and White Ghettos and Slums* (Englewood Cliffs, N.J.: Prentice-Hall, 1971), p. 78.

14. Luigi Laurenti, *Property Values and Race* (Berkeley, Calif.: University of California Press, 1960).

15. "Reality: Era of the Specialist," *Black Enterprise*, 3 (August 1972), p. 44.

16. Jack Greenberg, *Race Relations and the American Law* (New York: Columbia University Press, 1959), p. 276.

17. *Ibid.* Also see Herbert M. Franklin, "Zoning Laws, *Black Enterprise*, 3 (August 1972), p. 25.

18. Greenberg, *op. cit.*, p. 283.

19. Karl E. Taeuber and Alma Taeuber, "Negro Population in the United States," in J. P. Davis (ed.) *The American Negro Reference Book* (Englewood Cliffs, N.J.: Prentice-Hall, 1966).

20. Pierre DeVise, *Chicago's Widening Color Gap: 1971 Status Report* (Chicago: The Inter-University Social Research Committee).

21. Charles Abrams, "The Housing Problem and the Negro," *Daedalus* (Winter 1966), pp. 64–66.

22. George Greer and Eunice Greer, *Housing Segregation and the Goals of the Great Society* (Chicago: Quandrangle Books, 1966), p. 52.

23. Karmen, *op. cit.*, p. 48.

24. *Ibid.*

25. Juliet Saltman, *Open Housing as a Social Movement: Challenges, Conflicts and Change* (Lexington, Mass.: Heath Lexington Books, 1971), pp. 531–539.

26. *Thirty Years of Building American Justice* (New York: The NAACP Legal Defense and Educational Fund, 1970).

27. *Black Enterprise*, August 1972, p. 44.

6 | BLACK CAPITALISM AND HUMAN RESOURCES

In recent years much has been said about black capitalism and the need for human resource development as instruments for eradicating economic poverty and underdevelopment in the black community. Of major concern are issues such as the present state of black businesses, their capacity to survive in a manner to serve needs of black people, their ability to become economically viable institutions within the American economic system, and the articulation of strategies or programs that will help to create a well-trained manpower base among blacks. This chapter focuses on the structure of the contemporary black enterprise system and some of the factors that affect both its survival and viability as well as on problems of manpower development.

The structure of present-day black enterprises has its foundation in the construction of parallel institutions described in earlier chapters. Hence because of institutionalized segregation, blacks necessarily formed a business structure that catered almost exclusively to personal service functions (for example, accommodations, barbering, cosmetics, burial establishments, small-scale retail establishments) not provided by the larger society.[1] Primarily because of their disadvantaged economic condition, particularly the paucity of capital, blacks have not generally been involved in producing, manufacturing, and large-scale manufacturing. Nor have they owned huge corporations or become mining industrialists, for example. Rather, black businesses were forced to become and remain relatively small scale, highly focused, and limited in their capacity to generate either capital or large-scale employment of black people.

CONTEMPORARY STRUCTURE OF THE BLACK ENTERPRISE SYSTEM

Studies of businesses within the black community reveal: (1) that whites, not blacks, still own a significant majority of businesses in the black community; (2) that white owners more often tend both to reside elsewhere and to hire persons from outside the black community and, in general, white people continue to dominate the economic life of the black community. In this way whites again play the role of domestic colonizers controlling the business life within the ghetto colony.[2] According to a 1969 survey of the U.S. Department of Commerce, as reported in the population census of 1970, the 163,000 black-owned businesses in America represented a mere 2 percent of the total number of enterprises in the United States. The majority of these firms are concentrated in retailing, selected services, contract construction, transportation and other utilities, finance, insurance, real estate, and in a variety of unspecified industries. An examination of Table 6-1 indicates that blacks own less than 2 percent of the contract construction businesses, two-tenths of 1 percent of wholesale trade establishments, and slightly more than 2 percent of the retail trade firms. In addition, not even 5 percent of those businesses engaging in transportation and public utilities are black owned, and blacks own a mere six-tenths of 1 percent of all organizations combined involved in finance, insurance, and real estate. A further examination of types of black businesses shows that they are less likely to involve a high degree of technology and that they are more noncorporate in character.

The combined businesses owned by blacks receive not even one-half of 1 percent of the total gross receipts of all businesses in the United States. This observation is of great significance at a time when some Americans strongly believe that a significant class of black capitalists has emerged and that most black Americans are now middle class. It is only in the area of selected services, as Table 6-2 shows, that the proportion of gross receipts received by black businesses in relation to the total gross receipts exceeds 1 percent (1.1 percent).

Black-owned businesses are chiefly concentrated in the personal services today as they have always been in the past. Specifically, more than a third of them are in this category, but they account for only 9 percent of all

TABLE 6-1.

Number and Gross Receipts for All and Black-Owned Firms, by Industry Division: 1969

(*Numbers in thousands. Receipts in millions of dollars*)

Industry Division	Firms			Gross Receipts		
	All Firms[1] (Number)	Black Owned Firms (Number)	Percent Black of All Firms	All Firms[1]	Black-Owned Firms	Percent Black of All Firms
All industries	7,489	163	2.2	$1,497,969	$4,474	0.3
Contract construction	856	16	1.9	92,291	464	0.5
Manufactures	401	3	0.8	588,682	303	0.1
Transportation and other public utilities	359	17	4.7	106,040	211	0.2
Wholesale trade	434	1	0.2	213,196	385	0.2
Retail trade	2,046	45	2.2	320,751	1,932	0.6
Finance, insurance, and real estate	1,223	8	0.6	86,670	288	0.3
Selected services	1,803	56	3.1	61,858	663	1.1
Other industries and not classified	367	17	4.5	28,481	228	0.8

[1] Based on data from IRS statistics of income for 1967.

SOURCE: U.S. Department of Commerce, Social and Economic Statistics Administration, Bureau of the Census.

gross receipts of black enterprises. Eating and drinking places, comprising slightly more than one-sixth of black enterprises, account for one-eighth of gross receipts. Food stores are second in importance in terms of numbers and gross receipts. But the fact that automobile dealers and service stations comprise less than a tenth of all black-owned firms but rank first in gross receipts may suggest that black entrepreneurs may wish to expand their investments in this area. However, the impact of the energy crisis on this sector may be so severe as to discourage expansion.

TABLE 6-2.

Ten Most Important Industry Groups of Black-Owned Firms Ranked by Receipts: 1969

Rank	Industry	Firms (Thousands)	Gross Receipts (Millions)
	All industry groups	163	$4,474
	Ten most important industry groups	97	3,072
	Percent of all industry groups	60	69
	Percent	100	100
1	Automotive dealers and gasoline filling stations	7	21
2	Food stores	12	14
3	Wholesale trade	2	13
4	Eating and drinking places	15	12
5	Personal services	35	9
6	Special trade contractors	14	9
7	Miscellaneous retail stores	7	9
8	General building contractors	2	5
9	Trucking and warehousing	7	4
10	Insurance carrier	–	4

– Rounds to zero.

SOURCE: U.S. Department of Commerce, Social and Economic Statistics Administration, Bureau of the Census.

Black businesses tend to be small, self-owned, unevenly distributed in the country, and, characteristically, employ small numbers of individuals. Blacks are sole proprietors in more than nine-tenths of all black-owned businesses. According to the U.S. Department of Commerce, almost four-fifths of them (77 percent) do not have paid employees and, therefore, do not provide new jobs for members of the black community. The 152,000 paid employees of black businesses indicate that the ratio of paid employees to the number of black businesses is less than one per establishment. Obviously, most black establishments are mainly operated by a number of unpaid family members. Individually owned institutions are much more likely to engage paid employees than those businesses described as partnerships. Regionally, more than half of the black-owned businesses are located in the South, where institutionalized racial separation is more endemic and where the majority of blacks still live. That the North Central region of the country has the second largest concentration of black-owned businesses is consistent with population distribution trends and, perhaps, with opportunities afforded by the establishment of business in urban areas of the Midwest. (The reader's attention is called to the annual publication of a list of the top 100 black businesses by *Black Enterprise*. Space does not permit a listing of that sort here.) An examination of the top 100 black businesses indicates that only 15 percent are located in Washington, D.C., and Deep South states and, further, that the more successful in terms of size and assets are concentrated in New York, California, Illinois, and Michigan.

A discussion of aggregates of businesses does not tell the whole story concerning the present state of black enterprises. A more definitive perspective regarding this matter can be gleaned from a descriptive analysis of specific categories of black enterprises. This kind of analysis, which follows next, also conveys more vividly major changes and, possibly, improvements in the efforts of blacks to become economically assimilated into American society.

Black Banks. As early as 1888 blacks were directly engaged in banking. In that year W. W. Browne, a Richmond, Virginia, minister, organized the first black-managed bank in the nation. Several banks were established, particularly in the South, over the next several decades so that by the outbreak of World War I approximately 55 black-owned banking institutions existed in the United States. The majority of them had been organized in close association with black churches, fraternal organizations, and insurance firms. Their survival rate was relatively short, primarily because of inadequate capital, poor clientele, and problems associated with management philosophy (for instance, stress given to investments in low-yield securities, doubtful real-estate ventures, and loans generating small returns to black banks).

The overwhelming majority of black-owned banks are a phenomenon of the post–World War II era. Almost two-thirds of them were organized after 1960, and more than one-half of the nation's 37 black-controlled banks were organized after 1965. Slightly less than one-half were established in 1968 and later, a manifestation of the growth of a black economy as well as the intervention of external agencies for economic advancement within the black community. The combined assets of the 37 banks are approximately $600 million, in contrast to the $700 billion for the American banking industry as a whole. This is equivalent to less than 1 percent of total bank assets in the nation's banks. In 1972 no black-controlled bank had assets of $50 million or more. Assets of four banks were between $40 and $49 million; two were between $30 and $39 million; four were between $20 and $29 million; and the rest had assets between $4 million and $19,999,000. Thus despite this growth, assets in black-controlled banks are relatively small. The significance of black banks, however, lies in both their present services as well as their potential for aiding in the rehabilitation of major segments of the black community—especially in black ghettos and depressed areas.

All presently existing black banks organized prior to World War II can be found in the South, specifically in North Carolina, Georgia, Tennessee, South Carolina, and the District of Columbia. None were in the North or border states until 1947, when the Douglass State Bank was organized in Kansas City, Kansas. It was not until 1964 that the Far West had its first black-controlled bank with the establishment of the Bank of Finance in Los Angeles. However, the majority of those organized after 1946 are located in the North and West. Five are in Chicago. One explanation for the seemingly disproportionate number found in Chicago may be the prohibitions against branch banking* in the state of Illinois.[3]

The paid work forces of the Seaway National Bank of Chicago, the nation's largest black-controlled bank, of New York's Freedom National Bank, and of Atlanta's Citizen's Trust Bank each exceed 100 employees. Of these three banks only the Atlanta bank was in existence prior to World War II. In general, the older banks have remained comparatively small in number of employees and assets; the most notable exception is the Mechanics and Farmers Bank established in 1907, which is also the sixth highest-ranking black-owned bank in total assets. The total number of persons employed at the 37 banks is 1,307 as of 1972. However, the five banks located in Chicago account for slightly more than a fifth of all persons employed in these institutions.

Traditionally, and in the most recent times, black banks have been founded theoretically to serve the exclusive needs of black people. But the day-to-day realities of business transactions within banking institutions contradict the theory. One of these realities is the disinclination of the established black banks to encourage loans for black community development. They seem to be much more conservative in their loan portfolios, less inclined to take risk applications, and much more oriented toward relatively safe time-proved investments. The older banks will more readily finance new automobiles and home mortgages, for example, than an application to develop a new business enterprise. In this respect they do not differ from the conservative white banks, which are more likely to approve a loan for a man's vacation than for his new business venture. The famous case of George E. Johnson, who founded the $20 million Johnson Cosmetics Company, illustrates this point. He tells the story of how he attempted to obtain a loan of $500 to initiate a new cosmetic firm. The bank manager

---

* Branch banking is maintaining complete banking facilities away from the main office. Prohibitions against branch banking permit establishment of more independent banks in contrast to subdivisions of others.

refused, considering a black man a high business risk. Later, he went to another branch and applied for the same sum but this time to take his wife on a vacation trip to California. The loan application was immediately honored. He used that sum to launch an amazing career. Today, less than a generation later, his firm has more than $20 million in annual sales of such commodities as Afro-Sheen and Ultra Sheen and is listed on the New York Stock Exchange with more than 1,000 stockholders.

In contrast to the more established black-controlled banks, the higher failure rate of newer banks is undoubtedly attributable to their seemingly greater responsiveness to make loans for black community development. They will invest more heavily in business loans, which do, in fact, have a much higher risk than either consumer or real-estate loans. Nevertheless, this more liberal orientation, in contrast to the more conservative philosophy of older institutions, reflects a commitment to help stimulate a more diversified business structure in the black community, which might, in turn, possibly broaden the base of the bank's wealth. But the problem of taking greater lending risks is miniscule when compared to the problem of under-capitalization, which is common to black-controlled banks. It is this perpetual undersupply of capital that forces some black bankers into a cautious and overprotective posture regarding loan portfolios. This situation also stimulated much agitation from community development advocates for greater assistance from white institutions doing business in the black community. It is one of the primary justifications for insistence by Reverend Jessie Jackson and the late Dr. Martin Luther King that whites who do business in black ghettos should help increase assets for black banks by depositing some of their profits in black banks. That the need for capital is serious is further shown by the load that black-controlled banks are expected to carry. As was mentioned earlier, the total assets of black banks are a minute share of the $700 billion in assets of the banking industry. White-controlled banks, with less than 1 percent of their assets directed in this manner, actually provide a small fraction of loans, on a comparative basis, for blacks and other minorities during the course of the year. By contrast black banks use approximately 10 percent of their assets for business loans.

Savings and Loan Associations. These financial institutions have larger assets but smaller numbers of employees than regular banks and trust companies. Their assets range from a high of more than $60 million to a low of $230,000. The number of persons employed does not exceed 60 but is as low as 1 full-time person. The 44 existing savings and loan associations originated as early as 1888 (the founding date for the Berean Savings Association in Philadelphia). The most recently established was the Security Federal Savings and Loan Association in Chattanooga, Tennessee in 1971.

Geographically, the associations are not well distributed, since almost 30 of them are located in the South and border states; the remaining 12 to 14 are unevenly dispersed in the North Central region, the East, and the Far West. Although they are located predominantly in urban communities, the absence of these associations in several cities having a large black populations illustrates the relative inaccessibility of banking institutions purportedly established to serve the needs of black people. For example, no savings and loan associations controlled by blacks exist in Newark and in Gary, Indiana, whose black population is in excess of 50 percent of the total population or in New Orleans or in Savannah, Georgia, which have approximately 45 percent black populations. Moreover, the savings and loan associations that do exist share the same shortcomings as the banks and trust companies discussed in the preceding section.

Life Insurance Companies. Without a doubt, throughout the history of the participation of black people in business ventures in the United States their most successful and largest enterprises have been and continue to be life insurance companies.[4] Like all other parallel institutions within the black community, they arose because of the discriminatory practices of a segregated society. As with banking institutions, life insurance companies originated in association with black churches, lodges, free masons, benevolent societies, and other voluntary associations. Also, they were not infrequently associated with funeral establishments. Throughout the South, for example, where black undertaking establishments were among the more successful enterprises, associated life insurance and burial companies arose in conjunction with them and flourished.[5]

Three factors account for their continued success and prosperity as economic enterprises: (1) prejudice, (2) discrimination, and (3) appeal to the emotions of black people of all socioeconomic groups. This appeal was addressed to a basic wish to see loved ones "put away" as stylishly as possible. This desire often resulted, even now, in a form of economic exploitation by the management of funeral or burial establishments, which often persuaded blacks, irrespective of social class identification, to provide the best arrangements for their deceased relatives. Expensive capital outlays would be required for a coffin, limousines, a wake, and other items. Thus the business of burying the deceased could become unimaginably costly. Burial insurance became an imperative. Fortunately, such insurance is usually expensive in terms of cost-benefit ratios per family member.

As of 1973 only 42 of all insurance companies in the United States are black controlled or black managed. Their combined assets are less than one-half of 1 percent of total assets for the insurance business in America. The most successful and second oldest company is the North Carolina Mutual Life Insurance Company, headquartered in Durham, North Carolina. Its total assets in 1972, about 73 years after its founding, were in excess of $129 million. The founders of this company also established the Mechanics and Farmers Bank and the Mutual Savings and Loan Association of Durham, thus making this city one of the centers of black capitalism in the nation. The success of the North Carolina Mutual Life Insurance Company can be attributed to its ability to exploit a segregated market and, equally important, to sound management and fiscal responsibility by those persons who controlled the organization throughout its life. Astute men such as John Merrick, Asa T. Spaulding, Joseph W. Goodloe, and William J. Kennedy brought to Durham an acumen for high-quality banking and insurance that assured a successful operation.

The second most successful insurance company is the Atlanta Life Insurance Company. Although it is six years younger than the North Carolina company and has smaller total assets ($81 million), it provides employment for almost four times as many people (1,000 as opposed to 276) as the larger company does. This company is also noted for shrewdness of fiscal management, for excellent service to its customers, and for having as its chief executive officer N.B. Herndon, the richest black man in the United States, with a reputed fortune of about $20 million.*

Black insurance firms are also unevenly distributed throughout the nation. Less than a third of the 50 states have at least 1 company, but Louisiana contains about a third of the total number of black insurance companies, having 15 out of the total of 42. The concentration of insurance companies in Louisiana is partially explained by somewhat liberal laws that permit the establishment of insurance companies. However, only one insurance company in Louisiana has assets of $4 million or more, and that one ranks 15th among the total number of black insurance companies. Moreover, in terms of location, the South as a whole accounts for about 80 percent of black insurance companies, which once again reflects the legacy of discrimination and caste social arrangements.

Other Entrepreneurial Activities. In recent years there has been a movement away from the traditional "mom and pop" types of businesses that have repeatedly formed and disappeared in the black community. This has meant placing considerably less emphasis on neighborhood grocery stores, shoe-repair shops, dry-cleaning establishments, barber shops, beauty salons, and greater stress on other enterprises, such as automobile dealerships, advertising and public relations firms, cosmetic industries, publishing, or by filling the vacuum in the supermarket business left in the black ghetto following the white exodus to the suburbs. But, as we shall see presently, two

---

* In fact, the city of Atlanta, which has an impressive array of black business ventures—newspapers, radio stations, insurance and banking institutions, real-estate developers, and the like—is reported to have the largest concentration of known black millionaires in the nation.

contradictory perspectives on black businesses were simultaneously in operation. One called for diversification at a time when money was tight and not particularly forthcoming for new business ventures. The other called for the establishment of small businesses, more or less of the old mom and pop type, designed to create a larger but relatively economically powerless capitalist class.

Among the former types of business activities were the supermarkets. Literally hundreds, perhaps thousands, of them throughout the country were either abandoned or relocated as a consequence of the urban uprisings of the mid-1960s, mainly in the black ghettos. Consequently, the poor lost precious jobs as well as convenient shopping areas.

At the beginning of the 1970s there were almost 9,000 black-owned grocery stores with combined gross receipts of approximately $376 million. But these were essentially small businesses rather than supermarkets, since none had sufficient sales, floor space, or types of business necessary for classification as a supermarket. In several cities across the nation, despite the tight money problem, black entrepreneurs were able to purchase supermarkets and build new ones with capital obtained from bank loans. For example, following the disturbances of the 1960s, big chain supermarkets such as FEDCO, Shop Rite, Safeway, Grand Union, and Kroger moved away from the areas of conflict. In New York, an interracial group, led by Bruce Llewellyn, a black attorney, purchased the FEDCO-operated markets in the Bronx and Manhattan and subsequently expanded the number of stores outside the low-income areas originally served. The Shop Rite chain lost three stores during the Watts conflagrations and later decided to sell its surviving complement of four stores to black purchasers, the Watts Labor Community Action Committee. Similarly, the Big V Management, a black cooperative, purchased markets previously owned by Safeway and Grand Union.[6] And in Cleveland, in the strife-torn Hough Area, black proprietors opened up the JET Supermarket, a new firm. In the same city, in the Glenville area, scene of the famous "Cleveland shoot-out" of July 23, 1968, the New Republic of Libya acquired a small market vacated by former owners who were white.

This pattern has been repeated again and again in many cities, but not without major problems. A common observation is that for a short period of time following the transfer of ownership from whites to blacks, the support from the black community tends to be remarkable. Then, almost as suddenly, black customers begin to disappear, and since few white customers remain in the inner-city area, these establishments find themselves encumbered with massive financial difficulties. Theirs is a common complaint shared by almost all black-owned enterprises—in many ways a staggering paradox—the failure of the black community, which cries for self-development and economic control, to support black-controlled business enterprises. Customers claim that they must pay essentially a few pennies more for commodities at black businesses, but at the same time they do not perceive the contradiction in paying more in public and other transportation costs incurred in shopping in fringe and surburban areas where the white supermarkets are relocated. Their rationalization of this paradox is highly suspect, and actually this behavior is symptomatic of a much more deeply rooted reason—namely, that many black persons have historically internalized the same notions of black inferiority and the doubtful capability of blacks to manage financial institutions or anything else requiring mental acuity that are characteristic of majority group stereotypes. In other words, they feel that if the local supermarket is black owned or black managed, it must be inferior in quality. Those enterprises that do manage to survive do so largely because they are supplying the needs of a captured market behind the ghetto walls. (And this is a direct consequence of housing patterns, which have the paradoxical function of racial isolation *and* containing blacks in an area that makes it possible for viable black institutions to flourish.)

Primarily because substantial capitalization is required for organizing radio-television businesses, blacks have been slow to establish or buy controlling interests in them. There are about 300 black-oriented stations scattered across the country, but blacks own a controlling interest in only approximately 10 percent of them. The Sheridan Broadcasting Company of Pittsburgh purchased station WILD (Boston), WUFU (Buffalo), and WAMO in Pittsburgh in the early 1970s. However, the largest network of black-controlled stations is the Unity Broadcasting Company, which has a network of 38 affiliate stations in the nation and reaches almost 50 percent of the total black population. Both the Sheridan company, the Unity company were established with the assistance of more than a million dollars in bank loans and venture capital investments.

Blacks have not been as successful in acquiring control or management of television stations as they have in radio. Of the 692 commercial television stations in the United States, only 1 has a black manager. Two own cable TV networks. Of the some 220 public television stations in the continental United States, none has a black manager. Underrepresentation of blacks in the radio and television industry is largely due to lack of capital. Apparently, those persons who may have the necessary financial resources, such as the 116 black millionaires, are not oriented toward this industry as a business enterprise. Unless black capitalists either buy out existing stations outright or establish new ones, it is highly unlikely that blacks will, in the foreseeable future, obtain the controlling stock in currently operating stations and thereby reclassify such stations as black owned.

The Movie Industry. The latter half of the 1960s and the first years of the 1970s brought with them a relatively new phenomenon in the movie industry—motion pictures owned, produced, and directed by blacks and starred in by black actors and actresses. During this period, the black movie was revived. Earlier films having predominantly black casts—such as *Cabin in the Sky* and the original Mantan Moreland flicks—had been viewed in black neighborhoods by black audiences during the 1930s and 1949s. But these earlier films were distortions and exploitations of another kind. They either depicted black people as childlike, happy-go-lucky, free spirited, and addicted to Saturday night fish fries and weekend parties ending with a fight to recapture a deserting or stolen lover; or they relied on all the most debasing stereotypes of the black subculture as if they were reality and generalized throughout the entire black community.

The public believes that the black films of the 1970s are the work of black capitalist ventures into the movie industry. This is not necessarily the case, for black people do not always own or produce them. The real power behind these films rests in the hands of nonblack entrepreneurs who control production, marketing, distribution, and the recruitment of talent for the films. They also have the major control in film advertising and in the determination of bookings in various theatres throughout the country. Of the more than 75 black films produced between 1965 and 1973, for example, blacks did not have a major share or full ownership.

Black films reap huge financial rewards on low budgets and appear to be the most viable form of production that Hollywood can successfully undertake in the early 1970s. (*Sweet, Sweetback Baadasssss Song* grossed more than $11 million in the first year, and on a $500,000 investment; *Shaft* grossed in excess of $17 million during its first year.) Other financially successful black films include *Super-Fly, Nigger Charley, Comeback, Charleston Blues*, and Barry Gordy's *Lady Sings the Blues*. They have also provided numerous opportunities for black actors and actresses, screenwriters, producers, directors, and a variety of technicians to obtain employment in the film industry. Hence the magnitude of their success would suggest that the movie industry might provide new opportunities for black entrepreneurs.

ROLE OF THE FEDERAL GOVERNMENT AND THE EXTERNAL CORPORATE STRUCTURE IN BLACK CAPITALISM

Four interrelated factors account for the growth and expansion of black-owned enterprises in the latter half of the 1960s and the early 1970s. These are: (1) a shift in emphasis of the civil rights movement, (2) the assassination of Dr. King, (3) increasing aggressiveness of blacks in business, and (4) the overall response of the federal government to black economic ventures. In brief, after the successes of the early 1960s the civil rights movement had begun to redirect its emphasis from strictly civil rights issues toward the problems of urban poverty, unemployment, and "getting a piece of the action" for minority businesses. This new direction coincided with pressures exerted by leading black businessmen and with complaints from blacks on the periphery of the business world that they were not receiving their share of direct benefits from government largess. The enactment of the Small Business Act during the Johnson administration did stimulate the development of business enterprises among members of minority groups. Funds were relatively slow in coming, however, and a significant proportion of fund applicants soon became disenchanted with bureaucratic red tape and other impediments to immediate capitalization and startups. Shocked, undoubtedly, by the assassination of Dr. King and stirred by the violent eruptions triggered by his death, the federal government began to take concrete steps that at once appeared to be more responsive to the needs of urban minorities.

The Small Business Act established the Small Business Administration (SBA), which was empowered to stimulate, through loans and loan-development programs, enterprises in the minority ghettos. Further, through its section 8A, or the "set-aside" program, the federal government was to give priority to minority group businessmen in the awarding of federal contracts. By making low-interest loans available to blacks and other minorities and by giving them access to federal contracts, the SBA sought to increase the number of black capitalists. However, it was not until the late 1960s that the SBA began to assist minorities to any appreciable degree. Community business development organizations, local structures established to promote black capitalism, were not even conceived until 1966, and they also expanded slowly.

The federal government also established the Office of Minority Business Enterprise (OMBE) by an executive order issued by President Nixon in April 1969. This order was highly suspect from the beginning because President Nixon was not regarded as a supporter of causes that the black community deemed important. It was also believed that the Nixon administration was not especially eager to promote black capitalism, even though on an earlier occasion, the President had used the rhetoric of black militants and promised black businessmen "a piece of the action." When the OMBE began operations with an initial budget of approximately $3 million under a white director, suspicions were confirmed. Moreover, for approximately two years the office floundered without specific directions and without a clear mandate other than that of coordinating already existing agencies within the federal government whose function it was, in part or entirely, to increase the development of black enterprises. The office was intended to coordinate and conduct public relations, to function as an information clearing house that might direct interested minorities to specific sources of funding. Its power was limited, since it could not release funds, force existing agencies to capitalize new business ventures, or guarantee support for proposed business start-ups. Later, the task force of the National Advisory Council on Minority Business issued a report calling for major and substantive alterations in the structure of OMBE and for redirecting it from an impotent and powerless agency to one capable of generating sound economic development within minority communities. Little happened.

Pressure from various sources mounted for stronger governmental support. In 1971, after two directors had resigned, President Nixon appointed a black Tennessee lawyer, John L. Jenkins, as the new OMBE director and, at the same time, requested major budgetary improvements for fiscal years 1972–1973 for OMBE. The President also issued another executive order to strengthen the agency and make it a more effective tool for stimulating enterprise capitalization. OMBE did not remain an autonomous, independent entity, however, but became housed in the Department of Commerce. Under Nixon's executive order, the office could appropriate funds directly to technical and managerial assistance organizations, help locate technical assistance for minority enterprises, and develop business resource centers throughout the country. These centers were to disseminate information about governmental services available for business ventures, continue to stimulate and coordinate funds at the local level, and assist in the packaging of business plans and loan applications. Thus in fiscal year 1973 the OMBE was budgeted for approximately $43 million, and by fiscal year 1972 the federal government had obligated about $900 million in toto for minority business programs. Further, in 1969 the Minority Enterprise Small Business Investment Company (MESBICS) had also been created as another mechanism of venture capitalization.[7]

An examination of federal intervention, therefore, shows that by 1973 approximately 8,000 new minority business groups, most of them black, were organized by virtue of federal assistance. During the 1968–1972 period, federal loans from all sources increased to more than $400 million, and federal procurement from minority businesses also showed substantial increases. White private corporations also supplemented and augmented the work of the federal government during the 1960s and the early 1970s. The American Bankers Association, for instance, established Minbancs* to come to terms with the problem of undercapitalization. The National Alli-

* Minbancs are capital corporations that permit minority institutions to use expanding deposits for loans. This is done to help minority enterprises to obtain new capital for operation, development, and expansion.

ance of Businessmen, with Henry Ford II as chairman, was established to create more jobs for the hard-core unemployed, and the National Urban Coalition was established to improve business technology among black entrepreneurs. Of course, other banking institutions, such as the Bank of America, and manufacturing organizations and huge companies, such as IBM and Xerox, also provided technical assistance programs and some start-up or promotional finance. In addition, the government aided the National Negro Business League, comprising about 78 chapters and 15,000 members, in its Project Outreach through financial support at the rate of $1 million per year. All these efforts helped pave the way for the achievements made by black capitalists.

Unmistakably, these accomplishments are impressive but the other side of the business coin is not so positive. It may indeed be, as Andrew Brimmer once commented, "a cruel hoax" to perpetrate upon black people the hope of black capitalism as a major method of escaping the depths of poverty and economic deprivation under present conditions.[8] Certainly, the SBA finds itself perpetuating a paradoxical situation that calls for the end of mom and pop businesses while at the same time its loans go essentially to sole proprietors or to individually managed small establishments. Further, the failure rate of black businesses in this period has been six times as high as normally expected. This failure stems primarily from the lack of experience and business training, lack of management skills, and the inability of many new ventures to attract competently trained staffs for management and day-to-day operations. They also fail because of racial exploitation of many black business. The inexorability of undercapitalization, despite government and white corporate intervention, continues to plague black business ventures and leads directly to their demise. All too often, the government seems to expect swift and miraculous achievements within the first or second year, and if these are not forthcoming, funds and loan support subside. Significantly, the majority of black business failures occur during the first year because they lack adequate capital. Once they have been initiated or started-up the expectation appears to be that they should be able to function independently. Obviously, with such a high failure rate, support is withdrawn all too soon.

The social milieu and economic condition of the ghetto, which is the locus of the majority of new business ventures, raise serious questions about the ability of black communities to support both small businesses and huge corporate structures despite the $51 billion consumer market located there. The market is not concentrated, but is widely dispersed, not in a single black community or two or three, not even among a dozen black communities, but among hundreds of pocket areas where blacks are located. Success and failure are related to income disparities; to unemployment and low occupational status; to limited financial assets among blacks; and to their relatively high famly debts, low saving capacities, and unwise spending patterns.

Because the entrepreneurial class is so small, the black community's most fundamental gains will be largely psychological, being derived from the satisfaction that a few black brothers and sisters are "making it" in areas once monopolized or controlled by whites in the black community. But these gains do not begin to deal with the issue of white control of the lion's share of business enterprises in the black community.

SELF-HELP ORGANIZATIONS: ADAPTIVE RESPONSES

To ameliorate the conditions of poverty, undercapitalization, inadequately trained management/personnel and operations, and to stimulate broader participation by blacks in finding solutions to such problems a number of adaptive responses evolved in the form of self-help organizations. The diversity of these responses is reflected in the broad range of activities they have encompassed within a relatively short period of time. The omission here of such programs as the Black Panther food and medical services program for the urban poor and the Urban League's Jobs for Vietnam Veterans does not deny their importance. In some ways, these programs overlap with others selected for a somewhat more detailed analysis that follows.

Black Cooperatives. Advocated as a road to "the salvation of the black community,"[9] black rural cooperatives represent an adaptive response to the economic plight of rural blacks. Of the more than 100 formed during the 1960s, 90 are organized under the Federation of Southern Cooperatives. Their basic objectives are to: (1) retain and sustain the farm population, (2) produce enough food to make this population self-sufficient, (3) provide adequate jobs and thus increase earned income for members, (4) promote diversification of agricultural enterprises, and (5) help to raise the overall standard of living among the rural population.

Achieving these goals is a difficult process, especially since the catalog of problems found generally in black businesses are magnified in rural cooperatives. Further, the cooperatives have not always owned land sufficient for both cash-crop production and diversifying economic activities. Land is of major importance, especially since blacks in the South now own only approximately one-third of the 15 million acres of farmland they once controlled. One-fifth of the 5 million acres now remaining is in the state of Mississippi.

Despite these problems, some cooperatives are achieving modest degrees of success. For example, the North Bolivar County Cooperative of Mound Bayou, Mississippi, has attacked problems of poor nutrition and stimulated the production of cash crops. Much of its work has been done with assistance from Tufts Medical School, grants from the Office of Economic Opportunity, 300 acres of land donated by the Ford Foundation, and financial aid from countless American citizens interested in the problems of the rural poor. The Southern Consumers Cooperative of Lake Charles, Louisiana, initiated by Father Albert McKnight, a black priest from Brooklyn, has attempted to find marketing outlets for products from the 90 Southern cooperatives. The success experienced can also be in part attributed to the tireless efforts of Charles Prejean, a leader in the Black Cooperative Movement. Thus the People's Development Foundation (New York City), organized to assist black cooperatives, serves as a broker for Southern cooperatives and facilitates the full spectrum of the economic process, including production, packaging, marketing, advertising, distribution, and financing. Other cooperatives (for example, the West Georgia Cooperative of Harris County and the Eastern Central Committee for Opportunity) have established pig and catfish farms, a processing plant, and a concrete manufacturing facility; they have also constructed housing and enabled members to purchase goods and services at a much reduced rate.

Opportunities Industrialization Center (OIC), People United to Save Humanity (PUSH), and its parent body, Operation Breadbasket, and the Black Economic Union (BEU) are essentially urban-type responses. The Black Muslims respond to both rural and urban issues through their extensive business ventures in cities and the farms they operate in the South.

Opportunities Industrialization Center. This is essentially a manpower development and a job-generating enterprise founded by the Reverend Leon Sullivan in Philadelphia in the late 1960s. Its basic orientation is that of self-help through training, preparation, and building as prerequisites for job attainment. Its appeal is to urban grassroots individuals in need of skill development before they seek full-time employment. Thus OIC provides basic skill training in computational analysis (mathematics), communications, business education, computer techniques, offset printing, drafting, graphic arts, photography, cosmetology, and techniques of job interviewing so that applicants will be self-composed during job interviews. The center is now represented in more than 100 cities across the nation and is supported by a $32 million subsidy from the U.S. Department of Labor. As a result of its efforts, thousands of black people have found better jobs.

Operation Breadbasket. This program was inaugurated during the late 1960s as the civil rights struggle shifted from the South to the North. Established first in Atlanta by the Southern Christian Leadership Conference, under the late Dr. King, it soon spread to Chicago and to cities in the North. Its primary purpose was to gain employment for blacks in white businesses located in black communities. It operated on the rationale that such businesses were morally obligated to share some of their profits with those from whom the profits were made. Perhaps the most widely known chapter was located in Chicago, where the young Reverend Jesse Jackson was assigned. Responding to the relative ineffectiveness of moral suasion as a tactic for goal attainment, Reverend Jackson shifted to the utilization of such pressure resources as boycotts, picketing, and generalized demonstrations. Many ghetto businesses acceded to Operation Breadbasket demands and entered into covenants with blacks. These agreements went far beyond the acquisition of jobs and extended to depositing money in black-owned banks, stocking commodities produced by blacks, advertising in black news media, and contracting with other black businesses, particularly in service areas. The success of the Chicago chapter far exceeded that of others and, undoubtedly, stimulated the ideological schisms subsequently developed in the organization.

People United to Save Humanity. This organization known as PUSH was an outgrowth of the leadership and ideological conflicts that emerged full-blown after the assassination of Dr. King. Established in 1971, it is essentially an extension of the work commenced by the Chicago chapter of Operation Breadbasket and is headed by Reverend Jackson. As we have seen, he has enjoyed marked success in bringing about a sharing of the profits, whether this is accomplished through new jobs or other means.

The first notable success along these lines was the covenant reached with General Foods, signed on September 21, 1972, which is comprised essentially of ten commitments made by General Foods: (1) to add a total of 360 jobs for black people; (2) to continue its black college recruitment program; (3) to seek out ways of employing rehabilitated offenders; (4) to contract with black janitorial, pest control, and waste removal firms; (5) to hire black lawyers or to work, when possible, with institutions that had black lawyers as members of their firms; (6) to retain a minimum of five black physicians and black paramedical assistants to provide for the medical needs of employees and, further, to patronize black-owned medical supply firms; (7) to deposit some half million dollars immediately in black-owned banks and to increase that sum to $1.2 million over the next few months; (8) to immediately transact some $20 million in business with black insurance companies and to increase this amount to $50 million within a one-year period; (9) to donate at least about $100,000 to predominantly black colleges; and (10) to initiate immediately about $600,000 in business with black advertising and public relations agencies and to increase this amount to $1 million in the future.[10]

Since that time PUSH has negotiated covenants with several other firms, including the Schlitz Brewing Company, and met with similar success. Its annual expos, or trade fairs, are commendable exercises in organizational skill, development, and intergroup-intragroup cooperation. PUSH is presently attempting to extend its program into the depressed areas of black Africa.

The Black Economic Union. This organization was founded in 1966 largely by a group of enterprising athletes and ex-athletes who were committed to the philosophy of black capitalism. The list included Jim Brown, John Wooten, and Brady Keys. Its original purposes were to provide a dependable source for capitalizing black entrepreneurs; to stimulate the development and participation of blacks in new black enterprises (for instance, the movie industry); to maintain blacks' control over their own businesses once they were appropriately capitalized; and to encourage blacks to acquire businesses vacated by whites in the black ghetto. Branches were established in Washington, D.C., Cleveland, Oakland, Kansas City, Los Angeles, and New York City.

Within a few years BEU acquired or became associated with All-Pro Chicken with approximately 25 branches scattered in various cities; it stimulated the establishment of AFMIR, a cosmetic organization in New York City; it sponsored J.I.M., a summer youth-employment program for inner-city youth; and it promoted the acquisition of a number of franchises previously owned by white merchants in the black community. One result of its movement into franchises has been the acquisition by blacks of 75 McDonald franchises in cities such as Cleveland and New York. The BEU is essentially oriented toward conservative enterprises that have a high degree of success, and it is less inclined to support high-risk or even moderately risky categories of businesses.

The Black Muslims. It is difficult to measure the full economic impact of the Nation of Islam on the black community. The financial structure of this essentially religious body has never been opened to full public scrutiny. It has a highly diversified business structure comprised of farms, bakeries, meat-processing and packing plants, restaurants and cafés, retail stores, an egg-processing plant, hospitals, schools, the newspaper *Muhammed Speaks*, and other significant enterprises. The organization embraces much of the philosophy of the Protestant ethic and displays a special admiration for business procedures and practices attributed to the white population. It stresses financial independence, economic achievement, and fiscal autonomy. Moreover, one of its underlying assumptions is self-development through economic self-sufficiency and independence.

Problems and Prospects. Aside from the already discussed problems, the most serious issue, without a doubt, revolves around crime in the ghetto. High ghetto crime rates raise insurance premiums to astronomical proportions and are the direct cause of many business failures in the black ghetto.

A survey conducted by the SBA revealed some alarming statistics on criminal attacks on ghetto businesses and owners. Thirty-two of every 100 retail businesses in the ghetto were burglarized in 1972, with losses totaling almost a billion dollars. Nine percent of ghetto businesses were robbed, resulting in a $77 million loss. The damages from vandalism reached $813 million; losses from shoplifting approximated $504 million, while employee thefts from ghetto businesses amounted to $381 million. In addition, ghetto businesses lost about $316 million through bad checks. These financial losses do not begin to measure the psychological and social damages done to black businesses by the fears that people have, real or unreal, about shopping and conducting business in the urban ghettos. As we shall see in Chapter 9, some measures are presently under way that are designed to combat and control both the extent and structure of ghetto crime.

One final aspect of black businesses deserves our attention. Illegal business operates in the black community in much the same way that it does in the white community. It is believed that a huge share of black revenue comes from organized crime, gambling, drug trafficking, stolen property, prostitution, and other illegal activities. No one actually knows the extent of the holdings possessed by the lords of the underworld and by those who control the "shaded society." Moreover, even though exorbitant sums of money are generated in the black community, little remains there, since these illegal business ventures tend to be controlled by forces external to the community itself.

HUMAN RESOURCE NEEDS

Expanding opportunities for skilled and professional blacks, which resulted from the civil rights movement of the 1950s and 1960s and from the enactment of fair employment legislation, demonstrated in a most fundamental manner how extensive critical shortages in human resources are in the black community. These shortages extend to almost all skilled and semiskilled occupations and often reflect the legacies of past injustices against the black community. Similarly, they point to the failure of many blacks to take advantage of training and educational opportunities that were available to them even in more recent times. In this section the focus is primarily directed to professional needs and, secondarily, to human resources needs in skilled occupations.

Manpower Training Programs. These are among the first specific and concerted efforts designed to reorient training, to correct the mistakes of the educational system, and to expand the pool of trained persons for available jobs. Some programs are addressed to vocational needs, stressing skills provided by organizations such as the OIC. Others, such as the Urban League's on-the-job training program initiated in 1969, are directed specifically to hard-to-place clients (for example, veterans without honorable discharges, convicted felons, and former welfare clients). The Urban League has claimed a rate of 75 percent for training completion and job retention of hard-to-place veterans, 81 percent for male felons, and 91 percent for male and female former welfare clients between 1969 and 1971. But these successes are the exception rather than the rule. All too frequently, manpower programs have been reduced to temporary funding techniques for persons more interested in receiving the weekly or monthly stipends granted them for program participation than in learning the skills provided by the programs. Thus when funds ran out or were slow in coming, participants failed to show, and this is the basis for the commonly heard expression: "If we don't get the jelly (money), we don't jam (show)!" This expression is also the basis for erroneous assumptions about the quality of these training programs. Nevertheless, regardless of how misplaced and misguided certain allegations may be, it is true that these programs not infrequently have trained individuals for jobs that are no longer available, resulting in deepening frustrations related to unfulfilled aspirations. The situation highlights the critical need for manpower programs and on-the-job training geared specifically to positions available to individuals upon their satisfactory completion of training programs. Even after successfully completing programs, blacks have no guarantee of a position. They encounter discrimination in many unions and, particularly in the construction industry, in hiring policies. These policies can take the form of the demand for participation in apprenticeship programs, as if *all* employees were required to do so prior to employment; of giving hiring priorities to relatives and members of friendship cliques; of requiring blacks to demonstrate relative experience in order to be hired or to advance. The latter requirement creates a vicious circle—a treadmill as it were—from which it is almost impossible to escape. Individuals who complete training and have no work experience may be disqualified for jobs on the ground of lack of experience and those with experience may very well be informed that they are overqualified for the position. They remain unemployed, without income, and unimaginably disillusioned.

THE PROFESSIONALS

As we saw earlier, the nation is experiencing a severe and critical shortage of black professionals. The extreme shortages in every field are likely to worsen by 1980 unless gigantic steps are immediately taken to train more black professionals. Since we cannot examine all the professions here, we will focus on a few of the more important ones.

Medicine. In the past 100 years approximately 90 percent of all black physicians were trained at Howard University in Washington, D.C., and Meharry Medical College in Nashville, Tennessee. Even as late as 1967, these two institutions were still training more than 80 percent of black physicians. The situation is undergoing radical change today as several predominantly white medical colleges embark on a deliberate recruitment effort to attract black medical students. As a result, the proportion of black medical students rose from 2 percent to about 5 percent of the total number of medical students in a three-year period ending in 1972. During the 1972–1973 academic year, about 2,100 black students were enrolled in the 107 medical colleges.

Although such an increase is impressive, the 6,500 to 7,000 black physicians in the United States in 1973 comprised only about 2 percent of the nation's 332,000 physicians. Moreover, there is only one black physician for every 2,800 black persons in the country, while there are five physicians for every 2,800 white persons. Current projections indicate that the overall shortage of physicians will reach between 50,000 and 100,000 by 1980. By using American Medical Association (AMA) standards of one physician for every 1,500 persons, a shortage of fairly close to 25,000 black physicians already existed in 1972. A monumental effort will be required to alleviate deficits of such magnitude.

In order to recruit more black students into the medical profession, a number of special projects are under way at medical schools with the cooperation of medically related professional organizations. For example, Meharry Medical College is operating a program for early identification of potential medical students—as early as high school years. This program includes encouragement for medical careers, special premedical training with an Associated Arts degree granted at the end of the sophomore year of college, and possible early admission into medical school in certain specialized areas of training.

Similar programs are sponsored by the Urban Coalition (for high school students interested in medical careers) and by the National Medical Association, a parallel medical society formed by blacks when the AMA refused to admit black physicians, which jointly sponsors Project 75 with the AMA, the American Hospital Association, and the Association of American Colleges. The goal of this program is to increase the number of medical student enrollees of minority group origins to 12 percent by 1975. To accomplish this goal tutorial and counseling centers have been established in places such as Seattle, Tucson, California State University campuses at Northridge, Long Beach, and Los Angeles to assist students in dealing with subjects such as chemistry, biology, physics, and mathematics. Further, special fund-raising programs are sponsored to provide scholarships for black students, especially those from the lowest-income families, interested in careers in medical and allied health professions. This effort is especially significant given the low-income status of most black college students and the high cost of medical education (for example, the average cost of a medical education at Howard or Meharry is about $4,500 per year, but it is substantially higher in other institutions).

Dentistry. Blacks comprise approximately 2.5 percent of the nation's 121,000 dentists. Like black physicians, the overwhelming majority of dentists were also trained at Meharry Medical College and Howard University. The severe shortages of black dentists is likely to increase in the black community in the near future. Programs similar to those mentioned previously are presently under way under the sponsorship of the National Dental Association (NDA), the black counterpart to the American Dental Association, and under the sponsorship of regional and statewide chapters of the NDA. In addition, some formerly all-white dental schools have mounted major recruitment programs aimed at increasing the proportion of black dental graduates in the immediate future.

Allied Health Professions. Lucille Tunstall points out in a recent paper that there are more than 125 specialized occupations in the health-care field.[11] Although the allied health fields employed approximately 900,000 persons in 1971, critical shortages are predicted in several of them in the near future. Her study indicates that by 1980 the United States will find itself with approximately 432,000 unfilled positions in allied health, ranging from the 130,000 specialists in pharmacy and pharmaceuticals to 117,000 dieticians. Shortages are presently experienced in the fields of occupational therapy, medical data assistants, hospital and clinical staff, pharmacology, food nutrition, toxicology, biomedical science, health-care administration, radiology, and radio therapy, among others. To illustrate these shortages only eight black persons in the country are nationally certified as pharmacologists and toxicologists. Further, the black students enrolled in the historically white colleges of pharmacy in 1969 comprised seven-tenths of 1 percent of the total number of pharmacy students in the nation. The majority of black students of pharmacology outside those institutions were receiving training at Texas Southern University and Xavier University of New Orleans. In short, blacks constitute about 2 percent of all allied health professionals. We also know that black registered nurses constitute 7 percent of all registered nurses; blacks also provide 15 percent of all practical nurses in the United States and 50 percent of all nurses' aides. These figures illustrate the unequal distribution of black professionals from top to bottom in the health-services field. To reduce this shortage and alter the distribution pattern major efforts are under way to enlist and train blacks in career-oriented programs at institutions such as Clark University in Atlanta, Lincoln University in Pennsylvania, Meharry and Howard medical schools, Case Western Reserve University, and the UCLA schools of medicine, dentistry, and allied health.

Law. The 3,845 black lawyers in the United States comprise about 1.5 percent of the 325,000 lawyers in the nation. The paucity of black lawyers can be partly explained by the historical acts of discrimination that either prevented or discouraged blacks from entering predominantly white institutions for acquiring legal training. Furthermore, establishing a legal practice among essentially a low-income population has always been problematic economically. Hence many blacks, realizing that they might have to work in some other job while possessing a law degree, were persuasively discouraged from entering the profession. During the 1940s and 1950s, as an effort to sanctify the notion of separate but equal, several states established law schools at their state-supported black institutions. For instance, law schools were set up at Texas Southern University, South Carolina State or Orangeburg, Southern University, and North Carolina Central University. These complement Howard University Law School, which was long the seat for the training of the nation's black lawyers. Today, many predominantly white law schools, including those at Harvard, Yale, Berkeley, and the University of Washington, are training more black students than they did in the past.

Most black lawyers were traditionally trained to handle divorce cases, negligence, and criminal defenses. Changing state statutes may eventually make training in divorce law and negligence law obsolete, thus necessitating career changes for a number of lawyers if they plan to continue practicing. Since 50 percent of the court cases pertaining to criminal offenses, according to Julius Debro, involve black individuals,[12] there should be a continuing need for black lawyers to handle these cases, assuming that blacks in trouble seek out black lawyers, which is, of course, not always the case. Debro points out, for instance, that black militants in trouble turn to white lawyers rather than black lawyers for their defense on the grounds that whites are better respected and more knowledgeable about the system—attributes needed for exoneration or acquittal.[13]

Higher Education. The supply of blacks trained for roles in higher education is grossly inadequate to meet the demand. For example, black Ph.D.s constitute about 4 percent of all sociologists holding Ph.Ds, 5 percent of psychologists holding Ph.Ds, 2 percent of the economists, and less than 1 percent of the historians, mathematicians, physicists, biologists, and chemists. Yet black student leaders across the nation are demanding the hiring of black professors. To meet this demand several white institutions have raided predominantly black colleges to such an extent that their accreditation has been threatened. Some raided other white institutions, which only served to exacerbate the problem rather than to confront it with more long-term solutions.

What is needed is a national program designed to recruit and train a large number of black college students for careers as professional educators. One proposal is that institutions provide funds for graduate training in return for a commitment to assume teaching responsibilities for at least the number of years equal to the period of support granted for completing graduate and professional work. Another way of opening college teaching opportunities to blacks is to revamp the requirements for teaching to take advantage of enormous reservoirs of resources among professional practitioners who do not hold the Ph.D. degree.

In passing, it should be mentioned that excellent programs are presently functioning for business-administration training at institutions such as Atlanta University, the Xavier-Tulane Joint Business Administration Degree, the Harvard Graduate School of Business Administration, the Wharton School of Finance, and at Columbia University. In the field of social welfare, which has 10,500 trained black social workers, some highly successful programs are now in operation to deal with the need for professionally trained black social workers (for example, at Atlanta University, Howard University, Case Western Reserve University, and the University of Michigan).

In sum, then, major efforts are imperative for training a greater supply of black Americans to fill expanding job opportunities in the 1970s and 1980s. Unless new job opportunities are opened and the legitimacy of training and hiring blacks is recognized, serious intergroup conflicts will result. Skilled training and professional expertise, reinforced by an actualized commitment to change, are a *sine qua non* for maintaining a viable black community.

NOTES

1. Gunnar Myrdal, *An American Dilemma* (New York: Harper & Row, 1944), pp. 308–316.

2. Howard E. Aldrich, "Employment Opportunities for Blacks in the Black Ghetto: The Role of White-Owned Businesses," *American Journal of Sociology*, 78 (May 1973), pp. 1403–1425.

3. "Banks," *Black Enterprise*, 3 (June 1973), p. 57.

4. Among the research done in this area Theodore Cross' *Black Capitalism* is highly recommended.

5. Myrdal, *op. cit.*

6. "Banks," *loc. cit.*, pp. 3–34.

7. *Ibid., passim.*

8. Andrew Brimmer, "Economic Integration and the Progress of the Negro Community," *Ebony*, 25 (August 1970), pp. 118–121.

9. Robert Allen, *Black Awakening in Capitalist America* (Garden City, N.Y.: Doubleday Anchor Books, 1971), p. 52.

10. See *Amsterdam News*, September 30, 1972, B-B, for the text of the covenant.

11. Lucille Tunstall, *Increasing the Options in Health Professions* (Atlanta, Ga.: Clark College, 1973).

12. Julius Debro, "Black Lawyers—Black Militants," an unpublished paper presented at the annual meetings of the American Sociological Association, New Orleans, La., August 1972, p. 11.

13. *Ibid.*

7 | BLACK POLITICAL POWER

The slogan "black power," first echoed during the summer of 1966, escalated fear and strained social relationships between the races and within the black community primarily because its meaning was so widely misunderstood. When rationality finally supplanted emotionalism, many black persons could agree that a major focus of black power was how to gain access to the political power structure of American life and to effect economic and social changes. This consensus made explicit the manifest significance of political leverage in transforming power relations between groups of unequal status.

This chapter examines a number of issues related to changing power relations between black and white participants in the political process. Among the issues raised are: historical political roles of the black populace and black struggle for political inclusion, strategies for increasing political participation, factors accelerating or impeding political involvement by black Americans, and structures that facilitate power redistributions among societally determined unequals.

THE DEVELOPMENT OF A CRITICAL MASS

It is often argued that the acquisition of political power depends upon, among other things, the presence of numbers of people. Essentially, according to this thesis, distinct groups of people may achieve group power if they vote collectively and uniformly on the same issues over time and for one of their own group. In this sense group solidarity is manifested in a "consciousness of kind" as it relates to political behavior. If such groups persist in collective or bloc-voting behavior over time and if their numbers are large enough to affect voting outcomes, they may in time gain partial or complete control of the government especially at local levels. This thesis is fundamentally a politics of numbers predicated upon the assumption that the participants are both sufficiently well organized and motivated to mobilize their resources, whether in terms of individual voters, financial support, or whatever else is needed, and that their activities will be oriented toward a common goal, the acquisition of power. It also assumes that people aspire for political participation mainly because the rewards and gratifications anticipated are worth the energy expended in the process. Thus if the anticipated rewards are inadequate and the probability for goal attainment is not high, then groups are less likely to be motivated to gain political power than if the situation were the reverse.[1] In other words, the acquisition of political power by a minority is a highly complex phenomenon involving numbers of people, the strength of their social organization, the effectiveness to which whatever resources they possess are mobilized for goal attainment, and the position assumed by the dominant group in this process.

One of the basic problems that the black community has had to confront since emancipation is that of acquiring and maintaining a critical mass —that is, a sufficient number of people for influencing political outcomes or decisions in regard to collective black interests. This need was implicit in the equal rights conventions conducted by blacks during 1865 in such states as Virginia, South Carolina, North Carolina, Tennessee, and Mississippi. However, it was the Fifteenth Amendment to the Constitution (1870), which guaranteed the rights of black men to vote, that paved the way for large-scale participation of blacks in the political process. In general, the mood of the First, or Radical, Reconstruction was such that newly enfranchised blacks felt that their rights would be protected and that positive consequences would redound to them if they exercised political prerogatives. Hence blacks voted in such large numbers, particularly in the South, that black elected officials served in the U.S. Congress and Senate until 1901, interrupted only by a two-year period (from 1887 to 1889) when no blacks served in either branch of Congress. Although Hiram R. Revels and Blanche K. Bruce, who represented Mississippi as U.S. senators (between 1870 and 1881), are the most familiar names of national politicians during the period, some 20 black men served in the House of Representatives between 1869 and 1901. Most of these men came from the upper Southern states, particularly the Carolinas; however, others represented such Deep South states as Alabama, Georgia, Florida, Mississippi, and Louisiana.

During Reconstruction, in addition to national elective positions, blacks held innumerable state and local offices (for example, state senators and representatives; mayors, judges, members of all state courts, education superintendents; and one, P. B. S. Pinchback, served as acting governor of Louisiana for a short time). Hence this form of political leverage, relative to the power and prestige of the positions held, enabled blacks to promote a number of political and educational reforms of far-reaching significance (namely, the democratization of state constitutions and educational systems during Reconstruction).

The political power achieved by blacks in the South was short-lived. By virtue of a series of events commencing with the Compromise of 1877, Southern whites took systematic steps to disfranchise Southern blacks and, subsequently, to retard their political integration into American life. The Compromise of 1877 was essentially an agreement by the North to remove the federal troops, which had protected rights of black people, and to reestablish home rule in the South in exchange for Southern support for Rutherford B. Hayes, whose election to the presidency was hanging in the balance. With federal troops removed, the white South was not only free to establish home rule but to revert to its previous position of complete dominance over the black population. Also, Northern Republicans thereby abdicated responsibilities for the social, economic, and political development of black people by devolving it to white Southerners. The result was that whatever external support blacks once counted on for the attainment of a just life was no longer available.

The process of disfranchising blacks in the South assumed essentially eight forms: (1) Blacks were not permitted to vote in many places following changes in state constitutions. (2) The Enforcement Act of 1870 and the Civil Rights Act of 1875 were declared unconstitutional, both of which had protected the principle of universal suffrage. (3) A *grandfather's clause* was enforced whereby eligibility for voting was determined on the basis of having an acknowledged grandfather who had voted in federal elections prior to 1866. (4) *White primaries* were held that excluded all but members of the Democratic party from participating in an election, a strategy that made that party a private all-white club. (5) A *poll tax* was required of potential voters, which varied in sum from state to state and from jurisdiction to jurisdiction; but the enormity of the tax precluded most blacks and a sizable number of whites, when it was applied to them, from exercising the rapidly attenuating right of franchise. (6) *Literary tests* demanded that potential voters be able to read and recite from memory previously unspecified sections of either a state or federal constitution, as was done under the Boswell Amendment of 1946 in Alabama. (7) *Gerrymandering* permitted a jurisdiction to redistrict voters in such a way as to neutralize black voters by reducing their proportion in the new district. (8) *Violence* was used, either through the Ku Klux Klan (KKK) or other more spontaneously organized groups or hostile individuals—all of which effectively deterred blacks from voting. Often, violence took the form of lynchings, physical assaults, and various reprisals against potential black voters. By the turn of the century the majority of black Southerners were effectively eliminated from the polls, and their political power had been totally destroyed at local, state, and national levels. In the meantime, although Northern black citizens continued to participate in the electoral process, the impact of their votes was inconsequential. Their political power was severely limited and would so remain until the advent of the mass black exodus from the South to the North during World War I.

Despite these impediments to political participation, blacks neither acquiesced to white dominance nor resigned themselves to a subordinate political status. For example, the racially integrated Niagara Movement gave rise to the NAACP, organized in 1909 to restore political rights to black Americans.

For 60 years the NAACP has been a major force for regaining and maintaining political rights for black people. It may also be said that literally all of the contemporary minorities have benefited from legalistic battles won by the NAACP even though its plaintiffs have usually been black. The value of this organization as an instrument for social change can be gleaned from cases representative of its many victories: (1) the elimination of the grandfather's clause in the case of *Guinn* v. *the United States* (1915); (2) first, the reduction of the impact of white primaries as a restraining factor against black voters in *Nixon* v. *Herndon* (1927) and *Nixon* v. *Condon* (1932) and, then, the destruction of white primaries in *Smith* v. *Allright* (1944) followed by *Rice* v. *Elmore* (1947), in which the U.S. Supreme Court invalidated them as a violation of the Fifteenth Amendment; (3) attacks against obstructionist tactics involving abbreviated time periods for black registrants as in *Lane* v. *Wilson* (1939); (4) the abrogation of gerrymandering by the U.S. Supreme Court, which involved Tuskeegee in Macon County, Alabama, in the case of *Gomillion* v. *Lightfoot* (1969); (5) and the enactment of the Twenty-fourth Amendment to the U.S. Constitution, which abolished all poll taxes. Moreover, the association's sustained attack against lynchings and physical abuse substantially reduced or curtailed such occurrences to sporadic episodes.

The effectiveness of the NAACP in reenfranchising a fairly large number of blacks can be attributed to its highly organized internal structure and its ability to mobilize numerous resources to attain its goals. It welcomed whites to its ranks and valued their financial support. The organization has retained its interracial membership, despite adverse publicity in the late 1960s, and has oriented itself toward the goal of a racially integrated society in which black Americans would become full and equal participants. Its primary tactic for attaining this goal has been and continues to be legalistic. Its financial support is based upon membership fees and voluntary contributions. However, its resources extend far beyond finance and a strong membership to include a large pool of talented personnel, most especially a core of legal tacticians and strategists.

Two immediate consequences resulted from the persistent efforts to enfranchise blacks: (1) Blacks did begin to register in such a manner as to become an important political force. And (2) a shift in party affiliation occurred. Black importance as a political force was reflected in the degree to which the large political machines courted their votes in every region of the country. The shift from the Republican party to the Democratic party probably began as early as 1928 and was all but a *fait accompli* by 1940.

Party Machines. By virtue of the successes of the NAACP in enfranchising an increasingly larger number of black voters in the South, the number of black voters in 1932 was a substantial increase over the decimated residue existing in 1901. Southern machines courted black voters on the promise that their support would result in what Dahl calls both divisible and indivisible benefits to them.[2] Undoubtedly, the attainment of jobs was the more important divisible benefit for low-status blacks, whereas the acquisition of community needs, such as a playground, was among the more valued indivisible benefits. (Divisible benefits seem to be synonymous with William Wilson's adaptation of Hubert Blacock's concept of competitive resources.)[3] Thus the Byrds of Virginia could promise blacks a denunciation of the KKK or sponsor antilynching legislation in exchange for black votes. William C. Hartsfield in Atlanta could promise a better economic life for blacks in his meetings with the boss of the black machine there, A. T. Walden, in return for black support at the polls.[4] But these were largely paternalistic overtures, and, as Banfield observes, people like Hartsfield, for example, never provided either divisible or indivisible benefits for black Atlantans.[5] Some machine bosses, such as Boss Crump in Memphis, abided by segregationist principles when the alternative was integration or segregation (in one instance Crump refused to support Dr. T. E. Walker, his black counterpart in Memphis, in Walker's bid to ensure a desegregated seating arrangement for a Marian Anderson concert in 1940).

Machine politicians in the North relied more on political patronage as a means of attracting black voters. Through the patronage system blacks could be placed in low-level positions and be guaranteed dependable, although low-paying, employment. Occasionally, more influential black supporters would be rewarded with a relatively important judgeship, or some black person might be elected as an alderman or city councilman. These factors were crucial elements in the election of Republican Oscar DePriest of Chicago in 1929 as the first black congressman since 1901. He was succeeded by a black Democrat, Arthur W. Mitchell, who served from 1935 to 1943. He, in turn, was succeeded by William Dawson, who was joined by Adam Clayton Powell from New York in 1945. They, as well as other blacks who were to follow them to Congress, owed their political success to the conjoining of demographic/ecological factors with machine politics and a rising black consciousness.

The Shift to the Democratic Party. Historically, blacks have always been affiliated more predominantly with one political party than another. Primarily because of the historical association of President Lincoln with emancipation, blacks were loyal for a half-century or more to the Republican party. Black allegiance to the Republicans was fostered by solid evidence that the Democratic party was for three-quarters of a century, largely antiblack. However, in the period of reenfranchisement, beginning from about 1915 to the present time, the Democrats initiated programs and policies that successfully severed blacks from the Republican party and drew them within the orbit of Democratic politics. The Republicans themselves abetted this process by practices that favored privileged classes or appeared to be antiblack. Hence they excluded blacks from the inner circles of local Republican activities, isolated them at meetings, and treated them with disdain and contempt. Simultaneously, Democrats, especially from the 1928 presidential election on, overtly wooed black voters.

Following Roosevelt's victories in 1932 and 1936, he made two shrewdly conceived political moves that accelerated the shift of blacks toward the Democratic party. First, he established a black cabinet comprised of highly respected black leaders, who were advisers on black affairs, many of whom were prestigious educators like Mary McCloud Bethune, founder of Bethune-Cookman College in Florida. Dr. Bethune was the Director of the Division of Negro Affairs of the National Youth Administration (NYA) and was, for all practical purposes, the head of Roosevelt's black cabinet. President Roosevelt appointed more than 100 blacks to federal positions in the period between 1933 and 1940. Although subordinated to white directors of heads of agencies and without significant political authority, black appointees perceived themselves as participants in the decision-making process; they received high status and prestige in the black community and were regarded by whites as respectable black leaders who were a credit to their race. In addition to specific appointments, Roosevelt initiated meetings in the White House with black leaders. Members of the established cabinet were encouraged to seek the advice of black leaders on matters of direct concern to them. In this manner disenchanted blacks were somewhat placated, since it appeared that the Roosevelt administration was concerned with the plight of the poor and with including blacks in decision-making processes.

The second step was the inclusion of blacks in many New Deal program benefits. As expected, blacks, hard hit by the Great Depression, were in need of substantial relief. Many found employment through the various Public Works Administration projects. Charges of discrimination in the Civilian Conservation Corps were duly investigated, and discrimination there somewhat abated. But discrimination was rampant in several federal agencies during FDR's administration. Black farmers and sharecroppers were also adversely affected by New Deal agricultural policies (for example, discriminatory soil conservation programs, unequal incomes between black and white farm workers, underrepresentation of black agricultural extension workers, and so on). Even so, a spirit of optimism prevailed when blacks were made aware of frequent public appearances of Eleanor Roosevelt with Mary McCloud Bethune despite criticisms in the white community. This apparent genuine concern by Eleanor Roosevelt accelerated black movement toward the Democratic party. This process, initiated in the 1928 election, was discernible in 1932, quite apparent in 1936, and complete by 1940. Blacks had abandoned the Republican party—and were safely ensconced in the Democratic stronghold and committed to the position that greater social, economic, and political benefits were to be derived from their support of the Democratic party.

Similarly, Democratic party bosses were quick to perceive the pivotal character of the black vote in closely contested elections at all levels. Largely because of this capacity to influence political outcomes, blacks have to some degree benefited from Democratic machine politics, patronage, and party support but not to the degree of success experienced by white ethnics in earlier times. For example, presidential decisions to expand black participation in the military (FDR) and to desegregate the armed forces (H. S. Truman) were motivated in a large measure by the desire for support of black voters. White ethnics, on the other hand, were more successful in gaining control over entire systems and subsystems within municipal and state governments (for example, teaching, public works, fire and police departments).

The pivotal nature of blacks in closely contested elections can be illustrated by several instances: (1) In 1940 black votes helped Roosevelt gain 190 electoral votes that proved to be the margin of victory over Wendell Willkie.[6] (2) Black voters undoubtedly provided much of the narrow margin of victory for Truman over Dewey, Strom Thurmond, and Henry Wallace in 1948 after Truman insisted upon a strong civil rights platform at the Democratic national convention. (3) The fact that blacks gave John F. Kennedy from 68 to 80 percent of their votes helped him win the 1960 election by a margin of 112,827 out of 68,770,294 votes cast. (Significantly, the 250,000 blacks who voted for Kennedy in Illinois helped him carry that state by 9,000 votes; the 95,000 who voted for him in Texas enabled him to defeat Nixon by 45,000 votes there; similarly, they provided margins in South Carolina and Michigan. Had Kennedy lost those states or even suffered slight shifts in black votes or if a significant number of blacks had stayed at home, as they did in 1968, Richard M. Nixon might have been President eight years sooner than he was.[7]) It is apparent that by 1960 blacks had begun to exert themselves in a "politics of participants."[8] They had begun to form a collective political conscience regarding the relationship of their votes to quid pro quos from the Democratic party.

CONFRONTATION POLITICS

Background. As blacks shifted to the Democratic party, the achievement of political, economic, and social integration in American life was far from reality. Institutional racism, discrimination, and systemic segregation persisted throughout the American social system. Race riots had resulted in the deaths of several black persons during the 1940s; many were unjustly imprisoned attempting to desegregate public accommodations and buses; while others were brutally murdered (as was Emmett Till in Mississippi in 1955 for "disrespecting a white lady"). When Mrs. Rosa Parks, a black seamstress in Montgomery, Alabama, refused to relinquish her bus seat to a white man and was arrested, the stage was set for the emergence of confrontation politics by black citizens. The impulsive act of a tired black woman who defied the tradition of blacks' vacating their seats for whites catapulted Dr. King to international prominence as the leader of the Montgomery Improvement Association, head of the Southern Christian Leadership Conference (SCLC), the personification of passive resistance, and the articulate spokesman of the civil rights movement. But Mrs. Parks' act was an experience with which the masses of Southern blacks could immediately identify; her arrest aroused their indignation and anger and, as a result, provided the basis for the group cohesion so vital in social movements. The decision by blacks in Montgomery to boycott buses stimulated blacks in other cities such as Tallahassee and Florida to undertake similar acts of protest. School systems erupted in violence in several Southern and border cities; President Eisenhower mobilized federal troops in Little Rock;[9] Dr. King's home was bombed; so was that of his aide, Reverend Fred Suttlesworth, in Birmingham. The more violent white Americans became, the more determined black Americans seemed to protest racial injustice and inequality in American life.

In this context an understandable rationale was provided for disavowing total dependence on legalistic forms of social protest, which created gradual social change, and for their replacement by more direct forms of political activism. Undoubtedly, the most significant single event that escalated political activism among blacks and redirected strategies of protest was the sit-in movement that started with four black college students from North Carolina A & T College in a dime store in February 1960. Here was begun an effective use of pressure resources (that is, those that drew upon such practices as sit-ins, boycotts, picketing, and so on) as a means of changing power relations. Just as the bus boycotts had forged interracial coalitions among intergroup organizations, the sit-in movement captured the attention of black students throughout the South, of liberal and radical white students in other parts of the country, and accelerated the drive to break down the barriers of racial apartheid. This movement had the psychological impact of transforming a seemingly passive, amorphous population into a highly activist and cohesive group.

Escalation of Conflict. The white South responded to the sit-in movement by massive arrests of college students, expulsions, and physical violence. Student supporters of the movement met at Shaw University and formed the Student Non-Violent Coordinating Committee (SNCC) later in 1960. The committee (often called SNICK) first followed Dr. King's philosophy of passive resistance but subsequently disavowed that strategy for CORE's tactics of direct action. The "in-movement" encompassed a broad range of activities that attacked segregation in public accommodations—all single-tactic, direct-action, and goal-specific. Hence sit-ins were followed by "wade-ons," "kneel-ins," "dwell-ins," and "jail-ins." CORE joined the movement, providing attacks against structured segregation on several flanks. The most notable of the forays were the freedom rides through the South, particularly Alabama, in 1961. Freedom riders were viciously assaulted in Birmingham, Alabama, and McComb, Mississippi, and their bus was upended and burned in Anniston, Alabama, in May 1961. An increasing number of blacks and whites joined the freedom riders and the movement while white violence escalated and resistance stiffened.

Mass direct action, such as freedom rides, was accompanied by public demonstrations, boycotts, and picketing. Although techniques seemed somewhat diffuse, each tactic was goal-specific—desegregate a certain facility or open up jobs for blacks and other minorities. Constraint goals were employed to attain competitive rewards. Black protest organizations, including the NAACP, CORE, SNCC, SCLC, coalesced to form informal coordinating councils of human rights to reconcile differences and maintain a cohesive structure. Yet each organization remained relatively specialized in its approach to identical goals. (King's SCLC, for instance, touched the nation's conscience through passive resistance and nonviolence; the

NAACP provided legal services and bail money for freedom riders and other protesters and joined with CORE and SNCC in massive demonstrations against institutions such as five-and-ten-cent stores and Sears Roebuck.) Throughout all the demonstrations, boycotting, and picketing, blacks were unerringly peaceful. They withstood without aggressive retaliation the German shepherds unleashed by Bull Conners in Birmingham, physical assaults in Anniston, firehoses in Orangeburg, electric cattle prods in Plaquemines Parish, Louisiana, and police brutality in several places. As "law-and-order" men abused them, blacks responded with "We shall overcome."

In terms of national unity, coordination of civil rights organizations, and concerted efforts to achieve the goal of integration, perhaps the finest hour came on August 27, 1963, when more than 250,000 peaceful demonstrators of all races, religious creeds, and ethnic origins joined to protest racial discrimination and segregation in a massive march on Washington. Those who assembled there had heard the NAACP's futile slogan, "Free by '63," and they had heard President Kennedy's televised broadcast telling the nation in June 1963 that "discrimination was morally wrong"; they also knew that blacks had neither attained occupational and income parity nor ended discrimination in all public accommodations through freedom rides. Leaders like Roy Wilkins, Bayard Rustin, James Farmer, and John Lewis addressed these issues and the frustrations of the masses. But it was Dr. King's ringing indictment of ubiquitous racial apartheid, political injustice, and inequalities of opportunities in American society in his "I Have a Dream" peroration that electrified the nation and raised the level of the consciousness of guilt on that fateful day in August—the same day that the tireless militant, great black intellectual W. E. B. DuBois died in Accra, Ghana. But the nation all but returned to business as usual shortly afterwards.

Within a matter of weeks bombs killed four black school girls who were attending Sunday school in Birmingham, Alabama. Within a matter of months in Dallas an assassin's bullets felled the one President whom blacks uniformly perceived as their friend. But had it not been for these two events, cruel as they were, many doubt whether or not Congress would ever have passed the Civil Rights Bill of 1964.

This measure, which many believe was enacted as a final gesture to the liberalism of John F. Kennedy, was of immense importance. It was designed to end all forms of discrimination and segregation in public accommodations, as well as in employment in which agencies received any form of federal support, and to further limit the evasions of the 1960 civil rights voting bill.

The 1960 act had made violations of court orders in voting a federal crime. It also authorized the appointment of referees to assure the registration of properly qualified blacks. The Civil Rights Bill of 1964 strengthened the earlier voting bill by demanding uniform standards for registering voters in federal elections; it made a sixth-grade education proof of literacy unless otherwise proved by election officials in court; and it guaranteed rights of appeal against denials of voter registration through the articulation of an appeals procedure involving legally constituted panels, the U. S. Attorney General, and, if necessary, a direct appeal to the Supreme Court. The immediate impact of this measure was that blacks began to register to vote in unparalleled numbers.

Although voter registration projects in Mississippi and other Deep South states were effective in increasing the number of black registered voters, white resistance remained. Black workers were intimidated by the use of economic reprisals or sanctions against them by their employers as well as by both threatened and actual violence. Registrars attempted to curtail the number of black registrants by such devices as slowing down the registration process, closing the office earlier than scheduled, or by simply hiding when blacks came to register.[10]

Much to the astonishment of many blacks, President Lyndon Johnson seemed serious in his public pronouncements about creating a just and Great Society for all people irrespective of race, religion, or ethnic origin. Thus his political acumen, coupled with the increasing pressure from civil rights groups, accounted for the passage of the Civil Rights Act of 1965.

The 1965 act suspended literacy tests as a requirement for voting, authorized the use of federal examiners in the South to protect the rights of potential black voters, and extended several provisions of the 1964 act to cover state and local, as well as federal, elections. Thus the way was paved for even more significant increases in the proportion of eligible black voters. Organizations such as SNCC, the Voter Registration Project, individuals such as Julian Bond and John Lewis, and an enormous army of volunteers from all parts of the country cooperated in voter registration drives throughout the South.

Again, a crisis precipitated, to some degree, both the passage of the voting rights bill and the outpouring of manpower assistance from various parts of the country. During the summer of 1964, three young civil rights workers—James Chaney (black) and Michael Schwerner and Andrew Goodman (both white and, perhaps, representative of the large number of Jewish activists involved in the movement at this stage)—were murdered in Mississippi; a series of urban disruptions that imperiled national peace shocked the country. In early 1965, prior to the enactment of the new voting rights law, Malcolm X was assassinated; federal intervention was necessary in the confrontation of civil rights marchers at the Selma, Alabama, bridge so that a peaceful march to Montgomery could proceed. During that march, three white Unitarian ministers were mercilessly assaulted, and one, Reverend James Reeb, subsequently died. Mrs. Viola Liuzzo, a white civil rights worker who had joined the Selma-Montgomery marchers from Detroit, also met death as a result of gunshot wounds inflicted upon her by white terrorists in an ambush on Highway 80. Aside from the responses of a conscience-pricked white Northern public, the federal government was increasingly worried about its international image, since every act of violence in the United States, directed against civil rights groups or individuals, was front-page news in the world press. The international reputation of the United States as a multiracial society structured on high principles of justice, freedom, and equality was becoming severely tarnished. As a result, the government began to respond more quickly and more forcefully to the demands of protesters and to protect their rights.

However, a combination of circumstances further explains the favorable response of the federal government to the demands advanced by various civil rights groups. First, the civil rights movement until the mid-1960s had directed its major thrust toward a specific goal, the elimination of discrimination and segregation in such areas as public accommodations, libraries, schools, and voting. Second, these demands neither contradicted nor countervailed the basic principles of freedom and equality implicit in the American Constitution, especially in the Fourteenth Amendment. Third, the larger white society did not perceive assenting to the demands made by civil rights groups as a major threat to its welfare, since, for one thing, the white society continued to improve its status by moving into higher-paying, more prestigious positions. Thus blacks tended to fill positions vacated by whites rather than to move into highly competitive situations with them. Fourth, the federal government, as well as several local jurisdictions, recognized the growing political strength of black voters gained by virtue of well-orchestrated voter registration drives—also evidence of the movement of blacks toward a kind of participation politics.

However, the responses through legislation addressed to specific demands by civil rights groups primarily benefited the black middle and upper classes. Enacted legislation had the unintended function of raising the level of aspirations and expectations among black lower classes, who would soon cry for "a piece of the action." In time, for instance, they would seek to seize control of the antipoverty programs and an array of community-oriented programs stimulated by Johnson's Great Society legislation as their exclusive domain. However, federal and local government responses were both conciliatory and restricted to rather narrow parameters. Yet aspirations remained high. It is the disjunction between heightened aspirations or expectations and limited observable gratifications for the masses of people that paved the way for violent confrontations in urban centers.[11] This was particularly true for urban blacks in the North who felt excluded from civil rights gains.

URBAN REBELLIONS

Although the conditions of urban blacks in the North were in a sense objectively better than those of Southern blacks, deprivation is relative. Blacks in the North and West are not inclined to measure their objective condition by standards under which blacks in the South are believed to live. They measure their economic, social, and political advancement by the norms and standards prevailing in their local communities in the North and West. It makes little difference to a black man in Watts, California, that his median income may be $2,000 more than the median income of a black man of equal education, training, and experience in Alabama when his own median income is $4,000 less than that of his white counterpart in West Los Angeles. Blacks in Cleveland or Detroit care far less that their housing conditions may be superior to housing provided rural blacks in Mississippi than that their own situation is decidedly substandard in comparison to housing available to white citizens in Cleveland and Detroit. Thus the conditions encountered depict the relativity of deprivation and point to the fundamental basis for differential expectations and reward systems. When conditions of deprivation converge with conditions of police brutality, ghetto exploitation by unscrupulous landlords, dishonest merchants, pressures of overcrowded dwellings, and fear of crime, the essential ingredients for rebellion prevail.

Beginning with the "riots" of the summer of 1964, urban unrest escalated in severity and proportion in each year through 1968. It began in New York's Harlem in July 1964 and spread to the Bedford-Stuyvesant section of Brooklyn. Then incipient revolutions of black masses shook other communities, including Rochester, New York; Patterson and Elizabeth, New Jersey; Chicago; and Philadelphia. In the summer of 1965 the six-day uprising in the Watts section of Los Angeles nearly immobilized parts of Los Angeles in what became known as the Watts insurrection. The human toll included 34 dead and more than 1,000 injured. Almost 4,000 people were arrested in this rebellion, and property damages totalled approximately $40 million. What triggered the uprising was the allegedly unwarranted arrest of a black person who was subjected to police brutality, but actually the underlying causes went much deeper—they were the culmination of all the deprivations and denied opportunities blacks perceived in relation to white privilege and advantage. And more uprisings were forthcoming. In

1966 they occurred from Omaha to Lansing, Michigan, and from Chicago to Atlanta. The summer of 1967 witnessed a carnage probably never previously duplicated except in times of open warfare in the United States. Destruction, disaster, and hopelessness gripped this nation, which seemed unable to determine appropriate remedies. In Detroit alone in the events of the summer of 1967 about 42 people died, 386 were injured, 5,567 were arrested, and scores of buildings were burned and looted, with property damages in excess of $45 million. Newark was the scene of devastating destruction of human life and personal property. In all, during the first nine months of 1967, racial disturbances ripped apart approximately 164 American communities,[12] and during the summer months alone rebellions occurred in approximately 35 cities.[13]

Then came that fateful day of April 4, 1968, when an assassin felled the most revered civil rights leader of modern times, Dr. Martin Luther King. His death precipitated immediate and retaliatory responses by black people of all ideological dispositions and social classes. The United States was quickly engulfed in a national crisis in which rioting, rebellion, insurrections, carnage, looting, and burning were at the epicenter. Major rebellions occurred in Washington, Chicago, and more than 100 other cities, resulting in at least 46 persons killed, thousands injured, and millions of dollars of personal property lost. More than 50,000 federal troops and National Guardsmen were summoned to quell the disturbances throughout the United States. Later that summer, 11 persons were killed in a shoot-out in Cleveland. And the National Guard was mobilized for action during a riot in Miami while the Republican national convention was in session. When the insurrections were spent, blacks realized more than ever that the nation had moved into a more repressive state, taking on many attributes of a police state in which reactionary law-and-order forces had gained control of all levels of government. Indeed, some feared the possibility of incarceration in World War II concentration camps reportedly being reactivated for just that purpose.

The riots, rebellions, and insurrections were more directed to retail stores than to public institutions primarily because the retail establishments symbolized institutionalized exploitation of blacks in their day-to-day lives. As it became clear that white-owned establishments in black ghettos were under attack, black owners of businesses hastily scribbled signs on doors and windows, such as "Soul Brother" and "Black Owner," as a means of protecting themselves from total destruction. In many instances white merchants admired for their support of black people in employment and in achieving other goals were also spared. However, many innocent victims of black despair were not so fortunate.

Perhaps an unintended consequence of the urban rebellions was that they left the civil rights movement in shambles. The traditional black leadership seemed incapable of containing the century of controlled frustration that exploded on the urban scene. The loss of Dr. King was a crushing blow to black and white people alike, even though his leadership was being subjected to serious attack by militant blacks particularly and by those who disagreed with his apparent alignment with the Students for a Democratic Society antiwar activists. It has often been said that blacks lost their most effective leader and whites lost their closest friend and ally with King's assassination. With his death new forms and new approaches already in the offing two years earlier began to gain strength as a political force among black people.

BLACK POWER AND
BLACK LIBERATION

No one knew what Stokely Carmichael meant in 1966 when he pronounced his intention to claim black power for American blacks, not even the American press. In what has been described as "press-orchestrated hysteria,"[14] however, black power immediately became a divisive, extremely feared, and much maligned concept. A great part of the fear sprang from the use of the expression by a person who had encouraged blacks to take up arms in self-defense against white oppressors. With leadership changes SNCC had long since abandoned nonviolent advocacy and supplanted it with a freedom-by-whatever-means-necessary posture. Many Americans, white and black, interpreted the speeches and addresses given by Carmichael and H. Rap Brown as inflammatory and racially divisive. Moreover, the fragile coalition between black and white student members of SNCC disintegrated under the increasing militance assumed by the black leadership of SNCC. Thus when Carmichael shouted "black power," bored newspapermen covering the civil rights march through Mississippi had a story tailored for national attention.

White people in America interpreted black power as antiwhite, a demand for shared values at their expense, as blacks "getting something for nothing," as an infringement on their prerogatives, or as an impending physical assault on white people in general.

Black militant advocates of black power sensed that the American white public was perturbed but probably reluctant to escalate violent attacks against black Americans for fear of adverse publicity. The strategy, however, called for a rhetoric of militance and revolution as a new instrument for effectuating change. They explained, also, that black power meant the development of self-determination, a rekindled sense of personal worth, pride in one's blackness, a glorification of black culture, and a need for utilizing the black experience as a unifying force in the black community. For many of this group the only authentic black experience, however, resulted from socialization and social nurturing in a lower-class black ghetto. Middle-class blacks were highly suspect; integrationists became "toms" and "aunt saras" or "oreos." This group demanded avowed blackness as defined by ghetto experience and adherence to much of the philosophy articulated by the late Malcolm X. Indeed, a new cult of personality emerged in Malcolm X, who achieved status as a national hero and who was somewhat beatified in death largely because of his strong emphasis on black self-acceptance, black self-awareness, and the positive dimensions of black identity.

If the concept raised questions and doubts in the minds of white Americans, it aroused mixed reactions in the black community. Some blacks thought at first that black power smacked of racism in reverse; others viewed it as a highly separatist philosophy; others appreciated its more nationalistic fervor and its efficacy for severing the umbilical cord between white liberals and predominantly black organizations. In this category were those persons who questioned the sincerity of those white liberals in the movement who showed a penchant for eschewing conflict situations and who seemed to have relied instead on the critical element of their financial support to dictate to blacks how to behave and what strategies to call upon in specific situations. Black power was an opportunity for blacks to assert their independence and to move rapidly toward self-determination. CORE opted for this movement and almost immediately lost much of its financial support, which led to internal problems. The NAACP and the National Urban League slowly accepted a revised conceptualization of the slogan "black power," attributing to it, and rightly so as it turned out, a renewed thrust for economic, political, and social advancement by black people for black people. But the Black Panthers claimed that the only possibility for revolutionary change was through a coalition between blacks and white socialist radicals.

The black power movement spawned a new type of militance in the black urban community, captivating rhetoric, ideological schisms, and a demand for black studies programs as well as innumerable disruptions when these demands were not readily met. Most important of all, the black power movement spawned black liberation, which came to address itself as a movement for the unification of blacks of all ideological perspectives, social classes, and shades of color into a new single cohesive structure with the primary goal of reordering power relations within American society. As a result, the traditional black establishment structure diminished in power as a more amorphous leadership structure evolved at the grassroots level. But a quiet revolution beginning at the ballot box was to raise blacks to a new level of a politics of participation toward a politics of governance.[15] To move blacks toward that goal during the 1960s two major black power conventions were held: (1) Adam Clayton Powell convened the first major black power conference in Washington on September 3, 1966. This conference attracted about 169 representatives from approximately 64 organizations and 18 states. (2) The National Conference on Black Power was convened at Newark immediately following the insurrection there in July 1967. Among the more salient conference demands were those that called for an immediate tripling of the number of blacks in Congress, the election of black mayors, more city and state elected officials, and the appointment of a greater number of blacks to high federal positions.

In effect, blacks were calling for an end to what Chuck Stone described as "the revolving-door Negro" in federal appointments. This term refers to a long-established pattern of appointing a few blacks to breakthrough positions in the federal government without appointing black replacements when they later vacate such positions. As a result, the number of blacks in high-level governmental positions is restricted to a few individuals who are shifted from one position to another, and the net gain for blacks remains minimal.[16] Significantly, these demands were addressed to "getting into the system" rather than destroying the system per se. Blackness, too, meant using the power of the ballot, as ethnic immigrants had done before them, for the election of black officials and in the appointment of other black individuals to responsible leadership roles. Thus black power achieved a new level of respectability in the black community.

VOTER PARTICIPATION
AND BLACK OFFICE
HOLDERS

Compared to the proportion of white registered and actual voters, black voting behavior has until recently left a great deal to be desired. The black vote has always been smaller than normally expected in terms of the size of the black population for reasons previously explained in this chapter. In addition, voting among blacks has traditionally been much more pronounced among the smaller middle and upper classes and among the better educated than among the larger lower classes, which possess a higher proportion of the voting-age black population. The basic goal of participation was to reduce apathy and increase motivation for expanded political involvement. However, with the enactment of the previously described enabling voting rights legislation, combined with favorable decisions by the U.S. Supreme

Court and voter registration drives mounted in the 1960s, the increased proportion of registered black voters has made them a political force of substantial potential power.

Using 1952 as a base year, it is possible to illustrate the impact of voting rights legislation and voter registration drives on the fluctuations in the number of black voters in the South, for example. The estimated number of black voters in the South during 1952 was about 1,008,614. By 1958 the number had climbed to 1,303,627, and by 1964 Southern black registered voters almost doubled at 2,174,200. In those years less than half of all potentially eligible black voters had registered and voted in national and local elections. In 1966, following the enactment of the Civil Rights Act of 1965, the number of registered black voters in the South almost tripled as it climbed to 5,684,000 and climbed again in each year thereafter. Fully 60 percent of all blacks of voting age in the U.S. registered by 1966 (53 percent in the South). During the 1968 election year, 72 percent of all blacks in the North and West had registered. Table 7-1 illustrates these facts.

TABLE 7-1.

Reported Voter Registration for Persons of Voting Age, by Region: 1966, 1968, and 1970

(*Numbers in thousands*)

Subject	Negro			White		
	1966	1968	1970	1966	1968	1970
All persons of voting age:	10,533	10,935	11,473	101,205	104,521	107,997
North and West	4,849	4,944	5,277	72,593	75,687	77,158
South	5,684	5,991	6,196	28,612	28,834	30,839
Number who reported they had registered:						
United States	6,345	7,238	6,971	72,517	78,835	74,672
North and West	3,337	3,548	3,406	54,125	58,419	54,591
South	3,008	3,690	3,565	18,392	20,416	20,081
Percent of voting-age population:						
United States	60	66	61	72	75	69
North and West	69	72	65	75	77	71
South	53	62	58	64	71	65

SOURCE: U.S. Department of Commerce, Social and Economic Statistics Administration, Bureau of the Census.

In the meantime, voter participation by blacks increased as reflected in Table 7-2. Clearly, blacks, like whites, are more likely to participate in national elections than in the off-year local and state elections. However, the proportion of blacks actually voting, although increasing from year to year, remains lower than the proportion of whites who actually vote.

TABLE 7-2.

Reported Voter Participation for Persons of Voting Age, by Region: 1964, 1966, 1968, and 1970

(*Numbers in millions*)

Subject	Negro				White			
	1964	1966	1968	1970	1964	1966	1968	1970
All persons of voting age:	10.3	10.5	10.9	11.5	99.4	101.2	104.5	108.0
North and West	5.4	4.8	4.9	5.3	72.8	72.6	75.7	77.2
South	5.8	5.7	6.0	6.2	26.6	28.6	28.8	30.8
Number who reported that they voted:								
United States	6.0	4.4	6.3	5.0	70.2	57.8	72.2	60.4
North and West	3.9	2.5	3.2	2.7	54.4	44.8	54.4	46.1
South	2.6	1.9	3.1	2.3	15.8	12.9	17.9	14.3
Percent who reported that they voted:								
United States	59	42	58	44	71	57	69	56
North and West	72[1]	52	65	51	75	62	72	60
South	44[1]	33	52	37	60	45	62	46

[1] For Negro and other races.

SOURCE: U.S. Department of Commerce, Social and Economic Statistics Administration, Bureau of the Census.

Black Elected Officials. As a consequence of substantial increases in the proportion of registering and voting blacks, heightening levels of political consciousness of blacks, their increasing tendency to vote for black candidates, and their utilization of voting power as a mobilized resource, a quiet revolution occurred in the number of blacks who were elected to public office since 1965. Table 7-3 indicates the changes from 1969 to 1973. On the national level, for example, one black senator was elected in 1966 but largely from a white constituency in Massachusetts. However, the number of blacks elected to the House of Representatives more than tripled between 1964 and 1973, rising from 5 to 16, including four black women. By 1974, there were more than 200 blacks in the state legislatures of the country, two lieutenant governors (Colorado and California), approximately 110 mayors and almost 3,000 other elected officials, including, among others, vice-mayors, county officials, law enforcement officers, judges, and school superintendents. Blacks had indeed moved toward a politics of governance involving control over the decision-making apparatus in selected communities, though to a lesser degree at the national level.

T A B L E   7 - 3 .

Black Elected Officials in the United States, 1969–1973

Year	Total	Difference from Previous Year	Percentage Increase	
			Previous Year	1969
1969	1,185	0	0	0
1970	1,469	284	19%	19%
1971	1,860	391	26%	56%
1972	2,264	404	22%	91%
1973	2,621	357	15%	121%

SOURCE: Prepared by Office of Research, Joint Center for Political Studies, 1426 H Street, N.W., Washington, D.C. 20005.

One of the more disturbing features of the ascent of blacks at the local level is that they are gaining control of cities when the urban communities are enmeshed in poverty, unemployment, and experiencing terrifying losses of tax bases, on the one hand, and increasing problems of public transportation, high crime, and housing on the other hand. Their rise to political power at the local level coincides with a decision by the federal government to diminish federal aid to cities and states under a policy of a "New Federalism." The immediate outcome of this policy is to create a sense of hopelessness on which nationalistic movements thrive. This, in turn, may lead to new outbreaks of public confrontations despite the fears of powerful governmental repressive tactics that subdued demonstrations following the inclusion of antiriot sections in the Civil Rights Act of 1968. It is dangerous to misinterpret the withdrawal of blacks from public activism as a sign of growing satisfaction with tokenism or resignation to the inevitability of a public policy of benign neglect, for the probability is strong that the closer a dispossessed group gets toward goal attainment, the more frustrated it becomes as goals are blocked and the more likely it is to accelerate its demands for immediate compliance to its objectives. The failure of entrenched power structure to respond with immediate gratification may necessitate either the utilization of a crushing display of awesome power or acquiescence to all demands of minority groups. Conciliatory mechanisms are no longer as operative as they once were.

THE NATIONAL BLACK POLITICAL AGENDA AND THE BLACK BILL OF RIGHTS

Partially in recognition of the possibility of further conflict and partially to stimulate greater political participation by blacks in both the electoral and governmental processes black leaders convened a series of national conferences in the early 1970s. Perhaps the most important of these was the National Black Political Convention at Gary, Indiana, during March 1972. The congressional black caucus, formed by 12 congressmen and 1 congresswoman following the 1968 elections, had suggested such a meeting to reunite disaffected civil rights groups in preparation for the 1972 national elections. Newark blacks, led by Baraka, also called for a national unity meeting. Finally, in the official absence of the congressional black caucus, more than 8,000 delegates, observers, and media people convened at Gary.

The primary purposes of the 1972 national conference were to: resolve old conflicts, unify all black people under one national organization with objectives expressive of common needs; prepare for the 1972 national election through which the objective of black political power could be enhanced; and enable blacks to take control over their own political destiny. The 2,782 officially certified delegates adopted about 88 resolutions, almost all of which were clearly reformist in nature. However, vociferous and uncompromising ideologists, sponsoring resolutions against busing and Israel, almost succeeded in driving out the more moderate delegates. Shouts of "nationtime," symbolizing black nationalism rather than "unity without uniformity," and efforts to forge an all-black political third party[17] threatened to undermine the goal of national black unity. Indeed, several delegates walked out of the convention, returning only after a hard fought rapprochement had been won. An antibusing resolution was picked up by a press bent on sensationalizing every aspect of the conference, and all national television networks interpreted it as being in support of the Nixonian philosophy against forced busing to achieve integration. In reality, the thrust of the resolution was to expose the busing issue as a mask for other issues such as those pertaining to defiance of orders to provide both desegregated schools and quality education. It was a repudiation of notions of black inferiority and white supremacy. The anti-Israel resolution was a misguided demand for the "dismantling" of Israel and was presented undoubtedly as a symbolic nationalistic gesture of support for the Arab world. The National Political Agenda, which emerged from this conference, was a commitment to social reform through participation within the American political and economic system. It called for political empowerment through "proportionate black congressional representation, the continued election of blacks to national and local offices; economic empowerment through reparations, jobs, a reasonable minimum wage, rural development and self-determination; prison reforms, educational and social change, a better life for black youth and self-government for the District of Columbia; and end to police brutality and political surveillance of blacks by federal agencies and community control over those institutions which affect the destiny of black people in America."[18]

The Black Bill of Rights. This was the work of the black congressional caucus, which did not officially participate in the National Black Political Convention. However, this document included many issues outlined in the National Political Agenda. Essentially, it called for substantive improvements in the condition of black people in the following twelve areas: (1) jobs and income, including full employment and a guaranteed annual income of $6500; (2) foreign policy, including the end of the Vietnam War and support of African liberation; (3) the right to quality education; (4) radical improvements in housing and the alleviation of urban problems; (5) health and health-care delivery systems; (6) minority businesses; (7) the right to drug-free lives; (8) penal reform; (9) proportionate appointments of blacks by the Democratic administration; (10) justice and civil rights; (11) self-determination for the District of Columbia; and (12) the end of injustice in the military.[19]

The National Political Agenda and the Black Bill of Rights were prepared for inclusion in the platform of the Democratic national convention. The transfer of unity from Gary to the Miami convention sites did not materialize, however. Instead, the quest for unity was subordinated to personal agendas and self-aggrandizement as individual blacks bartered for personal power at the expense of the black masses. As a result, the Democratic national platform accommodated neither the bill of rights nor the agenda because the white power structure recognized that a few black opportunists had undermined the will of the masses in order to promote themselves.[20] Once again, the strategy of divide and conquer had managed to subvert the attainment of group goals and demands made by black people. Black Republicans had no such agenda and accomplished little more than an exchange of social pleasantries during their convention. Indeed, some prominent blacks, including Sammy Davis, Jr. and Floyd McKissick as well as many black businessmen, enthusiastically supported Nixon's election. Others supported Nixon for fear of withdrawal of financial support from business ventures. Nevertheless, black Republicans did not play a major role in the decision made during the Republican Convention.

Despite the setbacks in Miami, blacks voted in larger numbers than ever before in 1972, displaying a continued commitment to the Democratic party as well as *their* disdain for the elitism, conservatism, and general antiblack posture attributed to the Republican party. Eighty-seven percent of black voters supported George McGovern not only because of their alignment with his policies but because of the belief among many that Nixon remained unequivocally antiblack. This claim seemed to be supported by Nixon's opposition to busing for school desegregation, his skillful use of welfare arguments to arouse antiblack sentiments, and a general insensitivity to issues affecting the black poor. Three new blacks came to Congress, including a black female from Texas, another from California, and the first black sent from the Deep South to the U.S. Congress since 1901. Later, when Representative George Collins (Democrat, Illinois) was killed in a plane crash, his wife won his vacated seat and went to Congress in 1973. Blacks voted in such large numbers that by 1973 approximately 2,621 black elected officials, representing less than 1 percent of the 522,000 elected officials in the United States, were holding office. By April 1974 approximately 2,991 black elected officials were serving in 45 states.[21]

A second national political convention was convened in Little Rock, Arkansas, in March 1974. Less than one-half of the number of delegates who attended the Gary convention were in Little Rock. Gone was the rhetoric that was so divisive at Gary and gone were many of the national black leaders who had played prominent roles at the first convention. Representatives John Conyers and Ronald Dellums and Mayors Hatcher and Jackson of Gary and Atlanta, respectively, were among the leading political figures present. The delegates defeated a resolution that urged the establishment of a black political party. However, they passed resolutions that called for, among other things, home rule in the District of Columbia, African studies in public schools, opposition to psychological testing in public schools and colleges, the use of special courts to handle cases of political prisoners, and the creation of a black united fund to assist black institutions and aid projects in Africa.

Black political power has been transformed from fiery rhetoric without substance to the reconstruction of a critical black mass capable of influencing political outcomes and of electing an ever-increasing number of blacks to national, state, and local positions. This situation in itself is indicative of the power of the political process to effect social change; but blacks have yet to transfer that political power for substantial economic betterment of the black masses.

NOTES

1. For an extensive discussion of power and related theories see Hubert M. Blalock, Jr., *Toward a General Theory of Minority Group Behavior* (New York: Wiley & Sons, 1967); William J. Wilson, *Power, Racism and Privilege* (New York: Macmillan, 1973); and James C. Davies, "The J-Curve of Rising and Declining Satisfaction as a Cause of Some Great Revolutions and a Contained Rebellion," in *Violence in America: Historical and Comparative Perspectives*, Hugh Davis Graham and Robert Gurr (eds.) (New York: Bantam Books, 1969).

2. Robert Dahl, *Who Governs?* (New Haven, Conn.: Yale University Press, 1961), p. 21.

3. Wilson, *op. cit.*

4. Hanes Walton, *Black Politics* (New York: J. P. Lippincott, 1972), pp. 58–69.

5. Edward Banfield, *Big City Politics* (New York: Random House, 1965), p. 301.

6. Henry Lee Moon, *Balance of Power: The Negro Vote* (Garden City, N.Y.: Doubleday, 1948), p. 198.

7. For a discussion of both fluctuations in and influences of black voter participation cf.: Chuck Stone, *Black Political Power in America* (New York: Dell Publishing Co., Inc., 1948); Thomas Pettigrew, "White-Negro Confrontations," in Eli Ginsbert (ed.), *The Negro Challenge to the Business Community* (New York: McGraw-Hill, 1964), pp. 39–55; Theodore White, *The Making of the President 1960* (New York: Atheneum, 1961), p. 323; John Dean, *The Making of a Black Mayor* (Washington, D.C.: The Joint Center for Political Studies, 1973); and Daniel P. Moynihan, "Political Perspectives," in Eli Ginsbert (ed.), *The Negro Challenge to the Business Community* (New York: McGraw-Hill, 1964), pp. 71–80.

8. For a discussion of the politics of participation and the politics of governance cf. Charles V. Hamilton, "Racial, Ethnic and Social Class Politics and Administration," *Public Administration Review*, 32 (October 1972), pp. 638–648.

9. Wilson Record and Jane Cassels Record, *Little Rock, U.S.A.* (San Francisco: Chandler Publishing Company, 1960), pp. 35–119.

10. Cf. Charles V. Hamilton and Stokely Carmichael, *Black Power: The Politics of Liberation in America*, for a discussion of the restraints posed upon blacks in Lowndes County, Alabama, during the mid-1960s for an elaboration of efforts to curtail black political participation in the South. It should be stressed, however, that with successful voter registration in that county blacks in 1973 controlled major sections of the decision-making structure, including the county sheriff position.

11. This discussion is essentially in agreement with positions taken by several writers such as Wilson, *op. cit.*, Pettigrew, *op. cit.*, and William Gamson, *Power and Discontent* (Homewood, Ill.: Dorsey Press, 1968).

12. *Report of the National Advisory Commission on Civil Disorders* (New York: Bantam Books, 1968), pp. 112–115.

13. Stone, *op. cit.*, p. 24.

14. *Ibid.*, p. 16.

15. Hamilton, *op. cit.*, refers to the politics of participation as the use of the electoral process as a means of involvement in local and national politics, whereas governance is the result of sustained bloc voting, which creates political leadership roles by blacks to the degree that they control the instruments of government at one level or another.

16. *Op. cit.*, p. 75.

17. This was not the first attempt by blacks to form political parties. Indeed, blacks historically have formed political parties at either the state or national level for approximately 100 years. However, in more recent times state-level political parties included the Mississippi Freedom Democratic party, which challenged the seating of white Democrats at the 1964 Democratic convention in Atlantic City; the Black Panther party in Lowndes County, Alabama; and the National Democratic party of Alabama, which has been responsible for the rapid increase in the number of black elected officials since 1967. At the national level blacks formed the National Independent Political League (1912), the National Labor Congress (1924), the National Negro Congress (1936), the Afro-American party (1960), the Freedom Now Party (1964), and the Freedom and Peace Party (1968), which represented a coalition among Eldridge Cleaver, the Black Panthers, and the peace movement in the United States. Cf. Walton, *op. cit.*, for a more detailed discussion of black political parties.

18. *The National Black Political Agenda*, mimeo. (Gary, Indiana), 1972.

19. *The Black Bill of Rights* (Washington, D.C.: The Congressional Black Caucus, 1972).

20. Paul Delaney, "Black Politics 72," *Black Enterprise*, 3 (February 1973), pp. 30–33.

21. *Focus*, (April 1974), p. 2.

8 | THE MILITARY AND BLACK LIFE

Although blacks have always served in the armed forces of the United States, their roles have depended upon government policy. The government has followed a pattern that progressed from official segregation and discrimination to a policy of integration, which has in recent times permitted "voluntary separatism," which will be explained shortly. This shift in government policy occurred not always because of a more liberal governmental philosophy but often as an appropriate response to pressures or conditions that threatened the cohesion of the American military system. Changes within the military system have historically and characteristically transpired slowly, grudgingly, and cautiously. During the past century the increasing aggressiveness and militancy of the American black community has played a profound role in moving the American military toward change.

Four themes seem to emerge regarding black experiences in the armed services, namely, (1) blacks have been moving, although with resistance and interruptions, toward assimilation into the military; (2) a high correlation exists between racial identity and the experiences of people in the military system and as ex-servicemen or women; (3) the black community has never displayed organized opposition toward military service per se (rather, its protests have tended to be directed against its systematic patterns of discrimination, racism, segregation, and exclusion); and (4) racial conflict within the military community is not a recent phenomenon and, further, may reveal racial animosities or prejudices only temporarily allayed by needs for protection in combat situations.

This chapter examines the historical roles performed by blacks in relation to governmental policies and their consequences for contemporary black experiences in military life. Primary attention is devoted to blacks in the military during and since American involvement in the Vietnam War.[1]

GOVERNMENTAL POLICY
AND HISTORICAL ROLES

For more than 150 years U.S. government policies of exclusion and segregation prevented blacks from gaining full participation within the military system whenever they were permitted entry. This observation may be illustrated by brief examples from wars in which the United States has paricipated.

First, with the courage displayed by blacks such as Crispus Attucks, the first American to die in the cause of the Revolution, many blacks sought to volunteer for service with the Revolutionary army. General George Washington expressed his opposition to their inclusion in four orders issued through the Council of General Officers of the Continental Congress. It was only after the threat posed by Lord Dunmore's proclamation (issued November 7, 1777) guaranteeing unconditional freedom to male slaves who volunteered to serve with the British that Washington recommended the enlistment of blacks. The 5,000 blacks who served in the segregated army and the 1,500 or more who served in the navy were not only involved in combat but performed innumerable service roles. They worked as cooks, construction laborers, servants, and in other support capacities. But when the new nation's freedom had been won, Congress prohibited blacks from serving in any branch of the armed service, including state militias, the navy, and the marines.[2] A similar pattern of threats followed by exclusion occurred during the War of 1812 but on a much smaller scale.

Second, during the Civil War, decisions relative to the incorporation of blacks in either the Confederate army or the Union army were complicated by the issues of slavery, manumission, and fugitive slaves. No consistent governmental policy existed regarding either those issues or the conscription of blacks. Inconsistencies reflected regional policy distinctions as well as different perceptions of the importance of black people in achieving either the goal of national unity or of regional secession. Policy changes occurred solely because of changing definitions of the situation as couched in terms like "acts of military necessity." Therefore, the Confederacy, motivated by the need to combat external threats to internal security, initially responded by impressing blacks into support services (for example, construction of military installations, work as railroad repairmen, cooks, mechanics, hospital aides, and so on). Thousands of able-bodied slaves escaped rather than submit to this new form of tyranny with no promise of manumission. General Robert E. Lee reluctantly approved an order to permit the enlistment of 2,000 blacks into the Confederate army, with freedom being exchanged for loyalty, only after his army had encountered serious military setbacks. Thus official inclusion was made an act of military necessity.

Early in the Civil War Northern blacks were permitted to enlist in the Union army but on a segregated basis, whether in combat or in service roles. Initially, however, a primary concern regarded appropriate dispositions to be made of fugitive and captured slaves. The problem was resolved by the Confiscation Act of 1861, which authorized Union troops to free captured slaves. President Lincoln's Emancipation Proclamation (which he called an "act of military necessity" and which became effective on January 1, 1863) undoubtedly helped swell the ranks of the U.S. Coloured Troops. Although incorporated into the Union army structure, blacks still did not enjoy equal status. Inequities were observed in the paucity of blacks certified as commissioned officers (a total of 100 throughout the war), in the inequality of pay (the salary of whites ranged from $13 to $100 whereas that of the 178,975 black soldiers was established at $7 per month), in the inferior supplies assigned to blacks, and in the health conditions under which blacks labored, resulting in a mortality rate among blacks believed to be 40 percent higher than that of whites. Indeed, 38,000 black soldiers lost their lives, and thousands more were seriously wounded.[3] It is interesting to note, however, that during the Civil War in contrast to World Wars I and II, when the nation was presumably considerably more enlightened, 16 black soldiers and 5 black sailors were awarded the Congressional Medal of Honor. None was so honored in either of the world wars.

Third, the roles of blacks in the Indian wars illustrate how blacks, a subordinate group themselves, were forced to subordinate another group attempting to protect itself from territorial encroachments and violations of its sovereignty. Simultaneously, the migrant superordinates, white settlers, whose authority over the subordinated blacks had already been established in other territories and states, used that subordinate group for protection against native Indians who resisted their encroachments. Specifically, the four black units that remained after the Civil War (there had been as many as 150 during the war) were added to the regular army in 1866, sent initially to protect carpetbaggers in the South, and later transferred to the rapidly expanding Western frontier to protect white settlers against "hostile" Indians. Reaction of white settlers to a black military were both peculiar and expected as defined by the nature of the social and territorial situations.

The white people of the Western domain, for example, treated blacks of the 9th Cavalry with open hostility as they arrived in Wyoming in 1885.

Their internalization of stereotypes and prejudices against blacks is reflected in their love for watching "coon dances," a major recreation in that locale in that period. According to substantial evidence, nevertheless, attitudes were far less hostile and considerably more accommodating the closer the communities were to the Indian reservations. In those instances, under the threat of hostile Indian tribes, blacks and whites learned to subordinate racial animosities and to become more tolerant of each other.[4] Thus by the time that the 24th Cavalry of blacks and the 10th Cavalry of blacks arrived in Cheyenne to eliminate cattle wars, interracial hostility had somewhat abated at least on a superficial level. It was, however, the white citizens of Wyoming who called blacks "buffalo soldiers" because they believed that a similarity existed between the hair of blacks and that of the buffalo who roamed the Western territory. Unmistakably, hostility was only temporarily suppressed, since blacks were lynched in Wyoming in 1913 and that state early enacted laws prohibiting interracial marriage and integrated schools.

As the war with Spain broke out, the army ordered the four black regiments stationed in the Western states and territories to assist in the conquest of Cuba and Spanish territories in the West Indies. In addition 16 regiments of black volunteers also distinguished themselves in battle. Their primary motive for joining the military was economic betterment in the face of mounting discrimination associated with the return of white supremacy and agricultural displacements resulting from an economic recession, the spread of the boll weevil, and changing demographic patterns.

Fourth, the Brownsville incident illustrates the unwillingness of dominant group members to accept authority roles of low-status minorities over them and also illustrates how accusations against black men of sexual abuse of white women may be used to heighten animosities and lead to brutalities against the innocent. Briefly, the 25th Infantry Regiment, comprised of black soldiers and white officers, was stationed at Fort Brown near Brownsville, Texas, in 1906. Widespread resentment over their assignment to that area soon escalated into physical abuse, racial epithets, and discriminatory acts. One night in August, during an alleged raid on Brownsville, Mrs. Evans, a white woman, claimed to have been "almost raped" by a black man believed to have been from the infantry. However, the allegations were never substantiated during a jury trial. President Roosevelt, undoubtedly motivated by political considerations because of the forthcoming elections, sent General G. A. Garlington to Brownsville to initiate further investigations of the matter. Despite General Garlington's persistent questioning, none of the blacks spoke up. Nonplused by what he called "a conspiracy of silence," Garlington recommended that all 167 black members of the regiment be punished. President Roosevelt thereupon dishonorably discharged them—the first and only incident of mass punishment in American military history.[5] Sixty-six years later in 1972, under the leadership of Congressman Augustus Hawkins, Army Secretary Froelkhe revoked the dismissal order and exonerated all 167 men. Only two of the men were living at the time, however, and one has since died. They subsequently received a paltry sum in back pay—a small recompense for the years of hardship and intolerable conditions they and their compatriots had endured for a lifetime.

Fifth, an organized protest movement among dispossessed blacks who sought assimilation or integration into American life arose on the heels of the Brownsville incident. It originated with the formation of such organizations as the NAACP and the Urban League, whose causes were advanced by militant leaders such as W. E. B. Du Bois, A. Philip Randolph, and Elijah Muhammad—the latter two men refusing to serve in a segregated military during World War I. The stated goal of blacks was still full assimilation, not exclusion, into a military that had denied them entry except under extreme pressure and on a segregated basis. These organizations and individuals joined with several others to force abrogation of exclusionary policies and to guarantee equal rights to men who served in the military. As a result of the Selective Service Act of 1917, about a third of the 2,290,525 blacks who registered were summoned for service during World War I. Further, the enactment and implementation of the Selective Service Act of 1940 was required to assure that blacks would be called into active duty during World War II because the policy of exclusion had been reimposed between the two wars. Thus 800,000 blacks went into the army, 165,000 into the navy, 17,000 into the marines (which had barred blacks in World War I), 24,000 into the merchant marine, 3,000 into the Coast Guard, 1,-000 into the air force (trained primarily at a segregated base in Tuskeegee, Alabama), and 4,000 women each into the WACS and WAVES.[6]

In both world wars blacks encountered barriers of segregation and discrimination both on and off base at home and abroad. The units were segregated; training was initially segregated (and would remain so until limited integration occurred in World War II); proportionately fewer blacks were commissioned as officers, never reaching even 1 percent of the total officer force; discrimination occurred in housing both on and off base (barracks, clubs, mess halls, and recreational facilities were segregated and unequal, and black soldiers were often pushed to extremes to locate off-base housing in hostile communities); transportation services were not readily available to blacks; and separate USOs reflected traditional barriers to social integration. Moreover, the pattern of assigning blacks to low-status occupational roles in the military, which was so evident as early as the Revolutionary War, still persists even now. For example, important and distinguished combat units such as the 92nd and 93rd army divisions (both world wars), the 369th, 371st, and 372nd regiments (World War I), and the 99th Pursuit Squadron (World War II), made outstanding contributions in foreign battle zones. Collectively, they won hundreds of symbols of recognition for outstanding military performances—the Croix de Guerre, Distinguished Flying Cross, the Navy Cross, the Purple Heart—but not one Congressional Medal of Honor. Often the 92nd army division was maligned and falsely accused of cowardice. During World War II, blacks constituted 9 percent of all enlisted men, 2.8 percent of all ground combat troops, but almost half (45 percent) of the Quartermaster Corps. Almost four-fifths (78.1 percent) of all black army males were assigned to service branches. And in the navy they were largely radiomen, yeomen, shipfitters, quartermasters, stewards, carpenters, gunner's mates, and stockkeepers.[7]

American prejudice and institutionalized dominance were transported by the military to foreign shores. As a consequence, various myths and stereotypes regarding black Americans were employed to prevent the establishment of equal-status relationships between American blacks and Europeans. For example, a letter from General Pershing's headquarters to the French military under the title "Secret Information Concerning the Black American Troops" suggested to the French that they should not become too socially compatible with blacks and under no circumstances should they "spoil the negroes." The "secret information" warned the French against violating American social etiquette governing black-white relations: Taboos included shaking hands, eating together, and other forms of socializing.[8] The French were told that blacks were apelike, prone to sexual violence, and they were also told of accentuated notions of black male virility as measured by presumed excessive genital size. Such statements were designed to create effective barriers between blacks and the French, to reduce competition for French women, and to reinforce stateside notions of white supremacy. However, there is no evidence that such statements were effective restraints against social relationship across color lines in Europe. Similar ideas during World War II were frequently the basis of violent interracial confrontations, riots, and maltreatment of black military personnel. Numerous confrontations occurred and seemed to have subsided only when troops were involved in prolonged combat situations necessitating harmonious relationships for mutual survival. It is this type of imposed social situation that has in many instances led to a reduction of prejudice.[9] This thesis is under serious attack though, by virtue of the exigencies of black involvement in the Vietnam War.

Although the marines desegregated in 1942, other branches of the military did not. Protest organizations stepped up the attack against segregation and discrimination in the military and began to exploit the power implicit in the pivotal character of the black political position. Their work, coupled with the influential publication *To Secure These Rights* (1947), authored by the newly created U. S. Civil Rights Commission, helped to persuade President Harry S. Truman to issue Executive Order 9981 on July 26, 1948, which banned discrimination in the armed forces on the basis of race, religion, color, or national origin. On July 27, 1948, General Omar Bradley avowed his intention to resist this policy and to continue military segregation.[10] Despite his opposition, desegregation occurred and was complete six years later, but discrimination remained in the military. In the larger society, in the meantime, civil rights organizations and human relations associations continued their attack against off-base discrimination in housing, transportation, and educational facilities. Discrimination was attacked both as a constitutional violation and as a violation of morality explicit in the spirit of the American Creed. How could one be demanded to defend democracy abroad when segregation and discrimination ravaged people at home? It was this type of inconsistency that weighed so predominantly in the disillusionment of returning black soldiers who participated in the Red Summer of 1919 and the riots of the 1940s. It was the recognition of injustice involved in job discrimination at military installations and in war-related industries during and following the wars that provided the rationale for many fair employment practices statutes. As a consequence of protestations and legal actions against discrimination, many barriers to desegregation began to disintegrate. Directives were issued promoting desegregation in housing for military families, both on and off base, and by 1963 the USOs that occupied federal buildings were also integrated. School desegregation on military bases became more widespread. American blacks' experiences in the Vietnam War, however, particularly at its height during the late 1960s, reflected in microcosm the fundamental character of black-white relations at home, where confrontation politics escalated to alter power relations between blacks and whites.

THE VIETNAM PERIOD

Black Americans did not express discernible opposition to American involvement in the Vietnam War until the mid-1960s. Failure to oppose the war may have been due to the fact that many black persons worked in military installations and service-related industries. For them the primary factor was economic security. But as these facilities were closed or as cutbacks in them resulted in widespread unemployment, the concerns of blacks heightened. The opposition to the war stemmed from the continuing reports on (1) the disproportionate number of blacks being shipped to Vietnam and (2) the disproportionate number of blacks being killed during the war. Perhaps the opposition of blacks was based to a lesser degree, upon an identity with the darker-skinned "enemies" with whom some blacks may have felt a kindred relationship based upon color. They raised serious questions as to why one low-status people of color should be fighting another people of color in order to maintain the dominance of essentially white superordinates over both groups. Other blacks may have felt more constrained to die in the struggle for black liberation at home than to die fighting in another man's war 10,000 miles away. This may have been especially the case among those who realized that blacks sustained an estimated death rate as high as one-fourth of the American total and accounted for about one-sixth of the total number of casualties during a 1965–1966 period. Blacks were outraged by these mortality and casualty rates. A deeply rooted pattern of inequities which placed a disproportionate number of blacks in front-line combat conditions was also a source of focal concern.[11]

This situation—involvement in Vietnam—revealed multiple patterns of discontinuities, strains, and polarization within all branches of the military, which not only reflected conditions external to the military system itself but also deeply ingrained internal problems. Further, it was apparent that many of the highly publicized pronouncements of planned changes and improvements in social conditions within the military were at best superficial, having no direct impact on the fundamental issues of equality of opportunity and military justice. This situation may be illustrated in a number of ways.

STRUCTURE OF BLACK PARTICIPATION

Let us examine the structure of black participation at various levels of the Vietnam War. During the first five years of the 1960s, blacks comprised about 15 percent of all persons drafted into the military even though their proportion in the total population never exceeded 11 percent during the same time. Their proportion in the army, where the majority of blacks went, approached 15 percent by 1965, and roughly the same proportion of blacks acted as combat troops in Vietnam from that point to 1970, the period of heaviest fighting there. Blacks constituted 20 percent of *all* combat troops in Vietnam at that time. During the five-year period 1965–1970, however, only 7.1 percent of white troops were assigned to Vietnam and, proportionately, were underrepresented in both casualties and deaths.[12] Simultaneously, the proportion of black officers in the army, for example, showed a steady decline from 3.6 percent of the total number of army officers in 1966 to 3.2 percent in 1969, and rose only to 3.4 percent in 1970. This pattern existed despite the promulgation by the army of policy AR0600-21, which stipulated equal opportunity and equal treatment —clearly illustrating a contradiction between policy and behavior. In each of the other branches of the military the proportion of black officers was less than 1 percent of the total. Therefore, a disproportionately higher percentage of blacks were drafted, sent into combat in Vietnam, and died or suffered wounds, while they were underrepresented in the higher echelons of the command and overrepresented at the bottom layers of the system.

STRUCTURE OF THE
SELECTION PROCESS

The structure of participation is inextricably linked with the structure of the selection process and subsequent assignments in the military following formal induction. The failure of blacks to qualify for skilled training as measured by tests administered during the selection process may partially explain the preponderance of those assigned to combat duty. Racial and cultural biases are suspected of being so severe in the Armed Forces Qualification Tests (AFQT) as to reduce substantially the number of blacks, already victims of inadequate educational preparation in many school systems throughout the country, who can be assigned to technical and skilled jobs. The armed forces provide an array of approximately 237 occupational fields in almost 300 specialty and technical training schools. Despite these apparent opportunities, blacks are still overrepresented in low-skilled positions and combat branches. As late as 1971, which presumably showed improvements over the 1966–1970 Vietnam period, blacks performed 16.3 percent of low-skilled combat services and 19.6 percent of service and supply specialties, even though they comprised slightly more than 12 percent of all enlisted personnel. At the same time, they were underrepresented in the higher-skilled technical fields, constituting 7 percent of communications and intelligence specialists and 4.9 percent of the electronics equipment specialists.[13]

The overwhelming majority of black officers were similarly assigned to the supply-and-procurement sections, which in itself raises serious questions of the meaning of "professionalization of the military" as the concept applies to blacks. On the other hand, some evidence suggests that some blacks who qualify for special training do not wish to undergo it for a variety of reasons ranging from the time commitment to a desire to remain with friends in other nonspecialty low-skilled areas. Since this group seems to be in the minority, there is inadequate support for the rationalization that blacks do not want specialty training to account for inequities in job assignments within the military.

THE PROMOTION SYSTEM

The promotion system within the military has not permitted substantial upward mobility of blacks, although some blacks have used the military to enhance their opportunities for upward mobility in the larger society. Blacks seem to be locked into a promotion system that white military officials control. Black servicemen and officers often complain that they have been discriminated against in the promotion process, especially when it is apparent to them that less qualified whites are advancing to higher grades with undue rapidity. An examination of Table 8-2 shows that blacks are disproportionately clustered around the lower pay grades as well as the lower-status grades in all armed services. In 1970, for example, blacks constituted only 2.2 percent of all officers in the armed services, which is only slightly more than double the proportion they held during World War II. The change is significant only in the sense that the proportion was abysmally inadequate in the first instance. But even at the levels of E-2 and E-3 blacks state that they have often waited a year or more to move, for instance, from E-2 to E-3, whereas a white enlisted man often received an immediate promotion upon his arrival in Vietnam.

One consequence of discrimination in the military is the profoundly negative impact on attitudes among blacks regarding the military. In a detailed study[14] conducted in Vietnam, Wallace Terry surveyed 833 white and black servicemen, 392 enlisted men, 175 black officers, 181 white enlisted men, and 85 white officers. He found little distinctions in attitudes among blacks regarding military service, namely, that black enlisted men consistently agreed that the military was a poor place for blacks to be. This response was found among enlisted men in the army (75 percent), the air force (77 percent), the marines (73 percent), and the navy (64 percent). Black officers tended to support the view expressed by enlisted men when asked about difference of treatment between the races, but not to the same degree. Almost three-quarters (72 percent) of black enlisted men and slightly less than half (48 percent) of black officers believe that the military treats whites better than blacks. They were closer in agreement regarding opportunities for promotion inasmuch as almost two-thirds (64 percent) of black enlisted men and slightly less than half (45 percent) of black officers claimed that whites were being promoted at a faster rate. Further, about 50 percent of the enlisted men and nearly 30 percent of the black officers maintained that blacks were given more dangerous assignments. Terry also noted that a significant majority of blacks preferred to eat and live with other blacks, thereby pointing to racial polarization in Vietnam.[15]

White officers and enlisted men did not uniformly share these perceptions. For example, only about 2 percent maintained that blacks were given

TABLE 8-1.

Percent of Black Servicemen by Pay Grade and Branch of Service, 1970

Pay Grade and Rank		All Services	Army	Navy	Marine Corps	Air Force
All Officers (O)		2.2	3.4	.7	1.3	1.7
0-7 and above	Generals & Admirals	.2	.2	.0	.0	.2
0-6	Colonels & Captains	.6	1.2	.1	.0	.4
0-5	Lt. Cols. & Commanders	2.3	4.7	.3	.2	1.2
0-4	Majors & Lt. Commanders	2.6	5.2	.5	.3	1.7
0-3	Captains & Lieutenants	2.4	3.7	.6	1.4	2.2
0-2	1st Lieutenants & Lts. Junior Grade	1.7	2.5	.6	1.5	1.4
0-1	2nd Lieutenants & Ensigns	1.5	1.7	1.2	1.9	1.2
WO	Warrant Officer	3.2	3.4	2.1	3.0	1.8
All Enlisted Men (E)		11.0	13.5	5.4	11.2	11.7
E-9	Sergeant Major	3.6	6.0	1.5	2.3	3.0
E-8	Master Sergeant	7.1	11.8	3.1	5.3	4.4
E-7	Sergeant First Class	10.8	17.8	5.3	10.5	6.2
E-6	Staff Sergeant	13.5	22.0	6.8	13.4	10.1
E-5	Sergeant	10.9	11.3	4.4	10.6	14.7
E-4	Corporal	9.1	10.9	2.8	8.1	10.7
E-3	Private First Class	10.2	13.4	5.0	10.4	11.8
E-2	Private	13.6	15.0	10.2	13.6	14.8
E-1	Private	13.8	13.3	13.0	14.2	18.3

SOURCE: Prepared by the National Urban League Research Department from data in U.S. Department of Defense (Equal Opportunity), *The Negro in the Armed Forces: A Statistical Fact Book, 1971.*

more dangerous assignments; 5 percent of white officers in contrast to 41 percent of the black officers believed that whites were being awarded more medals than blacks. Other data indicated that white enlisted men and officers felt that conditions in Vietnam were worsening, but they seemed to deny changes in racial problems.[16] Apparently, then, perceptual discontinuities exist between blacks and whites regarding conditions in the military system. Moreover, it is undoubtedly true that divergences in viewpoints tend to widen with increases in experiences with the military since socialization patterns among blacks and whites in the military may vary markedly and thereby influence differences in attitudes toward the military.

STRUCTURE OF
GRIEVANCE

Divergent attitudes regarding privilege and prerogatives are often reflected in the structure of grievance. Aside from the areas already identified, grievances can be categorized into six overlapping areas, namely: (1) social relations, (2) violence and physical confrontations, (3) sensitivity to identity needs, (4) housing and medical services, (5) access to the command structure, and (6) injustices in the military justice system. It is the failure to make appropriate responses to one or more of these intertwining systems of grievances that has led to outbreaks of violence that have further had an untoward effect on veterans discharged into civilian life.

Social Relations. On a social level blacks complain that whites are more favored in the dispensation of leave privileges. But whites complain that blacks may avoid punishment for such minor infractions as not wearing a hat, taking more food than is allowed on the first serving, or not queuing up properly. Though these are extremely minor complaints, they are important, nonetheless, within the given social context we are discussing. Moreover, they have a way of expanding, and under prolonged tensions or unrelieved anxieties only one relatively minor incident, such as a person cutting a line, may trigger violent confrontations.

Both on and off base, many other observers, including the writer, have substantiated the polarization observed by Terry. Cleavages are often indicative of estrangement and alienation between the races rooted in patterns of social relationships observed almost immediately upon induction. Whereas blacks and whites may appear to be totally devoid of prejudice and bigotry under fire and when it is to their mutual advantage to each other, this camaraderie is not necessarily transferred back to the base or to social activities in surrounding communities. In fact, frequently, manifestations of racial intolerance appear in various forms on and off military installations, for example, in the KKK-style cross burnings at Cam-ranh Bay in 1968 on the heels of the death of Martin Luther King as well as at a navy base called Bien Bah Bay. Some whites also wore simulated KKK costumes at Que Viet in South Vietnam as a way of celebrating the death of Dr. King, and they raised Confederate flags on tanks, jeeps, and trucks at Da Nang. At first, aware of the stateside black power movement, blacks responded by making makeshift flags that predictably espoused black power, then with the formation of black organizations such as the Ju Jus, the Mau Maus, and others that remained nameless. They began to use complicated and intricate handshakes involving the use of the thumb, the palms of hands, and the slapping of fists. These greetings, referred to variously as the "power," the "dap," and the "pound," often angered whites who could not appreciate their symbolic value. Some sought to force discontinuation of black pride greetings. Whenever the opportunity arose, blacks dressed in specific identifying uniforms (for example, black shirts and gloves), which often symbolized both pride and self-determination.

Violence and Physical Confrontations. Blacks probably had their share of the 550 reported cases of "fraggings" in Vietnam.[17] (Fraggings consist of throwing a hand grenade at a superior officer or a hostile individual. The concept may also refer to almost any other form of attack except face-to-face encounters.) Physical confrontations occurred off base in Saigon, on other bases, in communities in Vietnam as well as Hong Kong, where many service people vacationed on "rest and recuperation," and on several Navy ships. The precipitating incident may have been an invasion of blacks into a white club or recreational area or competition for local women or a racial slur or physical attack on either a white person or a black serviceman. Whatever the overt triggering incident was, it was only a superficial manifestation of more deeply rooted conflict. Thus, the violence at Long Binh stockade, where blacks constituted 50 percent of the prison population, may have had its origins in injustices of the military justice system. A riot there resulted in the death of one white person and a destruction of most of the installation. Lives were lost in confrontations at Tenshaw and Piang Tri in Vietnam.

Not only in Vietnam but also in West Germany and in the United States, as we have seen, racial conflicts occurred. There were street brawls in Stuttgart and racial confrontations near Munich, Frankfurt, and elsewhere. They have taken place with increasing frequency from the mid-1960s to the present time. But it was during the summer of 1969 that the nation was literally gripped in cataclysmic episodes of racial explosions and violent confrontations at numerous stateside bases. They shook Forts Dix, Lee, Sheridan, Carson, Gordon, Hood, Jackson, Belvoir, Knox, Still, and Bragg.

In recent years the most notable episodes of racial conflict occurred on the U.S.S. *Kitty Hawk*, the U.S.S. *Constellation*, the *Hassayama*, the *Sumter* during 1972, and at Midway Island as well as at the naval correctional facility at Norfolk, Virginia. As a result of a 15-hour brawl on the *Kitty Hawk*, 46 persons were injured, and, at first, all 25 men charged with rioting were black. One white sailor, accused of assaulting a black petty officer, was added to the list approximately ten days after the trial commenced. The navy found it difficult to establish a riot charge by its own definition of the term; consequently, it gave most blacks lesser charges or cleared them altogether. The white sailor was freed after 23 minutes of deliberation by an all-white panel. In the *Constellation* case, perhaps the next most celebrated case, 130 sailors, including 123 blacks, staged a sit-in to protest inequities in the discharge pattern and job assignments on the ship. Essentially, these incidents were triggered by what appeared to be a relatively innocuous event such as stepping on someone's toe or requesting a sailor to take one sandwich at a time. However, they were only symptoms of much more fundamental problems. As a result, the navy has directed the implementation of major reforms.

Identity Needs. Blacks have often complained in recent years, especially since the new thrust toward black identity and black pride, that the military was not responsive to its needs. Specifically, the food in the dining hall was not satisfactory, the post exchanges (PXs) did not carry black literature or "rakes" for Afro hair and cosmetic supplies, or the barbers did not know how to style the hair of black people. All branches of the armed services, at home and abroad, have made substantial efforts to meet the demands for such supplies and facilities. They have added soul music to juke boxes; menus include soul food; PXs stock black magazines such as *Ebony, Jet,* and *Tan,* Afro hair products and cosmetics used by blacks, and wearing apparel such as dashikis and jewelry, including bracelets and black crosses. The Army and Air Force Exchange Service (AAFES) has sent barbers to innumerable installations in Europe and Asia, particularly to teach local barbers how to style the hair of blacks in military service. In this manner many apparent sources of unrest have been confronted.

Housing and Medical Services. It has been somewhat more difficult to control the responses of local citizens to blacks in the military, especially in the area of housing. In West Germany blacks seem to have experienced the greatest difficulties in finding suitable housing accommodations off base. This is attributed to the breakdown of those existing directives and regulations concerning listings of discriminating renters and owners. Housing discrimination persists in some instances because the command structure fails to follow through on registered complaints. And in other instances officials acquiesce to local practices that effectively discriminate against blacks in housing.[18] Perhaps to avoid problems the American government allegedly acquiesced to demands by the government of Iceland against sending blacks to NATO bases in that country.[19]

Insensitivity to the medical needs of blacks still persists to some degree. Except for the air force, the military has shown no apparent interest in research on sickle-cell anemia, which affects blacks almost exclusively. Nor has it uniformly recognized that pseudofolliculitis, exaggerated shaving bumps cured only by wearing a beard, affects a substantial proportion of black men. The military (except the air force) refuses to accept, for medical reasons, not shaving long enough to cure the condition.[20]

Command Structure. The military power structure is largely pyramidal and is characterized by a command structure that is so rigidly stratified that its subordinates are able to subvert and sabotage the mandates of those at its top. As a consequence, military personnel, in general, black and white, do not feel that they have access to the decision-making apparatus.

Many grievances go unheeded, and many directives such as the highly publicized Z-grams issued by the former chief officer of the navy, Admiral Elmo R. Zumwalt, Jr., are reportedly far short of implementation. As a result, planned improvements in the status and conditions of personnel are not made as rapidly as anticipated if they are made at all. Moreover, all branches of the service now have an Equal Opportunity (EO) officer of some kind, but even these officers do not have direct access to those having ultimate responsibility for decision making. At the level of the Pentagon, for example, the EO officer is a deputy assistant secretary rather than an assistant secretary, which means that the stratification system denies direct access to the Secretary of Defense. He must always transmit ideas, programs, and strategies for change through an intermediary. The system, therefore, makes lower-level servicemen even farther removed from the important functionaries in the chain of command. Therefore, many come to feel that no one in the system cares. The presence of black officers does not necessarily alleviate tensions created by strains between the enlistees and officials in the chain of command. Perceptions play a major role in determining the effectiveness of black officers with black enlistees as well as influencing the latter's assessments of black officers. These perceptions may be selectively influenced by age grades, the degree to which the officer is self-conscious of his status difference and his ability to maximize the advantages of status, his sense of objectivity, and, in sum, how he is regarded by the black enlistees (that is, Is he an "oreo," a "tom," "a committed black," "strictly a military man").

Military Justice System. It is in the structure of the military justice system, however, that we find the preponderance of problems confronting blacks, both those at present in the military and those who are veterans. It is estimated that of the nearly 500,000 Vietnam veterans who have returned to the United States with less than honorable discharges about 200,000 are black. The problem is even broader, for it embraces the entire fabric of the justice system, including who has the greatest likelihood of being charged with an offense, the nature of behavior classified as offensive, and the whole process of administering justice. Under Article 15 of the military code, officers may arbitrarily exact nonjudicial punishments, and service personnel may also accept these punishments without appearing for a court-martial. Unfortunately, many servicemen and servicewomen do not realize that an accumulation of such nonjudicial punishments may result in dismissal from service on the grounds of unsuitability or undesirability for continued service. Further, it may be only after they are discharged that they come to realize that the type of discharge a person possesses is of inestimable significance for adjustment as a veteran. Even then, they may not realize how difficult it is to remove the stigma of a bad discharge.

There is evidence that a disproportionate number of blacks receive Article 15 punishments. For example, as of June 30, 1972, blacks received more than a quarter (25.5 percent) of all nonjudicial punishments meted out in the armed forces. Moreover, in terms of specific Article 15 punishments, almost three-fourths of blacks (71.7 percent) in comparison to almost two-thirds (63.1 percent) of all whites who were AWOL received Article 15 punishments during the reporting period.[21]

Similar conditions existed regarding pretrial confinements. The proportion of blacks placed in pretrial confinement is greater (21.2 percent) than their percentage in the total armed services (13.1 percent). Discrepancies vary markedly from service to service. Blacks are also more likely to remain in pretrial confinement five days longer on the average than white enlisted men throughout the service, and white military personnel are much more likely to have their pretrial confinement terminated without any form of judicial or disciplinary action.[22] In many cases in Vietnam and West Germany blacks were held in pretrial confinement for up to 30 days on such trivial charges as having their hair too long or without ever having formal charges made against them.[23]

Similarly, blacks receive a disproportionate share of courts-martial. Tables 8-2, 8-3, and 8-4 illustrate these points.

It is the accumulation of Article 15 offenses resulting in nonhonorable or less than honorable discharges that is plaguing Vietnam veterans today. Across the board, from service to service, blacks receive a far greater share of such discharges than their proportions in each branch of the service would normally suggest. In contrast to white servicemen, the proportion varies from roughly five times the rate for white servicemen in the air force (10.3 percent blacks vs. 2.8 percent whites) to almost twice as many blacks than whites in the army (11.3 percent vs. 6.2 percent white), the navy (17.5 percent black vs. 9.8 percent white), and the marines (22.4 percent black vs. 13.4 percent white). However, it is in the marines that one observes that almost one-quarter (or 22.4 percent) of all blacks were discharged nonhonorably in the 1971–1972 period.[24] Many of them are the same men whose AFQT scores were so low as to place them in low-level jobs in the military, and they are less prepared to find jobs upon reentry into civilian life. The stigma of a bad discharge compounds the problem, since it inevitably means that they are the last to be hired and the first to be fired during periods of economic strain. Thus men who went into the service to obtain a marketable skill that would give them a modicum of upward mobility in civilian life now sense a deep frustration due to unfulfilled expectations. All too frequently, they come to feel that they have risked their lives and endured harassment or discrimination by superior officers for unfulfilled expectations in both the military life and the civilian life.

TABLE 8-2.

Racial Statistics by Specific Offenses: Specifications— Tried and Convicted

General Courts-Martial:

	White		Black		Other		Total	
	Tried	Conv	Tried	Conv	Tried	Conv	Tried	Conv
Art. 86	26	25	22	21	4	4	52	50
Art. 89–92*	54	44	27	16	—	—	81	60
Art. 128*	9	2	56	40	4	3	69	45
Totals:	89	71	105	77	8	7	202	155

*Three Blacks and one "Other" convicted of LIO.

Special Courts-Martial:

	White		Black		Other		Total	
	Tried	Conv	Tried	Conv	Tried	Conv	Tried	Conv
Art. 86	910	889	558	540	78	76	1,546	1,505
Art. 89–92*	270	201	265	212	36	29	571	442
Art. 128*	74	61	143	92	13	7	230	160
Totals:	1,254	1,151	966	844	127	112	2,347	2,107

*Five Whites, ten Blacks and one "Other" convicted of LIO.

Summary Courts-Martial:

	White		Black		Other		Total	
	Tried	Conv	Tried	Conv	Tried	Conv	Tried	Conv
Art. 86	16	10	22	15	—	—	38	25
Art. 89–92*	48	27	26	11	10	7	84	45
Art. 128*	3	2	2	1	—	—	5	3
Totals:	67	39	50	27	10	7	127	73

*One White and two Blacks convicted of LIO.

ALL COURTS-MARTIAL:

	White		Black		Other		Total	
	Tried	Conv	Tried	Conv	Tried	Conv	Tried	Conv
Art. 86	952	924	602	576	82	80	1,636	1,580
Art. 89–92*	372	272	318	239	46	36	736	547
Art. 128*	86	65	201	133	17	10	304	208
Totals:	1,410	1,261	1,121	948	145	126	2,676	2,335

*Six Whites, fifteen Blacks and two "Others" convicted of LIO.

SOURCE: Prepared by the National Urban League Research Department from data in U.S. Department of Defense (Equal Opportunity), *The Negro in the Armed Forces: A Statistical Fact Book, 1971.*

TABLE 8-3.

Racial Statistics on Article 15 Offenses

Article 15 Offenses:

White	Black	Other	Total
25,127	11,328	1,420	37,875
(66.3%)	(30.0%)	(3.7%)	

Article 15 Specific Offenses:

By Article:	White	Black	Other	Total
86(1)	12,103	6,975	681	19,759
86(2)	609	282	42	933
89	176	104	7	287
90(2)	144	73	5	222
91(2)	353	176	28	557
91(3)	338	229	34	601
92(1)	2,013	662	94	2,769
92(2)	1,570	669	101	2,340
128	338	347	30	715
128(1)	33	29	6	68
128(2)	26	27	3	56
134 — Disorderly in Public	102	47	6	155
— Dis. in Station	820	512	55	1,387
— Dis. in Quarters	48	27	8	83
— Drunk in Public	16	7	—	23
— Drunk & Dis. in Public	73	12	3	88
— Drunk & Dis. in Station	409	135	30	574
Totals:	19,171	10,313	1,133	30,617

Art. 86(3)—AWOL (not broken down by race):   Total—7,153

SOURCE: Prepared by the National Urban League Research Department from data in U.S. Department of Defense (Equal Opportunity), *The Negro in the Armed Forces: A Statistical Fact Book, 1971.*

PROBLEMS OF VIETNAM VETERANS

The picture for a significant proportion of black Vietnam veterans is not particularly bright. They are trapped in a multitude of adjustment problems encompassing a broad range of social and psychological conditions.

TABLE 8-4.

Disciplinary Statistics By Race
1 Jan.–30 June 1972, Navy and Marine Corps Combined

Type of Action	Caucasian	Negro	American Indian	Malaysian	Mongolian	TOTAL
General Courts-Martial	316	102	3	6	0	427
Special Courts-Martial awarding bad conduct discharges	668	185	11	3	0	867
Special Courts-Martial not awarding bad conduct discharges	2,689	747	50	40	8	3,534
Summary Courts-Martial	3,761	736	50	28	5	4,784
Nonjudicial Punishment (Article 15)	40,689	9,680	490	377	77	51,313

SOURCE: Prepared by the National Urban League Research Department from data in U.S. Department of Defense (Equal Opportunity), *The Negro in the Armed Forces: A Statistical Fact Book, 1971.*

Without a doubt, the two most critical problem areas are employment and education, for they are crucial links in the overall adjustment profile.

Unemployment. Unemployment among black Vietnam veterans has reached a crisis proportion. Although it is true that many black veterans do not wish to desert their homes in order to move to other areas where employment opportunities are greater, high unemployment prevails among veterans in every area of the nation. The problem is particularly critical for those veterans who have limited education and few marketable skills and carry nonhonorable discharges. They comprise a large segment of the younger veterans who cannot find employment at all or who are underemployed during most of the year. The pattern is quite similar to that for black nonveterans over a four-year period between 1969 and the first quarter of 1973, but it is only in 1973 that black Vietnam veterans appear to be faring better in employment than black nonveterans. In many cases, as Table 8-5 shows, the proportion of black unemployed veterans is generally twice as high as that for white Vietnam veterans. This condition conforms to the

TABLE 8-5.

Unemployment Rates of Men 20–29 Years Old, by Vietnam Era—
Veteran-Nonveteran Status and Age: 1969 and 1973
(Annual averages)

Age and Year	Negro and Other Races		White	
	Vietnam Era Veterans	Nonveterans	Vietnam Era Veterans	Nonveterans
Total 20 to 29 Years:				
1969	7.7	6.2	4.2	3.1
1970	11.6	9.5	6.4	5.5
1971	13.7	12.0	8.3	6.6
1972	12.6	11.1	6.8	6.2
1973 (1st quarter)	10.4	11.4	6.7	6.3
20 to 24 Years:				
1969	9.9	8.1	5.0	4.5
1970	15.2	11.9	8.7	7.4
1971	17.5	15.8	11.6	8.5
1972	16.3	14.2	10.0	7.9
1973 (1st quarter)	14.9	12.7	10.9	7.5
25 to 29 Years				
1969	4.2	4.1	3.1	1.7
1970	7.4	6.6	4.0	3.4
1971	10.0	7.2	5.3	4.3
1972	9.3	6.9	4.6	3.8
1973 (1st quarter)	6.6	9.7	4.3	4.7

SOURCE: U.S. Department of Labor, Bureau of Labor Statistics, *Employment Situation of Vietnam Era Veterans*, First Quarter 1973.

profile for the regular nonveteran population. Undoubtedly, the unemployment situation helps to explain why blacks have tended to reenlist in the military system despite claims of systematic injustice. In 1970 the proportions of black reenlistees were 12 percent for all services, 14 percent for the army, 3.8 percent for the navy, 15.3 percent for the marine corps, and 12.4 percent for the air force.[25] The unemployment picture is clouded still further, since as many as 60.000 black Vietnam veterans are in the category of the discouraged unemployed—that is, they have stopped looking for work because of protracted demeaning failure. The work situation has for them formed impregnable barriers that they are unequipped to surmount. Still another 33,000 black veterans join the lines at state employment offices, continuing to hope that work will become available.[26] Perhaps they would be in more propitious circumstances if they had received marketable skills while in the service, instead of being relegated disproportionately to combat and service divisions, and if so many employers in the private sector did not perceive Vietnam veterans as incurable "junkies."

The Concerned Veterans from Vietnam was organized in 1968 to assist black veterans in obtaining jobs and housing; however, because a large proportion of them have received less than honorable discharges and are, therefore, unable to locate suitable jobs, the concerned veterans are now directing their primary attention toward changes in military justice. The Veterans Administration operates the OUTREACH program, which is designed to assist veterans in, among other things, finding employment. The National Urban League received almost $10 million for supporting on-the-job training programs involving veterans in 32 cities, and the Opportunities Industrialization Centers also include veterans in their programs. With their collective assistance thousands of jobs have been located for veterans.

It is extremely difficult for the Vietnam veteran who is a college aspirant to pursue a college education unless he has saved a substantial part of his military pay or is able to obtain some form of outside aid, whether from family or public or private financial resources. The GI benefits provided the current veterans clearly are not as adequate as those provided the veterans of World War II, for example. GIs today receive benefits of $1,980 if they have no dependents, $2,349 with one dependent, and up to $2,682 with two dependents. Nevertheless, a million and a half educationally disadvantaged veterans—that is, high school dropouts—have received precollege training under the GI bill presently in force. Others do have the financial resources available and have completed college and professional training.

Aside from widespread unemployment and educational needs, many Vietnam veterans often experience mental, physical, emotional, and morale problems. (The next chapter also deals with this.) The Vietnam War was highly controversial almost from its inception, becoming an issue that divided the nation politically and emotionally as American involvement escalated. Except for the prisoners of war, veterans of this war, unlike veterans of any previous war, did not return to this country honored by ticker-tape parades on Fifth Avenue, Wall Street, or down Main Street, U.S.A. An uncompassionate federal government has done little or nothing to compensate the average GI for services rendered in a hated war. Many of them are ashamed of their participation and often attempt to disappear into the masses for fear of suffering the fate of the socially and politically outcast. Many suffered anxieties brought on by various forms of reentry crises—whether mental, physical, emotional, or moral. A significant number of the Vietnam veterans, however, were able to make suitable adjustments upon returning to the United States and have, of course, proceeded to continue developing useful and productive lives.

RACE RELATIONS IN THE
MILITARY TODAY

With the growing awareness of problems relative to prejudice, discrimination, and the opportunity structure, all branches of the military are apparently attempting to effect significant internal change. They have undertaken massive recruitment drives, through advertisements in the black press, for example, which point to the military as an employment alternative to the problems of civilian life. These advertisements describe in detail available opportunities for specialty training in the military, often in such a manner as to raise the inevitable question: Is this promise something more than can be delivered? They point to increases in the salaries or wages paid service personnel, which range from $307.20 per month for a private to $3,195 for a general. Undoubtedly, many young blacks will continue to be attracted to the military because of career opportunities and the fringe benefits coming from them. Indeed, the proportion of blacks in the new "volunteer army," formed after the abolition of the draft in December 1972, in comparison to the 13 percent blacks in the total draft-age population,[27] reached 35 percent in July 1973 but dropped to 24 percent in February 1974. However, in view of rising unemployment among blacks as related to the energy crisis, it is safe to predict that an increasing proportion of blacks will be lured to the volunteer army by the $2,500 enlistment bonus and the security of employment despite lingering problems of discrimination and racism. Thus the probability is high that the army will be comprised of a disproportionate number of the black poor just as it was during the Vietnam War, when the more well-to-do and influential escaped the draft.

The various service academies are making special efforts to increase the number of black cadets who, once accepted, are entitled to four years of free education. As of June 1973, West Point had 141 black enrollees; the Naval Academy at Annapolis had 130; and the Air Force Academy had 94. Reserve Officers' Training Corps (ROTC) programs, both for the army and the navy, are increasing rather than disappearing on black college campuses in an effort to increase the number of black officers.[28] Although these proportions are still a fraction of the total, they do show significant changes from the pre–World War II days, when most academies had none and West Point had one or two token, showcase blacks and when black schools were underrepresented in the training programs.

To improve race relations and to reduce interracial conflict the Department of Defense and all branches of the services have established special programs in which officers and many noncommissioned officers are expected to participate. A race relations institute has been established in Florida. Leadership training programs operate throughout the country. Seminars and encounter sessions dealing with intergroup tensions and conflict resolutions are widespread.

The power structure of the military is undergoing modest changes, as the proportion of black officers presently in the military suggests and as Tables 8-6 and 8-7 show. However, blacks remain grossly underrepresented in the leadership structure. And, further, it will perhaps require far more radical alterations of far greater substance to create a more democratic

TABLE 8-6.

Distribution of Officers and Enlisted Men by Service and Race in the U.S. Military, 1973

	Army		Navy		Marine Corps		Air Force	
	Number	%	Number	%	Number	%	Number	%
Totals								
Caucasian	678,351	83.9	526,784	90.2	170,707	86.2	638,230	81.6
Black	121,613	15.1	33,145	5.7	24,734	12.5	77,752	10.8
Other	8,021	1.0	23,895	4.1	2,496	1.3	5,466	7.6
Total	807,985	100.0	583,824	100.0	197,937	100.0	721,448	100.0
Officers								
Caucasian	116,005	95.7	72,204	98.7	19,164	98.0	118,875	97.7
Black	4,788	3.9	660	.9	285	1.5	2,118	1.7
Other	497	.4	291	.4	93	.5	681	.6
Total	121,290	100.0	73,155	100.0	19,542	100.0	121,674	100.0
Enlisted								
Caucasian	562,346	81.9	454,580	89.0	151,543	86.1	519,355	86.6
Black	116,825	17.0	32,485	6.4	24,449	12.6	75,634	12.6
Other	7,524	1.1	23,604	4.6	2,403	1.3	4,785	.8
Total	686,695	100.0	510,669	100.0	178,395	100.0	599,774	100.0

Note: Totals in Other column represent all other racial or ethnic groups. The above figures are expected to change with all-voluntary army.

SOURCE: Quoted with permission of Black Enterprise from *Black Enterprise*, 3:8 (March 1973), p. 60.

structure in the American military system than exists at the present time. However, the implementation of governmental policies in the military that provide concrete effectiveness in eliminating barriers to equal participation may have positive carry-over consequences for creating a more just civilian social system.

TABLE 8-7.

**Distribution of Women in the U.S. Military
by Race and Branches of Service**

Service	Total Enlisted Women	% Black	Total Officers	% Black
U.S. Army	13,000	19.1	4,500	5.5
U.S. Navy	6,000	6.4	3,000	1.9
U.S. Air Force	13,000	14.3	4,700	4.1
U.S. Marine Corps	2,000	17.0	250	5.0

Note: Above statistics are approximate figures.

SOURCE: Quoted with permission of Black Enterprise from *Black Enterprise*, 3:8 (March 1973), p. 63.

NOTES

1. Among the more extensive discussions of blacks in the military are: Richard Stillman, *Integration of the Negro in the U.S. Armed Forces* (New York: Frederick A. Praeger, 1968); Lerone Bennett, *Before the Mayflower*, 4th ed. (Chicago: Johnson Publishing Co., 1969); John Hope Franklin, *From Slavery to Freedom* (New York: Alfred A. Knopf, 1952); and Benjamin Quarles, *The Black American* (Glenview, Ill.: Scott Foresman & Co., 1967). I have relied heavily upon their data.

2. Stillman, *op. cit.* p. 8.

3. Franklin, *op. cit.,* 290.

4. Frank N. Schubert, "Black Soldiers on the White Frontier: Some Factors Influencing Race Relations," *Phylon*, 32 (Winter 1971), pp. 410–416.

5. Lewis N. Wynne, "Brownsville: The Reaction of the Negro Press," *Phylon*, 32 (Summer 1972), pp. 153–160.

6. For an excellent discussion of these issues and the discussion following cf. Peter G. Nordie et al., *Improving Race Relations in the Army* (McLean, Va.: Human Sciences Research Center, Inc., 1972), p. 68, and Franklin, *op. cit.*, p. 467.

7. *Ibid.* and see Bennett, *op. cit.*

8. Franklin, *op. cit.*, pp. 465–467.

9. Samuel Stouffer's classic study of the American soldier illustrates this point with highly significant data. Cf. Samuel Stouffer, *The American Soldier: Adjustments During Army Life*, Vol. 1 (Princeton, N.J.: Princeton University Press, 1949).

10. Nordie, *op. cit.*, p. 73.

11. Cf. Charles Moskos, Jr., "Deliberate Change: Race Relations in the Armed Forces," in Russell Endo and William Strawbridge (eds.), *Perspectives on Black America* (Englewood Cliffs, N.J.: Prentice-Hall, 1973), p. 62, and Charles Moskos, Jr., "Racial Integration in the Armed Forces," *American Journal of Sociology*, 72 (September 1966), pp. 133–148.

12. Lewis C. Olive, Jr., "Duty, Honor, Country But No Reward," *The Urban League News*, 3 (April 1973), p. 31.

13. These are Department of Defense figures cited in the hearings sponsored by the Congressional Black Caucus. See "Racism in the Military," *Congressional Record*, Vol. 118, No. 166, Part 11 (Washington, D.C.: U.S. Congress), October 14, 1972.

14. Wallace Terry, *The Bloods: The Black Soldier in Vietnam* (New York: Viking Press, 1973).

15. *Ibid.*

16. *Ibid.*

17. *Congressional Record, op. cit.*

18. *Ibid.*

19. *Ibid.*

20. *Ibid.*

21. Gilbert Ware, "The Spider Web and Racism in the Armed Forces," *The Urban League News*, 3 (April 1972), p. 5.

22. *Ibid.*

23. Ware, *op. cit.*

24. These figures were provided by the National Urban League Research Department and are based upon data in the "Administrative Discharges Study," *Task Force on the Administration of Military Justice in the Armed Forces*, October 13, 1972.

25. *Ibid.*

26. These studies were prepared by the National Urban League Research Department from data in the U.S. Department of Defense Report, *The Negro in the Armed Forces: A Statistical Fact Book, 1971.*

27. John W. Finney, "Gain Reported by All-Volunteer Army," *The New York Times*, February 21, 1974, p. 12.

28. The navy, for example, is establishing some 30 training centers at predominantly black colleges.

9 | DEVIANCE AND HEALTH-CARE PROBLEMS IN BLACK COMMUNITIES

One of the external images of the black community is that it exists in perpetually uncontrollable social pathology. Such images are reinforced by mass-media accounts of alleged deviant behavior of black persons while nonblack individuals also involved in nonconformist behavior are not identified. These images are sustained by a selective perception that attributes generalized deviancy to the entire black population on the basis of violations of the normative order committed by a relatively small number of black individuals. Images of black pathology are also created by conditions in the social structure that generate deviancy as the most efficacious adaptive mechanism for survival in a hostile society.

In regard to behavioral norms Americans as a whole are not perceptibly distinguishable from other groups. The overwhelming majority of black people in America, like the majority of Americans in general, conform to normative expectations in their social behavior. They are *normal*. They are *law-abiding citizens* engaged in the daily business of improving their social and economic status in American society. Others, due to a wide spectrum of reasons, deviate from societal norms in one or more of several different ways.

In this chapter we shall focus on the behavior of individuals who are conceived of as deviants within the larger social system because the behavior violates rules of the normative order beyond the limit of social toleration. Both definitions of deviancy and dispositions made of deviants are a function of power. Until recently, blacks have been powerless—a fact that may help to explain deviancy among them. Specific attention is given to criminality, problems of mental health, alcoholism, and drug abuse. We shall also discuss mortality rates and some of the more common causes of death among the black population of the United States. The final section of this chapter is devoted to an explanation of programs and issues relative to health-care delivery systems in the black community.

CRIMINAL BEHAVIOR

Numerous problems are associated with interpretations of data on crime and delinquency. One of the more universal problems is the inaccuracy of statistics relative to crime incidence. Generally, the sources of this problem reflect serious defects in the varied components of the criminal justice system itself. For example, one fundamental source of inaccuracy is the heavy volume of unreported crime. Criminal statistics are by no means uniform from one jurisdiction to another. There is no uniformity in the degree of record-keeping efficiency or even in the data collection process that is so fundamental to the reliability of incidence statistics. Inaccuracy in statistical data on crime and criminals may further depend on individual perceptions of behavioral patterns, which, in turn, lead law enforcement agents to render selective judgments of what does and does not constitute criminal behavior.

It is precisely this possibility of racial bias at the time an initial judgment regarding alleged criminality is made that makes criminal statistics pertaining to black Americans so highly suspect. Even so, we have come to accept the fact that the instrumentation of the law is the function of an interrelated network of decision makers who comprise a power structure including the police, prosecutors, judges, and jurors—all of whose judgments determine who is labeled a criminal. Objectivity is not always achieved in ascriptions of criminality, since subjective bias may consciously or subconsciously influence decisions. Subjective evaluations interfere with objectiveness and may help to explain why black Americans particularly are overrepresented in many forms of criminal behavior; this may also explain why blacks are more frequently suspected of an offense, apprehended, and booked. The very fact that blacks are more frequently brought to trial and sentenced, often without respect for rules of evidence and due process, reflects both their limited power and lack of influence on adjudication. The implications are broad and extend to other areas, since blacks are less often paroled but more likely to become recidivists. But blacks, as a group, are not more prone to criminal behavior. They are more often exposed to conditions in the social structure that may lead to their disproportionate representation in criminal statistics.

Arrest data over the past several generations reveal that blacks on an average are arrested four times as frequently as whites. This generalization holds true when age and sex variables are considered. Rates also vary with the type of offense committed and the area of the city within which violations of criminal behavior allegedly occur. Moreover, the arrest rates for whites are significantly lower for crimes against the black person than arrest rates are for blacks. If reports from Houston and Baltimore studies on juvenile delinquency hold true for adult criminality, then black arrest rates would be lowest in those areas of the city having the highest concentrations of blacks and highest in those areas having a greater proportion of whites.[1] One explanation for this disparity is that the tolerance level among whites for nonconformity among blacks is considerably lower in those communities where blacks are in the minority than is the case in communities where blacks are in the majority. Thus deviance is not only likely to be more noticeable, but it is also more likely to come to the attention of the police and lead to arrests.

Subjective definitions of deviance influence the initial decision that determines who is to be arrested. One of the more common complaints by blacks, revealed in a University of Michigan study, is that of police harassment by unwarranted stopping and questioning, searching, and arresting when there is no evidence that a crime has been committed. Sometimes the arrests of blacks are merely an effort on the part of police to save face.[2] This practice is likely to continue in the light of the tendency of the Nixon Supreme Court to give law enforcement officials great latitude regarding search and seizure.

Many unwarranted and discriminatory allegations and decisions will be made against blacks, as already claimed by civil rights organizations and the American Civil Liberties Union regarding the so-called zebra murders in San Francisco during 1973 and 1974. In that instance the police department with mayoral encouragement ordered a stop and search of *all black males* who supposedly fit the description of the zebra killers. (All the victims were white and their alleged killers were black.) There was an outcry of indignation over this practice, since there was no evidence that mass numbers of whites suspected of killing blacks would have been similarly treated, and, further, the practice was a violation of the rights of the almost 600 black men stopped under this directive. Most blacks who were stopped were given passes indicating that they had cleared police inspection—reminiscent of the pass system under apartheid in South Africa. Moreover, civil rights and civil liberties groups asserted that no similar procedures had been implemented in San Francisco against white men who may have fit the description of the zodiac killer who began his terror in 1969. Essentially, a double standard operates when the victims are white and the accused are black. Police bias enters the initial determination to suspect and arrest blacks. This bias and the unrestrained employment of police power coalesce to inflate arrest rates of black Americans. Therefore, the acknowledged high volume of crime in the black community must be understood within the framework of the foregoing observations.

VIOLENT AND
AGGRESSIVE CRIMES

The Uniform Crime Reports of violent crimes include offenses of murder, forcible rape, robbery, and aggravated assault. These may also be referred to as aggressive offenses, since they may do violence to persons. Although blacks constitute approximately 12 percent of the total population, the ratio between their population proportions and arrest rates for violent crimes is excessive.[3]

Criminal Homicide. This is usually subdivided into two categories: (1) murder and nonnegligent manslaughter and/or felony murder and (2) manslaughter by negligence. Sixty-two percent of all persons arrested for murder in 1971, the last year for which we have relatively accurate national statistics, were black. Thirty-eight percent were white. By contrast, whites constituted almost four-fifths (78.2 percent) of all persons arrested for manslaughter by negligence, but less than a fourth (23.2 percent) of persons arrested in this category were black. As Table 9-1 shows, of the 13,302 murder arrests in the United States 8,278 were black and 4,718 were white.

Differences between black and white populations in rates of murder and negligent manslaughter may be partially explainable by social and economic advantages of whites when appearing in a court of law. Because whites are generally able to hire more competent lawyers and have greater success at plea bargaining, killings by white people are more likely to be defined as negligent homicides than as felonious murders. On the other hand, poor blacks are often not informed of evidentiary rules or not apprised of due process. They are often unable to afford competent lawyers or secure legal aid from persons who have a vested interest in their welfare. As a result, they are not as successful in plea bargaining or in having felonious murder crimes reduced to ones that are considered less serious or less socially injurious.

Felonious murders, those murders resulting from robberies, sex motives, and premeditation, and from other felonious acts—and crime in

TABLE 9-1.

Total Arrests by Race, 1971—Continued

5,610 agencies; 1971 estimated population 146,564,000

Offense Charged	Total Arrests							Percent Distribution					
	Total	White	Negro	Indian	Chinese	Japanese	All Others	White	Negro	Indian	Chinese	Japanese	All Others
Stolen property; buying, receiving, possessing	61,434	38,582	21,969	313	37	20	513	62.8	35.8	.5	.1		.8
Vandalism	115,516	90,463	23,153	757	38	43	1,062	78.3	20.0	.7			.9
Weapons; carrying, possessing, etc.	105,781	49,650	54,057	723	57	28	1,266	46.9	51.1	.7	.1		1.2
Prostitution and commercialized vice	44,874	16,219	28,132	158	22	14	329	36.1	62.7	.4			.7
Sex offenses (except forcible rape and prostitution	48,153	36,603	10,477	332	37	43	661	76.0	21.8	.7	.1	.1	1.4
Narcotic drug laws	354,783	273,733	76,652	1,230	208	358	2,602	77.2	21.6	.3	.1	.1	.7
Gambling	74,911	20,370	51,594	76	183	425	2,263	27.2	68.9	.1	.2	.6	3.0
Offenses against family and children	55,674	38,593	16,384	371	8	6	312	69.3	29.4	.7			.6
Driving under the influence	480,801	383,106	81,394	8,608	137	341	7,215	79.7	16.9	1.8		.1	1.5
Liquor laws	226,148	196,993	23,747	4,056	43	82	1,227	87.1	10.5	1.8			.5
Drunkenness	1,472,917	1,085,153	291,335	87,617	512	209	8,091	73.7	19.8	5.9			.5
Disorderly conduct	606,318	387,620	200,504	7,675	211	115	10,193	63.9	33.1	1.3			1.7
Vagrancy	60,144	43,234	15,285	1,026	19	19	561	71.9	25.4	1.7			.9
All other offenses (except traffic)	837,231	599,289	220,690	8,269	372	533	8,078	71.6	26.4	1.0		.1	1.0
Suspicion	53,184	37,503	15,035	378	61	14	193	70.5	28.3	.7	.1		.4
Curfew and loitering law violations	97,884	75,665	19,859	1,138	49	160	1,013	77.3	20.3	1.2	.1	.2	1.0
Runaways	186,628	161,614	20,741	1,969	86	146	2,072	86.6	11.1	1.1		.1	1.1

[1] Violent crime is offenses of murder, forcible rape, robbery and aggravated assault.
[2] Property crime is offenses of burglary, robbery and auto theft.

SOURCE: L. Patrick Gray, *Crime in the United States: Uniform Crime Reports 1971* (Washington, D.C.: Government Printing Office, 1972), p. 127.

TABLE 9-1.

Total Arrests by Race, 1971

5,610 agencies; 1971 estimated population 146,564,000

Offense Charged	Total Arrests							Percent Distribution					
	Total	White	Negro	Indian	Chinese	Japanese	All Others	White	Negro	Indian	Chinese	Japanese	All Others
TOTAL	6,626,085	4,623,891	1,791,494	138,677	3,274	3,832	64,937	69.8	27.0	2.1	......	0.1	1.0
Criminal homicide:													
(a) Murder and nonnegligent manslaughter	13,302	4,716	8,276	88	7	4	211	35.5	62.2	.7	0.1	......	1.6
(b) Manslaughter by negligence	2,698	1,974	626	19	2	6	71	73.2	23.2	.7	0.1	.2	2.6
Forcible rape	15,468	7,386	7,781	142	2	5	152	47.8	50.3	.9	......	......	1.0
Robbery	83,936	26,524	55,745	624	25	39	979	31.6	66.4	.7	......	......	1.2
Aggravated assault	126,673	64,502	59,443	1,369	64	32	1,263	50.9	46.9	1.1	0.1	......	1.0
Burglary—breaking or entering	297,147	192,827	98,666	2,371	133	177	2,973	64.9	33.2	.8	......	.1	1.0
Larceny—theft	640,421	432,018	195,438	4,925	695	791	6,554	67.5	30.5	.8	.1	.1	1.0
Auto theft	121,773	75,949	42,596	1,254	144	122	1,708	62.4	35.0	1.0	.1	.1	1.4
Violent crime[1]	239,379	103,128	131,245	2,223	98	80	2,605	43.1	54.8	.9	......	.1	1.1
Property crime[2]	1,059,341	700,794	336,700	8,550	972	1,090	11,235	66.2	31.8	.8	.1	.1	1.1
Subtotal for above offenses	1,301,418	805,896	468,571	10,792	1,072	1,176	13,911	61.9	36.0	.8	.1	.1	1.1
Other assaults	290,836	174,279	111,128	2,488	79	66	2,796	59.9	38.2	.9	......	......	1.0
Arson	10,638	7,588	2,882	63	15	5	85	71.3	21.1	.6	.1	......	.8
Forgery and counterfeiting	41,142	27,848	12,872	270	12	15	125	67.7	31.3	.7	......	......	.3
Fraud	93,095	68,976	23,418	347	16	12	326	74.1	25.2	.4	......	......	.4
Embezzlement	6,575	4,914	1,595	21	......	2	43	74.7	24.3	.3	......	......	.7

general—have reached such staggering proportions in the black community that they constitute a major social problem. Indeed, murder is the fifth leading cause of death among black male adults. It is peculiarly ironic that at this moment in history, when a vast array of black Americans express apprehension about whites practicing systematic genocide against American blacks and when everyone is exhorted to "get things together," black Americans are criminally victimizing other blacks. This victimization is in criminal homicides, felonious murders, physical assaults, maiming, rapes, and crimes against property owned by black people. Fifty-five of every 100 murder victims in the United States are black individuals. The perpetrator of such offenses is usually in the prime of his life: a young male between the ages of 20 and 24.

A clear pattern emerges from the analysis of victimization data. For example, the offender and the victim are usually known to each other. One-fourth of all persons killed in 1971 were within-family killings. More than 50 percent of violent deaths involved interspouse killings, while the remainder included parents' killing of children, children's killing of parents, and other within-family murders. When murders involve spouses, 52 percent of the victims are women and 48 percent are men. In cases of felonious murders, however, including gangland slayings and murders committed in connection with robberies and involving a sex motive, 62 percent of the victims are white and 37 percent are black.

The arrest rates for murder vary according to demographic characteristics. For example, blacks account for more than two-thirds (67.7 percent) of all arrests for murder reported in the city; they account for less than half (43.3 percent) of suburban murders and less than one-third (30.9 percent) of murder arrest in rural areas of the United States. Comparable figures for white murder arrest rates are 30 percent in the city, 55 percent in the suburbs, and 64.9 percent in rural areas. By contrast, arrest rates for manslaughter by negligence clearly demonstrate higher proportions for whites. They account for 71.1 percent of such arrests in the city, 83.7 percent in the suburbs, and 76.4 percent in the rural areas.

The homicide rate for the American black man living in the city is approximately ten times that of the American white male in metropolitan communities. This observation is, to a large degree, supported by data from specific cities. For instance, New York data show that a black resident of that city is eight times more likely to be a murder victim than whites also living there. This study also revealed that intraracial homicides account for more than four-fifths (82 percent) of the total. Forty-eight percent of the sample total involved blacks killing blacks; 21 percent involved Hispanics killing Hispanics; and 13 percent were whites murdering other whites. However, three-fifths of all persons arrested for murder in New York City during the study year, 1971, were black Americans. Half of all murder victims during the same period were black.[4]

Most of the persons arrested for murder, as reported in the New York study, were either unemployed (39 percent) or classified as laborers (34 percent). Occupational profiles indicated that the remainder were classified as students, housewives, drivers of taxicabs, trucks or buses, or businessmen.[5] *This occupational profile supports the theoretical position that intrarace murders originate in frustrations related to economic deprivations or stem from the devastating consequences of poverty and resulting social alienation.* Aggressive responses to frustrations originating in conditions within the social structure obviously are not always directed toward the sources of the frustration; rather, such frustrations are intrapunitive and turned inward toward members of one's own group.[6] These behavioral patterns may also have their roots in a socialization process in which studied manifestations of masculinity are highly prized. They typify subconscious internalization of negative self-value and images attributed to blacks by the dominant group as well as a deeply ingrained subconscious belief system that leads the offender to believe that his offense against a member of his own group will not be as severely punished as one perpetrated against a member of the majority population. The discussion of rape cases, as we shall see, illustrates this point.

Fratricide. Intragroup murders, or fratricide, reflect an inner turmoil of societally induced rage that ultimately reduces many young black men to walking time bombs ready to explode in violent behavior at what appears to be the most insignificant incident, such as an argument over a dime or the use of racial epithets. Also, unresolved love triangles and suspicions of infidelity may precipitate a sudden release of rage resulting in murder.

The general finding reported in the New York City study supports findings revealed in earlier localized studies conducted in Philadelphia and replications of such studies conducted in Chicago. In both of the latter studies a significant majority of the criminal homicides were fratricidal or intragroup in nature.[7]

Aggravated Assaults. These are unlawful attacks upon a person for the purpose of inflicting severe bodily injury to him. As a rule, the attack is accompanied by the use of a weapon capable of producing serious bodily injury or even death. As in the case of criminal homicides, the greater frequency of such assaults observed in 1971 was in the South, in cities of more than 250,000 regardless of region of the country, and among persons aged 21 and over, who account for 69 percent of the nation's total population. Black Americans account for 46.9 percent in comparison to slightly more than one-half (50.9 percent) of the 126,373 cases of aggravated assault reported in the United States committed by white persons.

Like criminal homicides, in most cases the offender and the victim in aggravated assaults are known to each other—either as members of the family unit, as neighbors, or as acquaintances. This situation creates a problem in arrest clearance, since it is difficult to persuade the victims to testify against the alleged offender. It is undoubtedly for this reason that four of every ten cases of arrests for this offense result in either an acquittal or a dismissal. Only 43 percent of adults prosecuted for aggravated assault are convicted. Others may be convicted on a lesser charge as a consequence of plea bargaining or because of the refusal of the victim to press charges against the offender.

Forcible Rape. This type of rape refers to the employment of force or the threat of force in order to have carnal knowledge of a female. It is to be distinguished from statutory rape, which refers to having carnal knowledge of an underage female with her consent and without force.

Research on forcible rapes shows: (1) a steady climb in rates in recent years (for example, an increase of 64 percent in reported cases between 1966 and 1971); (2) variations in rates among regions of the country (for instance, 31 percent of the total forcible rapes occurred in the South; 26 percent in Western and North Central states; and 17 percent in the Northeastern states); (3) racial distinctions in victimization (for example, the victim is likely to be a black female); and (4) intraracial cases of sexual assaults are treated less severely than interracial rape cases, especially if the accused and convicted is a black male.

Slightly more than half of the 15,468 persons arrested in the United States in 1971 for forcible rape were black, and 47.8 percent were white. Again, variations reflect demographic locations. For instance, white rates rise dramatically from 40.7 percent of the total in the city to 69.5 percent in suburbs to 76.8 percent in rural areas. Irrespective of demographic factors, the victim is likely to be black, since black women have an 18-to-1 chance of becoming a rape victim. Similarly, the proportion of blacks arrested for this offense is excessive as evidenced, for example, by their overrepresentation in suburban arrests in relation to the size of their population there. However, we do not know what proportion of the accused actually reside in the suburbs as distinguished from the number of transients among accused rapists.

One must, however, be extremely cautious about these statistics in view of the historical fact that the credibility of white females accusing black men as rapists has seldom been challenged. But the black female's veracity is suspect whether she points the accusing finger at a black or white male. Consequently, as shown by the following discussion of a Baltimore study, disparities and inequities in the adjudication of rape cases exist.

Judge Joseph C. Howard, Sr., examined indictments involving allegations of rape covering a five-year period between 1962 and 1966 in Baltimore, Maryland. The accused were categorized as blacks against whites, blacks against blacks, whites against whites, and whites against blacks. Of all indictments Howard reported that the overwhelming majority of the cases were intragroup acts of sexual violence. Specifically, 505 cases involved blacks against blacks, 175 involved whites against whites, 61 involved blacks against whites, and 9 cases involved whites against blacks.[8]

Inequities in the disposition of rape cases between the races become apparent from the moment of trial, in indictments to final disposition. Although 54.1 percent of the blacks accused of raping white persons were indicted, almost four-fifths (78.8 percent) resulted in convictions, and more than nine out of ten (92.3 percent) convictions permitted the imposition of the death penalty at the discretion of the judge. In the black-against-black cases almost nine out of ten (88.9 percent) resulted in indictments, while slightly fewer than six out of ten (57.5 percent) brought convictions, and slightly more than six out of ten (60.8 percent) convictions could have brought the death penalty at discretion. More than half (57.4 percent) of white men accused of raping white women were convicted, and slightly less (54.3 percent) could have been given the death penalty. The number of cases involving white male sexual attacks against black females was relatively small when compared to all other categories. However, of the nine cases, six were indicted at trial, and more than 80 percent were subject to the death penalty at the discretion of the trial judge. Clearly, interracial rape cases are treated as much more serious offenses than are intraracial ones.[9]

Regarding probation for the convicted, only 1 black male (less than 4 percent) of the 26 blacks convicted of sexual assaults against white women had his sentence suspended and probation invoked. In this one instance the case involved two white boys also charged with the same attack. By contrast, 120 (or 46.5 percent) of 258 blacks convicted of sexual assaults against black women were immediately returned to the community. This study also showed that only five of the nine cases involving white men sexually assaulting black women "ever reached the sentencing stage of trial."[10]

Inequities in sentencing are as pronounced in rape cases as they are in other criminal offenses. Historically, whenever a black male was accused of raping a white female, the death penalty was almost always automatically imposed. Even up to World War II, black men were lynched, hanged, castrated, or subjected to brutal physical assaults. Lynchings (such as the 1957 lynching of Emmett Till in Mississippi) have resulted from such curious allegations as "reckless eyeballing" of white women or of making flirtatious passes at white girls. The average sentence imposed upon blacks accused of raping white women is approximately five times as severe as that imposed upon a black who rapes a black or a white who rapes a white. The enormity of this disparity undoubtedly reflects the rigidity of social taboos related to transgressions of the black male against the white female. This situation perpetuates the "white-females-on-a-pedestal syndrome," which serves as a social control and results in harsh sanctions against deviants who veer from the norm regarding black male-white female sexual relations. In the Baltimore study four-fifths of the whites who raped black women received a sentence of 5 years, and none received a penalty of 20 years to life or sentences of life or death. On the other hand, none of the blacks who raped white women received a sentence shorter than 5 years; half received sentences of 20 years to life; 11.5 percent were sentenced to life imprisonment; and 3.8 percent received a sentence of death. By contrast, slightly more than one-fourth (28.6 percent) of blacks who raped black women received terms shorter than 5 years; 5 percent received sentences of 20 years to life; and three-tenths of 1 percent had sentences of either life imprisonment or death.

Since 1923, in fact, of the 30 persons executed in Maryland on a charge of rape, 23 were black, 5 were white, and 2 were classified as "other."[11] Similar findings relative to the impositions of the death penalty were observed in studies conducted in Florida, Georgia, and New York. In Florida between 1940 and 1964, 48 of the 54 men sentenced to death for rape were black. Twenty-nine of the black men and one of the six white males were actually executed during that period. In New York in the five-year period from 1957 to 1962, 80 percent of the 50 persons sentenced to death for rape were black and Puerto Rican. Of the total, all of whom were either black or Puerto Rican, 11 were actually executed. In Georgia in a 30-year period from 1930 to 1961, 58 of the 61 persons actually executed for rape were black; 3 were white; but not 1 white person was executed for raping a black female.[12] Once again, persuasive evidence exists for the argument that intraracial cases of sexual assaults are indeed treated less severely than interracial rape cases, especially when the accused and convicted is a black male.

ACQUISITIVE CRIME

Robbery. Defined as a "vicious type of crime" occurring in the victim's presence, robbery is committed to obtain valued property by the use of force or the threat of force. Robberies, including assault to commit robbery as well as attempted robberies, comprise almost half of the crimes of violence. But it is *also* acquisitive, since its primary motivation is the acquisition of money or property through illegal means. Almost 386,000 robberies were committed in the United States during 1971 according to

Uniform Crime Report data. Most occurred in the Northeast (37.7 percent), but, irrespective of regions, 70 percent of all robbery cases occur in cities of 250,000 or more. More than half occur in the streets, and two-thirds (65 percent) are armed robberies. Notable increases can be observed in the five-year period from 1966 to 1971 in robberies occurring in banks, holdups of gas or service stations, chain stores, residences, and other commercial establishments.

Persons arrested for robbery are relatively young; approximately 55 percent are under the age of 21, and almost a third (32 percent) are under the age of 18. Robbery arrestees are also likely to be black, since blacks account for almost two-thirds (66 percent) of all such arrests throughout the nation, while whites account for approximately 32 percent. While blacks are more often arrested for robbery in the city (70 percent of all cases), whites are more frequently arrested in the suburbs (67.4 percent). Reverse racial arrest patterns occur as we move from the city to rural areas and back.

Burglary. This occurs when there is an unlawful entry into a structure, not involving force, to commit a felony or theft. More than 2,368,000 burglaries were recorded in the United States during 1971. Like robbery, burglary is among the most frequently committed of all crimes in the United States and accounts for 40 percent of all Crime Index offenses and 46 percent of all property crimes recorded. The burglary rate has increased 62 percent over that in 1966. The total volume of burglary seems to be almost uniformly distributed throughout each region of the country with no more than 3 percent regional variation. As in the cases of other serious offenses, the young—persons under the age of 25—account for a disproportionate number of burglaries. Nationally, they account for 83 percent of all burglary arrests. Persons under the age of 18 account for more than half of the total arrest figures. In this instance, white Americans are arrested for burglary twice as often as are black Americans. More than one-half of city arrests, four-fifths of suburban arrests, and almost nine-tenths of rural arrests for burglary involve whites.

Whites also outnumber blacks by a margin of two to one in arrests for larceny-theft as well as in arrests for auto theft.

CRIMES AGAINST BLACKS IN THE BLACK COMMUNITY

Throughout the United States residents of black communities perceive black-on-black crime as a major social problem. Increasingly, they realize their high vulnerability to crimes of murder, robbery, rape, assault, and generalized burglary. This heightened sense of awareness has produced an immeasurable amount of fear of crime within the black community. Black women fear being raped even when unaware of their much higher chances of being victimized. Men and women, young and old, fear physical assaults and muggings whether they reside in the upper middle-class Baldwin Hills district of Los Angeles, the upper-class Shaker Heights district of metropolitan Cleveland, or in the working-class areas of Harlem.

Nationally, black businessmen live with their increasing vulnerability every day. Recent survey data point out that more than a fourth of all ghetto businesses (28 percent) were burglarized in a single year. Similarly, one-fifth of city businesses elsewhere were victimized by burglaries. Inner-city and central businesses are also robbed more frequently. Collectively, 12 percent of the inner-city and central city businesses were robbed during the study year. As stated in Chapter 6, robberies, burglaries, shoplifting, and other felonious activities place a heavy financial toll on businesses in the ghettos and central cities of America.[13] Hence such crimes have serious consequences for the overall economy of the black community (businesses are forced to relocate and to pay higher insurance rates and higher prices for poorer services).

From Washington, D.C., to Detroit to Los Angeles the fear of crime is widespread in the black community. Residents have often followed the pattern of ghetto businessmen by placing guard bars over doors and windows of their dwellings. Some houses and businesses install two or three heavy padlocks on doors as deterrents to burglars and robbers. Businessmen who can afford to do so construct expensive security systems. Many "mom and pop" grocery storeowners wear handguns or keep them readily available in case of attack. Occasionally, when an elderly man in distress is forced to use his weapon in self-defense, the result is the loss of life or serious bodily injury. Gas stations, record shops, package liquor stores, cleaning establishments, and drug stores are constant targets. The homes of many black community residents, the poor and the economically privileged alike, stand a good chance of being victimized by thievery of some kind during the course of any year.[14] And with each occurrence the quality of life in the city deteriorates a little bit more!

One explanation for the increase of crimes by blacks against blacks and other groups in the black community is the lack of enforcement of laws by the police. The problem is seriously exacerbated by the limited amount of security and by the paucity of police assigned to the black community. A prevalent attitude among black community residents is that the police force is comprised of unconcerned whites who may, themselves, be partially responsible for the innumerable rip-offs occurring within the black community on a daily basis. The distrust of policemen is ubiquitous, and it also extends to black policemen who seem unsympathetic to the exigencies and vagaries of ghetto life.

Throughout the country, from city to city, the proportion of blacks on police forces is considerably lower than their proportion in urban populations. This generalization is illustrated by data from a number of places. In Washington, D.C., for instance, where blacks constitute 71.1 percent of the total population, only about 25 percent of its 4,409-member police force is black. In Detroit, which has a black population of approximately 42 percent and where the murder rate has reached staggering proportions, only 14 percent of its police force is black. Atlanta is more than 51 percent black but less than one-fourth (22 percent) of its police force is black. St. Louis, whose population is more than 40 percent black, has only 300 black policemen out of a total of 2,200. Bridgeport, Connecticut, a city in which minorities comprise more than a quarter of the total population, has only 3.7 percent minorities on its police force. The same situation exists in New York City, which with a total police force of nearly 30,000 and a black population of nearly 22 percent has a mere 7 percent of blacks on the police force. In Philadelphia, where law and order was the resounding theme of recent political elections and where the black population is more than a third of the total city population, blacks comprise only about 17 percent of the total police force. Given these statistical realities, it is relatively easy for blacks to conclude that they are indeed administered, manipulated, and controlled by a white occupation force. It provides evidence for the theoretical claim that the ghetto is a colony policed largely by white mercenaries.

There is a growing fear within the black community that crimes such as burglaries, armed robberies, muggings, and felonious assaults are clearly associated with the problem of drug abuse. In Detroit, for example, it is estimated by some that between 40 and 80 percent of all burglaries and robberies are drug related. Specifically, many individuals staunchly defend the view that these crimes are committed by persons addicted to drugs.[15] This same belief system pervades the Harlem community in New York and the Bedford-Stuyvesant section of Brooklyn. There it is claimed that as much as 70 percent of all incidents of crime are drug related. It is maintained by policemen and citizens alike that addicts steal, burglarize, mug, and rob in order to support a heroin habit whose cost ranges upward from $40 to $200 per day. The cost of addiction to heroin (or scag or horse) is extremely prohibitive. Crime does finance a large portion of the money needed to support the habit. However, all aggressive crime is surely not drug related; there is evidence provided in a study by Mark Moore, in a paper prepared for the Hudson Institute, which raises serious doubts about such an assumption. Moore maintains that addicts obtain only 2 percent of revenues required to support their habit through muggings and armed robberies. Peddling dope is the principal method of obtaining much needed funds, accounting for about 50 percent of all revenue required. However, addicts do rely upon such additional revenue sources as burglaries, shoplifting, and prostitution.[16] Some drug addicts, in desperation for funds, have been known to sell their own children. Drug users are not likely to be as involved in violent crimes, such as homicides and aggravated assault, as nonusers because they realize that conviction of these crimes will result in extended incarceration—a price they cannot afford in view of their dependency on drugs.

Gang-related Crimes. These kinds of crimes are also on the increase in the black community. During 1972 and 1973, several major cities of the United States, including Los Angeles, New York, Chicago, and Philadelphia, experienced a resurgence of gang activity. In recent years hundreds of deaths, homicides, and manslaughters have been attributed to juvenile and young-adult gang activities. Gangs have committed a major portion of the violent crimes for which young blacks have been arrested. The gangs of the 1970s are somewhat different from those of the 1950s in the sense that the more recent gangs are better equipped wth more sophisticated weaponry and are often expert in professional killings. Police have confiscated such weapons as zip guns, rifles, automatic pistols, and, in some instances, submachine guns from huge arsenals of weapons owned by gang members. The gangs of the 1970s are also reported by police to provide protection for drug users and guard service for drop-off stations. Some members have become sophisticated in hustling, whether it is defined as pimping for prostitutes or simply making an easy living as a human parasite or "con artist."

The new gangs persist because they are a source of personal belonging for homeless, nomadic, jobless youths who at an early age have already become alienated from the social system. They persist because the need to be accepted by a group and to have one's masculinity fulfilled through courage, "heart," and sexual prowess is fundamental to the subculture in which they live. These are not Albert Cohen's nonutilitarian gangs out on a lark.[17] They are purposeful and goal oriented as evidenced in their determination to protect their members or to rob and burglarize in order to survive in what for many of them is an extremely cruel and rejecting social milieu. They also persist because the conditions of deprivation in the social structure sustained through prolonged abject poverty and limited access to legitimate means for achieving culturally defined success goals have nurtured them. But the devastating brutalities of gang life dramatize with chilling force the degree of anomie, normlessness, and alienation that engulfs black youths at an early age.

Organized Crime. Since the post-World War I period organized crime has existed within the black community. Information on this subject is understandably scanty and fragmented. Historically, it has always been assumed that organized crime in the black community was controlled through black front men by white mobsters who lived outside the community. They controlled prostitution and gambling rings, loan sharking, the numbers game, narcotics trafficking, organized burglary gangs, bookmaking, and other forms of organized criminal behavior. All of these activities continue to be highly lucrative enterprises in the black neighborhood—so much so that some police officials now claim that black mobsters are attempting to seize control over organized crime in the black community.

Organized crime cannot operate without some form of police corruption. Wherever it exists, whether in black or white communities, whether controlled by blacks or whites, it is reasonable to assume that law enforcement agents at one level or another are being paid for protective services. Accordingly, prostitution rings, burglary rings, drug trafficking, and the numbers game, for example, are permitted to flourish because corrupt police officials give tacit if not formal approval in exchange for regular, lucrative payoffs.

Perhaps of all the forms of crime alleged to be controlled by organized crime forces now institutionalized within the black community, "playing the numbers" is the most common. It is estimated that in New York City alone fully 40 percent of black and Puerto Rican community members play the "policy game," or make parimutuel bets. The numbers system is functionally organized into three components: runners, controllers, and bankers. Runners, who comprise the largest segment of this structure and who rank at the bottom in social standing, are collectors of bets and money. They, in turn, report their funds to controllers, the second largest component. After coding bets, controllers turn them over to bankers whose major responsibility is covering bets and record keeping. Bankers are believed to have the most direct association with organized criminal elements. Functional differentiation extends to responsibilities for paying-off different levels of law enforcement agents for protection. Thus the local patrolmen are paid by runners; uniformed policemen and detectives are paid by controllers; and bankers distribute payoffs to city and police officials at high levels. In essence, the numbers game is big business involving about $2 billion in annual receipts obtained from thousands of bets ranging from a nickel or a dime up to hundreds of dollars. Despite its possible connections with organized crime, the numbers game flourishes also because people like it. Many of its participants do not perceive it as illegal behavior; or they find it indistinguishable from church bingo games or race-track betting—both of which are legal in several states. They do not believe that society is in any way socially injured by their betting on numbers. Many hope that the numbers game will provide a big "hit" that will give them a ticket out of the ghetto plus a new lease on a much better life.[18]

White-Collar Crime. A further illustration of race-class distinctions in crime is this unique kind of crime, which is committed by middle- and upper-class individuals in the course of their daily occupations. It includes offenses such as embezzlement, fraud, and forgery. The white population accounts for more than two-thirds of all cases of forgery and three-fourths of all cases of embezzlement and fraud. These are not physically violent crimes; they are crimes committed by "respectable" persons who are usually regarded as upstanding citizens. The degree of social injury resulting from white-collar crime is considered less harmful than that resulting from violent crimes. Yet the amount of money lost through forgeries, frauds, and embezzlement each year is in the billions of dollars. However, society has a high toleration level for such offenses and for such offenders and is less inclined to stereotype the white middle and upper classes as criminals, as is often done in the case of the black population, especially of the lower class. One need only recall the all-white cast of the alleged offenders in the infamous Watergate case to realize the magnitude of white-collar crime even in high places. The only black person involved in that sordid episode was a watchman who notified the police of the break-in.

Even though a banker in Los Angeles or Chicago may be convicted of embezzlement involving several million dollars, he may often be granted a lighter sentence than a young black or poor white adult who is convicted of burglary or robbery. This inequity in the administration of justice has a profound impact on poor blacks and whites, whose observations of such blatant disparities lead to the inevitable conclusion that the law is made by the privileged and well-to-do for the benefit of the rich and powerful.

RACISM AND THE ADMINISTRATION OF JUSTICE

Discriminatory practices and prejudice in the administration of justice remain a serious problem. Evidence suggests that approximately 75 percent of white police officers assigned to predominantly black precincts expressed some form of prejudice or antipathy toward black people. About 10 percent of black officers assigned to predominantly black precincts harbor extreme antiblack attitudes. Given these antiblack sentiments, the chances of blacks coming to the attention of the law are excessive even under the most ordinary circumstances. Once confronted by the police, blacks frequently claim to be subjected to status degradation, physical and verbal abuse, and to be referred to in terms of racial epithets.[19]

Our discussion of rape cases demonstrated the magnitude of discrimination against blacks in the relative infrequency with which probation is awarded. Discrimination also occurs in the comparatively higher bails required of blacks for relatively minor offenses; in longer sentences given to blacks than to whites for the same offenses, averaging about 15 to 18 months longer for blacks than for whites; in the tendency for a greater proportion of blacks to be imprisoned and to serve out most of their terms than whites. It is estimated, for example, that, nationally, more than 50 percent of all inmates in the nation's prisons are blacks. Even in prisons, until recently, racial segregation was the norm. Black inmates are still demeaned and brutalized by the prison system and, once again, by its power forces comprised predominantly of authoritarian white guards and administrators. As at Attica in 1971, black inmates often claim physical attacks by guards, racism among administrators, a differential privilege and work assignment system based upon race, and a low probability of attaining parole. Others fear victimization by psychosurgery related to behavioral modification programs. Many become highly political, defining themselves as political prisoners victimized by a capitalist, racist society. Not only is white racism magnified, but interethnic conflicts exacerbate deeply rooted prejudices. Thus racism is associated with the criminal justice system at all levels— from policemen to trial judges to parole boards and probation officers.

How, then, can criminal behavior among blacks be explained? Explanations of human behavior are invariably fraught with problems, and no single theory can completely account for either conformity or deviance from the normative order.

Aggressive offenses, such as crimes of murder and aggravated assault, may indeed be the result of deeply embedded frustrations that originate in social deprivations and interpersonal conflicts induced by the social structure. Proponents of *deprivation theory* argue that frustration induced by abhorrent forms of economic and social discrimination may lead to aggressive acts against a victim who at a critical moment in time is defined as weak.[20] Similar to *learning and reinforcement theory,*[21] deviance is viewed as a response to environmental pressures. Certain types of stimuli call for specific types of responses. In this case, the response is defined deviant behavior.

Another claim is that criminal behavior, aggressive or acquisitive, is learned behavior. It is learned in association with other criminals, and it is assumed that the socializing experiences of individuals who become criminals have permitted them to internalize an excess of definitions favorable to violations of the law over those definitions that are unfavorable to illegal behavior. This is a major theme in *differential association theory*.[22] Essentially, most offenders have had contact with other offenders, who socialize them into deviancy, and they, in turn, become socializers for others. This is the basis for both the cause and the cycle of recidivism among offenders. Accordingly, criminal behavior among blacks may be related to social and economic conditions in the social structure that force blacks to live in communities where the frequency and intensity of deviant behavior induce a socialization pattern that is at variance with the normative order. Furthermore, whereas certain traditions common to a given locale may be in conflict with the morality of criminal law, they are not defined as criminal by local norms. But criminal behavior is also a function of *differential opportunity*, since all persons and groups do not have equal access to attain culturally prescribed goals or rewards through legitimate means.[23]

Both differential opportunity and goals-means theory are forms of *congruence theory*, which regards social systems as highly integrated and as having priority over individuals. However, individuals may experience personal strains in cases of ambiguity in the norms of the group or when the norms seem contradictory or logically incongruous. Presumably, certain goals are culturally prescribed as normative, and the routes prescribed for their attainment are legitimated by the social system. Even in the face of disjunctions between the end—a socially accepted goal—and the means— an illegal method of achieving means—individuals are presumed to possess cognitive orientations. Individuals have alternatives. They may conform to societal expectations; they may innovate; they may engage in ritualistic behavior irrespective of consequences (retreatism); or they may rebel by rejecting the goals and the means. Persons who are poor, limited in money, economically deprived, and who, in general, do not have the means to achieve culturally defined success and who endorse success as an acceptable goal select alternative routes such as criminal behavior for goal attainment. In this sense, acquisitive crime—burglary, robbery, thievery—among blacks may be partially explained. But these are precisely the people who are the victims of repressive measures for the most minute forms of deviant behavior. Repeated acts of repression may have a reinforcing effect in the sense that once *labeled* a criminal, the individual may come to believe that he is indeed a criminal and, consequently, reorder his behavioral system in such a way as to conform to that deviant expectation.[24]

An important point should be reiterated here. Although the primary focus of this section has been on crime among blacks, it should never be assumed that the sole argument is that blacks are *more* criminal than whites or that crime is a peculiarity of the black community. A discussion of this kind is inescapable, though nonetheless painful, in an examination of diversity in the black community. Clearly, the overwhelming majority of black

Americans are law-abiding citizens and will remain so even in the face of relentless economic deprivations and ravaging racial discrimination. Historical experiences demonstrate beyond a shadow of a doubt that blacks have an infinite capacity for adaptation and have employed a variety of adaptive responses to racial prejudice and subordination. Criminal behavior itself may in fact be one mode of adaptation to the myriad stresses and strains of living in a racist society that still denies blacks equal access to socially defined shared values.

GHETTO CONTROL PROGRAMS

Black Americans are undoubtedly more greatly disturbed by the disproportionate volume and rate of crimes attributed to blacks in the black communities than are any other groups of American people. The very presence of high rates of both aggressive and acquisitive crimes as compared to high rates of white-collar crimes and burglaries by whites in the white communities is no valid justification for the pervasive stereotypes about blacks and criminality. Yet these stereotypes persist because of their convenience or because of racist thinking that allows individuals to accept them as unequivocal truths.

In recent years in an effort to combat increasing rates of both aggressive and acquisitive types of criminal offenses black community residents organized a number of preventive programs. In response to inadequate protection by police to black community residents, blacks organized citizens' task forces in many cities throughout the nation. Such groups attempt to improve police surveillance and to ensure prompt action by law enforcement agencies when criminal behavior is suspected. They also organized radio patrols as crime alert systems. Organized largely as a response to the urban revolts of the 1960s, youth patrols function primarily in many cities as a buffer between the black community and the police, protecting property, disseminating information, and "monitoring police activities." In few places have youth patrols found it easy to maintain an effective balance between themselves and the police mainly because police have limited control over them.[25] Vietnam veterans organized groups called Vietnam Veterans Against Crime and many joined De Mau Mau for the purpose of combating or controlling drug trafficking and crimes against the black poor and elderly. Radio programs, such as "Buzz the Fuzz," broadcast over an all-black Chicago radio station, tend to foster attitudinal changes of blacks toward police and to promote responsibility among black community residents to report suspected criminal offenses to the police. Concerned Citizens

Organizations and Friends of the Police stress the acquisition of better street lights and improvements in the social justice system as well as in the social structure as first steps in eliminating the conditions that give rise to criminal behavior. Groups of this kind have become disenchanted with some organizations such as Detroit's STRESS, an acronym for Stop the Robberies—Enjoy Safe Streets, primarily as a result of the transformation of this organization from a decoy system for apprehending criminals in the act of criminal behavior to a perceived antiblack organization. One basic explanation for the opposition to STRESS is that between 1971, when it was first organized, and the first half of 1973, most of the 17 persons killed by policemen assigned to STRESS teams were blacks. This situation gave ample credence to the view that so many policemen are prone to violence when confronted with black suspects.

This tendency toward violence and unwarranted employment of force against black suspects raises serious questions about the credibility of many policemen as law enforcement officers, strengthens perceptions of racial prejudice among police officers, and escalates allegations of police brutality. Indeed, disharmonious relationships between the black community and law enforcement officers originate most fundamentally in charges of police brutality. Vociferous blacks claim that police are "trigger happy" when confronted with black people and that their ingrained hatred or fears of black people stimulate more brutalizing responses when encountering blacks suspected of criminal offenses. This situation—combined with alleged corruption and disregard for the welfare of black people—has prompted proponents of community control to focus attention on the police as an important institution requiring direct accountability to local community people. It is mainly by virtue of these persistent efforts that personnel changes in the police force assigned to black communities have occurred and city-wide programs designed to alter radically the negative images of police officers are forming.

MENTAL HEALTH AND
HEALTH CARE

Mental Health. Our knowledge of the prevalence and distribution of emotional health problems within the black population is seriously limited. This problem stems largely from inconsistencies in interpretations of what behavior actually constitutes psychotic and psychoneurotic behavior. It is embedded in our confused understandings of the relationship between socioeconomic status and social behavior. Furthermore, rates of some forms of mental disorders among blacks often result from overdiagnosis (labeling a disease more severe than it actually is), particularly by white psychiatrists. The tendency among white psychiatrists to overdiagnose psychoses among blacks is a manifestation of one way in which cultural bias impedes objective perceptions. It also shows the inability of white psychiatrists to understand the various nuances of black culture and the persons socialized in the American black culture.[26] If there were more than the 100 known black psychiatrists in the United States and if they, by virtue of their being black, could comprehend the nuances of black culture, perhaps prevalence and incidence data relative to the types of emotional health problems among blacks would be more reliable.

Most studies on mental illness have established a linkage between social class, or socioeconomic position, and both the incidence and the prevalence of certain types of mental illness. In general, the highest rates of mental disorders are found among the lowest socioeconomic and occupational groups, and, conversely, the lowest rates are among the more economically advantaged. From the early studies conducted by Robert E. L. Faris and H. W. Dunham, who followed an ecological approach to this problem in determining prevalence distribution, to more recent investigations, this theoretical position appears to be substantiated. For instance, R. E. Clark claimed that the higher the occupational level, the lower the rates of schizophrenia and, conversely, schizophrenic rates are highest among persons with low-status occupations.[27] Confirmations on this finding appeared in a plethora of studies including research conducted by August B. Hollingshed and F. C. Redlich in New Haven,[28] the widely known Midtown Manhattan Study conducted by Leo Srole and his associates,[29] and in the more recent investigations undertaken by Dunham[30] and W. A. Rushing.[31] One could therefore draw the inference that since blacks are concentrated in low-status occupations as well as residentially confined to the central city, rates of mental disorders would be high among them.

Although evidence strongly endorses the linkage between social class and mental illness, there are other serious ramifications of the association. First, the prohibitive cost of psychotherapy or psychiatric care is often beyond the capacity of all but comparatively few black Americans to afford. Consequently, only those persons whose aberrant behavior is sufficiently serious, in terms of personal injury to others, or who are personally destructive so as to require societal intervention are likely to obtain psychiatric care. Evidence indicates that these individuals tend more often to be institutionalized and are less likely to receive private psychiatric treatment. Second, since a disproportionately large number of blacks who suffer from mental health problems are institutionalized, they have a greater probability of being disproportionately represented in most categories of mental disorder and of being overdiagnosed as psychotics rather than psychoneurotics. Thus one would expect the rates of nonwhite or black mental illness to be higher than rates for whites when data from state hospitals are analyzed.

Conversely, though, as Benjamin Pasamanick has observed, in 1962, rates of mental illness, both psychotic disorders and psychoneurotic behavior, are highest for whites in private institutions and Veterans Administration (VA) hospitals. White admissions for psychoneuroses in private and VA hospitals were at the rate of 62.29 per 1,000, while the rate for blacks was 27.35 per 1,000, but the overall rates of admission of psychoses for whites and blacks were 9.46 and 7.04, respectively. However, the most remarkable disparity occurred in the analysis of noninstitutional data. Here, Pasamanick observed that the rate of serious mental illness among whites at 5.20 per 1,000 is ten times greater than that of blacks at 0.5 per 1,000.[32] Third, if one holds the social class variable constant, prevalence by types as related to racial identification appears more distinctive. Benjamin Malzberg, in holding social class constant, observed higher rates of schizophrenia, general paresis, and alcoholic psychoses among blacks. He also observed higher rates of old-age psychoses, involutional psychoses, senile psychoses, and manic-depressive behavior among whites.[33] Thus different types of psychoses are found within each group. Undoubtedly, these responses are a function of different cultural experiences.

Melvin Kohn and John A. Clausen raised the question as to whether or not rates of mental illness in various occupational groups and in different parts of the city more accurately reflect *concentration* of cases in the lowest socioeconomic strata. Examining data on schizophrenia in Hagerstown, Maryland (with a population of 36,000), and several studies regarding area characteristics and rates of schizophrenia, they concluded that there was a much stronger correlation between social class and schizophrenia in large urban communities than in smaller communities. Thus the larger the city, the greater will be the probability of a strong association between the prevalence of schizophrenia and lower-status groups.[34] It is also suggested by this finding that stresses and strains brought to bear on individuals who are concentrated in poverty-stricken, low-income, and highly congested areas of the cities result in various forms of mental illness. However, the evidence is as yet too inconclusive to draw definitive generalizations regarding either incidence or prevalence of specific types of mental health problems among various groups. More reliable conclusions await extensive national research.

ALCOHOLISM, EXCESSIVE DRINKING, AND DRUG ABUSE

Atlhough thousands of dollars have been expended in support of research pertaining to alcoholism and heavy drinking, our knowledge of this subject remains limited and incomplete. Contradictions and uncertainties prevail in terms of what actually constitutes alcoholism, its etiological bases, its relative incidence, and the effects of alcohol upon the physiology of the drinker. These shortcomings are due largely to serious methodological weaknesses inherent in much of the research. In recent years, however, more sophisticated research has broadened our understanding of the nature of alcoholic addiction and heavy drinkers. There is still a strong tendency, nevertheless, to treat heavy drinking and alcoholism as if they were conceptually interchangeable.

Heavy drinking is excessive drinking that may over the long run, often as long as 15 or 20 years, lead to alcoholic addiction. By alcoholic addiction, or alcoholism, we mean dependency upon alcohol as a means of retreat or escape from the daily responsibilities and demands of life. This dependency is so pronounced that the individual feels unable to enjoy life or to establish satisfying social relationships without relying upon alcohol.

The estimated incidence of alcoholism in America ranges from 5 or 6 million to 9 million Americans. This is considerably more than even the best estimates of the number of drug addicts in the United States. Social scientists know less about alcoholism, excessive drinking, or social drinking among American blacks than perhaps about any other racial or ethnic group in America.[35] Research conducted during the 1960s, though, has provided illuminating findings regarding drinking among black Americans. The estimated proportion of white Americans who drink alcoholic beverages is 69 percent of the adult population. The proportion among blacks approximates 62 percent. About one-quarter of black alcohol consumers (23 percent) are classified as heavy drinkers in comparison to 17 percent of the drinking white population.[36]

Although evidence regarding racial differences in rates of alcoholism is contradictory, most studies seem to indicate that both rates of heavy or excessive drinking and alcoholism are higher among blacks than among whites.[37] Many findings are highly suspect relative to comparative rates reported and, not infrequently, serve to perpetuate the mythical "black pathology syndrome." But more scientifically sound investigations lend tentative support to the hypothesis that alcoholism is increasingly a social problem in the black community. For example, a 1965 Manhattan borough study reported that the rate of alcoholism among blacks was 28 per 1,000 persons while that for whites was 16. However, dramatic reversals occur in rates when measured against amounts of education. That is to say, when whites and blacks with ten or more years of education were tested, the rate for whites was 20 alcoholics per 1,000 persons but only 12 for blacks.[38] This finding suggests that more highly educated whites are more likely to become alcoholics than are more highly educated blacks. Conversely, one may also assume that alcoholism is more widespread among the less educated blacks than among those having more years of schooling. High educational attainment is a deterrent to alcoholism among blacks but does not appear to have the same effect on whites.

Although alcoholism is largely a male phenomenon, it is by no means peculiar to men. The high visibility of male alcoholics may actually inflate their disproportionality as related to the low visibility of women alcoholics and heavy drinkers in American culture. Most studies of sex differences in drinking behavior tend to agree that black women are more likely to be abstainers than are white women, for example. Less than one-half (49 percent) of black women are drinkers in comparison to 61 percent of white women. It is interesting to note, however, that although fewer black women drink, the proportion of heavy drinkers among them is about three times the proportion of drinking white females classified as heavy-escape drinkers. The actual percentages were 11 and 4 for black and white females, respectively.[39] The sex ratio for alcoholism appears to be greater among whites than among blacks. For instance, among whites there is only 1 female alcoholic to every 6.2 male alcoholics, but among black alcoholics there is 1 female to every 1.9 male alcoholics.[40] More recent observations about skid-row women who are heavy drinkers illuminate this subject further. Gerald Garrett and Howard Bahr found evidence among New Yorkers that shows, contrary to expectations, that black men are not overrepresented on skid row. The proportion of black men on skid row in the Bowery is approximately the same as the proportion of black men in New York. One of every four New Yorkers is a black male; and, proportionately, one of every four skid-row inhabitants is a black male. But black women are overrepresented there, constituting approximately 40 percent of the skid-row female population. The researchers also found evidence to support previous investigations that both black men and women drinkers have a higher proportion of the heavy drinkers among skid rowers. It should be stressed that Garrett and Bahr did not conclude that black men and women on skid row are disproportionately found among the alcoholics there.[41] The comparatively lower proportion of drinking black women is explained by several factors. It is hypothesized, for example, that the greater degree of religiosity among black women, coupled with cultural expectations of the female role, restrains them from indulging in drinking. Another assumption is that black women have a greater responsibility thrust upon them by adverse economic factors that are not only conducive to abstinence but only allow heavy drinking rather than alcoholism among those black women who do drink.[42]

As has been suggested, then, one must be cautious in interpreting comparative data about rates of both alcoholism and heavy drinking among blacks and whites. Higher rates of drinking behavior among blacks may be more of a reflection of high visibility among black consumers than would normally be the case if they had the same opportunity to receive private care as do many white alcoholics, male and female. Furthermore, the measures of heavy drinking as opposed to socially acceptable drinking are not clearly delineated from one study to another. Societal toleration of excessive drinking among the white population may be so flexible as to deflate the proportion of whites who are defined as either heavy drinkers or as confirmed alcoholics.

According to deprivation and congruence theory, alcoholism among blacks may be an adaptive response to frustrations that have their roots in racial oppression and exploitation. It may also represent escape or withdrawal (retreatism) from the exigencies of a social world that shuts them out or makes life itself somewhat intolerable. We know that many alcoholics experience status inconsistency and that others attempt to endure downward mobility. Alcoholism may once again be an adaptive response to both situations. Because of economic deprivations, lower incomes, and low-status occupational pursuits, black alcoholics seeking treatment more frequently become wards of the state or public treatment centers. Thus their visibility in statistics is heightened.

Drug Abuse. The American public has become increasingly conscious of the prevalence of drugs and the reported higher incidence of drug abuse in the United States during the past decade. Many would argue that comparatively little attention was paid to the problem of illegal drug use until the drug crisis victimized the sons and daughters of the white middle class. According to this argument, which is frequently heard among street people, there was no concerted effort to study the causes of drug addiction and no organized program to legalize either stimulants or narcotic drugs as long as drug abuse was believed to be a problem of black ghetto dwellers and white musicians. Although the argument has merit, it should be pointed out that during the 1950s Alfred Lindesmith[43] and others argued unsuccessfully that the basic problem of drugs in America is the law itself and not the people who use them. Society establishes definitions of legality and illegality as it chooses. Thus the associative problems of drug addiction, such as organized crime and other forms of deviant behavior, did not arise when the use of drugs was not societally defined as deviant behavior. Nevertheless, today, the use of certain types of drugs is considered illegal in the American society and is, therefore, in violation of the normative social order.

Statistics on drug behavior, like statistics on deviant behavior in general, tend to be contradictory and misleading. The illegality of drug use makes drug-abuse statistics all the more unreliable, since violators of drug laws tend to function as furtively as possible. There is evidence, however, that the use of illegal drugs has been steadily increasing since the beginning of the decade of the 1960s. Then it was estimated that the number of drug addicts in the United States varied from 20,000 to 60,000. By the end of the 1960s, with the rise of a drug culture in mecca cities such as San Francisco and with the return of Vietnam veterans reportedly exposed to drug abuse, law enforcement agents raised the alarm of a rapidly expanding drug-abuse crisis. Some estimates ran as high as 600,000![44]

However, the best available evidence indicates that there are about 200,000 heroin addicts in the United States. Approximately 50 percent of them are believed to be residing in New York. The remaining ones are concentrated primarily in California, Illinois, Michigan, Maryland, Pennsylvania, and the District of Columbia. It is also claimed that about 51.3 percent of opiate offenders are black Americans.[45] For this reason residents of many black communities, particularly the depressed urban ghettos, maintain that drug abuse has reached epidemic proportions.

Drug abuse is primarily a phenomenon of urban communities. It extends beyond the downtrodden neighborhoods of the inner city to suburban communities. Within cities both drug addiction and illicit drug use appear to be located in areas characterized by low income, poor housing, and high rates of crime and delinquency. These neighborhoods also contain a greater proportion of broken homes, high rates of unemployed men, working women, and relatively low educational attainment levels.[46] Whether the focus is on illicit use or on dependent drug addiction, statistics on the locations of drug abuse must be interpreted with care because of the transient nature of users. This is especially the case in the black community, to which a fairly substantial transient population flocks due to the unavailability of drugs in other communities or to hide the drug more effectively.[47]

Drug addicts tend to be young males concentrated in the 21 to 30 age bracket; however, the average age at which the onset of heroin addiction occurs may fluctuate over time. During the 1930s, for example, persons between 16 and 20 accounted for slightly more than 1 percent of narcotic violators, but by the beginning of the 1950s persons in this age group accounted for more than 13 percent of the total.[48] Hospital data show a decreasing age of admission for drug addiction. Law enforcement agents indicate that in some cities the problem has become severe not only among the teenaged and young-adult groups but even among preteens as well. Initial reports from Vietnam indicated that as many as 60,000 soldiers were regular heroin users. Later surveys, however, suggested that most soldiers kicked the habit upon returning home. Probably, no more than 1 or 2 percent of Vietnam veterans are confirmed addicts. The number of reported users is considerably higher. Despite the plethora of publicity given to the alleged epidemic of drug addiction and the extensive use of marijuana among members of the armed services in Vietnam, we have no precise data as to the actual extent of either addiction or narcotic abuse among them. But it would seem that a distinct majority of veterans discontinued drug use upon returning home.

For the Vietnam veteran who did return home with a drug problem, adjustment has been fraught with difficulty. For many the initial problem is how to continue to mask or disguise narcotic addiction. For others dependency upon drugs intensifies to an unmanageable degree, finally resulting in the need for hospitalization or private treatment or in street crime. Maintaining steady employment continues to be a source of unrelenting personal and social pressure. Many lose their jobs as unsympathetic supervisors become aware of their addiction to narcotic drugs.

It is the alleged involvement of addicts in crime, particularly street crime, that has perpetuated the public notion of an intimate association between criminality and drug addiction. The victim is once again blamed! Thus the junkie, or addict, has become a symbol of street crime, and for many black community residents this perception is, indeed, real. (The same notion reverberates endlessly in black exploitation films, too.) Law enforcement data from New York City indicate that, during 1970, thefts by addicts approximated $2.3 billion, about $1.8 billion of which was lost in Harlem. It was also reported that addicts accounted for slightly more than a fifth of burglary arrests, somewhat less than a fifth of robbery arrests, more than a tenth of the homicides.[49]

The ineffectiveness of treatment and rehabilitation is implicit in the observation that only one-sixth of the known addicts are involved in treatment programs throughout the nation. Those hospitals that have historically attempted to rehabilitate the addicted, located at Lexington, Kentucky, and Forth Worth, Texas, have not enjoyed notable success in controlling the spread of addiction. Methadone maintenance centers, which sponsor a program that fosters the substitution of the drug methadone for heroin as a means of reducing heroin dependency, are under attack for their apparent inability to produce total withdrawal from drugs. Heroin maintenance has its advocates as well as its adversaries in the United States. Proponents of heroin maintenance, or providing heroin to addicts at no cost, claim that this program will inevitably reduce criminal activity associated with addiction and, subsequently, destroy the involvement of organized crime in drug trafficking. The Bureau of Narcotics and Dangerous Drugs vehemently opposes such programs with the assertion that even in Great Britain, where heroin maintenance was attempted and abandoned, it failed as an effective weapon for combating drug abuse.

The federal government has finally recognized that drug abuse is not confined to the black ghettos. Consequently, increasing sums of money are allocated to public and private universities and agencies to research the all-encompassing dimensions of the drug-abuse problem and to develop programs of rehabilitation. Such programs are funded by the National Institute of Mental Health, the Office of Economic Opportunity, the Veterans Administration, the Department of Defense, the Law Enforcement Administration Agency, and the Department of Housing and Urban Development. But the black community, impatient with the slow process of research, and wearied from being the subjects of too much research, has declared war on drugs. It is distressed by the presumed disproportionate number of black veterans who are hooked and immobilized by their dependency on narcotizing drugs. Pitiful and poignant cases of black babies born as addicts because of the addiction of their mothers and the knowledge that, in some treatment centers, one in eight narcotics addicts is aged 15 and under have demanded immediate ameliorative action within the black communities of urban cities. In response to this situation organizations such as the Mothers Against Dope, Vietnam Veterans Against Drugs and Crime, Black Citizens Patrol, and Citizens Protective Organizations were formed. These voluntary associations are oriented toward eliminating the suppliers, pushers, and corrupt police known to be involved in drug trafficking as well as those who seem unconcerned with the self-destruction of blacks.

Rehabilitation, treatment, and maintenance programs will be absolutely useless unless we are willing to confront head-on those conditions in the social structure that create in some individuals the need to escape through the use of narcotic drugs. These structural conditions involve economic deprivation, limited access to employment or to the opportunity system in general, and oppressive racism. For those who are already hooked on drugs, the first step is to create an environment that will encourage them to seek assistance in coming to terms with those situations that fostered drug dependency as an adaptive response.

Mortality. The mortality rates of blacks are higher than those for whites in every age group, from infancy to the age of 74. Such rates seem to be increasing for specific age groups among the black population. For example, the age-specific death rate for blacks between the ages of 15 and 24 was 1.6 per 1,000 in 1960 but rose to 2.1 per 1,000 in 1969. Increases of similar magnitudes were observed in the 25-to-34, 35-to-44, and 65-to-74 age groups. These changes may reflect higher incidences of specific types of physical disorders that affect blacks at certain ages. The leading causes of deaths among black people today are major cardiovascular diseases and malignant neoplasms. According to census data, the rate of death resulting from major cardiovascular diseases was 34 percent greater among whites. The rate of deaths among blacks from malignant neoplasms was 25 percent higher than for whites in 1970.[50]

One explanation for the high incidence of deaths from cardiovascular disorders among blacks is the excessive rate of hypertension, or high blood pressure, in the black population. It is estimated that from 5 to 6 million or at least one-quarter of all black adults are affected by hypertension. In some age groups deaths directly attributed to hypertension have reached alarming proportions. For example, within the 25-to-44 age groups among males deaths attributed to high blood pressure are more than 15 times greater among blacks than among whites. Among black females in the same age bracket, the death rate is approximately seven times greater than among white females in the same age group.

Explanations that account for the fact that 25 percent of blacks above the age of 18 suffer from hypertension in contrast to 15 percent of the whites afflicted this way are far from conclusive. Efforts have been made to associate highly seasoned soul-food diets of blacks with high blood pressure. Some researchers attribute the condition to obesity, while others claim that it has its origins, perhaps, in genetic characteristics. Still others maintain that hypertension is a response by blacks to the bottled-up rage, frustrations, and anxieties induced by pervasive racism, discrimination, and functioning in a hostile environment. All of these explanations may be useful, but the validity of the assumptions upon which they are based has never been satisfactorily borne out by empirical investigations. What we do know is that, except for that form of hypertension resulting from kidney disease and glandular abnormalities, the causes of hypertension are not clear. And it is not hypertension related to kidney disease or glandular abnormalities that affects blacks to any noticeable degree. That form of hypertension is apparent in only about 15 percent of known cases, which means, of course, that in the overwhelming majority of cases of hypertension affecting blacks we neither know the causes nor have an effective cure. Thus more than 13,000 blacks will die from hypertension during the course of a year.[51]

Robert Hill adjusted census data on "Negro and other races" in order to determine the leading causes of deaths among blacks. He found that heart disease is specifically the leading cause of death among blacks as well as whites. The rate for blacks is 280.1 per 100,000, while that for whites is 257.1 per 100,000. Men of all races are more vulnerable to death by heart disease than are women. The same generalization holds true for cerebrovascular disease as well. Other leading causes of deaths among blacks per 100,000 are malignant neoplasms (134.9), cerebrovascular disease (106.1), accidents (70.2), early childhood disease (43.6), influenza (43.2), homicide (41.3), cirrhosis of the liver (19.0), and arteriosclerosis (9.6).[52]

HEALTH CARE AND
HEALTH-CARE SYSTEMS

It is evident that far too little attention has been given to the delivery of health care to the black population. This has been a low-priority matter in America. Thousands of black people die needlessly because of grossly inadequate health-care systems, while others are allowed to suffer unnecessarily because of discrimination and segregation in health care.

The inadequacy of health care reveals, among other things, extreme shortages of health-care workers as well as malfunctions in the distribution of health-care systems (see Chapter 6). The increasing numbers of black physicians and dentists, limited as that rise is, have been accompanied by increasing specialization and the urbanization of the black population. This, in turn, has not only inflated the cost of medical and dental care but has also meant the shifting of black medical and dental services to urban areas. As a consequence of this movement, there are 134 rural communities or more in the United States without a doctor.

Blacks see physicians and dentists less often than whites, and when they do come in contact with them, it is more likely to be in hospital clinics and emergency rooms. A recent survey indicated that in 1970, 21 percent of the black population had not seen a physician in two years or more. More than seven out of ten whites who saw physicians visited them in their offices, and less than 9 percent saw physicians in clinics or emergency rooms. In contrast, slightly more than six of ten blacks saw physicians in offices, and almost a fourth had contacts limited to emergency rooms or clinics.[53] Other studies show that blacks tend to use medical services less frequently and more episodically than other ethnic groups. This tendency may be accounted for by different degrees of cosmopolitanism and parochial group structures or a greater folk orientation toward medical care among blacks than among whites[54] or the higher degree of skepticism among blacks about both the availability of medical services and the quality of services given to them.[55]

The problem of inadequacy in health-care delivery is evident in other areas such as in health insurance and available hospital services. For example, in 1970 almost four out of ten blacks over the age of 65 had no hospital insurance, and more than six out of ten black families with annual incomes under $5,000 were without coverage. Moreover, of the 50 black hospitals established when medical care was more segregated, no more than 30 remain, and these are fighting merely to survive. They are in extreme difficulty primarily because of diminishing financial resources, accessibility of integrated facilities to blacks, and their abandonment by black physicians who have flourishing private practices and affiliations with larger, often better-equipped, predominantly white hospitals. Nevertheless, many black physicians have a strong commitment to improving health care and health-care institutions within the black community. Also, many black communities are attempting to gain their share of benefits granted under a series of federal acts designed to improve the quality of community health care. For instance, they are taking advantage of research opportunities provided under the National Sickle Cell Anemia Control Act in order to contain a disease whose two types, sickle-cell trait and incurable sickle-cell anemia disease, are said to affect 2 million blacks as carriers and from 40,000 to 50,000 blacks who have the disease itself. This research is crucial, since the disease usually results in death by the age of 20, and sickle-cell trait victims are often unaware that they are carriers.[56] Also, black community members, including health professionals and practitioners, have taken advantage of laws that provided for the establishment of comprehensive health-planning agencies, community health services, consumer education and training programs, neighborhood health centers, community mental health centers, and health maintenance organizations. These groups attempt to involve both consumers and providers of health care in a cooperative enterprise in which both share in decisions regarding community health needs and how to meet them. Intelligent responses to such needs may occasionally require community lay individuals to be trained to participate on health boards or in hospital management and administration or to devise implementable strategies for effective disease prevention and control. They must also learn ways of stimulating community members to be less episodic in taking advantage of available health-care services and of reducing the degree of skepticism regarding these services. Health-care personnel have also established on-site community services in which they work for specified periods of time in neighborhood centers, whether in housing projects or in storefronts or in local clinics. Greater use is also being made of outpatient services for those persons who cannot afford to lose valuable work time for prolonged periods of hospitalization. Still greater use should be made of psychiatric services to combat rising rates of suicide among black Americans. (Although black rates are generally 50 percent less than white rates, suicide rates among black men between the ages of 25 and 35 are double that of whites in the same age group.)[57] Thus prevention programs are needed to control black suicides too.

On another level blacks have begun to attack the problem of discrimination in the employment of medical personnel in health-care systems and to increase their representation among higher-level professional and administrative positions in the health-care field. Blacks are also attempting to prevent further occurrences of the exploitation of subjects in medical research such as the case of the U.S. Public Health Services Study of syphilitics in Tuskegee, Alabama, and in alleged illegal sterilization of mentally retarded black girls in Montgomery, Alabama.[58] However, improvements in health care of the black population will require a steady infusion of funds for health maintenance, for research to combat debilitating diseases, a stepped-up pace of training health professionals and practitioners, a better distribution of services throughout the nation and within cities, and effective programs that result in wider use of available health-care services by the black population closer to their places of residence.

NOTES

1. Edwin Sutherland and Donald Cressey, *Criminology* (Santa Barbara, Calif.: University of California Press, 1970), p. 139.

2. Marvin Wolfgang, *Crime and Race* (New York: Institute of Human Relations Press, 1970), p. 70.

3. The discussion that follows relies heavily upon data presented in L. Patrick Gray, *Crime in the United States: Uniform Crime Reports, 1971* (Washington, D.C.: U.S. Government Printing Office, 1972).

4. David Burnham, "Black Murder Victims in the City Outnumber White Victims 8 to 1," *The New York Times*, August 5, 1973, p. 1. This study was based upon a computer analysis of police records for 1971.

5. *Ibid.*

6. Cf. Alvin Pouissant, M.D., *Why Blacks Kill Blacks* (New York: Emerson Hall Publishers, 1972); Kenneth Clark, *Dark Ghetto* (New York: Harper, 1965), Chap. 5; and Gresham M. Sykes, *Crime and Society* (New York: Random House, 1956).

7. Wolfgang, *op. cit.*, pp. 43–45.

8. Joseph C. Howard, Sr., "The Administration of Rape Cases in the City of Baltimore and the State of Maryland," a paper prepared for the Monumental Bar Association, Baltimore, August 1967.

9. *Ibid.*, pp. 6–9.

10. *Ibid.*, p. 7.

11. *Ibid.*, p. 16.

12. Sol Rubin, "Imposition of the Death Sentence for Rape," in Marvin Wolfgang and Leon Radzinowicz (eds.), *The Criminal in the Arms of the Law* (New York: Basic Books, 1971).

13. "Crime and Black Business," *Black Enterprise*, 3 (April 1973), pp. 17–22.

14. *Ibid.*

15. *Ibid.*, p. 19.

16. James M. Markham, "Heroin Hunger May Not a Mugger Make," *New York Times Magazine*, March 18, 1973, p. 39.

17. Albert Cohen, *Delinquent Boys: The Culture of the Gang* (Glencoe, Ill.: Free Press, 1955).

18. "Crime and Black Business," *op. cit.*, pp. 41–44.

19. The topics discussed in this section are amplified in references such as: William A. Bonger, *Race and Crime* (New York: Columbia University Press, 1973); Wolfgang, *op. cit.*; Wolfgang and Radzinowicz, *op. cit.*; and *The U.S. Civil Rights Commission Reports, 1961* (Washington, D.C.: Government Printing Office, 1962).

20. Cf. Gordon Waldo and Simon Dinitz, "Personality Attributes of the Criminal: An Analysis of Research Studies, 1950–1965," *Journal of Research in Crime and Delinquency*, 4 (1967), pp. 185–202.

21. Irvin G. Sarason, "Verbal Learning, Modeling and Juvenile Delinquency," *American Psychologist*, 23 (1968), pp. 254–266.

22. Cf. Sutherland and Cressey, *op. cit.*, p. 142.

23. For a discussion of differential opportunity theory and goals-means theory cf. Richard Cloward and Lloyd Ohlin, *Delinquency and Opportunity* (Glencoe, Ill.: The Free Press, 1960), and Robert K. Merton, *Social Theory and Social Structure* (Glencoe, Ill.: The Free Press, 1957).

24. For an elaboration of the major themes previously presented see Clarence Schrag, *Crime and Justice: American Style* (Rockville, Md.: National Institute of Mental Health, 1971).

25. Ann Knopf, *Youth Patrol: An Experiment in Community Participation* (Waltham, Mass.: Brandeis, 1969).

26. Benjamin Pasamanick, "A Survey of Mental Illness in an Urban Population," *The American Journal of Psychiatry*, 119 (1962), pp. 299–305.

27. R. E. Clark, "The Relationship of Schizophrenia in Occupational Income and Occupational Prestige," *American Sociological Review*, 13 (1948), pp. 325–330.

28. August B. Hollingshead and F. C. Redlich, *Social Class and Mental Illness: A Community Study* (New York: John Wiley and Sons, 1958).

29. Leo Srole et al., *Mental Health in the Metropolis: The Midtown Manhattan Study* (New York: McGraw-Hill, 1962).

30. H. W. Dunham, *Community and Schizophrenia: An Experimental Analysis* (Detroit: Wayne State University Press, 1965).

31. W. A. Rushing, "Two Patterns in the Relationship Between Social Class and Mental Hospitalization," *American Sociological Review*, 34 (1969), pp. 533–541.

32. Pasamanick, *op. cit.*

33. Benjamin Malzberg, *Statistical Data for the Study of Mental Diseases Among Negroes in New York State* (Albany, N.Y.: Research Foundation for Mental Hygiene, 1964).

34. Cf. Melvin Kohn, "Social Class and Schizophrenia: A Critical Review and a Reformulation," *Schizophrenia Bulletin* (Winter 1969), pp. 60–79, and John A. Clausen and Melvin L. Kohn, "The Ecological Approach to Social Psychiatry," *American Sociological Review*, 60 (1954), pp. 140–151.

35. Harrison M. Trice, *Alcoholism in America* (New York: McGraw-Hill, 1966), p. 22.

36. Don Callahan, *Problem Drinkers* (San Francisco: Jossey-Bass, 1970), p. 139.

37. Julian Roebuch and R. G. Kessler, *The Etiology of Alcoholism: Constitutional, Psychological and Sociological Approaches* (Springfield, Ill.: Charles C Thomas, 1972).

38. *Ibid.*, p. 203.

39. Don Callahan, Ira H. Casin, and Helen M. Crossley, *American Drinking Practices* (New Brunswick, N.J.: Rutgers Center of Alcohol Studies, 1969), pp. 48, 142.

40. Margaret Bailey, Paul Halberman, and Harold Alksne, "The Epidemiology of Alcoholism in an Urban Residential Area," *Quarterly Journal of Studies on Alcohol*, 26 (1965), pp. 19–40.

41. Cf. Howard Bahr and Gerald Garrett, *Disaffiliation Among Urban Women* (New York: Bureau of Applied Research, 1971), and Gerald R. Garrett and Howard Bahr, "Women on Skid Row," *Journal of Studies on Alcohol* (forthcoming).

42. Roebuch and Kessler, *op. cit.*

43. Alfred Lindesmith, *The Addict and the Law* (New York: Random House, 1965), pp. 99–134.

44. Note that there are problems with such statistics, for they are based largely upon reports of individuals who come to the attention of the law, persons who are hospitalized in public institutions, and projections based upon such data. They do not take into consideration the relatively higher proportion of whites who receive treatment in private institutions or from private physicians. Thus it is possible that these statistics are highly distorted.

45. Norman E. Zinberg and J. A. Robertson, *Drugs and the Public* (New York: Simon and Schuster, 1972), p. 14.

46. Cf. *Task Force Report: Narcotics and Drug Abuse*, the President's Commission on Law Enforcement and Administration of Justice (Washington, D.C.: Government Printing Office, 1967), pp. 3, 48–49; I. Chein et al., *The Road to H.* (New York: Basic Books, 1964); I. Chein and E. Rosenfeld, "Juvenile Narcotic Use," *Law and Contemporary Problems*, 22 (1957), pp. 52–68; and Harold Finestone, "Kats, Licks and Color," in M. Stein et al., *Identity and Anxiety* (Glencoe, Ill.: The Free Press, 1960).

47. Clark, *op. cit.*, p. 90.

48. *Task Force Report: Narcotics and Drug Abuse, op. cit.*, p. 50.

49. "Crime and Black Business," *op. cit.*, p. 22.

50. *The Social and Economic Status of the Black Population in the United States, 1972*, U.S. Department of Commerce Series, p. 23, No. 46 (Washington, D.C.: U.S. Government Printing Office, July 1973), p. 90.

51. John Fried, "The Blood Pressure on 22 Million Americans," *New York Times Magazine*, February 25, 1973, pp. 14.

52. Robert Hill, "Health Conditions of Black Americans," *Urban League News*, 3:5 (May 1973), p. 5.

53. *Ibid.*

54. Cf. Edward Suchman, "Socio-medical Variations Among Ethnic Groups," *American Journal of Sociology*, 70 (November 1964), pp. 319–331, and Edward Suchman, "Social Factors in Medical Deprivation," *American Journal of Public Health*, 55 (November 1965), pp. 1725–1733.

55. Herman James, "Health Orientations, Health Opportunities and the Use of Medical Services: Toward a Clarification of the Relationships," an unpublished manuscript based upon a study of black and white subjects in Pittsburgh, 1967–1970.

56. "Sickle Cell Anemia: Blood Disease Gets Dollar Transfusion," *Black Enterprise*, 2 (June 1972), pp. 23.

57. Herbert Hendin, *Black Suicide* (New York: Basic Books, 1969), p. 4.

58. The Tuskegee syphilis study was brought to national attention in 1972 when it was discovered that 431 black men had been denied treatment for syphilis over a 40-year period between 1932 and 1972. The purpose of the study was to determine the long-range effects of syphilis on the human body. However, as a result of this study, at least 28 of the participants died, but the number of possible deaths resulting from participation and lack of treatment could approximate 100 if further investigations were undertaken. Further, a charge of illegal sterilization was brought against an OEO-funded family-planning clinic in Montgomery, Alabama, in 1973. The allegation was that two teenage black girls, one of whom was mentally retarded, were sterilized without the consent of their illiterate parents. This case focused on what was believed to be a much wider practice of sterilizing mentally retarded girls and the forced use of sterilization by women on welfare as a requirement for continued support through public assistance.

10 | THE BLACK COMMUNITY IN A WHITE SOCIETY

I n various ways throughout this book, we have attempted to address the nine essential questions posed in the foreword. We defined the black community, showed how it was formed and held together, and demonstrated the immense diversity within a community united by both the external threats and impositions of white racism and its inner resources. Each preceding chapter demonstrated the inapplicability of singular theoretical models to the analysis of the black community. But it was clear that in some instances one theory more so than another—whether social systems theory, internal colonialism theory, or parallel institutions theory—may have been more useful. Other theoretical referents were employed in the analysis of deviance in the black community.

In addition to reviewing some of the basic ideas posed in previous chapters, we shall now focus primarily on the process of radicalization of the black community in America.

It was argued that the black community in America is a product of white oppression, racism, and patterned repression. Black people have been systematically excluded from equal participation in the life and culture of American society as an assimilated minority because of the imposition and subsequent institutionalization of sociolegalistic policies never before directed against other minority groups. These policies involved, at varying stages of time, chattel slavery, manumission with gradual or orthodox assimilation, segregation, integration, and benign neglect. The alternatives open to black Americans at once were reduced to a form of accommodation that necessitated the formation of separate, parallel institutional arrangements as functional requirements for meeting their basic and fundamental needs.

A boundary-maintenance system was established between blacks and whites in the United States, not by black people, but it was imposed upon them by whites in control of the American power structure. This system was predicated on one factor alone—RACE. A close scrutiny of black-white relations in the United States reveals the high salience of the race factor It is the factor of race that historically divided the American republic. It is race that gave rise to and nurtured theories of group supremacy and group inferiority. It is race, with its derivative of "color purity," that forged distinctions within a nascent black community through the imprimatur of an aristocracy of color among black people. It was this latter distinction that originated the first antagonistic class lines among black people that so disunified blacks that the formation of a true community built upon group solidarity was delayed. It was race that permitted white Americans and social science theoreticians either deliberately or subconsciously to come to regard black people as a monolithic undifferentiated mass (and for others to change their positions with the acquisition of more scientific knowledge). Hence race and racism provided the impetus for the development and enforcement of a segregated social structure sustained by legalized discriminatory social policies without due regard for intragroup distinctions.

Two kinds of forces have always been at work in the black community: (1) centripetal forces—elements that draw members of a minority group toward their own group, and (2) centrifugal forces—those elements that magnetize minority group members in the direction of the dominant group's cultural values, societal norms, and institutional arrangements. Centripetal forces facilitated black community formation; embodied the commonality of experiences of black people with white racism and racial oppression; included a desire to escape the debilitating psychological consequences of day-to-day contact with repressive conditions, as well as a need to belong to an accepting and status-rewarding group, and a wish to participate in the process of institution building and cultural revitalization. These forces were abetted by proscriptive norms such as sanctions by the white community against exogamous marriages, which, of course, almost always minimized social interaction.

Hence, black Americans were posed with the dilemma articulated by Du Bois three-quarters of a century ago—the dilemma of "twoness." Blacks, according to Du Bois, are *within* America but not *of* America; they have the soul of an American by virtue of limited acculturation that containment on American soil has necessitated and encouraged. Yet cognitively, their blackness is inescapable. They recognize what blackness portends in a society in which privilege is a function of color differentiation. For many then, there is an obvious contradiction implicit in the utilization of race as the basis for categorical treatment, patterned segregation and discrimination, and condemnation to exile from the opportunity structure when theoretically the United States is touted as an open society. Because of this contradiction, Du Bois' view that the problems of the color line would be the most significant domestic issue facing the American populace in the twentieth century has been vindicated by the events of the century's first 75 years.

Early on, beginning with the differentiation between house and field slaves and continuing through emancipation/Reconstruction, blacks embarked upon a course that tacitly recognized this duality. On the one hand, blacks responded to the policies of exclusion by constructing institutional arrangements that *included* blacks. Out of these arrangements emerged a viable black community—segregated, isolated, and contained as a unique colony within the larger white society. This community is primarily comprised of (1) the family, a social structure predicated upon a system of social stratification and intragroup inequality, (2) economic organizations and occupational pursuits, (3) educational institutions, (4) organized religion, and (5) political behavior. It has also developed systems for maintenance through housing, health care, recreation, and participation in those suprasocietal institutions oriented toward mutual protection and the control of deviance. The institutional arrangements of the black community are designed to serve both expressive and instrumental functions related to the fulfillment of human needs of black people as a people. However, we should stress again that there is no single black community and that communities over time have come to be differentiated in terms of social class variables, color, size (for example, small rural, large urban, and intermediate types), as well as a sense of identity and ideological perspectives.

Black Americans, however, have never been totally satisfied with policies and practices of exclusion, since throughout their history in America the majority of them have embraced the belief that they are indeed Americans entitled to all the advantages and responsibilities entailed in American citizenship. Since the First Reconstruction the overwhelming majority have acceded to the orthodox view that they, like white ethnic immigrants, are to become assimilated into whatever is defined as mainstream America. This meant to the rank-and-file black person access to what sociologists call shared values and scarce resources. More specifically, it meant structural and civic assimilation into a society relatively free from the restraints of prejudice and discrimination plus the right to make the free choice to engage in courtship, cohabitation, and marriage across racial and ethnic lines as desired. In the long and protracted history of this struggle to become an American, integration was substituted for assimilation primarily because the goal was to *become a part of the society* rather than to *become engulfed by the society.*

The black American's systematic struggle against virtually implacable racism has highlighted the goal of integration of black people as part of the larger American society. This struggle spawned protest movements and protest organizations, which were, at the initial stages of their formation, united in that common purpose. Resistance to integration and desegregation also resulted in violence and social strains. At the outset the NAACP, CORE, the National Urban League, the Southern Christian Leadership Conference, and the Student Non-Violent Coordinating Committee were committed to the goal of an integrated society. As we shall see once more, it was the failure of this objective or its perceived unattainability that inevitably led to a politicization and radicalization of the protest movement among black people in the United States.

The evidence that an integrated American society has not been achieved is irrefutable. This fact was demonstrated in a variety of ways: (1) Barriers to employment opportunities, which lead as expected to income inequity, have not disappeared. Proof of this assertion is found in the excessive rates of unemployment, subemployment, and underemployment among black adults, teenagers, male and female. It is also found in the disproportionate number of blacks still mired below the low-income levels despite the important income gains made by some blacks during the 1960s. (2) Although significant improvements have been made in the educational structure of the South, now, two decades after the 1954 Supreme Court desegregation decision, white flight to the suburbs and Northern resistance to school desegregation have created a dual school system almost as severe as any that operated in the South prior to 1954, and resegregation has occurred in many desegregated systems. (3) Despite the enactment of remedial housing legislation, housing in the urban ghetto is abysmally bad, and the increase of blacks in suburbia is miniscule. Urban renewal has been a disaster frequently accentuating urban blight through abandonment and unalterable decay. This physical environment also has an affective impact on the human condition and human spirit, for no person can live in such a social and physical milieu every day without experiencing some form of alienation and discontent. (4) Black capitalism, which had an auspicious beginning, has not been as productive as its architects anticipated. It has not generated the predicted economic viability in spite of hundreds of new venture start-ups, many of which have failed due to undercapitalization, lack of community support, crime, and governmental impatience. Black capitalism generated a number of successful ventures, but their direct dividends for the masses of black community residents are open to serious question. Finally, whether we speak of problems and successes (and there are many) in all of these areas or in the military and the political arena, one fact is indisputable—a major portion of the black population did not achieve measurable benefits from the civil rights movement of the 1960s.

THE RADICALIZATION OF BLACK AMERICA

It is precisely because of the persistence of the types of problems just reviewed and the failure of the black masses to feel included that an increasing number of black Americans of all social classes now look askance at integration. For those persons who see an interchange of integration with assimilation the orthodox view of the inevitability of assimilation is now seriously challenged. The new goal substituted for integration/ assimilation is LIBERATION. In this view integration is nothing more than a strategy that may be called upon to achieve a liberated status *within* the United States.

Liberation means the complete freedom of black Americans and entails an "equal distribution of decision-making power."[1] The liberated black is more concerned about freedom as an individual and of blacks as a group of people than he is about physical proximity to white people. He is especially concerned about his capacity to obliterate white oppression as well as his ability to challenge cherished American values that are inconsistent with the black experience in white America. He is committed to the unity of blacks as a people living in a nation that is as much his as it is that of any other group of people inhabiting it. But implicit in the liberated person's demands for the right of self-determination is the willingness to take his stand for that cause on American soil.

The liberationists have come to adopt this position because they feel that the integrationist philosophy or strategy has not achieved its ultimate goal of an open society in which people compete as equals and are in fact judged on the basis of merit. They have come to this position because they can observe that even more than a century after emancipation black Americans remain a *subordinate* group ranking near the bottom of the social scale. Even the black stratification system is a subordinate, essentially proletarian system. Here we are speaking of the position of a group rather than individual achievements. The exceptions to the rule are merely that and nothing more! The goal is to achieve a just and free society in which people have an equal chance to obtain equal results—in which people can indeed achieve to the best of their abilities. But the exclusionary practices of the past remain with us. The promises of a Great Society have not been fulfilled for the masses of black people. The failures in employment, income maintenance, housing, and opportunities to provide for the instrumental needs of the family, combined with limited opportunities in the business world, inadequacies in the political system, the administration of justice, and provisions for decent health care—all have forced black Americans to take another look at integration. We cannot conclude however that integration is no longer an appropriate strategy. Nor can it be claimed with any degree of certitude that the majority of black Americans are disenchanted with integration. The evidence suggests that from three-quarters to nine-tenths of all blacks remain committed to integration. But this is not the entire picture.

The civil rights movement achieved its greatest success in breaking down the barriers of institutionalized segregation in the Deep South, particularly in the areas of public accommodations, personal services, school desegregation, and in broadening the scale of job opportunities. It failed, however, to recognize the impact of limited gains on the rising expectations of the masses of blacks. It failed to anticipate either the gravity or the magnitude of the frustrations that followed the awareness of Northern urban ghetto blacks that somehow they had been left behind in the process of the second emancipation of Southern blacks. They were still the victims of social injustice in every aspect of life—mired in poverty and crime-infested ghettos. The movement had little meaning for them. Rising rates of unemployment, perpetually low incomes, the inability to hold jobs, and the lack of resources to escape an ever-widening ghetto with all of its problems exacerbated the fundamental problem of second-class citizenship and magnified the tensions and anxieties that characterized blacks' daily existence. The few black congressmen in Washington prior to 1965, such as Adam Clayton Powell and William Dawson, were more symbolic to the rank-and-file Northern black than directly beneficial. Governmental patronage is unknown to the masses of blacks—few jobs ever came their way because of the election of a black congressman. The net effect of this pattern of denial predictably exploded in the previously described urban unrest, violent deaths of the 1960s, and systematic repression of the 1970s. With that explosion came a new turn of events in black protest: Black Power was the clarion cry.

The fears provoked by the emergence of black power as a slogan and as a philosophy must be placed in the context of the institutionalized fear that has historically characterized the lives of countless of thousands of black people both prior and subsequent to the civil rights movement of the 1960s. Those fears stemmed unalterably from the abuses of white power, which were manifested, for example, in physical assaults, lynchings, maiming, raping of black women, and castrating black men. These are the conditions that spawned such radical groups as the Deacons of Defense, De Mau Maus, Afro-Sets, and black paramilitary groups in general. While whites were predictably puzzled by black power, black Americans used the slogan as a basis for nationalistic revitalization.

Black Nationalism. This phenomenon is a direct outgrowth of the interminable struggle of black Americans for inclusion in the American mainstream. It is the consequence of the failure to deal effectively with urgent problems in the black community. It represents failures of structural assimilation and the perceived unattainability of an integrated society. As an ideology, its major theme is the right to cultural, economic, social, and political self-determination and the control of black destinies by black people. The three major forms of black nationalism are: (1) separatism, (2) cultural nationalism, and (3) revolutionary nationalism. Like integration, each may be viewed as a strategy for the achievement of the ultimate goal of the liberation of American blacks.

Advocates of a *separatist philosophy* assert that it is not synonymous with segregation as is claimed by integrationists. The distinction between the two concepts is that segregation is an imposed condition, whereas people choose to be separated in order to be included within a group rather than to be excluded from another. The most fundamental aspect of separatist ideology is the right of self-determination, which embraces the freedom of black people to exercise control over their own destinies and welfare. Historically, separatist nationalism can be traced to the founding of the American Colonialization Society in 1816. This was an incipient back-to-Africa movement that managed to survive for almost half a century. The success of the movement can be gleaned from its relatively large expenditures of $205 million to accomplish the return of 12,000 blacks to Africa. A sizable proportion of those who returned to Africa were slaves whose manumission was contingent upon their departure from the United States.[2] In this century the most successful effort toward the formulation of a separatist ideology was led by Marcus Garvey in his "Back to Africa" movement. Between 1914 and until the virtual collapse of Garveyism in 1923 he launched the most successful black nationalist movement ever organized in the United States. Whereas the Harlem Renaissance* had a wide appeal among the black intelligentsia, mainly in the black middle class, as an aggressive response to the conditions of blacks during and immediately following World War I, Garvey made his strongest appeal to the black lower class. He convinced black people that black is beautiful a half century before Malcolm X, Stokely Carmichael, H.

---

* The Harlem Renaissance, occurring during the 1920s, was a period of unparalleled achievements by blacks in music, literature, and the arts. It was a kind of revival of learning among blacks in which cultural and intellectual attainments were viewed as the special mission of American blacks.

Rap Brown, or James Brown came into national prominence. Garvey instilled self-acceptance through an elaborate system of titles, honors, and social rewards. He glorified everything black that created a sense of self-worth among a lower-class black population that was so victimized by the brutalities of racial hatred, segregation, and discrimination. An inspirational and spellbinding orator, his speeches enthralled the audience so convincingly that many believed that the realization of their dreams of freedom and liberation was imminent. He was, indeed, their black Moses! Anywhere from 3 to 6 million blacks followed him until he was convicted for mail fraud and later deported. The collapse of Garveyism, forced by the federal government, which feared the mass organization of black people as a clear and present danger, deepened the sense of pessimism and disillusionment among the nation's impoverished blacks. It undoubtedly affected middle-class black Americans, too, even though they had been in the forefront of the opposition to Garveyism, denouncing him as a demagogue. The protest literature of the period, primarily that produced during the Harlem Renaissance is, in fact, a vindication of Garvey's observations of the inhumane conditions inflicted upon black people in white America. The radicalization process, however, was undoubtedly kept alive by protest literature such as in the writings of Claude McKay, Sterling Brown, Langston Hughes, Richard Wright, and, three decades later, in the eloquence of James Baldwin's *The Fire Next Time* and *Nobody Knows My Name*. Although these writers did not espouse a separatist social thought, they were instrumental in focusing attention on the pernicious forms of social injustice and racism that prevailed throughout the United States.

Garveyism was an expression of *physical separation*, which stressed the goal of the establishment of a territorial base, a kind of national homeland, within which the right of self-determination could be assured. Physical separation may take one of at least three different forms. First, it may involve a "Back to Africa" movement as more recently advocated by Stokely Carmichael. But this is not likely to happen, since a significant majority of black Americans have cast their lot in America and are not inclined to engage in a mass immigration to Africa as the motherland. Furthermore, the major key to internal unity within African states is tribal identity, not national identity. Without the ability to establish prerogatives of tribal affiliation and with the improbability that American blacks will be received as a "long-lost tribe," notions of a mass return of American blacks to Africa are illusory.

Second, physical separation may also connote the creation of a separate black nation out of five or six Deep South states in the continental United States. This position is advocated by the Republic of New Africa and by the Nation of Islam—the Black Muslims. Within this proposed homeland, created by partitioning the United States, blacks would be free to rebuild their own institutions, develop a separate culture, and simultaneously emancipate themselves from their mental enslavement to white America. Their desire to establish a homeland through partitioning the United States is an admission of the futility of mounting an effort to persuade American blacks to engage in a new "Back to Africa" movement, which, of course, places this group in conflict with those who espouse the return of blacks to the African motherland. It may also be construed as acquiescence to white racism—a signal that blacks have tired of the struggle to claim their social, economic, and political entitlements as American citizens.

The Black Muslims, in more recent times, were the first black nationalist group to advocate the creation of a separate black nation through partitioning the United States. (However, the Communist party has intermittently suggested this goal since about 1920.) Undoubtedly, the Southern states were selected because of their higher proportion of blacks from other areas who would return to the South as the new black nation. In the late 1950s and during the early 1960s national attention was called to the Muslim philosophy primarily through the fiery, exciting, and captivating oratory of Malcolm X. To the black proletariat working class and to the thousands of black prisoners throughout the nation's jails and prisons who were already in despair of American justice, the Muslims carried their message of black pride, positive self-images, and the necessity to free oneself from mental enslavement by white devils. They offered an opportunity for blacks to rediscover themselves as a people through understanding the greatness of their African heritage. Their religion was enshrouded with a mysticism overlaid by a philosophical justification for relegating white society to the status of the devil. In their view, as articulated by Malcolm X in the early 1960s, the white man should be avoided and hated for evils visited upon Afro-Asian people, and it was incumbent upon black people to be prepared to fight white people if necessary in self-defense.

This philosophy provoked widespread fear among white Americans, which was translated into systematic harassment by local, national and federal officials of Black Muslims and their followers. However, the movement continued to grow and is now estimated to have more than 100,000 members who worship at approximately 40 mosques and Black Muslim temples throughout the United States. The Lost-Found Nation of Islam in the Wilderness of North America, which is the formal name of the Black Muslims in the United States, reaches more than 600,000 individuals through its publication, *Muhammed Speaks*, and hundreds of thousands more through its impressive array of business enterprises. Thus they have managed to blend a mystical religion with black capitalism, ideas for self-help, and black pride into an attractive black nationalist philosophy—at least for poor blacks, reformed prisoners, and those petite bourgeoisie who are frustrated with the exclusionary practices of white America.

The third aspect of physical separatism is that encompassed by the concept of community control. This may take the form of black control of entire cities or counties through capturing the majority of powerful elective positions (for instance, as mayors, councilmen, commissioners, and county sheriffs) and appointed positions (such as police chiefs) via the established political process, or it may mean the establishment of autonomous black communities within the geographical boundaries of a city controlled by a white power structure. In the latter type, advocated by CORE, the emphasis is on the ability of blacks to control the decision-making aspects of institutional life within the black community. Thus, as was pointed out in Chapter 4, community-control advocates would support separate all-black schools under the aegis of all-black administrators and staff. In essence, in this regard they would demand that an equitable share of city revenue be granted to black community leaders for the internal management of black institutional affairs. Simultaneously, they would seek to establish a separate black economic system and a political structure within the black community directly responsive to its crucial needs. Opponents of this position maintain that instead of liberating blacks from white society, community control would invariably force the dependency of blacks on the largesse of the white power structure. Instead of decolonizing blacks, community control would create even more highly visible black colonies within the boundaries of the larger political structure. Thus the goal of black self-determination and liberation would not be indistinct from that which exists after working hours every day in contemporary American society. There is, of course, nothing inherently objectionable about either community control or other efforts of blacks to force Americans to redistribute power and resources more equitably. It is also true that separatists provide a compelling argument that recognizes how separate all Americans now are and always have been in this country. Whereas community control might accomplish quasi-autonomy, there is no guarantee that those blacks in control of the economic system, for example, would be any less exploitative of other blacks than those whites in control of the present system. In this view black capitalism under community control is synonymous to capitalism in the larger society. Only the color is different!

A second major theme in nationalism is that of *cultural nationalism*. This term is often used interchangeably with cultural pluralism. Proponents of this position assert the need to revive the black cultural heritage. They envision a cultural liberation of black Americans by first persuading blacks to accept their own identity as black persons as well as through the establishment of cultural linkages with Africa, the mother continent. The ideology of cultural nationalists is in a sense a vindication of the Herskovits thesis of African survivals in the United States and in part a repudiation of the Frazier argument that blacks are uniquely Americans without significant traces of Africanism. Cultural nationalists celebrate the distinctiveness of black people as it is manifested, for instance, in soul music, a black value system, black literature, black theater, Afro-America studies, and various patterns of life in black America that identify and distinguish black people from others.

They seek neither integration nor physical separation; rather, they seek to practice black cultural forms while coexisting with other groups of people in the United States. However, their emphasis on the need to build a black culture is in a sense an admission that notable defects in the cultural organization of black American life stem largely from the disparate forces of isolation of one class from another, the diversity of the experiences of black people in America regarding confrontations with segregation, and rebuffs to attempted integration. It is similarly an acknowledgment of the presence of the essential elements of a culture that have not been structured or unified into an integral system.

Many individuals attempt to communicate their identity as cultural nationalists by giving high visibility to their blackness through such external symbols as Afro hair styles, corn-rolls, the wearing of dashikis and other African-style attire, and various forms of greetings and salutations. Others who also advocate cultural nationalism claim that external symbols possess primarily a psychological importance. For this group there is no necessary connection or correlation between identification through attachments to external symbols and the actualization of commitment to black unity, black identity, and black awareness or the ability to be of value to black people. In other words, the person with the biggest Afro hair style and the most dashing dashiki may in fact be devoid of a genuine commitment to black nationalism. These symbols may be useful only for whatever hustle the individual is involved in at that moment in time.

Notwithstanding, cultural nationalism is a movement toward black solidarity not too dissimilar from other forms of cultural revitalization. It is imperative as a process of reclaiming a past too long condemned and denied. This stress on cultural revival among black people finds expression in the philosophical articulations of such writers as Harold Cruse and among the leading advocates of the more than 1,200 college black studies programs and Afro-American cultural centers throughout the United States. The struggle to establish the legitimacy of black studies calls attention to the monumental problems facing cultural nationalists in the 1970s.

Finally, *revolutionary nationalism* is the third major theme of black nationalism. Proponents of this form of nationalism are equally committed to the goal of black liberation, but their strategy is a radical departure from those strategies advanced by either integrationists, separatists, or cultural nationalists. Revolutionary nationalists are convinced that the only effective strategy for black liberation is the complete overthrow of the present American political and social system and its subsequent replacement by what they perceive as a new and more just political and social form. On a most pragmatic level, revolutionary nationalists accept the fact that this process of overthrow and replacement will necessarily involve a protracted and bitter struggle, since its success depends upon the ability to destroy totally the social organization of the current social system. By the same token, a true revolution has as its necessary preconditions the ability of its potential organizers to dramatize the dysfunctions of the current systems; to demonstrate the abuses of power and authority by those who have political and economic power within the social system; to attack systematically that power structure in such a manner as to communicate to others that power is eroding and authority is disintegrating and that the best interests of the masses can be served by the overthrow of the incumbents. These conditions must, in turn, generate a mass following—a significant group of adherents who are willing to escalate the incipient struggle into violent activity to accomplish the downfall of those in power.

Assuming, then, that these factors are necessary preconditions to a true revolution, it should be apparent that the episodic urban conflagrations of the 1960s were not revolutionary. They were revolts, riots, or perhaps insurrections. But depending upon the degree of social organization developed by the leaders and the resources mobilized by such groups over time, the riots and revolts may be classified as precursors to an incipient revolution. The early history of the Black Panthers in the United States suggests that they should be called revolutionary nationalists. Yet the present schism within the Black Panther organization seems to be deepening to such an extent that the early Marxist-Leninist perspectives of its spokesmen have been modified by the Huey P. Newton-Bobby Seale faction in contrast to the more militant faction led by exiled Eldridge Cleaver. The entry of Seale in the 1973 mayoralty campaign of Berkeley, California, marked a radical departure from the Seale revolutionary posture communicated during the trial of the Chicago Seven, when he was gagged to prevent violent outbursts in the courtroom. Other revolutionary nationalists are localized groups that modeled themselves after the Panthers in stressing self-defense. Numerous organizations of this type are scattered across the country; one, the Black Liberation Army, symbolically views the police as the enemy—the brutal enforcers of social and political injustice who seem to be committed to black annihilation. Other self-defense organizations effect a militantly nationalist posture with their affinity for inflammatory rhetoric and highly sophisticated weaponry. In fact, many could be correctly called paramilitary organizations.

To what extent is the liberation of black people through revolution possible in the United States? This approach seems doomed to failure for a number of reasons. First, its theoreticians have tied themselves ideologically to the cause of all Third World peoples both in continental United States and in other parts of the world. Although there is great merit in this association, given the collective experiences of blacks in the Western white world, it is absolutely foolhardy to assume that other Third World nations will, at least in the forseeable future, intercede directly in the internal affairs of the United States in behalf of the black cause. The history of the relationships between the United States and other nations does not suggest this possibility as an acceptable alternative despite the evidence that the United States has been repeatedly guilty of doing precisely that—interfering in the internal affairs of another nation. But this is a question of the use of not only power but force at the expense of expendable and relatively powerless groups. Moreover, many Third World groups will in all probability find it more expedient in promoting self-interest to pay only lip service or give a sympathetic ear or offer political asylum to blacks in their struggle rather than mount a direct intervention strategy.

Second, the success of a revolution depends upon effective mobilization of major resources such as military power, modern war instruments, mechanized warfare, and financial support. Even though the estimated monetary value of the black economy in the United States is about $51 billion, it is naïve to conclude that blacks are unified or in agreement on revolution as the most efficacious strategy for black liberation. Probably no more than 5 percent of the black population—and the majority of these are among the economically downtrodden who invariably are attracted to revolutionary causes but are devoid of the economic capability to support a revolution of major proportions—have become dedicated revolutionaries. Thus in open warfare the military might of the United States would be too powerful against revolutionary blacks.

Third, the repressive forces of the federal government and its ability to destroy militant groups through infiltration and the use of agents provocateurs have already been demonstrated in a number of ways. Leaders are usually jailed on "trumped-up charges" and removed from direct action for substantial periods of time. Unanticipated police raids have resulted in the deaths of leaders, while others have died of mysterious causes. Infiltrators, obviously paid informers, all too frequently have revealed plans, strategies, and programs of militant groups before they could be effectively implemented. To be successful revolutionaries must be able to provide satisfactory solutions to such problems.*

---

* They may also need either the support or neutrality of white working classes, which are now the source of much antiblack sentiment.

What then is left for black revolutionaries to do? Two alternatives are open to them. They can either accept the inevitability of their failure or engage in protracted guerrilla warfare, which, if successful, can unnerve a community, a city, or a nation that believes itself to exist in a state of seige by a powerful enemy of revolutionary guerrillas. They may engage in political kidnapping, ambushing, and sniper attacks designed to frustrate and effect retaliatory harassment against the authority system. But this type of activity is not likely to gain support from the masses of people unless it proves effective in goal attainment. It is likely to alienate sympathizers to their cause among the black elite, the petite bourgeoisie, and the lumpen proletariat which envision the possibility of massive retaliation by the reactionary forces of the larger society, forces that feel threatened by this activity.

The rhetoric of unity has been replaced with unity without uniformity —a clear recognition of the extreme diversity prevalent in the black community of America—and with the right of black people to choose from a number of alternatives, be they adherence to integration, absorption through assimilation, or black nationalism with its components of separatism, cultural nationalism, and revolutionary nationalism. As things now stand, blacks seem to be more committed to both integration (that is, becoming a part of the American society as distinguished from assimilation, or being absorbed by the American society) and cultural nationalism than they are to other available alternatives. And they see themselves as black Americans!

Whatever the choice, blacks are increasingly united around the commonality of their experiences in America, particularly those experiences resulting from systematic exclusion, patterned denials, and deprivations structured on institutionalized racism and ubiquitous discrimination. These conditions have led blacks to organize for the attainment of group rights, individual choices, and the legitimation of their claim for institutional and psychological liberation.

We conclude as we began with the assertion that no single sociological theory or explanatory model is a sufficient tool for understanding the dynamic character of the black community and its relationship to the larger American society. Instead, we found considerable utility in drawing upon a variety of theoretical frameworks for explanatory purposes. Thus on either a microsociological or macrosociological level, a kind of synergism prevailed in our employment of theoretical constructs. Functionalism or systems theory and conflict theory tell us a great deal about the internal structure of the black community as well as its external relationship to the larger society, whether or not the black community is perceived as a subsystem with parallel institutions or as an internal colony. Furthermore, on a microsociological level, we used a variety of established theories and classification schemes, such as anomie, relative deprivation, differential association, and social learning, as instruments for understanding *behavior* as it relates to the social structure or macrosociological conditions.

Finally, it is the interaction among race, color, and class that has the most profound impact upon the internal structure of the black community, its social organization, its relationship to the larger society, and, ultimately, social interaction among individual members of both black and white communities. Race, color, and class establish and maintain relatively inpregnable boundaries between the two social systems. Historically, color was employed as a fundamental principle of internal stratification and social differentiation. However, in more recent times, color has been supplanted by economic and social class as the primary basis for intragroup differentiation. The resurgence of black nationalism with its diverse ideological positions reflects social class differentiation and social class position in many ways. *Hence it is once more evident that the black community is a highly diversified aggregate of people whose social organization and internal unity are a collective response to the external social forces unleashed by white racism, oppression, and systematic repression in the United States.*

NOTES

1. Lerone Bennet, "Liberation," *Ebony*, 25 (August 1970), p. 36.
2. Roy Wilkins, "Integration," *Ebony, op. cit.*, p. 54.

BIBLIOGRAPHY

Abrams, Charles. "The Housing Problem and the Negro." *Daedalus* (Winter 1966), 64–66.

Aldrich, Howard E. "Employment Opportunities for Blacks in the Black Ghetto: The Role of White-Owned Business." *The American Journal of Sociology*, 78 (May 1973), 1403–1425.

Alex, Nicholas. *Black in Blue: A Study of the Negro Policeman.* New York: Appleton-Century-Crofts, 1969.

Allen, Robert L. *Black Awakening in Capitalist America.* Garden City, N.Y.: Doubleday Anchor Books, 1970.

American Medical Association. *Allied Medical Education Directory,* 1972.

Amsterdam News, September 30, 1972, B-8.

Andreasen, Alan R. *Inner City Business: A Case Study of Buffalo, New York.* New York: Praeger, 1971.

Apter, David E., ed. *Ideology and Discontent.* New York: The Free Press, 1964.

Armor, David. "The Double Standard: A Reply." *The Public Interest,* 30 (Winter 1973), 119–131.

Axelrod, Morris. "Urban Structure and Social Participation." *American Sociological Review,* 21 (February 1956), 13–18.

Back, Kurt W., and Ida Harper Simpson. "The Dilemma of the Negro Professional." *Journal of Social Issues,* 20 (1964), 60–71.

Bahr, Howard, and Gerald Garrett. *Disaffiliation Among Urban Women.* New York: Bureau of Applied Research, 1971.

Baily, Margaret, Paul Halberman, and Harold Alksne. "The Epidemiology of Alcoholism in an Urban Residential Area." *Quarterly Journal of Studies on Alcohol,* 26 (1965), 19–40.

Banfield, Edward. *Big City Politics.* New York: Random House, 1965.

Banks, Rae. "New Directions in Education." *Freedomways,* 10 (Spring 1970), 8–14.

Barber, Bernard. *Social Stratification: A Comparative Analysis of Structure and Process.* New York: Harcourt, Brace, 1957.

Bardolph, Richard. *The Civil Rights Record: Black Americans and the Law, 1849–1970.* New York: Thomas Y. Crowell Co., 1970.

Baughman, E. Earl. *Black Americans.* New York: Academic Press, 1971.

———, and W. G. Dahlstrom. *Negro and White Children.* New York: Academic Press, 1968.

Bell, Carolyn. *The Economics of the Ghetto.* New York: Pegasus Co., 1970.

Bendix, Richard, and Seymour Lipset, eds. *Class, Status and Power.* Glencoe, Ill.: The Free Press, 1953.

Bennett, Lerone. *Before the Mayflower,* 4th ed. Chicago: Johnson Publishing Co., 1969.

———. "Liberation." *Ebony,* 25 (1970), 36–45.

———. "The Making of Black America: The Black Worker, Part X." *Ebony,* 27 (December 1972), 73–79, and (November 1972), 118–122.

Bernard, Jessie. *American Community Behavior.* New York: Holt, Rinehart and Winston, 1949.

———. "Marital Stability and Patterns of Status Variables." *Journal of Marriage and the Family,* 28 (November 1966), 421–439.

———. *Marriage and the Family Among Negroes.* Englewood Cliffs, N.J.: Prentice-Hall, 1966.

Bierstedt, Robert. "An Analysis of Social Power." *American Sociological Review,* 15 (December 1950), 730–738.

Billingsley, Andrew. *Black Families in White America.* Englewood Cliffs, N.J.: Prentice-Hall, 1968.

The Black Bill of Rights. Washington, D.C.: The Congressional Black Caucus, 1972, pp. 30–33.

The Black Economic Union. *Judicial Council Newsletter of the National Bar Association,* 2 (March 1973), Philadelphia: NBA.

Black Elected Officials in the United States. Voter Education Project, Atlanta, Ga.: Southern Regional Council, 1969.

Black Enterprise articles:

"Banks," *Black Enterprise* 3:11 (June 1973), 55–57.

"Black Athletes As Investors," *Black Enterprise* 4:3 (October 1973), 19–21.

"Black Business in Profile," *Black Enterprise* 4:3 (October 1973), 49–52.

"Black Consumer Market," *Black Enterprise* 4:7 (February 1974), 17–26.

Black Enterprise 4:10 (May 1974)—See the entire issue which is devoted to Dealerships and Franchises.

Black Enterprise 3:11 (June 1973)—See the entire issue which is devoted to the Nation's 100 Top Black Businesses.

"Black Farming in the Age of Agri-Business," *Black Enterprise* 4:1 (August 1973), 16–21.

"A Black GP Looks at Hypertension," *Black Enterprise* 4:12 (July 1974), 15–16.

"Black Movies," *Black Enterprise* 4:2 (September 1973), 47–53.

Clark, Christine and Leroy Clark, "The Black Lawyer," *Black Enterprise* 3:7 (February 1973), 14–18, 48.

"Crime and Black Business," *Black Enterprise* 3:9 (April 1973), 17–22.

Delaney, Paul, "Black Politics '72," *Black Enterprise* 3:7 (February 1973), 30–33.

"Economics of Health Care," *Black Enterprise* 2:11 (June 1972), 17–20.

"Farm Coops," *Black Enterprise* 4:1 (August 1973), 22–28.

Franklin, Herbert M., "Zoning Laws," *Black Enterprise* 3:1 (August 1972), 25–26, 55.

"High Blood Pressure," *Black Enterprise* 4:12 (July 1974), 9–14.

"Housing Policy at the Crossroads," *Black Enterprise* 4:7 (February 1973), 17–20.

"An Interview With Benjamin Hooks," *Black Enterprise* 3:7 (February 1973), 20–24.

Karmin, Monroe W., "Government Programs," *Black Enterprise* 3:1 (August 1972), 20–23.

"MESBICS," *Black Enterprise* 3:6 (January 1973), 18–22.

"Military Careers: A New Outlook," *Black Enterprise* 3:8 (March 1973), 57–64.

"New Towns: HUD Paves the Way," *Black Enterprise* 3:1 (August 1972), 27–32.

"OMBE," *Black Enterprise* 3:6 (January 1973), 14–18.

"Reality: Era of the Specialist," *Black Enterprise* 3:1 (August 1972), 44.

"Rural CDC's," *Black Enterprise* 4:1 (August 1973), 29–31.

Shorter, Charles, "Financing A Home," *Black Enterprise* 3:1 (August 1972), 33–36.

"Sickle Cell Anemia: Blood Disease Gets Dollar Transfusion," *Black Enterprise* 2:11 (June 1972), 23, 33.

"Supermarkets," *Black Enterprise* 2:11 (June 1972), 30–36.

"Will Black Hospitals Survive," *Black Enterprise* 2:11 (June 1972), 21.

Blackwell, James E., and Marie Haug. "Relations Between Black Bosses and Black Workers." *The Black Scholar,* 4 (January 1973), 36–43.

Blalock, Hubert M. "A Power Analysis of Racial Discrimination." *Social Forces,* 39 (1960), 53–69.

———. *Toward a General Theory of Intergroup Relations.* New York: John Wiley & Sons, 1967.

Blau, Peter, and Otis Dudley Duncan. *The American Occupational Structure.* New York: John Wiley & Sons, 1967.

Blauner, Robert. "Black Culture: Myth or Reality." In Norman Whitten and John Swed, eds. *Afro-American Anthropology.* New York: Doubleday, 1970, Chap. 19.

————. "Internal Colonialism and Ghetto Revolt." *Social Problems*, 16 (Spring 1969), 393–408.
Bogue, Donald J., and Jan E. Dizard. *Washington Post*, May 25, 1964, and March 10, 1965.
Bond, Horace Mann. "The Curriculum and the Negro Child." *Journal of Negro Education*, 4 (April 1935), 159–168.
Bonger, William A. *Race and Crime*. New York: Columbia University Press, 1973.
Bonilla, Seda E. "Social Structure and Race Relations." *Social Forces*, 40 (1961), 141–148.
Bowles, Frank, and Frank De Costa. *Between Two Worlds: A Profile of Negro Higher Education* (Carnegie Commission on Higher Education Report). New York: McGraw-Hill, 1971.
Boyd, William M., II. *Access and Power for Blacks in Higher Education*. New York: Educational Policy Center, 1972.
Branson, Herman R. "Producing More Black Doctors: Psychometric Barriers." Prepared for the Education Research Center Colloquium of M.I.T., December 19, 1969.
Brimmer, Andrew F. "Economic Integration and the Progress of the Negro Community." *Ebony*, 25 (August 1970), 118–121.
Browne, Robert S. "Black Economic Autonomy." *The Black Scholar* (October 1971), 26–31.
————. "The Case for Black Separatism." *Ramparts Magazine* (December 1967), 46–52.
Bryant, James W. *A Survey of Black American Doctorates*. New York: The Ford Foundation, 1970.
Buckley, Walter. *Sociology and Modern Systems Theory*. Englewood Cliffs, N.J.: Prentice-Hall, 1967.
Bullock, Henry A. *A History of Negro Education in the South*. New York: Praeger, 1970.
Bureau of the Census. *The Social and Economic Status of Negroes in the United States, 1970*. Washington, D.C.: U.S. Department of Commerce, Government Printing Office, 1971.
————. *The Social and Economic Status of the Black Population in the United States, 1971*. U.S. Department of Commerce (Series P-23, No. 42). Washington, D.C.: Government Printing Office, 1972.
————. *The Social and Economic Status of the Black Population in the United States, 1972*. U.S. Department of Commerce (Series P-23, No. 46). Washington, D.C.: Government Printing Office, July 1973, p. 90.
Burnham, David. "Black Murder Victims in the City Outnumber White Victims 8 to 1." *The New York Times*, August 5, 1973, p. 1.
Burrell, Berkeley, and John Seder. *Getting It Together*. New York: Harcourt Brace Jovanovich, Inc., 1971.
Callahan, Don. *Problem Drinkers*. San Francisco: Jossey-Bass, 1970.
————, Ira H. Casin, and Helen M. Crossley. *American Drinking Practices*. New Brunswick, N.J.: Rutgers Center of Alcohol Studies, 1969, p. 48.
Caplan, Nathan S., and Jeffrey M. Paige. "A Study of Ghetto Rioters." *Scientific American* (August 1968), 15–21.
Cayton, Horace M., and St. Clair Drake. *Black Metropolis: A Study of Negro Life in a Northern City*. New York: Harper & Row, 1945.
Chaneles, Sol. *The Open Prison*. New York: The Dial Press, 1973.
Chein, I., et al. *The Road to H*. New York: Basic Books, 1964.
————, and E. Rosenfeld. "Juvenile Narcotic Use." *Law and Contemporary Problems*, 22 (1957), 52–68.
Clark, Christine, and LeRoy Clark. "The Black Lawyer." *Black Enterprise*, 3 (February 1973), 14–18.
Clark, Kenneth. *Dark Ghetto*. New York: Harper, 1965, Chap. 5.

Clark, R. E. "The Relationship of Schizophrenia in Occupational Income and Occupational Prestige." *The American Sociological Review,* 13 (1948), 325–330.
Clausen, John A., and Melvin L. Kohen. "The Ecological Approach to Social Psychiatry." *American Sociological Review,* 60 (1954), 140–151.
Clinard, Marshall B., and Richard Quinney. *Criminal Behavior Systems: A Typology.* New York: Holt, Rinehart and Winston, 1973.
———. *The Sociology of Deviant Behavior.* New York: Holt, Rinehart and Winston, 1963.
Cloward, Richard, and Lloyd Ohlin. *Delinquency and Opportunity.* Glencoe, Ill.: The Free Press, 1960.
Cohen, Albert. *Delinquent Boys: The Culture of the Gang.* Glencoe, Ill.: The Free Press, 1955.
Cohn, Jules. *The Conscience of the Corporation: Business and Urban Affairs, 1967–1970.* Baltimore: Johns Hopkins Press, 1971.
Coleman, James S. *Equality of Educational Opportunity.* Washington, D.C.: Department of Health, Education and Welfare, U.S. Printing Office, 1967.
Coles, Flournoy. *An Analysis of Black Entrepreneurship in Seven Urban Areas.* Washington, D.C.: Prepared for the National Business League under the sponsorship of the Booker T. Washington Foundation, 1969.
Coles, Robert. *Children of Crisis.* New York: Dell Publishing Company, 1967.
Committee for Economic Development. *Education for the Urban Disadvantaged.* New York: March 1971.
Congressional Black Caucus. *Proceedings of the National Policy Conference on Education for Blacks.* Washington, D.C.: 1972.
Congressional Black Caucus. *What Our Priorities Should Be Forum.* Washington, D.C.: June 1972.
Congressional Record, Vol. 118, No. 166, Part II. Washington, D.C.: United States Congress, October 14, 1972.
Conyers, James, and T. H. Kennedy. "Negro Passing: To Pass or Not to Pass." *Phylon,* 24 (1963), 215–224.
Cowgill, Donald. "Trends in Residential Segregation of Non-Whites in American Cities." *American Sociological Review,* 21 (February 1956), 43–47.
"Crisis in Education and the Changing Afro-American Community" (special issue). *Freedomways,* 8 (Fall 1968).
Cronen, Edmund D. *Black Moses.* Madison, Wis.: University of Wisconsin Press, 1964.
Cross, Theodore. *Black Capitalism.* New York: Atheneum, 1969.
Crossland, Fred E. *Minority Access To College.* New York: Ford Foundation, 1970.
Cruse, Harold. *The Crisis of the Negro Intellectual.* New York: William Morrow, 1967.
———. "A Fantasy in Black and White," *Book World,* July 26, 1970, pp. 7 ff.
———. *Rebellion or Revolution.* New York: William Morrow, 1968.
Dahl, Robert. *Who Governs?* New Haven, Conn.: Yale University Press, 1961.
Dahrendorf, Ralf. *Class and Class Conflict in Industrial Society.* Stanford, Calif.: Stanford University Press, 1969.
Daniel, Johnnie. "Negro Political Behavior and Community Political and Socio-Economic Structural Factors." *Social Forces,* 47 (March 1969).
Davies, James C. "The J-Curve of Rising and Declining Satisfaction as a Cause of Some Great Revolutions and a Continued Rebellion." In Hugh Davis Graham and Robert Curr, eds. *Violence in America: Historical and Comparative Perspectives.* New York: Bantam Books, 1969.
Davis, Allison, and Burleigh B. and Mary R. Gardner. *Deep South.* Washington, D.C.: American Council on Education, 1940.
Davis, Allison, and John Dollard. *Children of Bondage.* Chicago: University of Chicago Press, 1941.
Davis, John P. *The American Negro Reference Book.* Englewood Cliffs, N.J.: Prentice-Hall, 1966.
———. "The Negro in American Politics: The Present." In John P. Davis, ed.,

The American Negro Reference Book. Englewood Cliffs, N.J.: Prentice-Hall, 1966, pp. 531–539.

Davis, Kingsley and Wilbert E. Moore, "Some Principles of Stratification," *American Sociological Review* 10 (1945), pp. 242–249.

Dean, John. *The Making of a Black Mayor.* Washington, D.C.: The Joint Center for Political Studies, 1973.

Debro, Julius. "Black Lawyers—Black Militants." An unpublished paper presented at the annual meetings of the American Sociological Association, New Orleans, La., August 1972.

Delaney, Paul. "Black Politics '72." *Black Enterprise,* 3 (February 1973), 30–33.

DeVise, Pierre. *Chicago's Widening Color Gap: 1971 Status Report.* Chicago: Inter-University Social Research Committee, 1971.

Directory of Black Businesses in San Francisco. San Francisco: Pact, Inc. 1970.

Directory of Black Businesses and Professional, Boston Vicinity, 1969. Boston: Roxbury Businessmen's Corporation, 1969.

Directory of Black-Owned Businesses in Washington, D.C., 3rd ed. Washington, D.C.: Howard University Small Business Guidance and Development Center, 1969.

Dollard, John. *Caste and Class in a Southern Town,* 3rd ed. New York: Doubleday, 1957.

Domhoff, William. *The Higher Circles: The Governing Class in America.* New York: Random House, 1970.

Draper, Theodore. *The Rediscovery of Black Nationalism.* New York: Viking, 1970.

Du Bois, W. E. B. "Does the Negro Need Separate School?" *Journal of Negro Education* (July 1935), 335–337.

Duncan, Beverly, and Otis D. Duncan. "Family Stability and Occupational Success." *Social Problems,* 16 (Winter 1969), 273–285.

Dunham, H. W. *Community and Schizophrenia: An Experimental Analysis.* Detroit: Wayne State University Press, 1965.

Edgar, Richard E. *Urban Power and Social Welfare: Corporate Influence in an American City.* Beverly Hills, Calif.: Sage Publications, 1970.

Edmonds, Ronald, et al. "A Black Response to Christopher Jenck's Inequality and Certain Other Issues." *Harvard Educational Review,* 43 (February 1973), 76–92.

Edwards, Harry. *Black Students.* New York: The Free Press, 1970.

Egeberg, R. O. "Allied Health Workers Now and Tomorrow." *Manpower.* Washington, D.C.: U.S. Government Printing Office, 1970.

Elkins, Stanley. *Slavery.* Chicago: University of Chicago Press, 1959.

Emblem, Roger. *Society Today.* Del Mar, Calif.: CRM Books, 1973.

Emeka, Maurice L. "Black Banks: Progress and Problems," *The New York Times,* June 10, 1973, Sec. 3, 15.

Endo, Russell. *Perspectives on Black Americans.* Englewood Cliffs, N.J.: Prentice-Hall, 1973.

Enloe, Cynthia H. *Ethnic Conflict and Political Development.* Boston: Little, Brown and Co., 1973.

Epps, Edgar G. *Race Relations.* Cambridge, Mass.: Winthrop Publishers, 1973.

Essien-Udom, E. U. *Black Nationalism.* Chicago: University of Chicago Press, 1964.

Fava, Sylvia Fleis. *Urbanism in World Perspective: A Reader.* New York: Thomas Y. Crowell, 1969.

Finestone, Harold. "Kats, Kicks and Color." In M. Stein et al., *Identity and Anxiety.* Glencoe, Ill.: The Free Press, 1960.

Finney, John W. "Gains Reported by All-Volunteer Army." *The New York Times,* February 21, 1974, p. 12.

Fisher, Sethard, ed. *Power and the Black Community.* New York: Random House, 1970.

Focus, 2 (April 1974).

Fogelson, Robert M., and Robert B. Hill. *Who Riots: A Study of Participation in the 1967 Riots.* Washington, D.C.: Government Printing Office, 1968.

Foner, Eric. "In Search of Black History." *New York Review of Books,* October 22, 1970, pp. 11–14.

Foner, Phillip S., ed. *The Black Panthers Speak*. Philadelphia: J. B. Lippincott, 1970.

Forman, Robert E. *Black Ghettos, White Ghettos, and Slums*. Englewood Cliffs, N.J.: Prentice-Hall, 1971, p. 78.

Forsythe, Dennis. "The Sociology of Black Separatism." An unpublished paper presented at the 1973 meetings of the American Sociological Association, New York City.

Franklin, Herbert. "Zoning Laws." *Black Enterprise*, 3 (August 1972), 25.

Franklin, John Hope. *From Slavery to Freedom*. New York: Alfred A. Knopf, 1948.

Frazier, E. Franklin. *Black Bourgeoisie*. New York: The Free Press of Glencoe, 1957.

———. *The Negro Family in Chicago*. Chicago: University of Chicago Press, 1932.

———. *The Negro Family in the United States*. Chicago: University of Chicago Press, 1939.

———. *The Negro Family in the United States*, rev. ed. Chicago: University of Chicago Press, 1966.

———. *The Negro in the United States*. New York: The Macmillan Company, 1949.

Freeman, L. C. *Patterns of Residential Segregation*. Cambridge, Mass.: Schenkman Publishing Co., 1970.

Fried, John. "The Blood Pressure on 22 Million Americans." *New York Times Magazine*, February 25, 1973, p. 14.

Fried, Joseph P. *Housing Crisis, USA*. Baltimore: Penguin Books, 1971.

Gamson, William. *Power and Discontent*. Homewood, Ill.: Dorsey Press, 1968.

Garrett, Gerald R., and Howard M. Bahr. "Women on Skid Row." *Quarterly Journal of Studies on Alcohol*, 34:4 (December 1973), 1228–1243.

Gist, Noel P., and William S. Bennett. "Aspirations of Negro and White Students." *Social Forces*, 42 (1963), 40–48.

Glaser, Daniel, Bernard Lander, and William Abbott. "Opiate Addicted and Non-Addicted Siblings in a Slum Area." *Social Problems*, 18 (Spring 1971), 510–521.

Glazer, Nathan. "Housing and Housing Policies." *The Public Interest* (Spring 1967), 21–51.

———, and Daniel P. Moynihan. *Beyond the Melting Pot*. Cambridge, Mass.: The M.I.T. Press, 1963.

Glenn, Norvall D. "Negro Prestige Criteria: A Case Study in the Bases of Prestige." *American Journal of Sociology*, 68 (1963), 645–657.

———. "Some Changes in the Relative Status of Nonwhites, 1940–1960." *Phylon*, 24 (1963), 109–122.

Glick, Paul, and Arthur Norton. "Frequency, Duration, and Probability of Marriage and Divorce." *Journal of Marriage and the Family*, 33 (May 1971), 307–313.

Goldfarb, Ronald, and Linda Singer. *After Conviction*. New York: Simon & Schuster, 1973.

Goldfield, David R., and James B. Lane. *The Enduring Ghetto*. Philadelphia: J. B. Lippincott & Co., 1973.

Goode, William J. *World Revolution and Family Patterns*. New York: The Macmillan Co., 1963.

Gordon, Milton M. *Social Class in American Sociology*. Durham, N.C.: Duke University Press, 1958.

Gray, L. Patrick. *Crime in the United States: Uniform Crime Reports 1971*. Washington, D.C.: U.S. Government Printing Office, 1971.

Greenberg, Jack. *Race Relations and the American Law*. New York: Columbia University Press, 1959, p. 276.

Greer, George, and Eunice Greer. *Equality and Beyond*. Chicago: Quadrangle Books, 1966. This book is the same as *Housing Segregation and the Goals of the Great Society*.

Grodzins, Morton. *The Metropolitan Area as a Racial Problem*. Pittsburgh: University of Pittsburgh Press, 1959.

Gwaltney, Corbin, ed. *The Chronicle of Higher Education*, May 30, 1972.

Hall, Raymond L. "Explorations in the Analysis of Separatist Movements." An unpublished paper presented at the 1973 meetings of the American Sociological Association, New York City.

Hamilton, Charles V. "Racial, Ethnic and Social Class Politics and Administration." *Public Administration Review,* 32 (October 1972), 638–648.

————, and Stokely Carmichael. *Black Power: The Politics of Liberation in America.* New York: Random House, 1967.

Hare, Nathan. *Black Anglo-Saxons.* London: Macmillan, 1970.

Heberle, Rudolf. "The Normative Element in Neighborhood Relations." *Pacific Sociological Review* (Spring 1960), 7–9.

Heer, David. "Recent Data on Negro-White Marriage in the United States." A paper presented before the American Sociological Association, Montreal, August 1964.

Henderson, Lenneal J., Jr. "Impact of Military Base Shut-Downs." *The Black Scholar,* 5 (October 1973), 9–15.

Henderson, Stephen. "Toward a Black University." *Ebony,* 25 (September 1970), 108–116.

Hendin, Herbert. *Black Suicide.* New York: Basic Books, 1969.

Herskowitz, Melville J. *The Myth of the Negro Past.* New York: Harper & Brothers, 1941; paperback ed., Boston: Beacon Press, 1958.

Herzog, Elizabeth. "Is There a 'Breakdown' of the Negro Family?" *Social Work,* 2 (January 1966), 3–10.

————, and Hylan Lewis. "Children in Poor Families: Myths and Realities." *American Journal of Orthopsychiatry,* 40 (April 1970), 375–387.

Hill, Robert. "Health Conditions of Black Americans." *Urban League News,* 3:5 (May 1973), 5.

————. *The Strengths of Black Families.* New York: Emerson Hall Publishers, Inc., 1972.

Hodge, Robert W., and Donald Treiman. "Class Identification in the United States." *American Journal of Sociology,* 73 (March 1968), 535–547.

Hollingshed, August B., and F. C. Redlich. *Social Class and Mental Illness: A Community Study.* New York: John Wiley and Sons, 1958.

Holloway, Harry. "Negro Political Strategy: Coalition or Independent Power Politics?" *Social Science Quarterly,* 49 (December 1969), 543–547.

Housing, 1961. Report of the U.S. Commission on Civil Rights. Washington D.C.: Government Printing Office, 1961.

Howard, Joseph C., Sr. "The Administration of Rape Cases in the City of Baltimore and the State of Maryland." A paper prepared for the Monumental Bar Association, Baltimore: August 1967.

Hughes, Everett C. "Dilemmas and Contradictions of Status." *American Journal of Sociology,* 50 (March 1945), 353–359.

Hund, James M. *Black Enterpreneurship.* Belmont, Calif.: Wadsworth, 1970.

Hunnertz, Ulf. *Soulside.* New York: Columbia University Press, 1971.

Hunter, Charlayne, "The Negro College Fund, A Success at Thirty, Running Harder Now," *New York Times,* October 18, 1974.

"Is the Black Public College Dying? " *Ebony,* 25 (September 1970), 92–103.

James, Herman. "Health Orientations, Health Opportunities and the Use of Medical Services: Toward a Clarification of the Relationships." An unpublished manuscript based upon a study of black and white subjects in Pittsburgh, 1967–1970.

Jellinek, E. Morton. *The Disease Concept of Alcoholism.* New Haven, Conn.: College & University Press, 1959.

Jencks, Christopher. "Busing—the Supreme Court Goes North." *New York Times Magazine,* November 19, 1972, pp. 40–127.

————, et al. *Inequality.* New York: Basic Books, 1973.

Johnson, Charles S. *Growing Up in the Black Belt.* Washington, D.C.: American Council on Education, 1941.

————. *Shadow of the Plantation.* Chicago: University of Chicago Press, 1934.

Johnston, Ronald J. *Urban Residential Patterns.* New York: Praeger, 1971.
Jones, Edward. *Blacks in Business.* New York: Grosset-Dunlap, 1971.
Josiah Macy Foundation. "A Proposal to Increase Significantly the Number of Negro Physicians in the United States." Document, New York, 1968.
Joyce, George, and Norman Govoni, eds. *The Black Consumer: Dimensions of Behavior and Strategy.* New York: Random House, 1971.
Kamil, Constance K., and Norma J. Radin. "Class Differences in the Socialization Practices of Negro Mothers." *Journal of Marriage and the Family,* 29 (May 1967), 302–310.
Karmen, Monroe W. "Government Programs." *Black Enterprise,* 3 (August 1972), 22.
Keech, William R. *The Impact of Negro Voting: The Role of the Vote in the Quest for Equality.* Chicago: Rand McNally, 1968.
Keller, Suzanne, and Marisa Zavalloni. "Ambition and Social Class Respecification." *Social Forces,* 43 (October 1964), 58–70.
King, Lucy Jane, et al. "Alcohol Abuse: A Crucial Factor in the Social Problems of Negro Men." *American Journal of Psychiatry,* 125 (June 1969), 96–104.
Knopf, Ann. *Youth Patrol: An Experiment in Community Participation.* Waltham, Mass.: Brandeis, 1969.
Kohen, Melvin. "Social Class and Schizophrenia: A Critical Review and a Reformulation." *Schizophrenia Bulletin.* Rockville, Md.: National Institute of Mental Health, Government Printing Office, Winter 1969.
Kolko, Gabriel. *Wealth and Power in America.* New York: Praeger, 1962.
Konvitz, Milton. *A Century of Civil Rights.* New York: Columbia University Press, 1961.
Kristol, Irving. "The Negro Today Is the Immigrant of Yesterday." *New York Times Magazine,* September 11, 1966, p. 50.
Kronus, Sidney. *The Black Middle Class.* Columbus, Ohio: Charles E. Merrill, 1971.
————. "Some Neglected Areas of Negro Class Comparisons." In Edgar G. Epps. *Race Relations.* Cambridge, Mass.: Winthrop Publishers, 1973, pp. 236–249.
Ladd, Everett C., Jr. *Ideology in America.* Ithaca, N.Y.: Cornell University Press, 1969.
————. *Negro Political Leadership in the South.* Ithaca, N.Y.: Cornell University Press, 1966.
Laurenti, Luigi. *Property Values and Race.* Berkeley, Calif.: University of California Press, 1960.
Lenski, Gerhard. "Social Participation and Status Crystallization." *ASR,* 21 (August 1956), 458–464.
————. "Status Crystallization: A Non-Vertical Dimension of Social Status." *ASR,* 19 (August 1954), 405–413.
Lewis, Hylan. *Blackways of Kent.* Chapel Hill, N.C.: University of North Carolina Press, 1955.
Lieberson, Stanley. "A Societal Theory of Race and Ethnic Relations." *American Sociological Review,* 26 (December 1961), 902–910.
Liebow, Elliott. *Tally's Corner: A Study of Negro Street Corner Men.* Boston: Little, Brown, 1967.
Light, Ivan. *Ethnic Enterprise in America.* Berkeley, Calif.: University of California Press, 1972.
Lincoln, C. Eric. *The Black Muslims in America.* Boston: Beacon Press, 1961.
Lindesmith, Alfred. *The Addict and the Law.* New York: Random House, 1965.
Lynch, Hollis R. *The Black Urban Condition.* New York: Thomas Y. Crowell Co., 1973.
McAllister, Ronald J., et al. "Residential Mobility of Blacks and Whites: A National Longitudinal Study." *American Journal of Sociology,* 77 (November 1971), 448–453.
McClelland, David. *The Achieving Society.* Princeton, N.J.: Van Nostrand, 1961.
McKee, J. B. "Changing Patterns of Race and Housing, a Toledo Study." *Social Forces,* 41 (March 1963), 253–260.

Maddox, George L., and Bernice Allen. "A Comparative Study of Social Definitions of Alcohol and Its Use Among Selected Male Negro and White Undergraduates." *Quarterly Journal of Studies on Alcohol*, 22 (September 1961), 418–427.

Malzberg, Benjamin. *Statistical Data for the Study of Mental Diseases Among Negroes in New York State*. Albany, N.Y.: Research Foundation for Mental Hygiene, 1964.

Marden, Charles F., and Gladys Meyer. *Minorities in American Society*. New York: American Book Co., 1962.

Markham, James M. "Heroin Hunger May Not a Mugger Make." *New York Times Magazine*, March 18, 1973, p. 39.

Martin, John B. *The Deep South Says Never*. New York: Ballantine, 1957.

Marx, Gary T. *Protest and Prejudice: A Study of Belief in the Black Community*. New York: Harper & Row, 1967.

Marx, Karl. *Capital*. Max Eastman, ed. New York: Modern Library, 1968.

———. *The Communist Manifesto*. Chicago: Regnery, 1969.

———. *Pre-Capitalist Economic Formations*. Eric Hobsbawm, ed. Jack Cohen, tr. New York: International Publishers, 1921.

Matthews, Donald R., and James W. Prothro. *Negroes and the New Southern Politics*. New York: Harcourt, Brace, and World, 1966.

Meer, Bernard, and Edward Freeman. "The Impact of Negro Neighbors on White Homeowners." *Social Forces*, 45 (September 1966), 11–19.

Meharry Medical College. *Report to the Nation: Meharry Medical College, 1967–1972*. Nashville, Tenn., 1973.

"Meharry Needs Help." *The New York Times*, April 8, 1973, E-5.

Meister, Richard J. *The Black Ghetto: Promised Land or Colony*. Lexington, Mass.: D. C. Heath & Co., 1972.

Merton, Robert K. "Insiders and Outsiders: A Chapter in the Sociology of Knowledge." *American Journal of Sociology*, 78 (July 1972), 9–47.

———. *Social Theory and Social Structure*. Glencoe, Ill.: The Free Press, 1957.

Metzger, Paul J. "American Sociology and Black Assimilation: Conflicting Perspectives." *American Journal of Sociology*, 76 (January 1971), 632 ff.

Miller, Andreas. "The Problem of Class Boundaries and Its Significance for Research Into Class Structure." *Transactions of the Second World Congress of Sociology II* (1953), 348–349.

Mills, C. Wright. *The Power Elite*. New York: Oxford University Press, 1959.

Mitford, Jessica. *American Way of Dying*. New York: Simon and Shuster, 1963.

Moon, Henry Lee. *Balance of Power: The Negro Vote*. Garden City, N.Y.: Doubleday, 1948.

Moore, Nancy L. "Cashing in on Blackness: The Dilemmas of Afro-American Education." *Freedomways*, 12 (Winter Quarter 1972), 283–288.

Moskos, Charles, Jr. "Deliberate Change: Race Relations in the Armed Forces." In Russell Endo and William Strawbridge, eds. *Perspective on Black America*. Englewood Cliffs, N.J.: Prentice-Hall, 1969, p. 62.

———. "Racial Integration in the Armed Forces." *American Journal of Sociology*, 72 (September 1966), 133–148.

Moynihan, Daniel P. *The Negro Family: The Case for National Action*. Washington, D.C.: U.S. Department of Labor, 1965.

Myrdal, Gunner. *An American Dilemma*. New York: Harper and Row, 1944.

NAACP Legal Defense and Educational Fund. *It's Not the Distance, It's the Niggers: Comments on the Controversy Over School Busing*. New York: 1972.

———. *Thirty Years of Building American Justice*. New York: 1970.

Napper, George. *Blacker Than Thou: The Struggle for Campus Unity*. Grand Rapids, Mich.: William B. Eerdmans Publishing Company, 1973.

National Black Political Agenda. Mimeo. Gary, Ind.: 1972.

National Urban League Research Department. *Special Reports on the Military*. Prepared for James E. Blackwell, July 1973.

"New Threat to Public Schools." *Ebony*, 25 (September 1970), 84.

Newton, Huey P. *Revolutionary Suicide*. New York: Harcourt Brace Jovanovich, 1973.

———. *To Die for the People*. New York: Vintage Books, 1972.

New York Times Magazine. "Just Teach Them to Read: Kenneth Clark's Revolutionary Slogan." March 18, 1973, pp. 14–65.

Nordie, Peter G., et al. *Improving Race Relations in the Army*. McLean, Va.: Human Sciences Research Center, Inc., 1972, p. 68.

Ohlin, Lloyd, ed. *Prisons of America*. Englewood Cliffs, N.J.: Prentice-Hall, 1973.

Olive, Lewis C., Jr. "Duty, Honor, Country But No Reward." *The Urban League News*, 3 (April 1973), 31.

Otto, Herbert. "What Is a Family?" *Marriage and Family Living*, 24 (February 1962), 72–89.

Parker, Seymour, and Robert J. Kleiner. *Mental Illness in the Urban Negro Community*. New York: The Free Press, 1966.

Parsons, Talcott. "The Distribution of Power in America." In *Structure and Process in Modern Society*. New York: The Free Press, 1960.

———. *The Social System*. New York: The Free Press, 1951.

Pasamanick, Benjamin. "A Survey of Mental Illness in an Urban Population." *The American Journal of Psychiatry*, 119 (1962), 299–305.

Pettigrew, Thomas F. *Racially Separate or Together*. New York: McGraw-Hill, 1973.

———. "White-Negro Confrontations." In Eli Ginsberg, ed., *The Negro Challenge to the Business Community*. New York: McGraw-Hill, 1963, pp. 39–55.

———, et al. "Busing: A Review of the Evidence." *The Public Interest*, 30 (Winter 1973), 88–118.

Phillips, Ulrich B. *Life and Labor in the Old South*. Boston: Little, Brown & Co., 1929.

Pinkney, Alphonso. *Black Americans*. Englewood Cliffs, N.J.: Prentice-Hall, 1969.

Pittman, David J., ed., *Alcoholism*. New York: Harper & Row, 1967.

———, and Harrison M. Trice. "Social Organization and Alcoholism: A Review of Significant Research Since 1940." *Social Problems*, 5 (Spring 1958), 294–308.

Pivin, Frances Fox, and Richard Cloward. *Regulating the Poor*. New York: Vintage Books, 1971.

Ploski, Henry A., and Ernest Kaiser, eds. "Predominantly Negro Institutions, Colleges and Universities in the United States." *The Negro Almanac*, 2nd ed. New York: Bellwether Co., 1971.

Pouissant, Alvin. *Why Blacks Kill Blacks*. New York: Emerson Hall Publishers, 1972.

———, and Carolyn Atkinson. "Black Youth and Motivation." *The Black Scholar* (March 1970), 43–51.

Powdermaker, Hortense. *After Freedom*. New York: Viking Press, 1939.

Project Seventy-Five. Chicago: National Office of Project 75, 1973.

Quarles, Benjamin. *The Black American*. Glenview, Ill.: Scott, Foresman & Co., 1967.

Radzinowicz, Leon, and Marvin Wolfgang, eds. *The Criminal in the Arms of the Law*. New York: Basic Books, 1971.

Rafky, David M. "The Black Academic in the Marketplace." *Change*, 3 (October 1971), 65–66.

Rainwater, Lee. "The Crucible of Identity: The Lower-Class Negro Family." *Daedalus*, 95 (Winter 1965), 258– 264.

———. *Soul*. Chicago: Aldine Publishing Co., 1970.

———, and William Yancy. *The Moynihan Report and the Politics of Controversy*. Cambridge, Mass.: The M.I.T. Press, 1967.

Rapkin, Chester, and William Gribsby. *The Demand for Housing in Racially Mixed Areas*. Berkeley, Calif.: University of California Press, 1960.

Record, Wilson, and Jane Cassels Record. *Little Rock, U.S.A.* San Francisco: Chandler Publishing Company, 1960.

Report of the National Advisory Commission on Civil Disorders. New York: Bantam Books, 1968.

Rinder, Irwin. "Minority Orientations: An Approach to Intergroup Relations Theory Through Social Psychology." *Phylon*, 26 (Spring 1965), 5–17.
Robbins, Lee, et al. "Drinking Behavior of Young Urban Negro Men." *Quarterly Journal of Studies on Alcohol*, 29 (September 1968), 657–684.
Roebuck, Julian, and R. G. Kessler. *The Etiology of Alcoholism: Constitutional Psychological and Sociological Approaches*. Springfield, Ill.: Charles C. Thomas, 1972.
Rose, Arnold. *The Negro in America*. New York: Harper & Bros., 1948.
Rose, Peter I., ed. *Americans from Africa: Old Memories, New Moods*. New York: Atherton Press, 1970.
———. *Americans from Africa: Slavery and Its Aftermath*. New York: Atherton Press, 1970.
———. *They & We: Racial and Ethnic Relations in the U.S.* New York: Random House, 1964.
Rosenthal, Robert, and Lenora Jacobson. *Pygmalion in the Classroom: Teachers' Expectations and Pupils' Intellectual Development*. New York: Holt, Rinehart and Winston, 1968.
———. "Self-Fulfilling Prophecies in the Classroom: Teachers' Expectations as Unintended Determinants of Pupils' Intellectual Competence." In M. Deutsch, I. Katz, and A. R. Jensen, eds. *Social Class, Race, and Psychological Development*. New York: Holt, Rinehart and Winston, 1968.
Rubin, Sol. "Imposition of the Death Sentence for Rape." In Marvin Wolfgang and Leon Radzinowicz, eds. *The Criminal in the Arms of the Law*. New York: Basic Books, 1971.
Rushing, W. A. "Two Patterns in the Relationship Between Social Class and Mental Hospitalization." *American Sociological Review*, 34 (1969), 533–541.
Rustin, Bayard. "The Failure of Black Separatism." *Harper's Magazine* (January 1970), 25–34.
———. "From Protest to Politics: The Future of the Civil Rights Movement." *Commentary*, 39 (1965), 25–31.
Ryan, William. *Blaming The Victim*. New York: Vintage Books, 1971.
Saltman, Juliet. *Open Housing as a Social Movement*. Lexington, Mass.: Heath Lexington Books, 1971.
Sarason, Irvin G. "Verbal Learning, Modeling and Juvenile Delinquency." *American Psychologist*, 23 (1968), 254–266.
Scanzoni, John H. *The Black Family in Modern Society*. Boston: Allyn & Bacon, Inc., 1971.
Schermerhorn, Richard A. *Comparative Ethnic Relations: A Framework for Theory and Research*. New York: Random House, 1970.
Schnore, L. F. *Class and Race in Cities and Suburbs*. Chicago: Markham, 1972.
———. "Social Class Segregation Among Non-Whites in Metropolitan Centers." *Demography*, 2 (1965), 126–133.
Scholnick, Jerome. *The Politics of Protest*. New York: Simon and Schuster, 1969.
Schrag, Clarence. *Crime and Justice: American Style*. Rockville, Md.: National Institute of Mental Health, 1971.
Schubert, Frank N. "Black Soldiers on the White Frontier: Some Factors Influencing Race Relations." *Phylon*, 32 (Winter 1971), 410–416.
Schulz, David A. "The Role of Boyfriend." *Coming Up Black: Patterns of Ghetto Socialization*. Englewood Cliffs, N.J.: Prentice-Hall, 1969, 36–144.
Shelling, Thomas C. *The Strategy of Conflict*. Cambridge, Mass.: Harvard University Press, 1960.
Shibutani, Tamotsu, and Kian M. Kwan. *Ethnic Stratification: A Comparative Approach*. New York: The Macmillan Company, 1972.
Shumpeter, Joseph. *Imperialism and Social Classes*. New York: Meridian Books, 1955.
Simpson, Richard, and Milton Yinger. *Racial and Cultural Minorities*. New York: Harper & Row, 1953.

Sklare, Marshall. "The Conversion of the Jews." *Commentary*, 36 (September 1973), 44–53.

Sowell, Thomas. *Black Education: Myth and Tragedies*. New York: McKay, 1973.

Srole, Leo, et al. *Mental Health in the Metropolis: The Midtown Manhattan Study*. New York: McGraw-Hill, 1962.

Stampp, Kenneth. *The Peculiar Institution: Slavery in the Ante-Bellum South*. New York: Alfred A. Knopf, 1958.

Staples, Robert. *The Black Family: Essays and Studies*. Belmont, Calif.: Wadsworth Publishing Co., 1971.

Starr, Paul. *The Discarded Army*. New York: Charterhouse, 1973.

Stetler, Henry. *Racial Integration in Private Interracial Neighborhoods in Connecticut*. Hartford, Conn.: Commission on Human Rights, 1957.

Stillman, Richard. *Integration of the Negro in the U.S. Armed Forces*. New York: Praeger, 1968.

Stone, Chuck. *Black Political Power in America*. New York: Dell Publishing Co., Inc., 1968.

Stouffer, Samuel. *The American Soldier: Adjustments During Army Life*. Vol. 1. Princeton, N.J.: Princeton University Press, 1949.

Stuckert, Robert. "The African Ancestry of the White American Population." *Physical Anthropology and Archaeology*. New York: Macmillan, 1964, pp. 192–197.

Suchman, Edward. "Social Factors in Medical Deprivation." *American Journal of Public Health*, 55 (November 1965), 1725–1733.

———. "Socio-Medical Variations Among Ethnic Groups." *American Journal of Sociology*, 70 (November 1964), 319–331.

Sutherland, Edwin, and Donald Cressey. *Criminology*. Santa Barbara, Calif.: University of California Press, 1970, p. 139.

Sykes, Gresham M. *Crime and Society*. New York: Random House, 1965.

Taeuber, Karl E., and Alma F. Taeuber. *Negroes in Cities*. Chicago: Aldine Publishing Co., 1965.

———. "The Negro Population in the United States." In J. P. Davis, ed. *The American Negro Reference Book*. Englewood Cliffs, N.J.: Prentice-Hall, 1966, pp. 531–539.

———. "Residential Segregation." *Scientific American*, 213 (August 1965), 12–19.

Task Force Report: Narcotics and Drug Abuse. The President's Commission on Law Enforcement and Administration of Justice. Washington, D.C.: Government Printing Office, July 1973, p. 90.

Taylor, Clyde. "Black Consciousness and the Vietnam War." *The Black Scholar* (October 1973), 2–9.

Taylor, Howard F. "Playing the Dozen with Path Analysis: Methodological Pitfalls in Jencks et al., *Inequality*." *Sociology of Education* (Fall 1973), 433–450.

Terry, Wallace. *The Bloods: The Black Soldier in Vietnam*. New York: Viking Press, 1973.

Travis, Dempsey J. "Barriers to Black Power in the American Economy." *The Black Scholar*, 3 (October 1971), 21–25.

Trice, Harrison M. *Alcoholism in America*. New York: McGraw-Hill, 1966.

Tunstall, Lucille. *Increasing the Options in Health Profession*. Atlanta, Ga.: Clark College, 1973.

Udry, J. Richard. "Marital Instability by Race and Income Based on 1960 Census Data." *American Journal of Sociology* (May 1967), 673–674.

———. "Marital Instability by Race, Sex, Education and Occupation Using 1960 Census Data." *American Journal of Sociology*, 72 (September 1966), 203–209.

Urban League News (March 1974).

U.S. 1970 Census of Population: General Social and Economic Characteristics. Washington, D.C.: U.S. Department of Commerce, Bureau of the Census, June 1972.

US. Civil Rights Commission Reports, 1961. Washington, D.C.: Government Printing Office, 1962.

U.S. Commission on Civil Rights. *Political Participation*. Washington, D.C.: Government Printing Office, 1968.

U.S. Department of Labor. *Health Manpower—1966–1975: A Study of Requirements and Supply*. Washington, D.C.: U.S. Department of Labor, 1967.

Valentine, Charles A. *Culture and Poverty: Critique and Counter-Proposals*. Chicago: The University of Chicago Press, 1968.

Vander Zanden, James. *American Minority Relations*. New York: Ronald Press, 1966.

Vanguard, 3 (July 1969).

Waldo, Gordon, and Simon Dinitz. "Personality Attributes of the Criminal: An Analysis of Research Studies, 1950–1965." *Journal of Research in Crime and Delinquency*, 4 (1967), 185–202.

Walton, Hanes. *Black Politics*. New York: J. B. Lippincott, 1972.

Ware, Gilbert. "The Spider Web and Racism in the Armed Forces." *The Urban League News* (April 1972), 5.

Warner, W. Lloyd, Buford H. Junker, and Walter A. Adams. *Color and Human Nature*. Washington D.C.: American Council on Education, 1941.

Warner, William L., and F. S. Lunt. *The Social Life of a Modern Community*. New Haven, Conn.: Yale University Press, 1941.

Warren, Roland. *The Community in America*. Chicago: University of Chicago Press, 1972.

Wattenberg, Ben, and Richard Scanlon. "Black Progress and Liberal Rhetoric." *Commentary*, 55 (April 1973), 35–44.

Weaver, Robert C. *The Negro Ghetto*. New York: Russell and Russell, 1948.

Weber, Max. *The Protestant Ethic and the Spirit of Capitalism*. Talcott Parsons, tr. New York: Scribner, 1930.

————. *The Theory of Social and Economic Organization*. A. M. Henderson and Talcott Parsons, trs. Glencoe, Ill.: The Free Press, 1947.

Weinstein, Eugene A., and Paul Geisel. "Family Decision Making over Desegregation." *Sociometry*, 25 (1962), 21–28.

"Which Way Black America?" *Ebony* (special issue), 25 (August 1970).

"Welfare Myth," *Boston Sunday Globe*, Nov. 26, 1968, Section 6A-1.

Wheeler, Robert R., "Public Schools, Public Policy, Public Problems: Some Observations and Suggestions." Proceedings of the National Policy Conference on Education for Blacks. Washington, D.C.: The Congressional Black Caucus, 1972.

"White Acquitted in Kitty Hawk Trial," *New York Times*. February 13, 1973, p. 40.

White, Theodore. *The Making of the President, 1960*. New York: Atheneum, 1961.

Wilenski, Harold, and Charles LeBeaux. *Industrial Society and Social Welfare*. New York: The Russell Sage Foundation, 1958.

Wilkins, Roy. "Integration." *Ebony*, 25 (August 1970).

Wilkinson, Doris Y., ed. *Black Male/White Female*. Cambridge, Mass.: Schenkman, 1974.

Willie, Charles. *The Family Life of Black People*. Columbus, Ohio: Charles Merrill, 1970.

Willie, Charles V., and Joan D. Levy. "Black Is Lonely on White Campuses." *Psychology Today*, 5 (March 1972), 50–56.

Wilson, Charles E. "Lessons of the 201 Complex in Harlem." *Freedomways*, 8 (Fall 1968), 399–406.

Wilson, James Q. "The Negro in American Politics: The Present." In John P. Davis, ed. *The American Negro Reference Book*. Englewood Cliffs, N.J.: Prentice-Hall, 1966.

————. *Negro Politics: The Search for Leadership*. Glencoe, Ill.: The Free Press, 1960.

Wilson, William J. *Power, Racism and Privilege*. New York: The Macmillan Co., 1973.

————. "Revolutionary Nationalism 'Versus' Cultural Nationalism; Dimensions of the Black Power Movement." *Sociological Focus*, 3 (Spring 1970), 43–51.

Wirth, Lewis. "The Problem of Minority Groups." In Ralph Linton, ed. *The Science of Man in the World Crisis.* New York: Columbia University Press, 1945, pp. 347–372.

————. "Urbanism as a Way of Life." *American Journal of Sociology*, 44 (July 1938), 3–24.

Wolfgang, Marvin. *Crime and Race.* New York: Institute of Human Relations Press, 1970.

Woodson, Carter G. *The Mis-Education of the Negro.* Washington, D.C.: Associate Publishers, 1969.

Woodward, C. Van. *The Strange Career of Jim Crow,* rev. ed. New York: Oxford University Press, 1957.

Wright, Erik Olin. *The Politics of Punishment.* New York: Harper Colophon Books, 1973.

Wright, Nathan, Jr., ed. *What Black Educators Are Saying.* New York: Hawthorne Books, 1972.

Wynne, Lewis N. "Brownsville: The Reaction of the Negro Press." *Phylon*, 32 (Summer 1972), 153–160.

Zeul, Carolyn R., and Craig R. Humphrey. "The Integration of Suburban Blacks in Suburban Neighborhoods: A Reexamination of the Contact Hypothesis." *Social Problems*, 8 (Spring 1971), 462–474.

Zimple, Lloyd, ed. *The Disadvantaged Worker: Readings in Developing Minority Manpower.* Boston: Addison-Wesley, 1971.

Zinberg, Norman E., and J. A. Robertson. *Drugs and the Public.* New York: Simon and Schuster, 1972.

AUTHOR INDEX

311

SUBJECT INDEX